CAMBRIDGE SOUTH ASIAN STUDIES

THE STATE OF MARTIAL RULE

D1628627

THE STATE OF MARTIAL RULE

The origins of Pakistan's political economy of defence

AYESHA JALAL

*Assistant Professor, Department of Political
Science, University of Wisconsin-Madison*

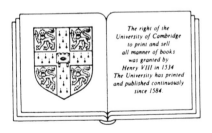

The right of the
University of Cambridge
to print and sell
all manner of books
was granted by
Henry VIII in 1534
The University has printed
and published continuously
since 1584.

CAMBRIDGE UNIVERSITY PRESS
CAMBRIDGE
NEW YORK   PORT CHESTER
MELBOURNE   SYDNEY

CAMBRIDGE UNIVERSITY PRESS
Cambridge, New York, Melbourne, Madrid, Cape Town, Singapore, São Paulo

Cambridge University Press
The Edinburgh Building, Cambridge CB2 8RU, UK

Published in the United States of America by Cambridge University Press, New York

www.cambridge.org
Information on this title: www.cambridge.org/9780521373487

First published 1990
This digitally printed version (with corrections) 2008

A catalogue record for this publication is available from the British Library

Library of Congress Cataloguing in Publication data
Jalal, Ayesha
The state of martial rule: the origins of Pakistan's political
economy of defence / Ayesha Jalal,
p.   cm. – (Cambridge South Asian studies)
Bibliography: p.
Includes index.
ISBN 0-521-37348-4
1.   Pakistan – Politics and government. 2.   Martial law – Pakistan.
3.   Pakistan – Defenses. 4.   Pakistan – Economic conditions.
I.   Title. II.   Series.
DS384.J36   1990
954.904 – dc19   89-7266

ISBN 978-0-521-37348-7 hardback
ISBN 978-0-521-05184-2 paperback

For Amijan

CONTENTS

PREFACE

Scholarly pursuits matched by the right inspiration and proper settings can be truly rewarding. I was fortunate to have had a good measure of both during the years that this work has been in preparation. It gives me special pleasure to put down these words of acknowledgement to my family, friends and colleagues who have sustained and supported the demanding process of research and writing, and to institutions that have at various stages facilitated the elaborate enterprise of producing this book.

Although this work has travelled with me across three continents my main debt is to the University of Cambridge which gave the most extended support. I began research on it while I was still a fellow of Trinity College, Cambridge. From 1984 to 1987 I was supported by a most generous grant from the Leverhulme Trust at the Centre of South Asian Studies, Cambridge. A grant from the Smuts Memorial Fund in the spring of 1986 enabled an initial foray into the National Archives of the United States of America in Washington, DC, while the enthusiastic support of the Third World Foundation made it possible for me to be based in London in order to more effectively mine the invaluable source materials in both the India Office Library and the Public Records Office. Between September 1985 and May 1986 I was a fellow of the Woodrow Wilson Center, Washington, DC, where I gained much not only from the proximity of the National Archives and the Library of Congress but also from the intellectual stimulation of excellent colleagues. The Leverhulme Trust made provision for my research trip to Pakistan in the winter of 1986–7. I am very grateful to all those individuals in Pakistan who took the time to talk to me at length about the events in which they had participated. The Department of Political Science at the University of Wisconsin, Madison, where I started teaching in the Fall of 1987, provided the institutional bridge for my intellectual crossing of the disciplinary frontiers separating history and political science. Its Graduate School funded a research visit to Pakistan in the winter of 1987–8 and gave salary support in the summer of 1988 for additional research and writing in London. The refinements and finishing touches were added during the fall of 1988 after my appointment as a Kukin

ix

scholar of the Harvard Academy for International and Area Studies at Harvard University.

I would like to express my gratitude to the staff of the following archives and libraries: the National Archives of Pakistan; the India Office Library; the Public Records Office; the School of Oriental and African Studies Library; the National Archives of the United States of America; the Washington National Records Center and the Library of Congress. I am particularly appreciative of Lionel Carter, the secretary/librarian of the Centre of South Asian Studies at the University of Cambridge, for competently handling every administrative detail. While at the Woodrow Wilson Center I was aided by the tireless efforts of Diane Ansell, my research assistant, in culling masses of information from the National Archives and the Library of Congress.

A number of friends and colleagues in the scholarly community took a deep interest in my work. I would especially like to mention Chris Bayly and Gordon Johnson at the University of Cambridge and David Washbrook at Harvard University and the University of Warwick who offered consistent support and encouragement. I have also benefited from exchanges with Anthony Low at the University of Cambridge; Robert Frykenberg at the University of Wisconsin, Madison; Prosser Gifford at the Woodrow Wilson Center; Altaf Gauhar at the Third World Foundation in London and Shuja Nawaz at the International Monetary Fund in Washington, DC. I presented papers based on research for this book at the University of Cambridge, the Woodrow Wilson Center, Tufts University, the annual Middle East Studies Association conference in Boston in 1986, the University of Texas, Austin and the Massachusetts Institute for Technology. Participants at these meetings made comments which helped sharpen my arguments. My greatest intellectual debt, however, is to Sugata Bose who spurred me on with his questions and constructive criticism but balanced it with unflinching faith and encouragement.

Long years of research and writing on Pakistan would have been impossible without the understanding and support of my family, especially my mother to whom this book is dedicated. She has boldly taken up the challenge of maintaining a keen interest in my scholarly endeavours in an attempt to minimise the impact of the loss of my father. The display of concern and interest by many friends in London and Lahore – specifically Nilufer Kuyas, Aamer Hussein and, above all, Nita Nazir – boosted morale and alleviated the inevitable strains that accompany scholarship. As a friend Sugata Bose has contributed immeasurably to this book; I cannot thank him enough for his advice, support and companionship during arduous moments in my years as a scholar gypsy.

Cambridge, MA   AYESHA JALAL
December 1988

ABBREVIATIONS

AIML	All-India Muslim League
BD	Basic Democracies
BPC	Basic Principles Committee
CAD	Constituent Assembly Debates
CRO	Commonwealth Relations Office
CSGID	Chief of Staff, General Intelligence Department
CSP	Civil Service of Pakistan
FO	Foreign Office
GHQ	Army General Headquarters
HAG	Harvard Advisory Group
ICA	International Cooperation Administration
IDA	Islamic Democratic Alliance
IOL	India Office Library (London)
JUI	Jamiat-ul-Ulema-e-Islam
JUP	Jamiat-ul-Ulema-e-Pakistan
LFO	Legal Framework Order
MAAG	Military Assistance Advisory Group
MEDO	Middle Eastern Defence Organisation
MLA	Member of the Legislative Assembly
NA	National Archives (Washington, DC)
NAP	National Awami Party
NEA	Office of Near Eastern Affairs
NWFP	North West Frontier Province
PRO	Public Records Office (London)
PNA	Pakistan National Alliance
PNP	Pakistan National Party
PPP	Pakistan People's Party
PRODA	Public Representatives Disqualification Order
RG	Record Group
SOA	Office of South Asian Affairs
UP	United Provinces
WNRC	Washington National Records Center

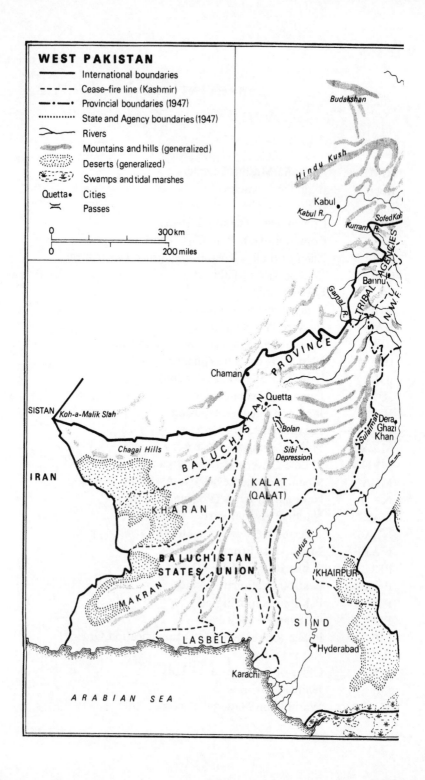

WEST PAKISTAN

———	International boundaries
– – – – –	Cease-fire line (Kashmir)
– · – · – ·	Provincial boundaries (1947)
··············	State and Agency boundaries (1947)
~~	Rivers
	Mountains and hills (generalized)
	Deserts (generalized)
	Swamps and tidal marshes
Quetta •	Cities
⤨	Passes

0 — 300 km
0 — 200 miles

Budakshan

Hindu Kush

Kabul •
Kabul R.
Kurram
Sofed Koh
Sofed Koh R.

Gamal R.

Bannu

TRIBAL AGENCIES

N.W.F. PROVINCE

Chaman •

Quetta •
BALUCHISTAN
Bolan

Sibi Depression

Sulaiman

Dera Ghazi Khan

SISTAN
Koh-a-Malik Slah

Chagai Hills

IRAN

KHARAN

KALAT (QALAT)

Indus R.

KHAIRPUR

BALUCHISTAN STATES UNION

MAKRAN

LASBELA

SIND

Hyderabad •

Karachi •

ARABIAN SEA

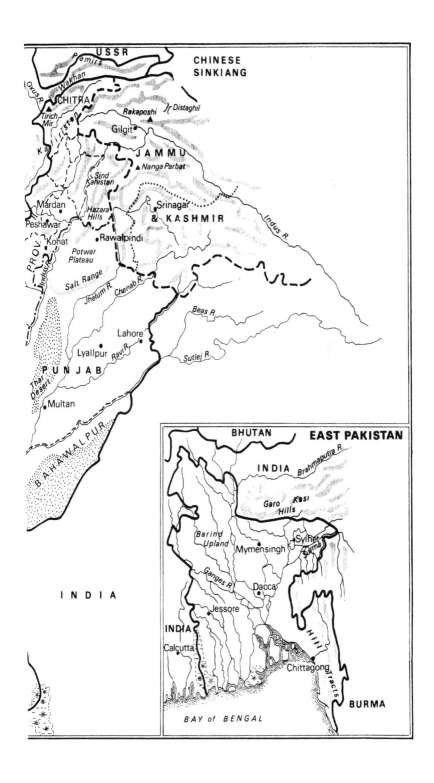

Introduction

Pakistan is an early and rather curious product of the post-war decolonisation process. Painfully carved out of the Indian subcontinent – ostensibly to provide a homeland for the Indian Muslims – Pakistan has been remarkable more for the tensions between its dominant and subordinate regions than for the purported unities of a common religion. Of the forty-two years since its creation, Pakistan has seen military or quasi-military rule for twenty-five; it has been governed under six different constitutions and has been at war with India on three separate occasions. In 1971 Pakistan lost a majority of its Muslim population with the breakaway of its eastern wing and the establishment of a new country, Bangladesh – the only successful secessionist movement in a newly independent state. A civil war in which Muslim slaughtered Muslim might seem to have exploded the notion that religion alone was sufficient cement to hold Pakistan together. There have been continuing tensions in its remaining provinces in the west. During the 1980s a government sponsored 'Islamic revival' led to a fierce debate about the form of government Pakistan should adopt, Islamic or secular.

The ideological debate was symptomatic of the difficulties Pakistan has continued to face in reconciling its self-professed Islamic identity with the imperatives of a modern state structure. The problem is all the more complex since state construction and consolidation in Pakistan has largely been on a collision course with the social dynamics underlying political processes. Pakistan had no well-developed political party organisations when it came into existence and it is still struggling to establish a party-based system of parliamentary democracy. It has not been able effectively to integrate its provinces or distribute resources equitably between the dominant Punjab and the subordinate provinces of Sind, the North West Frontier Province and Baluchistan as well as between the diverse linguistic groups within them. As in other post-colonial states where the unfolding of political processes has been hampered, Pakistan has relied on its civil service and, ultimately, on the army, to maintain the continuities of government. The institutional dominance of a predominantly Punjabi army and civil bureaucracy

1

within the state structure has exacerbated regional grievances, especially since representative government, which might have provided a better balance between the provinces and linguistic groups within them, has been kept in abeyance for long periods of time. Pakistan's precarious internal political balance has been accentuated by an adverse regional environment. Relations with India and Afghanistan have been cold, if not overtly hostile. After the Iranian revolution and the Soviet invasion of Afghanistan, Pakistan came to assume greater significance in Western security calculations. But, as has been the case throughout its history, the recent Western efforts to bolster Pakistan's strategic defences have only served to heighten its internal socio-economic and political dilemmas. The support lent by the military regime of general Zia-ul-Huq to the Afghan resistance movement, and the presence of some three million Afghan refugees on Pakistani soil, has spawned a parallel arms and drugs economy with devastating effects for the fragile weave of Pakistan's social fabric. Running battles between the security forces and disaffected youth in rural Sind, violent conflict between Sindhis and Urdu-speaking Muhajirs in Hyderabad and Karachi – that cauldron of a city ruled by armed narcotics kings and their moles in army intelligence and the metropolitan police – are simply the most startling manifestations of the seething hate that has in recent years pitted Sindhi against Punjabi, Muhajir against Punjabi, and Muhajir against Pathan. With drug money making Kalashnikovs accessible to increasingly larger segments of a politically repressed and psychologically battered and divided society, many had come to wonder whether Pakistan could survive, indeed whether it ought to survive.

In August 1988, Zia-ul-Huq's death along with senior military aides paved the way for national elections and the restoration of a party-based parliamentary government. The victory of the Pakistan People's party led by Benazir Bhutto in the general elections in November certainly boosted morale and raised hope. But the new prime minister has been left facing a menacing set of challenges on the domestic, regional and international fronts. A state structure dominated by the non-elected institutions – namely the military and the bureaucracy – is not easily amenable to a transformation that readily acknowledges the ascendancy of the elected institutions – parliament in particular. The apparent move away from the state of martial rule has simply given a new twist to the long-standing contradiction between the state structure and political processes. The next step in the resolution of this contradiction, if it is to be in favour of a party-based parliamentary system, will have to overcome a formidable wall of structural obstacles rooted in the very nature of the Pakistani state.

No understanding of contemporary Pakistan is possible without an historical analysis of the first decade after independence, a period of relative flux in the institutional balance of power between elected and non-elected institutions but during which the state structure was cast into an enduring, even rigid, mould. This work focuses on the dialectic between state construction and political processes while weaving in the related economic, strategic and ideological dimensions. Beginning its independent career without the semblance of a central government apparatus, Pakistan is a fascinating laboratory for studying the construction of a state. Alternating between detailed and more general levels of analysis the argument unravels the interplay of domestic, regional and international factors and how it weakened the position of parties and politicians within the evolving structure of the Pakistani state by tipping the institutional balance in favour of the civil bureaucracy and the military. The focus on institutional imbalances places the question of 'ethnicity' and provincialism in an altogether different light. In strategically situated countries like Pakistan, tensions between the centre and the provinces are not merely a reflection of the difficulties involved in integrating linguistically and culturally diverse constituent units. The problem is at the same time more basic and more complex – basic, because demands of provinces and linguistic groups within them are most often demands for a larger share of the state's financial resources; and more complex, because finances are generally limited, especially when the state's strategic perceptions have resulted in a political economy of defence characterised by the maintenance of defence budgets well beyond its resource capacities. The response in either case tends to be the centralisation of state authority and the pursuit of development policies aimed at maximising revenues rather than social welfare – a process which in Pakistan saw the non-elected institutions assuming dominance over the elected institutions of the state. These non-elected institutions carried a legacy of uneven recruitment patterns from the colonial era, thus exacerbating the problem of integrating diverse linguistic and socio-economic groups.

In the immediate aftermath of independence and partition the questions of sovereignty and state-building were inextricably linked in Pakistan. Notional sovereignty is not the same as the exercise of sovereignty. This work examines how a state, maimed and mutilated at birth, managed to survive and how in the process of exercising Pakistan's sovereignty the bureaucratic and military institutions rose to a position of dominance. The argument distinguishes between the phases of dominance and actual intervention by the military. After rejecting the common view that the weakness of political parties is the main variable explaining the first military intervention in Pakistan, it investigates how and why a military already dominant by 1951 decided to directly wield state authority in 1958. However, the political process was by no means a passive element; its complex dynamics contributed to the shaping of the Pakistani state structure, if only because it had to be thwarted and eventually aborted by the military and the bureaucracy operating within the constraints of constructing and consolidating a state in a difficult regional and international setting. The central concern is to show how the imperatives of the international political and economic system combined with regional and domestic factors in defining the nature of the Pakistani state. In other words, the answer to why the military and the bureaucracy came to assume the dominant role in decision-making within the state structure is attempted through a close and careful scrutiny of the different ways in which the interplay of regional and international factors influenced domestic politics and economy, distorting relations between the centre and the provinces in particular and the dialectic between state construction and political processes in general. The nexus between the top echelons of the military and the bureaucracy in Pakistan and the centres of the international system in London and Washington is of special relevance in this context. It is essential to take account of all the subtle and intricate influences that served to aid the senior bureaucratic and military officials in their efforts at derailing and then dismantling the political process during the first decade of Pakistan's independence. The more so since the institutional imbalances established in this period have proven to be of an enduring kind.

Five related themes have informed the analytical narrative throughout. The federal dilemma posed by the almost chronic tensions in the relations between the centre and the provinces, as well as between the provinces; the factors which have inhibited the growth and consolidation of a well-knit national political organisation; the role of the civil bureaucracy and the army in bolstering central authority; the extent to which the international connections of the civil bureaucracy and the military have influenced internal developments in Pakistan, and, finally, the recurrent resort to Islam as a political tactic which can at least provide the appearance of cohesion to an otherwise disparate people.

Most of these themes can be traced back to the decade preceding the partition of India in 1947. Chapter 1 concentrates on the political objectives of Mohammad Ali Jinnah, the founder of Pakistan, and the All-India Muslim League, and the extent to which these were realised. Three significant historical developments need underlining. Unlike India, which inherited British India's unitary central government in

New Delhi, Pakistan had to create a wholly new central apparatus if it was to survive as a sovereign entity. The All-India Muslim League, the party that took over the reins of government in Pakistan, had no effective organisational machinery in the provinces which became part of Pakistan. The particularisms of these provinces – their strong aversion to any outside central authority, Hindu or Muslim – rather than the attractions of a vague but simple cry of 'Islam in danger', were principal driving forces in the making of Pakistan.

The popular view that religious solidarities formed the basis of Pakistan has distracted attention from the problems it faced in creating a central government from scratch. Consequently it has never been fully established how central authority was imposed over territories separated by over a thousand miles. Chapter 2 delves into this issue by assessing the extent to which the administrative structure of the colonial state substituted for the lack of a political party with a high command reaching down into the provinces, districts and localities. The League's share of the assets of undivided India and the nature of the administrative structure inherited at the time of partition forms the basis for the analysis of state formation in Pakistan.

The absence of a well-developed national political party organisation had an important bearing on the process of state formation in Pakistan. While the provinces continued to be the main arenas of political activity, those who set about creating the central government apparatus were either politicians with little or no identifiable support at the base or civil servants versed in the old traditions of British Indian administration. Chapter 3 examines the disjunction between the formation of the new centre and political activity at the provincial levels in the context of the strategic and economic consequences of Pakistan's creation. The aim is not to provide consolidated information on provincial politics or the Muslim League. Provincial politics are analysed to the extent that they directly affected the nature of the Pakistani state and its relations with society. The purpose is to show how, while the state was being constructed, the institutional balance of power shifted in favour of the bureaucracy and the military. Through skilful manipulation of international connections, military-bureaucratic dominance within the state structure had already been achieved by the time of the assassination of prime minister Liaquat Ali Khan in October 1951.

Chapter 4 analyses the emerging disjunction between the wielding of state authority and established notions of representative government. It considers how positions within the non-elected institutions of the state, rather than bases of support in society, became the key to exercising political power in Pakistan. The sum total of provincial disaffections helped confirm the institutional imbalances. This chapter traces the links between domestic conflicts at various levels and the international compromises to which they led in 1954–5. By looking at the series of crises in the process of constitution-making, Chapter 5 illuminates the dialectic between state consolidation and political processes from a different angle. It questions interpretations which place the responsibility for the 1958 coup solely at the door of inept and corrupt politicians. Instead it investigates how the military and the bureaucracy railed and eventually broke down the political system to ward off challenges to which the state, dominated by these non-elected institutions, was still vulnerable. The negative impact of economic policies, geared to sustain needs of defence and requirements of international allies, had contributed in no uncertain way to a wide array of social disaffections which, on the eve of national elections, various political groups were seeking to mobilise. The analysis of the military intervention of 1958 is placed firmly in the context of these threats emanating outside the state structure but being quickly replicated within.

The balance between state and society could not be fully probed by focusing on the political process alone. By using Islam at the level of ideology and culture as the main point of reference, Chapter 6 considers the nature of the mutual accommodations worked out between state and society. This particular sort of search for legitimacy was fully explored in the first few years after independence and has become a time-honoured device ever since. The chapter offers a different perspective on state-society relations from that afforded by the study of the dialectic between state construction and political processes in the rest of the book.

Finally, Chapter 7, although in the form of an epilogue from the narrative point of view, provides the capstone to the various layers of argument woven together in the earlier chapters. It outlines a conceptual framework within which to place developments in Pakistan since 1958, and shows just how enduring the shifts in the institutional balances have proven to be in subsequent decades. Further it helps understand the subtleties underpinning the extended duration of the state of martial rule, and the conditions under which a reversal from direct intervention to a negotiated level of dominance might be possible.

The crucial first decade of Pakistan's independence lends itself particularly well to historical and political analysis now that important classes of source materials have become available. While most official documents in Pakistan have not found their way into archives where they can be consulted by scholars, this work has made use of all accessible primary sources – official and non-official. Interviews with participants in the events have helped in recapturing some of the flavour of the times, although these have not been relied upon to provide factual references. By far the most interesting and illuminating sources for the period up to 1958 were located in British and American archives in London and Washington, DC. Rich in information, these sources are quite indispensable for a thorough analysis of the complex interplay of domestic, regional and international factors in moulding developments in strategically important post-colonial states such as Pakistan. British officials had continued to serve in the Pakistani military and bureaucracy well into the nineteen-fifties while the Americans took a keen interest in Pakistani affairs for their own geopolitical reasons. While being sceptical of the interpretations of British and American diplomats the study has sought to make full critical use of the information and insights obtained from these sources – unlikely to be surpassed in the near future.

Although this is not a work of comparative politics it hopes to engage the interest of the student of comparative politics. An historical and political study of post-independence Pakistan, it should be of relevance to the broader issues of military intervention in politics and the nature of the state in the developing world. Most newly independent countries developed within the same international context as Pakistan. Moreover, many states in the third world experienced shifts in the institutional balance of power broadly analogous to those in Pakistan. So an analysis of Pakistan might well provide some unique insights into the evolution of state structures and political processes in the post-colonial world. Since Pakistan had no central government apparatus to begin with, the particularities of its case throw sharper light on the general problems of state formation, consolidation and the imperative as well as the potential for reconstitution.

1

The demand for Pakistan, 1940–1947

The demand for Pakistan was first voiced by the All-India Muslim League in March 1940.[1] Raised on behalf of all Indian Muslims, now deemed to be a nation rather than a minority, it led less than seven and a half years later to a communal carnage and a division of the subcontinent based on the partition of British India's two main Muslim-majority provinces of Punjab and Bengal. Underpinning this momentous but tragic event were some startling facts. Neither partition nor the creation of Pakistan had produced unqualified advantages for Indian Muslims. Punjabi and Bengali Muslims lost the economically vibrant non-Muslim majority districts in the eastern and western halves of their respective provinces. Redrawing India's political frontiers partly along religious lines had justified the exclusion of these districts from a state where Islam ostensibly was to be the main determinant of nationality. Yet the creation of a predominantly Muslim state left over a third of India's Muslims outside Pakistan's freshly demarcated frontiers.

As it emerged in 1947 Pakistan consisted in the north-west of western Punjab, Sind, the North West Frontier Province and Baluchistan, and in the north-east of eastern Bengal and the Sylhet district of Assam. The separation of Pakistan's western and eastern wings by over a thousand miles of Indian territory was simply the most glaring of the many curious features of the new state. Its creation apparently had conceded the claim that India's Muslim minority was a nation entitled to determine its own political future. But the 'two nation theory' – the popular explanation for the creation of Pakistan – does not explain how, while exercising their right of self-determination, the Indian Muslims ended up becoming citizens of two separate and mutually hostile states. Efforts to prove or disapprove the 'theory' have not only distracted from analyses of relations among Muslims but also of the varied regional and local contexts in which they tended to co-exist, cooperate or conflict with Hindus.

---

[1] For a detailed version of the argument of this chapter see A. Jalal, *The Sole Spokesman: Jinnah, the Muslim League and the Demand for Pakistan*, Cambridge 1985.

There is now overwhelming evidence to suggest that, regardless of whether or not Muslims were in fact a 'nation', the contradictory nature and structural peculiarities of their politics in the Indian context had a greater hand in the making of Pakistan. So it is important to be clear both about the context of Indian politics, and the uses made of the 'two nation theory' by the All-India Muslim League, and especially by its leader Mohammad Ali Jinnah, in the final decade of the British raj in India.

Undeniably the theory has historical antecedents predating the demand for Pakistan. But the view that India's geographically dispersed Muslims were a separate and identifiable community tended to appear and fade with equal ease at the level of political debate. As early as 1909 the British had granted separate electorates to Indian Muslims in all representative bodies. The principle survived the constitutional reforms of 1919 and was later incorporated into the government of India act of 1935. One large consequence of creating a separate political identity for the Indian Muslims was that it effectively consigned them to being a permanent minority in any constitutional arrangement. It also reinforced factional rivalries among Muslim politicians who elbowed for position inside the protected walls of specifically Muslim constituencies. To seek office Muslim politicians – landlords in the main – could deploy their local influence without let or hindrance from organised political parties at the centre or in the provinces. Throughout the first three decades of the twentieth century the Indian National Congress managed, albeit imperfectly, to impose its imprimatur on the old factional structures of local politics. By contrast, Muslim politicians were able to work successive constitutional reforms without any heed to the All-Indian Muslim League set up in 1906.

Indeed there is nothing to show that the local and provincial politics of Muslims ever developed within the context of an all-India Muslim political organisation until the last decade of British rule. Except for brief periods when it made sense to band together and claim to represent the communal interests which the British believed to exist, Muslim politicians continued to seek accommodations with members of other communities at the local and provincial levels. Supra-communal alliances often dictated against too close an alignment with the Muslim League's communal concerns. This was underlined by the Montagu-Chelmsford reforms of the nineteen-twenties which gave Indians a measure of self-government at the local and provincial level, but kept the centre firmly in British hands. The British largely succeeded in driving a wedge between the all-India high commands of the League and the Congress and their local and provincial bases of support. During the twenties a separatist Muslim politics held few attractions. Separate representation was no longer enough; the constitutional arrangements ensured against the dominance of the reformed councils by any single community. Alliances cutting across lines of community were forged not only in the United Provinces where Muslims were in a minority, but also in the Punjab and Bengal where they had bare majorities. The provincialisation of electoral politics was matched by fateful developments at the all-India level. Muslim concerns about the Turkish Khilafat found an unlikely spokesman in Mohandas Gandhi. The Mahatma's leadership of the Khilafat movement served to highlight the various possible combinations of religion and politics in the Indian context. The collapse of the movement saw the Muslim League moribund and the Congress split into warring factions over whether or not to enter the reformed provincial councils.

By the time of the constitutional negotiations of the early thirties there was no all-India Muslim political party which could put forth a plausible claim to speak for all Indian Muslims. Paradoxically, it was the Punjab Unionists, a supra-communal alliance of Muslim, Hindu and Sikh agriculturist interests, who dominated the political dialogue of this period. The Punjabi construct of 'Muslim interest' which found form in the communal award of 1932 and the government of India act of 1935 was unacceptable to Muslims in provinces where they were in a minority. The award left Muslims in the Punjab and Bengal in a strong position; they were allowed to retain their separate electorates and received more seats than any other community in the provincial assemblies. Muslim politicians in these two provinces, along with their counterparts in the newly created province of Sind and the North West Frontier Province, which was elevated to the status of a governor's province, could look forward to taking advantage of the provincial autonomy granted under the 1935 act. But full autonomy for the provinces placed Muslims in the minority provinces at a disadvantage. It involved scrapping the official bloc, the one effective safeguard for minority interests.

The revival of the All-India Muslim League in 1934 with Jinnah in the saddle was partly an attempt by disgruntled politicians in the minority provinces, the United Provinces in particular, to revise the new constitutional arrangements. The 1935 act had for the first time opened up the prospect of the British giving Indians substantial power at the centre on the basis of electoral success in the provinces. If Jinnah and the League could somehow link their concerns with those of Muslims in the majority provinces, minority province Muslims might still retrieve some of the old benefits by calling in the centre to redress their provincial grievances. But, until the British actually showed signs of devolving power at the all-India level, the Muslim-majority provinces saw no reason to ally with the All-India Muslim League.

Before the first elections under the 1935 act, Jinnah and the League tried not only to woo the Muslim-majority provinces but also to come to an understanding with the Congress at the all-India level. They failed on both counts. The Muslim provinces were not prepared to puff up the claims of a League which had no organisational presence in British India. Lacking a solid base of support in the Muslim-majority provinces, the League could not find the terms which might have paved the way for an agreement with the Congress at the centre. The results of the 1937 elections registered an embarrassing defeat for the Muslim League. It won a mere 4.4 per cent of the total Muslim vote cast and this despite the fact that Muslims had separate electorates. Except in Bengal where it managed to bag thirty-nine seats in the provincial assembly, the League met with a serious rebuff in the Muslim-majority provinces of the north-west. It did slightly better in the Muslim-minority provinces. But here the Congress did best and did not need help from outside quarters to form stable ministries. This left Jinnah and the League in the lurch, both at the centre and in the provinces.

There was some consolation for Jinnah. Congress also had failed to make an impressive showing at the polls in the Muslim-majority provinces. Ready and able to seize power at the all-India centre, Congress had to find a way of pulling in the Muslim provinces. The results of the 1937 elections underlined the attachment of these provinces to the autonomy granted to them by the 1935 act. They all had opted for provincial parties, some with only the most nominal links with all-India parties. This was one of the intended consequences of politics under the 1919 reforms. It was only with the broadening of the franchise under the 1935 act and, more specifically, the possibility of the British conceding self-government to Indians at the centre that there could be a real need for all-India parties. Congress alone amongst the all-India parties did well at the polls, a reward for the civil disobedience campaigns of the twenties and early thirties. Its success was seen by Jinnah as evidence of the eventual triumph of the centre over the provinces. If the League could make amends for its magisterial inactivity of the past, it could conceivably try and approximate Congress's example in the future.

Here Jinnah took advantage of the fact that the Indian Muslims, however divided, remained a separate political category within the existing constitutional set up. If the League could lend some credence to its claim to speak on behalf of all Muslims it might yet confirm its position as the representative organisation of Muslims in majority and minority provinces alike. It could do so by appearing to mediate on behalf of the Muslim provinces in the negotiations that were to determine India's constitutional future. In the process it might be able to rivet its own control over the majority provinces and hold out a bait to the Congress. These then were the objectives Jinnah had in mind when he began recasting the League's political strategy.

In October 1937 the Muslim premiers of the Punjab and Bengal, Sikander Hayat Khan and Fazlul Huq, gave Jinnah the semblance of a brief to speak for their provinces at the centre, but only if he kept out of provincial affairs. This was an indication that Muslim politicians outside the Congress ken in the majority provinces were coming to sense the danger in allowing their case to go unrepresented at the all-India level. So for the first time Muslim politicians in both the majority and the minority provinces were in tacit agreement about the need to back an all-India Muslim party. The federal provisions of the 1935 act were uncertain safeguards for Muslim interests, both at the centre for the Muslim provinces and in the provinces where they were in a minority. Separate representation offered no relief whatsoever. In the unlikely event that it gave Muslims an incentive to vote solidly for a single party – a display of unity that would be unprecedented in the history of Muslim politics in India – they would still be hopelessly outnumbered in the making of the new constitution. So there was no question of backing Congress's demand for independence to be organised by a single constituent assembly whose proceedings it almost certainly could dominate. What India's Muslims needed was a way of overcoming the constitutional problem of having been cast into the category of a political minority lacking both in organisation and unanimity.

One plausible way forward was to draw upon some of the old thinking and asserting that the Indian Muslims were not a minority but a nation entitled to equal treatment with the Hindu nation in the distribution of power and patronage. During the 1880s, Syed Ahmad Khan had used the argument of the 'two nations' to exhort Muslims to shun the Congress and to impress upon the British the need to view their importance in political rather than in numerical terms. In 1930, Mohammad Iqbal, the renowned poet and philosopher, had asked the All-India Muslim League's council to endorse the call for the creation of a Muslim state in the north-west of India, including Punjab, Sind, the NWFP and Baluchistan. His ideas failed to capture the imagination of Muslim politicians, but they inspired Chaudhri Rahmat Ali, a student at Cambridge, to conjure up the word 'Pakistan'. Literally, the 'land of the pure', 'P' stood for the Punjab; 'A' for Afghanistan or the North West Frontier Province; 'S' for Sind and 'tan' for Baluchistan. Yet unlike

Iqbal's scheme, which was placed strictly within the context of all-India, Rahmat Ali's envisaged a massive transfer of Muslim populations from other parts of India and was sneered at by Muslim politicians some of whom dubbed it 'chimerical' and 'impractical'. By the late nineteen-thirties, however, there were new and powerful reasons for appearing to go along, in part at least, with these shreds of Muslim political genius.

So the reappearance of the 'two nation' theory at the level of political debate has to be seen in the light of the very different circumstances of the late 1930s and 40s. The Congress victory in the 1937 elections had already forced Muslim politicians to assess the implications for their interests in the event of a British transfer of power at the centre. With the outbreak of war in Europe the context of Indian politics changed rapidly. The viceroy's decision to postpone all constitutional advance gave Jinnah and the League an opening. Once Congress had spelt out its terms for cooperating in the war effort, namely independence here and now, it became urgently necessary for the viceroy to justify keeping things as they were for the duration of the war. The League's claim to speak for all Muslims seemed a convenient excuse with which to challenge Congress's claim to speak for the whole of India. So the viceroy pressed Jinnah to outline the League's 'constructive policy'.

But any 'constructive policy' for divided Muslims had to steer a clear path between the contradictory requirements of Muslims in the majority and the minority provinces. All that Jinnah wanted at this stage was to secure recognition for the League as the sole representative organisation of the Indian Muslims. Forced prematurely to specify the League's policy, Jinnah kept it as vague and imprecise as possible. In March 1940, without specifying the exact geographical boundaries, the League formally demanded independent Muslim states in the north-west and the north-east of India, repudiating once and for all the minority status separate representation implied, and declaring instead that the Indian Muslims whatever their internal differences were a nation. This was Jinnah and the League's bid to register their claim to speak for all Indian Muslims, not only for Muslims in minority provinces where they had had their only electoral success in the 1937 elections, but also for Muslims in the majority provinces where they had been unequivocally rejected.

There was an obvious contradiction in a claim to represent all Indian Muslims and an apparently separatist demand for independent Muslim states. A closer analysis of the League's resolution adopted in Lahore hints at the thinking leading to the enunciation of the new policy. The resolution made no reference to a centre, weak or strong, an intriguing omission considering Jinnah and the League's centralist pretensions.

Even more significantly, the resolution made no mention of either partition or 'Pakistan'. The essence of the League's resolution was the assertion that all future constitutional arrangements be 'reconsidered de novo' on the grounds that Indian Muslims were a 'nation'. It was the League's 'considered view' that the Muslim-majority provinces in the north-west and the north-east of India should be 'grouped to constitute Independent States in which the constituent units...[would] be autonomous and sovereign'.[2] This was a concession to the Muslim-majority provinces. It was only by appearing to concede an even greater measure of autonomy than had been granted under the 1935 act that Jinnah and the League could expect to solicit support in the Muslim provinces. Jinnah's reluctance in making the concession can be seen by the care he took to ensure that the 'sovereignty' of these 'Independent States' would be something for the future. The League's working committee was to frame a scheme 'providing for the assumption *finally* by the respective regions of all the powers such as defence, external affairs, communications, customs and such matters as may be necessary'.[3] The choice of the word 'finally' was deliberate; it kept the door open for negotiations leading to different solutions.

Jinnah at least both wanted and needed a different solution. Throughout his political career his main concern had been the arrangements by which power was to be shared at the all-India centre. The problem of bringing the Muslim provinces behind the League's all-India purposes had been a main stumbling-block in Jinnah's repeated efforts to secure an agreement with the Congress at the centre. Once it became obvious that Congress had no intention of sharing power with a rival high command, as Jawaharlal Nehru's refusal to countenance a Congress-League coalition ministry in the UP had seemed to indicate, Jinnah took the risk of appearing to go along with the demands of the Muslim provinces. But the particularisms of these provinces posed an even greater threat to the role he envisaged for the League than to Congress's purposes at the centre. This is why Jinnah had avoided committing himself to the future shape of the centre. He knew all too well that the British and the Congress would stolidly resist the demand of the Muslim provinces for autonomy, much less that for outright sovereignty. The League's seeming denial of any kind of all-India centre would force the British and the Congress to negotiate with it when the time came to settle India's constitutional future. In the meantime the

[2] See the AIML's resolution of 23 March 1940 in Syed Sharifuddin Pirzada (ed.), *Foundation of Pakistan: the All-India Muslim League Documents: 1906–1947*, Karachi 1970, II, 340–41.
[3] Ibid.

notion that Muslims constituted a nation allowed Jinnah to trump Congress's claim to inherit power at the existing British Indian centre.

So far from abandoning the hope of winning a large share of power for Muslims at the all-India level, the League's Lahore resolution had in fact staked a claim for equality of status with the Congress in an independent India. The resolution had the additional merit of satisfying the Muslim provinces while at the same time alleviating some of the anxieties of Muslims in the minority provinces. It was based on the premise that the frontiers of the 'Independent States' would conform to the existing boundaries of the Muslim provinces. This would leave Muslims in the minority provinces outside the Muslim 'autonomous and sovereign' areas. It would also include large non-Muslim minorities in the predominantly Muslim 'Independent States'. The League envisaged a reciprocal arrangement to protect the interests of both sets of minorities, Muslim and non-Muslim. Interestingly enough, the resolution refers to 'the constitution' to determine safeguards for minorities both inside and outside the Muslim states.[4] This is proof that Jinnah had deliberately left open the option for a constitutional arrangement covering the whole of India.

After 1940 Jinnah argued that, since India contained two separate nations, a transfer of power would have to involve the dissolution of the unitary centre created by the British. Any reconstitution of that centre would require the agreement of the Muslim-majority provinces as well as the princely states. Once the principle of Muslim provinces being grouped to form a separate state was conceded, Jinnah was prepared to negotiate whether that state would seek a confederation with the non-Muslim provinces, namely Hindustan, on the basis of equality at the all-India level, or whether, as a sovereign state, it would make treaty arrangements with the rest of India. But, in either case, the League's demand for a 'Pakistan', the territorial expression of the Muslim claim to nationhood, had to be conceded prior to negotiations determining the shape and powers of the all-India centre. In sum, Jinnah was using the demand for Pakistan to negotiate a new constitutional arrangement in which Muslims would have an equal share of power at a centre reconstituted on the basis of a partnership between two essentially sovereign states, Pakistan (representing the Muslim-majority provinces) and Hindustan (representing the Hindu-majority provinces).

This was the strategy of a leader, taking his cues from constitutional law, but directing a party whose main bases of support were in the Hindu-majority provinces. If they were to play their role in the making

⁴ Ibid.

of India's constitutional future Jinnah and the League had to prove their support in the Muslim-majority provinces. Such support could not have been won by too precise a political programme since the interests of Muslims in one part of India did not suit Muslims in others. A socio-economic programme aimed at mobilising the rank and file could hardly enthuse the landed oligarchs who dominated Muslim politics. With no organisational machinery in the Muslim provinces, Jinnah and the League had little option but to advocate terms largely defined by landed notables in control of local politics.

Preoccupied with developments at the all-India level, Jinnah could not afford to wreck the existing structure of Muslim politics, especially since he had nothing plausible to replace it with. This is where religion came to the rescue of a politician whose secular leanings had won him the title of 'ambassador of Hindu-Muslim' unity, and who had on more than one occasion voiced his contempt for the mullahs and maulvis who tauted Islam in the bazaars and mohallas of Muslim India. Yet Jinnah's resort to religion was not an ideology to which he was ever committed or even a device to use against rival communities; it was simply a way of giving a semblance of unity and solidity to his divided Muslim constituents. Jinnah needed a demand that was specifically ambiguous and imprecise to command general support, something specifically Muslim though unspecific in every other respect. The intentionally obscure cry for a 'Pakistan' was contrived to meet this requirement.

During the remaining years of the war the demand for 'Pakistan' did come to have an appeal for most Muslims, whether in the majority or in the minority provinces. But there was no obvious connection between popular sentiments for an undefined demand for a 'Pakistan' and a matching political organisation striving to achieve it. Despite Jinnah's large claims the League achieved little in terms of effective control over the Muslim-majority province politicians, both inside and outside the provincial legislatures, as well as over the populace at the base. Concerned mainly with getting the appearance of support for his strategy at the all-India level, Jinnah had at each step to postpone building a party machinery linking the League's high command with the provincial and local levels.

The provincial Leagues in the Punjab, Bengal, Sind and the North West Frontier Province were rent with factional divisions and all that Jinnah could do was to claim allegiance of whichever combination temporarily emerged on top. In return he had to allow Muslim provincial factions an independence of manoeuvre which sooner or later threatened the very purposes for which their support had been sought in the first place. For one thing it meant that Jinnah could not afford to state precisely what the demand for 'Pakistan' was intended to accomplish. If the demand was to enjoy support from Muslims in the minority provinces it had to be couched in uncompromisingly communal terms. But the communal slant to the demand cut against the grain of politics in the Muslim provinces, particularly the Punjab and Bengal, where Muslim domination over undivided territories depended upon keeping fences mended with members of other communities. Without a measure of communal harmony in the Punjab and Bengal, Jinnah could not realistically hope to claim these provinces for 'Pakistan'. It is a commentary on Jinnah's priorities, and evidence that he was thinking of a strategy covering the interests of all Indian Muslims, that he made no effort to qualify the communal overtones of the League's programme and simply demanded the incorporation of undivided Punjab and Bengal in 'Pakistan'.

The Cripps offer of 1942, offering provinces and not communities the right to opt out of the Indian union, nearly succeeded in bringing out the basic contradiction in Jinnah's demands. Some Muslim politicians in the Punjab and Bengal could see that the provincial option was incompatible with following the lead of a communal party at the all-India level. But the Cripps mission failed and many Muslim politicians continued to nurture illusions of gaining more by backing the League at the centre than by coming to terms with the non-Muslims. Conveniently for Jinnah both the Congress high command and the British had other concerns at the time and preferred to ignore the inherent contradiction in the League's claims, namely that the communal slant to the 'Pakistan' demand might have to entail the partition of the Punjab and Bengal. The imposition of a communal line on what were essentially Muslim province demands to safeguard, and preferably strengthen, provincial autonomy was in due course to provide Congress the means with which to cut Jinnah's claims down to size. But even as early as 1944 C.R. Rajagopalachari, a veteran Congress politician from Madras, tried flushing out the contradictions in the League's demands when he offered Jinnah a 'Pakistan' carved out of the Muslim-majority districts of the Punjab and Bengal. Such a 'Pakistan' had still to seek common arrangements with the rest of India on matters to do with defence, communications and commerce. This was in part what Jinnah himself had in mind. But if he was to be Congress's equal and not a mere supplicant in the making of the future all-India arrangements he had to have undivided Punjab and Bengal. Without the non-Muslim-majority districts of these two provinces, the League could not expect to bargain for parity between 'Pakistan' and 'Hindustan'. So, although Pakistan's geographical boundaries in 1947 were not very different from those visualised by Rajagopalachari, Jinnah dismissed the scheme as 'offering a shadow and a husk – a maimed, mutilated and moth-eaten Pakistan, and thus trying to pass off having met our Pakistan scheme and Muslim demand'.[5]

Both Cripps and Rajagopalachari had in their different ways raised the vital question of what was to happen to the non-Muslim minorities in the Muslim-majority provinces if the demand for Pakistan was conceded. The demand was based on the Muslim right to self-determination and could not logically be denied to non-Muslims living in the Punjab and Bengal. Taking uncertain refuge under the separate political category assigned to India's Muslims, Jinnah in a sheer display of nerve declared that if a plebiscite was held to decide the future of the majority provinces Muslims alone would have the right to vote. Despite repeated warnings by the governors of the Punjab and Bengal, and also Assam, about the implications of the League's propaganda, nothing was done by New Delhi or London to challenge the false premises of the 'Pakistan' slogan. Let off the hook, Jinnah concentrated upon building the League's strength inside the Muslim-majority province legislatures in case these served as the electorate to determine India's political future.

By the time of the first Simla conference in the summer of 1945, Jinnah and the League had made little headway in dominating the legislatures in the Muslim provinces. Muslim League ministries in Bengal and the North West Frontier Province had been ousted. In the Punjab, the province which mattered most to the League, Jinnah had little support in the assembly and no influence at all over the provincial ministry. Sind was the only province with a League ministry still in office. The failure of the Simla conference on the issue of Muslim representation in the viceroy's executive council had as much to do with Jinnah's intransigence – his stubborn insistence that the League alone should select the Muslim members of the council – as with the inability of the British and the Congress to grasp the Pakistan nettle. It was at Simla that Jinnah was at his most vulnerable. The collapse of the conference fortified his credentials as the sole spokesman of Indian Muslims, even though the League's performance in the Muslim provinces had fallen badly short of Jinnah's most modest expectations.

During the war Jinnah's tactics had dovetailed neatly with British purposes. Once the war ended they posed the most formidable obstacle to them. Congress, put out of effective play for much of the war, became extremely important after it. The governors of the Punjab and Bengal

[5] Jinnah's address to the AIML council at Lahore, 30 July 1944, in Pirzada (ed.), *Foundations of Pakistan*, II, 493–5.

continued to urge New Delhi to state authoritatively that the creation of Pakistan would mean the partition of these two Muslim provinces. But neither New Delhi nor London cared to clarify HMG's position on the League's demand for Pakistan. And as for the Congress high command, it sanguinely reiterated the old line that the communal question would be settled after independence. With both the British and the Congress continuing to give short shrift to the League's demand for 'Pakistan', many Muslims, whatever their persuasion, saw the best security in having a single voice powerfully advocating the Muslim case in the negotiations to settle the all important question of how power was to be shared after the British transferred power in India. So Jinnah took a barely organised Muslim League, with no specific political programme except the vague cry for 'Pakistan', into the 1945–6 elections certain of capturing most of the floating Muslim vote.

Jinnah and the League won all the Muslim seats in the elections to the central assembly, and polled 75 per cent of the total Muslim vote cast in the provincial assembly elections; an impressive about turn considering the dismal showing in the 1937 elections. But the Muslim vote had not ratified a specific programme because no programme had actually been specified. No one was clear about the real meaning of 'Pakistan', let alone its precise geographic boundaries. Moreover, the elections had not been won by a well-organised political party, but by leaders of local factions with whom the ramshackle provincial Leagues had quickly made terms. The League's recent converts were just as capable of changing tack if circumstances called for different political accommodations. This was entirely within the realm of possibility in the Punjab and Bengal since here the League's communal line, anathema to the non-Muslim minorities, could lead to the partition of these provinces on the lines of religious self-determination.

Predictably, Jinnah interpreted the election result as a mandate for the League's demand for a 'Pakistan' based on undivided Punjab and Bengal. Yet the stridently communal overtones of the League's election propaganda, specifically the role of local religious leaders in stirring Muslim passions, had embittered relations between the communities beyond repair. Communal tensions did not strengthen Jinnah's hands in the constitutional negotiations at the centre – they weakened them further still. As it was Jinnah's priorities had left him in the precarious position of performing the final act without the backing of an effective political party organisation in the Muslim-majority provinces. Without the control from the centre which the League's high command had signally failed to exercise, there was nothing to stop the Congress from making terms separately with politicians in Muslim-majority provinces.

Indeed after the 1946 elections apart from Bengal which had a League ministry, but one that was ready to make overtures for a coalition with the Congress, Sind was the only province in the north-west where Leaguers were in office. The North West Frontier Province was under a Congress ministry and the Punjab, the 'corner-stone' of Pakistan, was under a coalition ministry of Unionists, Congressmen and Panthic Sikhs.

The cabinet mission plan of 1946 for a three-tier all-India federation came close to giving Jinnah what he needed. Compulsory grouping of provinces at the second-tier handed the League a potential centre capable of disciplining the Muslim provinces and deploying their weight at an all-India centre confined to dealing only with defence, foreign affairs and communications. But the Congress had long ago spotted the basic weaknesses in Jinnah's position. It was not persuaded that the League could swamp the provincialism of the Muslim provinces. Above all, its own imperatives called for the extension of the centre's powers so that real authority was vested at the all-India level, not with the group legislatures as the League demanded. When the mission took Congress's aims into account they could only offer Jinnah the choice between an undivided India with a weak federal centre and compulsory grouping of Muslim and Hindu provinces but without a guarantee of the Muslim share at the centre, or a sovereign Pakistan stripped of eastern Punjab and western Bengal (including Calcutta).

Significantly, Jinnah rejected the Pakistan on offer and on 6 June 1946 the All-India Muslim League took the momentous step of accepting the mission's plan. Indications that Congress intended to exploit divisions within the Muslim camp to break provincial grouping, however, convinced Jinnah that the mission's proposals were not a secure basis for a settlement. A sovereign Pakistan alone could give the League a centre capable of controlling the Muslim provinces. But a sovereign Pakistan had to include undivided Punjab and Bengal if it was to receive a large share of the centre's assets (particularly the Indian army). Without some such bargaining weight Jinnah could not hope to negotiate the broader all-India arrangements which he had always assumed would have to be made. He had also calculated that once the principle of Pakistan had been conceded there would be time enough at hand to offer safeguards to the non-Muslim minorities in the Punjab and Bengal. These were some of the reasons why in the fall of 1946, despite deep reservations about the mission's long-term proposals, Jinnah advised the League to join the interim government as a junior partner of the Congress.

But on 20 February 1947 the Attlee government, without first conceding a Pakistan based on undivided Muslim provinces, announced its decision to transfer power by June 1948. This left Jinnah hoping against hope that the British might yet make an award giving him the whole of the Punjab and Bengal. But by early 1947 London's main priority was to get out of India as quickly as possible. To do so it had to come to terms with a Congress high command which knew that the resources of the raj, already stretched to the limit, were insufficient to prevent it from shaping India's future according to its own design. The old administrative structure, once the 'steel frame' confirming British rule, but now emasculated by a delayed policy of Indianisation and uncertainties about service futures, could not be relied upon to cope with the swelling tides of communal disorder. The Indian army was an equally unreliable instrument in a political society on the brink of chaos. The need to strengthen central authority was the paramount concern dictating Congress's policy in the last few remaining months of the British raj in India. So there was a basis for an understanding between the Congress high command and London. The main obstacle was the demands of the Muslim-majority provinces as articulated by Jinnah and the League. Even before the arrival of Mountbatten as Britain's last viceroy to India, the Congress high command had laid down its terms for a settlement. It was not prepared to continue to share power with the League inside the interim government so long as Jinnah refused to accept the cabinet mission's proposals. Nor was it willing to view provincial grouping as the nub of the mission's proposals. The future constitution of India would be framed by the constituent assembly where the League would be given a chance to prove that grouping had the support of all the Muslim provinces.

The choice with which Jinnah was presented in the end by the Congress and the British was either an undivided India without any guarantee of the Muslim share of power at the all-India centre or a sovereign Pakistan carved out of the Muslim-majority districts of the Punjab and Bengal. Had Jinnah been more sure of his following in the Muslim provinces he might conceivably have decided to work the mission's plan for an all-India federal structure. In this way he could have prevented the partition of the Punjab and Bengal and used the weight of the Muslim provinces to secure safeguards for Indian Muslims in both majority and minority provinces. But Jinnah's fears of his own followers, his deep mistrust of the Congress high command and Mountbatten's decision to move up the date for the final transfer of power to August 1947, left him with no alternative but to acquiesce in the creation of a Pakistan shorn of eastern Punjab and western Bengal (including Calcutta) – the 'mutilated and moth-eaten' state which he had rejected out of hand in 1944 and then again in 1946.

A Pakistan without its large non-Muslim minorities in the Punjab and Bengal was hardly well placed to demand safeguards for Muslim minorities in the rest of India. Congress had agreed to the principle of partition on the condition that Jinnah and the League accepted it as a final settlement and would not make any further claims on behalf of Muslims in the minority provinces. Moreover, according to the Congress, partition did not entail a division of India into Pakistan and Hindustan as Jinnah had always maintained, but would merely mean that some areas with Muslim majorities were 'splitting off' from the 'Union of India' which already existed.[6] As far as Jinnah was concerned, the 'Union of India' could not exist without the Muslim areas. Congress's insistence and the British acceptance of the notion that the 'Union of India' would continue to exist without the Muslim-majority areas destroyed the entire basis of the 'two nation' theory as propagated by Jinnah. So the creation of Pakistan, far from being the logical culmination of the theory that there were two nations in India, Hindu and Muslim, was in fact its most decisive political abortion. It was only in an all-India context that the concept of the two nations could have survived the creation of a separate Muslim homeland. Congress's interpretation of partition cast Pakistan in the role of a 'seceding' state with the added implication that if it failed to survive the traumas of its creation the Muslim areas would have to return to the 'Union of India' severally, not help to recreate it on the basis of two sovereign states.

This is why it was vitally important for Jinnah and the League to create a viable central authority over the Pakistan areas. Mere references to Islamic solidarity were no substitute for the hard imperatives of building a new central government machinery for Pakistan's western and eastern wings. It was precisely because religion had not been a sufficient cement to bring the Muslim provinces solidly behind an all-India strategy aimed at safeguarding the interests of all Indian Muslims that Jinnah had been forced to abandon his larger political purposes and settle for a truncated Pakistan. This is not to deny that the slogan 'Islam in danger' was a useful rallying cry against the prospect of a Hindu dominated centre. But it cannot be argued that by a supporting a demand couched in Islamic terms, Pakistan's predominantly Muslim peoples, whatever their provincial affiliations, particular traditions or ideological convictions, had for religious reasons agreed to buckle under the tight central control which the new state had to establish if it was to survive. The particularisms of the Muslim provinces had been a

---

[6] Record of Henderson's conversation with Krishna Menon, 23 May 1947, *The Transfer of Power 1942–7*, X, 962, London 1981 (henceforth *TP* followed by volume and page number).

principal driving force in the making of Pakistan. In the absence of a well-knit party organisation linking the League's high command with those who wielded power at the local and provincial levels, these particularisms posed a serious threat to the establishment of central authority in the new state. This, together with the dislocations wrought by partition and the problem of resettling millions of refugees, underlines the monumental difficulties that were involved in creating a new centre over provinces which for so long had been governed from New Delhi.

2

Pakistan's share of the spoils

The plan to partition India announced on 3 June 1947 merely conceded the principle of a separate centre for the Muslim-majority areas. It offered no guarantees for Pakistan's creation, much less for its survival as an independent entity. Once the Muslim provinces had voted to join a new constituent assembly the creation of Pakistan might assume greater certainty. Yet voting to create a Pakistan was not the same as having the ability or the resources to sustain it as a sovereign state. If Pakistan was to survive it had somehow or other to build a central administrative structure capable of coordinating and regulating the affairs of territories separated by over a thousand miles. But the existing structures of administration, finance, communications and defence were on an all-India basis, all controlled from New Delhi, the future seat of the Congress government. Transferring power by 15 August 1947 instead of June 1948 on the basis of dominion status for both states confounded the task. The partition machinery set up to determine Pakistan's share of the assets of undivided India had seventy-two days in which to dismantle a government structure it had taken the British over a hundred years to construct. Settling who was to get what – a laborious business even in normal times – took place against the backdrop of an unprecedented communal carnage. With distrust shaping the perceptions of the two negotiating sides and the partition process constantly in danger of going off the rails, Pakistan moved towards independent statehood in less than auspicious circumstances.

Distrust of Congress designs was matched by disunities within. There was no certainty of the Muslim-majority provinces cooperating inside the new constituent assembly, especially on the critical issue of how power was to be apportioned between the centre and the provinces. It was only after Mountbatten, in deference to the Congress, revised the partition plan at the eleventh hour that efforts to keep Bengal united and independent were abandoned. In Sind, where there was a 'strong feeling among...[the] Leaguers that the Province would literally and figuratively find itself under the heel of the Punjab in any federated Pakistan',[1]

---

[1] R.D. Gatewood [American vice consul, Karachi] to the secretary of state, 3 May 1947, NND.842909, RG 59, Box 5955, 845.00/5-347, NA.

moves were afoot to establish a sovereign state. In the North West Frontier Province where a Congress ministry was in office, some Leaguers had joined their rivals in pressing for an independent 'Pathanistan'. Baluchistan was under the sway of tribal sardars who were not at all amenable to compromising their autonomy of action by buckling under any central authority, be it Hindu or Muslim. The Punjab, which like Bengal was facing an agonising amputation, did not have the dominant voice in the League's central high command which remained the preserve of Muslims from the Hindu-majority provinces.

So there was a high probability of tensions between the new centre and the provinces. If the centre was to triumph, Pakistan's early managers had to secure a substantial share of the financial and other assets of undivided India, especially the Indian army. A committee consisting of the viceroy and two representatives each from the Congress and the League was to supervise the partition process.[2] Once eastern Bengal, western Punjab and Sind had voted to join a new constituent assembly the partition committee was replaced by a partition council. It consisted of three representatives each from the League and the Congress with Mountbatten acting as chairman but without any powers to arbitrate. Similar committees were created in the provinces awaiting partition. A special arbitral tribunal was established to adjudicate on disputes arising from the partition process whether at the centre or in the Punjab and Bengal. In addition, a boundary commission under the chairmanship of Cyril Radcliffe was entrusted with the job of drawing the frontiers of the two states.

The question of sovereignty

Even with an elaborate machinery to push forward the partition process, snags and delays were inevitable. There were no rough and ready formulas at hand to divide the government of India's assets between the two dominions. For all the contrived urgency of the process the division could not be completed before power was transferred. This meant that Congress as the inheritor of British India's unitary centre

[2] The actual working out of the details was left to a steering committee of two senior civil servants, Chaudhri Mohammad Ali, representing the government of Pakistan, and H.M. Patel, representing the 'Union of India'. Both served as secretaries of the partition committee as well as the specially created partition secretariat with as many as ten different expert committees, each assisted by a number of subcommittees representing the various departments of the undivided government of India. Each of the committees had an equal number of Hindu and Muslim officials. Despite the sheer magnitude of the task, the committees had only a month in which to report their findings. These were then screened by the steering committee which made its recommendations to the partition committee – the final decision-making authority.

would assume control over the joint assets of the two dominions after 15 August. Anticipating Pakistan's problems in securing its share of the assets Mountbatten offered to continue as governor-general for both dominions. Yet sensing his impotence once formal power had been transferred he sensibly refused to arbitrate in disputes between the two sides. A common governor-general without the power to enforce decisions could do no more than plead for a just division of the assets.

The Indian independence bill, as Mountbatten himself confessed, had been drafted on the assumption that there was a continuing government of India under Congress control with Pakistan in the position of a seceding state.[3] Jinnah and the League saw no attractions in having a common governor-general for two states, one of which was regarded as the 'successor' and the other as the 'seceder'. If the Pakistan constituent assembly fell to pieces nothing could prevent its constituent units from seeking accommodations with the Indian union. Since it had been deemed impracticable to complete the division of the armed forces before 31 March 1948, seven and a half months after the transfer of power, Pakistan's sovereignty would be more fiction than fact if it shared the office of common governor-general with the rest of India. This was why Jinnah tried floating the idea of a supra-governor-general with authority to resolve disputes between the two states each of which would have its own governor-general. But a supreme arbitrator could not have authority over a dominion governor-general. So the Indian independence bill was premised on the acceptance by both sides of a common governor-general. The need for some executive authority to implement the partition process ensured that the governor-general was invested with powers more wide-ranging than those normally conferred upon a dominion governor-general.

Jinnah had insisted that the bill should state explicitly that the governor-general would not be liable to act on the advice of his ministers. But at Congress's intervention no such provision was made. Nor was it made clear how a common governor-general would function in the face of conflicting advice from the two governments. Confident about its ability to flout the governor-general's authority and keep Pakistan's share of the assets to a bare minimum, Congress wanted all disputes to be settled through arbitration. Mountbatten had hinted that, if both dominions had separate governor-generals, the two might meet to settle disputes on an equal footing. This persuaded Jinnah that a separate governor-general for Pakistan would be a better insurance against any efforts by Congress to withhold assets after the transfer of

[3] Harry F. Grady [American ambassador, New Delhi] to the secretary of state, telegram no. 475, 2 July 1947, NND.842909, RG 59, Box 5955, 845.00/7-247, NA.

power. It would at least enable the governor-general of Pakistan to present his dominion's case without also having to account for the interests of the union government.

But it was the extent of the governor-general's powers which ultimately determined Jinnah's decision.[4] If the bill had not been drafted on the mistaken assumption that there would be a common governor-general for both dominions it is doubtful whether the office would have been invested with such enormous powers. Once again it was Congress's imperatives which gave Jinnah an opportunity to consolidate the government of Pakistan's authority over its territories. Congress had wanted the bill to provide for a strong central government so as to avoid the possibility of the union constituent assembly limiting its sphere of authority in an independent India. Consequently, the Indian independence bill provided for the continuation of the government of India act of 1935 as the legal framework for both dominions until their constituent assemblies had drafted alternative constitutions. The governor-general of either state could adapt the 1935 act to suit the particular requirements of his dominion. Under section 9(1) of the Indian independence bill, the governor-general was given virtually dictatorial powers over the entire sphere of government (including the judiciary). These powers could be checked by the constituent assembly. But, until the Pakistan constituent assembly was in a position to do so, the governor-general could rule by executive decree and scotch any nascent revolt against the new centre.

A man of unquestionable constitutional acumen, Jinnah could see the perils ahead in letting anyone other than himself exercise the vast powers bestowed upon the governor-general. He knew only too well that there was no certitude that Pakistan would be able to pull through the crucial first few months of independence. The partition of Punjab and Bengal had already cut down drastically the League's share of the assets of undivided India. By exercising the powers of the governor-general, Jinnah could begin building real central authority over Pakistan's provinces and, in this way, confirm its independent existence. So on 2 July 1947, Jinnah informed the viceroy of his decision to become Pakistan's first governor-general. Rejecting the contention that this would rob Pakistan of crores of rupees worth of assets, Jinnah asked Mountbatten to accept Congress's invitation to remain as governor-general for the 'Union of India'. Jinnah indicated that 'unless there...[was] a steadying influence he was afraid of what the Congress

---

[4] For a detailed analysis of Jinnah's reasons for becoming Pakistan's first governor-general see A. Jalal, 'Inheriting the Raj: Jinnah and the Governor-Generalship Issue', in *Modern Asian Studies*, 19, 1, February 1985, 29–53.

might do to Pakistan'.[5] These were not the words of a man in the grips of 'megalomania' as Mountbatten suspected. They were the considered words of an old campaigner who had a measure both of the Congress leadership and his own followers and realised that the battle for Pakistan's survival had only just begun.

The limitations of Mountbatten's influence over the Congress and the soundness of Jinnah's decision to become Pakistan's first governor-general can best be seen by the tortuous negotiations to settle the broad principles of division. Every asset of undivided India was bitterly disputed. An immediate issue of controversy was the reconstitution of the existing interim government. Congress had repeatedly threatened to resign on the grounds that it could not be expected to share power with the League so long as Pakistan loomed on the horizon. So, once the independence bill was on the statute book, Mountbatten divided his executive council into two sub-committees representing the governments of India and Pakistan. Both sides were responsible for their respective territories and met jointly under the viceroy's chairmanship only on matters of common concern. But, until the actual division of all the departments, the government of India continued to function as a single entity. So after the reconstitution of the interim government the Leaguers were in effect ministers without portfolios in the existing secretariats of British India. As Jinnah had argued vehemently, a reconstitution at the centre prior to the transfer of power would reduce the League ministers to the 'invidious role of spies on behalf of Pakistan'; the Congress members could 'entrench themselves in possession of the machinery and assets in favour of the Pakistan Government, after the date of the creation of the two Dominions, on the principle of "what we have, we keep"'.[6]

The administrative legacy

The central reshuffle created the anomalous situation of a cabinet claiming to be a government, but as yet without any ground under its feet or a roof over its head. Mountbatten showed his contempt when he let slip that the government of Pakistan would have to make do with a 'tent' in the initial years of its independence. In the desperate search for a suitable camping ground to pitch the Pakistan government's proverbial 'tent', Karachi was an obvious choice. A burgeoning commercial city of some 600,000 at the time of partition, Karachi was the closest thing to a

[5] Mountbatten's report no.11, 4 July 1947, *TP*, X, 900, cited in ibid., 52.
[6] Jinnah's memorandum on the viceroy's proposal for the reconstitution of the interim government, 29 June 1947, *TP*, XI, 752–3, cited in ibid., 46.

cosmopolitan centre in the areas constituting Pakistan. Its harbour and airport afforded a much needed link with east Bengal and the outside world. But during the war there had been a virtual cessation of building activity in Karachi. So there was little in the way of office space or residential accommodation for the new government and its employees. The Sind League ministry, whether out of patriotism or plain calculation, offered to house the Pakistan central government. But the limits of Sindhi hospitality were reached sooner rather than later. The governor's house, the provincial assembly and a handful of other buildings were all the Sind government was ready to make available. An alternative plan to use the facilities of the army headquarters of the northern command in Rawalpindi was abandoned at Jinnah's insistence. Instead the Quaid-i-Azam ordered the Sindhis to throw open the gates of Karachi[7] to a central government they had worked so hard to resist.

With a semblance of a capital city the search for recruits and office equipment to run the new government began in earnest. The expert committee to divide the personnel, organisation and records of the undivided government of India came up with a series of unworkable formulas. Every government servant was given the choice of opting for either dominion irrespective of religious affiliation. But there were few bold enough to choose serving in a dominion as a religious minority. This was particularly true of non-Muslim civil servants in Pakistan. To prevent government employees running helter-skelter, a provision was made to ensure that the transfers took place over a period of time. A 'standstill' agreement to that effect was reached between the two sides until the reorganisation of the service cadres had been completed. The practical problems of relocating the government personnel, however, were small in comparison to the difficulties of moving equipment and records from New Delhi to Karachi.[8] It soon became impossible to move anything to Karachi where a Pakistan central secretariat of about 300 officers and 4,000 clerks was to be set up.[9]

So the government of Pakistan had literally to begin operations from 'hastily constructed tin sheds' without such basic items as typewriters,

---

[7] Chaudhri Mohammad Ali, *The Emergence of Pakistan*, Lahore 1973, 198–9.

[8] Pakistan was to have approximately 20 percent of the office equipment, furniture and stationary of the government of India's central secretariat. All other offices were to be divided equally between the two dominions. See minutes of the expert committee on 'Organisation, Records and Personnel', memorandum dated 17/19 July 1947, *Partition Proceedings*, I, 101, and 198–9.

[9] Ibid. The transportation system, such as there was, had been disrupted by disturbances and the movement of millions of panic-stricken refugees. Even the duplication of essential records of the most important departments was left unfinished.

telephones, pens or paper.[10] With no records to serve as precedent, government by trial and error became the norm for administering the affairs of the state. This added to the general confusion. Trainloads of junior government employees of varying degrees of technical skills poured into Karachi in search of jobs. What was needed were men with technical know-how and administrative experience; those who made their way to Karachi were largely unskilled or worse still, unlettered. Their main contribution was to strain the capacities of the city to breaking point, converting it overnight into a massive refugee camp.

The new government somehow managed to prepare a blueprint to forestall administrative anarchy. It was the brainchild of Chaudhri Mohammad Ali, a member of the steering committee and among the senior-most Muslim civil servants in British India. The aim was to establish a greater degree of administrative centralisation than in undivided India.[11] This was deemed essential to coordinate the work of the central ministries and the provincial governments. A special post of secretary-general, occupied by Mohammad Ali himself, linked the central cabinet with the overall administration in the country. The secretary-general was responsible for the posting of civil servants at the centre as well as in the provinces and served as the principal decision-maker on all matters to do with the administration. Consequently, the structure of government adopted at the very outset was prone to a certain arbitrariness in decision-making – a perfect formula for friction between the centre and the provinces.

Yet the need to enforce central authority had to be the main priority if Pakistan was to survive the initial tests of independence. In the absence of a basic machinery linking the makeshift central government with the provincial administrations, posting members of the central superior services to the lower rungs of the administrative hierarchy – an old and well-preserved tradition of British Indian administration – was the one effective means of establishing a chain of command from the secretary-general's office into the provinces, districts and localities of Pakistan. Authority vested in the civil servants who had opted for Pakistan, together with the powers of the provincial and local police, were the crutches holding up an inherently weak-kneed administrative system.

It has never been established conclusively just how many civil servants were engaged in the task of administering the new state. The best known estimate is of some 157 officers, including thirty-six British civil servants, forming the core of the Pakistan civil service.[12] But this is an

[10] Mohammad Ali, *The Emergence of Pakistan*, 247.
[11] Ibid., 242.
[12] Ralph Braibanti, *Research on the Bureaucracy of Pakistan*, Durham 1969, 97.

underestimate since it does not account for Muslim officials who came to Pakistan from departments other than the Indian civil service. A more reasonable figure might be somewhere in the vicinity of 200, and even more if the provincial services are taken into consideration. Whatever the precise number, no more than a few hundred got the government machinery rolling.

In any event, numbers bore little relation to the powers senior civil servants could exercise at the provincial, district and local levels as agents of the central government. Here the administrative legacy of the colonial state fitted the interests of the new central government perfectly. Apart from eastern Bengal where an administrative system approximating that in other parts of British India was in existence, Pakistan's north-western provinces had traditionally been governed by officials exercising vast discretionary powers without being inconvenienced by specific rules and procedures. The combination of revenue, executive, magisterial and judicial functions in a single district official responsible to the central government through the office of the provincial chief secretary, almost always a member of the central superior service, was conducive to much greater centralisation than in the regulation provinces of British India. Since all appointments, transfers and promotions of civil servants throughout Pakistan were handled by the secretary-general, Karachi's ability to impose administrative authority over far flung territories was by no means inconceivable.

The division of the financial assets

The effectiveness of the central government's authority of course ultimately depended upon the availability of adequate financial resources. Doubts about the economic viability of Pakistan had been expressed long before it assumed any concrete shape or form. A state carved out of British India's north-western and north-eastern Muslim-majority districts seemed destined to be an international liability incapable of paying for its defence, let alone its development requirements. Statements by Congress leaders predicting the early demise of the state, though long on rhetoric and short on specifics, did have a point. The areas which constituted Pakistan historically had been the agrarian backwaters of British India. With nothing remotely resembling an industrial infrastructure, the revenues accruing to the new central government would be hopelessly inadequate. Even with help from private capital, the state would have to incur vast amounts of expenditure to facilitate the process of capital accumulation. For the time being, however, the central government had to be content with whatever it could get as its share of undivided India's financial assets.

Both sides fought tooth and nail for every rupee worth of assets, one anxious to deny, the other determined to secure. The deliberations of the expert committee on assets and liabilities are an amazing instance of the tortured logic deployed by negotiators with only the most rudimentary knowledge of facts. It was not clear precisely how much the areas constituting Pakistan had contributed to undivided India's central revenues. This was estimated by Pakistan's representatives to be 11 per cent in the pre-war period and 7 per cent for the duration of the war. On the basis that its share of the public debt should represent the contributions made by its territories in the past, Pakistan's representatives wanted responsibility for only 7 per cent of the total financial liabilities.[13] As for the share of the assets, they nailed the argument on the claim that the per capita income of the Pakistan areas as a whole was 32 per cent less than in the rest of India. Pakistan had to pay for the upkeep of its defence forces, build an administrative structure and resettle the millions fleeing into its territories. It would take time to set up a workable taxation structure, not to mention an operational money market. In view of the unusual circumstances facing the new state, its representatives felt entitled to a weighted share of the assets.[14]

This was considered preposterous logic by the representatives of the Indian union. They were opposed to any straightforward correlation between the contribution of the Pakistan areas to the centre and their share of the public debt. It was surely more important to establish each dominion's capacity to shoulder the burden of the debt. Estimates provided by the Indian representatives suggested that the Muslim-majority areas with approximately 23 per cent of the population of undivided India had absorbed nearly 26 per cent to 27 per cent of its national income. In any case, the figures produced by Pakistan's representatives for the contributions made by their areas to the central exchequer were a gross underestimate. The actual contribution of the Muslim areas in the past had been closer to 15 per cent or 17 per cent since Pakistan could look forward to a substantial proportion of the centre's share of duties from jute grown in eastern Bengal. If the contributions of the princely states were taken into account, the figure

[13] 'Statement Showing the Contribution of the Pakistan Areas to the Central Revenues of the Government of India', prepared by the representatives of the government of Pakistan, *Partition Proceedings*, II, 36.
[14] Ibid., II, and minutes of the expert committee on 'Currency, coinage and exchange', memorandum on sterling balances submitted by Pakistan's representatives, ibid., III, 106.

could be pushed up to 20 per cent which was what the Indian representatives thought should be Pakistan's burden of the debt.[15]

A juggling of not very reliable statistics to score points against each other was all very well at the level of debate. But in order to unscramble the assets and liabilities some common ground had to be found between these mutually contradictory lines of argument. Immediately at stake were the government of India's cash balances worth nearly Rs. 4,000 million. Pakistan claimed one-fourth of this amount as its absolute minimal requirement. This was rejected by the Indian representatives who maintained that after accounting for inflation the real value of the cash balances was not more than Rs. 500 million. By trying to cover budgetary deficits with the cash balances rather than raising its own internal revenues or loans, Pakistan might act 'directly contrary to the considered anti-inflationary policy of the Indian Government'.[16]

There was force in this line of argument. It was impossible for Pakistan to print and circulate its own currency and coins in the first few months of its creation. So both states had perforce to share a common monetary system under the supervision of the reserve bank of India until the end of March 1948 and possibly up to the end of September 1948. Since the existing customs tariffs were also to be retained, and there was to be no restriction on the movement of goods and people between the dominions, the financial policies adopted by one government could adversely affect the economy of the other. The government of India was naturally keen to whittle down Pakistan's share of the cash balances. On the assumption that the contribution of the Muslim areas to the central revenues was in the order of 15 per cent, if not more, its representatives considered Rs. 90 million as adequate for Pakistan's cash-flow requirements. When pressed harder they were ready to acknowledge the difficulties the new state would face in setting up its own treasury bills market and offered Rs. 200 million as Pakistan's opening cash balances. This was thought to be well in excess of Pakistan's 'reasonable needs'.[17]

The dispute over the cash balances lingered on for months after the transfer of power. It is one example only of the many obstacles in reaching a financial settlement. There were fierce disagreements on how the material assets as a whole were to be allocated. These included immovable items like railways, posts and telegraph, defence and industrial installations, government buildings and workshops, etc. Amongst the divisible assets of the government of India were the bank balances, securities, investments and sterling balances held by the

[15] See ibid., II, 38–42.
[16] Ibid., 11.
[17] Ibid., 12.

reserve bank. Most of the immovable assets were located in the union of India. Anxious to secure a 'just and equitable distribution' of all the assets, Pakistan's representatives wanted joint control over the entire range of property belonging to the government of India. This was promptly dismissed by their counterparts on the grounds that the fixed assets could not be transferred without impairing their real value.[18] It was decided that each dominion would assume control of property within its territory after 15 August. With some reluctance the Indian representatives agreed to provide financial compensation for certain categories of stores and 'unique' institutions which could not be duplicated.[19] But, even with this concession, Pakistan had to face the prospect of paying cash for machinery to build a printing press, an ordnance factory and other vital establishments.

This was one reason why Pakistan's representatives had to try and maximise their share of the various financial assets held by the reserve bank of India. The government of India's representatives, for their part, insisted that the question of the assets was intrinsically linked with that of the uncovered national debt. There was no question of dividing the assets 'until Pakistan agreed to accept a proportionate share of the liability'.[20] Mindful of the grave consequences to its international credit worthiness, the Pakistan government accepted responsibility for the debt in principle. It, however, objected to India assuming full control of the national debt. This would, its representatives argued, erode Pakistan's claim to sovereignty,[21] make it a debtor to the government of India and place it in a 'weak bargaining position in any dispute about the ultimate distribution of [the] assets'.[22] It was only after the government of India agreed to reconsider Pakistan's share of the cash balances and stagger the repayment of the debt over a period of fifty years with a three year moratorium from the date of the transfer of power that the basis for a settlement was found. An order on property, rights and liabilities gave New Delhi the initial responsibility for all loans advanced to the undivided government of India. Mountbatten thought this was 'very fair and reasonable' from Pakistan's point of view.[23]

The reality for Pakistan was not nearly so reasonable. Afraid of

---

[18] See note of the steering committee for the special committee of the cabinet 16 June 1947, *TP*, XI, 407.

[19] See minutes of the expert committee on assets and liabilities, *Partition Proceedings*, 1, 8–11.

[20] Patel to Mountbatten, 6 August 1947, *TP*, XII, 549–50.

[21] See minutes of the expert committee on assets and liabilities, *Partition Proceedings*, 1, 8–11.

[22] See viceroy's report no. 16, 8 August 1947, *TP*, XII, 596–7.

[23] Mountbatten to Listowel, 10 August 1947, ibid., 651.

having no cash balances at all by the time power was transferred, the government of Pakistan became a signatory to the order on property, rights and liabilities. Its representatives had conceded Mountbatten's and Congress's point that a holding order on the issue of the national debt was vital for establishing the credit worthiness of the two governments. But, with the government of India inheriting the entire public debt, Pakistan in fact had no basis on which to establish its credit. Its share of the debt had still to be determined; a settlement on the cash balances was also pending. Since the two dominions were unlikely to resolve these matters smoothly or swiftly, Pakistan's financial prospects looked woefully bleak.

There was no comfort here for businessmen and holders of government securities in the Pakistan areas. Uncertainties about Pakistan's capacity to survive and the communal disturbances had already resulted in a flight of capital from the Muslim-majority areas into India. Since the announcement of the partition plan in early June, Rs. 3,000 million were estimated to have been sent out of the Punjab alone. Capital transferred from Sind amounted to Rs. 200 to Rs. 300 million.[24] And this was only the tip of the iceberg. The bigwigs of Indian business, G.D. Birla and P. Thakurdas, expressed their disquiet about the rapid movement of capital out of Pakistan. It would 'dislocate business in both Dominions' and was attributed to the 'fear of Pakistan imposing restrictive legislation on non-Muslims' business activities'. The trend could be discerned in the reluctance shown by traders to purchase cotton grown in Sind and the Punjab for mills located in India. Significantly, Jinnah 'resented the allegations...that non-Muslim industrialists in Pakistan would not get a fair deal'. He sought to dispel such notions by assuring non-Muslim businessmen that they would be 'allowed full facilities to carry on their normal business' without 'distinction or discrimination'.[25] Doubts about the economic policies of the new government were not limited to non-Muslim business. There was 'a very strong rumour' in Karachi business circles that the chief minister of Sind, Ghulam Hussain Hidayatullah, designated as governor of the province, had 'transferred a large sum of money to certain unnamed banks in New Delhi'.[26] Whatever the truth in the charge, it reflects the kind of thinking dominating business calculations on the eve of Pakistan's creation.

This was ominous for Pakistan, the more so since no immediate steps could be taken to offset the crisis of confidence about its financial and

---

[24] Gordon Minnigerode [American consul, Karachi] to the secretary of state, 8 July 1947, NND. 842 909 Box 5955, 845.00/7-847, NA.

[25] Meeting of the partition council, 19 July 1947, *TP*, XII, 259.

[26] Minnigerode to the secretary of state, 8 July 1947, NND. 842 909 Box 5955, 845.00/7-847, NA.

economic viability. Sprung on the world in the middle of the Indian fiscal year, which extended from April to March, Pakistan had to seek a series of awkward standstill agreements with the government of India. These pointed to the continuing economic integration of the two states and advertised Pakistan's uncertain claims to sovereignty. The existing all-India system of customs tariffs, import controls and inland trade was to remain intact until 31 March 1948. Pakistan had also to share a common currency with the rest of India. Until agreement could be reached on how Britain would release the sterling balances it owed to the government of India – estimated to be some £1,160 million in August 1947 – Pakistan was to have no independent foreign exchange reserves. Its foreign exchange earnings from raw jute and raw cotton, both of which were manufactured for export in factories located in India, as well as its share of the initial releases of sterling by London were to be held jointly with the government of India in a common pool at the reserve bank. Under the single system of import controls agreed upon in the standstill arrangement, all licences issued before 15 August 1947 for the Pakistan areas had to be revalidated by the government of India. Pakistan could issue new licences for commercial imports up to 31 December 1947 for an amount not exceeding Rs. 65 million (£775,000).[27] This was barely sufficient for the import of essential commodities, let alone the capital equipment Pakistan needed to begin building an industrial infrastructure. With a mere Rs. 200 million in the central treasury and a host of intractable problems that could not be tackled without considerable expenditure, Pakistan embarked upon the stony trek of establishing itself as an independent entity.

The division of the armed forces

It was an excruciatingly difficult task since the process of splitting up the Indian armed forces to create two self-sufficient defence establishments could not be completed in time for the transfer of power. As in the case of the financial and other assets of undivided India, delays in the division of the armed forces worked to Pakistan's disadvantage. Long before the political leaders in India agreed to a partition, the British chiefs of staff – both in New Delhi and London – had considered the implications of splitting up the Indian armed forces.[28] But, with an eye on the

---

[27] British high commissioner [New Delhi] to the secretary of state [CRO], telegram no. 780, 17 September 1947, L/F/7/2872, IOL.

[28] For the strategic consequences of Pakistan's creation see A. Jalal, 'India's Partition and the Defence of Pakistan: an Historical Perspective', in *The Journal of Imperial and Commonwealth History*, XV, May 1987, no. 3, 289–310 and chapter 3 below.

law and order problems and silent hopes for a political settlement leading to a united India, no plans were prepared for the actual division.

Until the very end, and indeed even after the transfer of power, Mountbatten continued his efforts to get the two sides to accept some sort of common defence arrangement. That objective influenced both the timing and the method of dividing the armed forces. There was an inconsistency in accepting the principle of a sovereign Pakistan and trying to keep the army undivided. Not one to be daunted by contradictions, Mountbatten's fertile mind had been angling for a way out of the cul-de-sac. One reason for retaining both parts of India inside the British commonwealth was the hope that this might persuade them to agree to an overall defence arrangement covering the whole subcontinent. If he could cap this by becoming the governor-general for both states, each enjoying dominion status, the division of the Indian army could be delayed if not altogether avoided.

These were precisely the reasons why Jinnah had been so insistent on becoming governor-general. Sensing the opposition within British military circles to a division of the Indian army, Jinnah was taking out an insurance against any move to stop Pakistan having an army of its own. He had been disturbed by rumours of a Congress inspired military coup d'etat to quash the League's movement for Pakistan.[29] So he told Mountbatten that he would happily consider a common defence arrangement, but only after Pakistan had been granted its full share of the Indian army and was given parity with Congress inside a common defence organisation.[30] Liaquat Ali Khan was more direct. While he had shown undisguised enthusiasm for Mountbatten's proposal for a common defence arrangement which would be financed by the two states in proportion to the size of their respective armies,[31] he later qualified this with the revealing assertion that a Pakistan without an army would 'collapse like a house of cards'.[32] If Pakistan was to have an army of its own, the Congress high command was not ready to do a deal with the League. A common defence arrangement based on parity between Pakistan and Hindustan was in any case unacceptable.[33] The Congress leaders were well aware of the League's weaknesses in the Muslim-majority areas – its ramshackle organisation might cave in under the pressure of building a state out of nothing. Allowing the

---

[29] See minutes of the viceroy's seventh miscellaneous meeting, 23 April 1947, *TP*, X, 381.
[30] See ibid., and record of Mountbatten's interview with Jinnah, 7 April 1947, also in ibid., 149.
[31] Mountbatten's interview with Liaquat Ali Khan, 19 April 1947, ibid., 331–3.
[32] Liaquat Ali Khan to Mountbatten, 7 April 1947, ibid., 152
[33] For Congress's attitude see A. Jalal, *The Sole Spokesman*, 260–2.

Pakistan central government a separate defence establishment was tantamount to equipping it with false teeth to bite and chew up the Muslim areas once and for all. What Congress wanted instead was the right to exercise control over the undivided Indian army.

Even a viceroy moving in rhythm with tunes emanating from the Congress high command's control room could not concede this dance. According to reports by military intelligence, any decision which could be interpreted as a declaration of war against the League would tear apart the unity of the Indian army.[34] The implications for the law and order situation would be catastrophic. And as for the political settlement, it would be back to square one all over again. Liaquat Ali Khan and Jinnah were both 'resolved that they would not take over the reins of Government in Pakistan unless they had an Army on the spot, and under their control',[35] an unequivocal comment on just how nervous Pakistan's leaders were about their ability to defend and control their territories. Once Jinnah had made known his intention to assume charge as governor-general of Pakistan, Mountbatten had to give the go ahead for the division of the army.

The armed forces reconstitution committee – consisting of the commander-in-chief, Auchinleck, the commanders-in-chief of the air force and navy, the chief of the general staff and one official each from the two sides – had been drawing up a plan for the creation of 'two separate, self-contained and self-sufficient forces'. Its terms of reference were intended as anaesthetics, making the operation as painless as possible, and so keeping alive the elusive goal of a common defence arrangement. The three forces were to remain under the administrative control of the existing commander-in-chief and the devolution of authority to the two dominions was to be 'gradual and progressive'. The personnel of the armed forces were to be divided on a territorial rather than on a communal basis. No Muslim living in the Pakistan areas could opt for service in India, nor could a non-Muslim in India choose to serve in the Pakistani armed forces. With a view to a possible stitching up job in the future, neither the organisation nor the functions of the three services were to be altered unless absolutely necessitated by the reconstitution. British officers were to be encouraged to opt for service in either state, thus assuring a 'successful reconstitution' with little or no break in continuity.[36]

---

[34] 'State of the morale and reliability of Muslim personnel in the three Indian Services', enclosed in it general Arthur Smith to general Mosley Mayne, 17 August 1946, L/WS/1/1030, 94–100, IOL.

[35] Ismay to Mountbatten, 20 June 1947, *TP*, XI, 534.

[36] Ibid., 411–12.

On 30 June the armed forces reconstitution committee's report was approved by the partition council. Since both dominions were insistent on having separate armies on the date power was transferred, they were given operational instead of full administrative control over units located in their territories. As ever, the compromise had its merits and demerits. It laid the basis for the sovereignty of the two states and extricated the British from the odious responsibility of maintaining law and order. But it raised the spectre of a breakdown of military discipline during the period of the reconstitution, particularly in the Pakistan areas. There were no units in the Indian army that were exclusively Muslim in composition. Any army for Pakistan would have to include non-Muslims. At a time when Hindus, Muslims and Sikhs were erecting walls of hatred against one another, banking on the allegiance of the non-Muslim personnel to a Muslim central government was a mirage no one was prepared to chase.

So the reconstitution had to proceed piecemeal. The first step was to despatch predominantly Muslim units to Pakistan. Then the non-Muslims serving in these units had to be given a choice whether or not to remain with the Pakistani armed forces. The reallocation of the major units was to be followed by an exchange of officers and junior personnel of the administrative services – a long-drawn out affair since otherwise there were risks of an administrative collapse. Amongst the remaining stages of the reconstitution was the duplication of training establishments in Pakistan and, most important of all, the division of movable military assets like stores, arms, munitions and equipment, most of which were in the dominion of India. The facilities of the northern command in Rawalpindi were to serve as the headquarters of the Pakistan army until provisions could be made for accommodation and communications in Karachi. To avoid confusion and chaos during the crucial period of the reconstitution, all area commands in Pakistan were to be retained with only the most minor adjustments. Although Pakistan's final share of the financial assets had yet to be determined, it had to bear the cost of the forces in its operational control apart from paying a proportion of the expenses of the central administrative machinery. It required no sophisticated knowledge of financial and military matters to realise that Pakistan's army would act as a drain on the central government's meagre financial resources without any certainty of it being able to perform its law and order duties.

The only consolation for military experts was the stipulation that the existing Indian army would remain under the administrative control of a central authority until it had been replaced by two separate and viable defence establishments. This authority could only be that of Auchinleck, who was to become supreme commander after 15 August so as to distinguish him from the commanders-in-chief of the two dominions. Assisted by the supreme commander's headquarters, Auchinleck was to implement decisions taken by the partition council. But there were constraints on his authority. After 11 August Auchinleck was directly responsible to the joint defence council, the final decision-making body in all matters pertaining to the division of the armed forces. Mountbatten was to be the chairman of the joint defence council which included the defence ministers of the two dominions – Baldev Singh and Liaquat Ali Khan – and Auchinleck himself. Under the general direction of the joint defence council, Auchinleck was entrusted with a series of responsibilities, commensurate with the task at hand but requiring a superhuman effort and commitment, neither of which could be expected of a man who was an ardent believer in the wisdom of keeping the Indian army undivided.

Administrative control over the two armies, which Auchinleck exercised on behalf of the joint defence council, was to be relaxed only after the dominion governments were in a position to maintain and equip their respective forces. This was expected to take at least seven and a half months after power had been transferred. The calculation, implicit because it could not have been made explicit, was that, if Pakistan crumbled during these months, there would have been no rupture in the administrative control of the Indian army. Mountbatten was at pains to emphasise that the plan for the division did 'not preclude arrangements or agreements between the two Governments for sharing any administrative or training establishments'.[37]

There was an obvious contradiction between British perceptions of their strategic imperatives in South Asia and the need to create two viable defence establishments. The joint defence council ostensibly had been set up to supervise the division. But Britain's strategic interests called for its retention as a permanent common defence authority for the whole of India. Both the Congress and the League had agreed to bear the administrative expenses of the joint defence council in accordance with the size of their armies. It was tempting to assume that everything else being equal this arrangement could be extended indefinitely. No steps were taken for a simultaneous division of the personnel and military stores of the Indian army. Granted all the difficulties this involved, keeping both armies tied to common sources of supply was also the best possible insurance for an overall defence arrangement. Of course all things were far from being equal. The military stores as well as the

---

[37] Mountbatten's note, ibid., 695.

ordnance factories were in India. Pakistan's dependence on supplies from India left it in the absurd position of being in possession of an army that was to have its share of manpower but without the matching firepower.

Pakistan's share of the Indian army came to roughly 36 per cent or approximately 140,000 out of a total strength of some 410,000 in 1947.[38] In the end, however, Pakistan settled for 30 per cent of the Indian army, 40 per cent of the navy and 20 per cent of the air force.[39] With some difficulty the partition council decided that all movable stores and equipment would be divided between the two dominions in proportion to their respective strengths. The stickiest issue was the surplus stores. Pakistan's representatives wanted joint administration of these stores. But New Delhi's representatives were not in the business of distributing firearms to enemies. When pressed harder they were prepared to concede no more than 7 per cent as Pakistan's share of the surplus stores. So the matter had to be referred to the arbitral tribunal.

Before the arbitral tribunal could arrive at a decision, circumstances compelled Auchinleck to resign and close down the supreme commander's headquarters, the one impartial authority which could plausibly supervise the division of the military stores.[40] The supreme commander's decision, taken within two and a half months of partition, was demanded by New Delhi, sanctioned by Mountbatten and fiercely opposed by the government of Pakistan. There were reasonable grounds for the Pakistani outcry. With no ordnance factories of its own, Pakistan desperately needed its share of the military stores. Liaquat Ali Khan urged Auchinleck and Mountbatten to reconsider the decision. A neutral machinery was essential to supervise the movement of the military assets; this was 'not a minor but a major matter'. After all, 'an Army without equipment was as much use as tin soldiers'.[41]

Pakistan's first prime minister was doing more than exercising his tongue in the art of rhetoric. Seen in the light of the massive internal and external security problems confronting the fledgling state, the outburst seems perfectly understandable. Communal massacres of horrific

---

[38] These are only very rough estimates. See minutes of the armed forces reconstitution committee, 9 August 1947, *Partition Proceedings*, IV, 493–4 and the meeting of the joint defence council, 1 November 1947, ibid., V, 515.

[39] Viceroy's report no. 15, 1 August 1947, *TP*, XII, 446.

[40] A less ostentatious organisation to oversee the movement of British troops but with no responsibility for the division and movement of the military stores was to be set up under British command. This was to close down automatically on 31 December 1948. Auchinleck's note, 13 October 1947, *Partition Proceedings*, V, 436–7.

[41] See minutes of the twelfth meeting of the joint defence council, 16 October 1947, ibid., 462.

proportions, both preceding and following the transfer of power, made it imperative for the new state to starch its limp security apparatus. The law and order situation was particularly chaotic in the Punjab. Organised gangs of armed thugs, in defiance of the boundary commission's arbitrary demarcation of frontiers, were engaged in the systematic extermination of hundreds of thousands of innocent men, women and children. The summary disbandment of the Punjab boundary force due to the fear of embroiling British troops in a futile attempt to preserve order along the newly drawn frontiers is a stark commentary on the sheer magnitude of the troubles.

Conditions were not much better in Pakistan's other provinces. In the North West Frontier Province, marauding tribesmen from the surrounding areas had interpreted the departure of the white rulers as a clarion call for looting and murdering non-Muslims with impunity. To seal western Punjab's borders from Sikh infiltrations as well as to stop the tribes running amuck was a taxing enterprise for the most effective of security forces. As it was the seemingly endless trail of refugees in their millions moving both ways between its two wings and India, and the law and order problems ensuing from these dislocations, were well beyond the capacity of Pakistan's nascent security apparatus.

With massive internal security problems, Pakistan's faintly demarcated frontiers were easy prey for trigger-happy neighbours. Apart from the obvious worries along the borders with India, the central government in Karachi had also to reckon with Afghanistan's irredentist claims on parts of the North West Frontier Province. In what was described by Mountbatten as 'a most disturbing paper', Pakistan's first British commander-in-chief, general Messervy, outlined a dreary picture of the defence potential of the new state immediately after 15 August. The total number of battalions in the Pakistan areas would be drastically reduced from sixty-seven (including five British battalions) to thirty-five. But these would have to be stripped of Hindu and Sikh companies, and, even with the recall of demobilised soldiers in the Punjab and the North West Frontier Province, they could not be brought back to their full strength in the foreseeable future. Mountbatten had 'no doubt' that there would be 'very considerable risk[s]' involved in defending Pakistan, especially from the north-west. So he took special care to send Jinnah 'a bowdlerised version' of Messervy's paper.[42]

It was not long before the Quaid-i-Azam had been put into the full picture. He received his first shock upon discovering that Pakistan was

---

[42] Viceroy's report no. 16, 8 August 1947, *TP*, XII, 599.

militarily incapable of securing the accession of Junagadh, a tiny maritime state some 300 miles from the coast of Karachi, whose Muslim ruler had briefly flirted with the idea of throwing in his lot with the Muslim League. More devastating for Jinnah was the news that the Hindu maharaja of Kashmir – a Muslim-majority state – had reacted to Pakistan's covert encouragement of tribal incursions into his domain by acceding to the union of India. In a flush of anger, Jinnah ordered general Gracey, who had replaced Messervy as commander-in-chief of the Pakistan army, to send troops into Kashmir. This brought Auchinleck flying into Karachi to warn Jinnah of the 'incalculable consequence' of any military action which could be construed as a violation of Indian territory.[43] Western Punjab and eastern Bengal alike would fall like overripe plums into the Indian basket. Learning the hard truths about Pakistan's military weakness, Jinnah sullenly withdrew his order. Both incidents, together with the dispute over Hyderabad, were sharp reminders of the hopeless inadequacies of Pakistan's strategic defences. Unless these could be strengthened, Pakistan could only look forward to being outmanoeuvred and ultimately overpowered by the big guns of the Indian union.

The economics of defence

The overlapping of the military and economic aspects of the partition process, and their impact upon the political climate, provide the final strokes on the canvas depicting Pakistan in the period immediately after independence. Once the possibility of military confrontation over the accession of Kashmir and Hyderabad had reared its head, it was unrealistic to expect releases of military stores from India. In a fit of hurt national pride, Pakistan's leaders were ready to scour the world markets to furnish the requirements of their gimcrack defence establishment. But the interim arrangements on financial and economic matters brought them to heel before their political ambitions could be given full play. There was nothing in the central exchequer to meet the most ordinary requirements of government, much less the extravagant demands of the armed forces. Claims for additional sums of undivided India's cash balances and Pakistan's share of the central revenues, in particular the export duties on raw jute from eastern Bengal, foundered on Indian intransigence. New Delhi's dictum of 'what it had it kept' and 'what it collected it also kept' made nonsense of Pakistan's pleas for justice and fair play. So on 13 November 1947 Pakistan levied its own export duty

---

[43] Note by brigadier B.G. Scoones, no date, L/WS/1/1187, IOL.

on raw jute earmarked for mills in Calcutta. But with no means of patrolling the border between the two Bengals, collection was a little difficult. The decision nevertheless signalled the beginnings of a mutually debilitating trade war, with the government of India more resolute than ever not to reopen dialogue on the final settlement of assets and liabilities.

The attempt to assert its economic independence was in large part a response to pressures building up within government circles to extricate Pakistan from what was considered to be a humiliating dependence on India. The failure of the Indian government to revalidate licences for imports into Pakistan persuaded officials in Karachi that New Delhi's 'dilatory attitude...[was] designed to embarrass Pakistan'.[44] There were demands for a separate allocation of foreign exchange for Pakistan. Those with imagination thought Pakistan should divert its exports of raw jute, raw cotton and foodgrains from India to other markets and earn the foreign exchange it needed to purchase defence stores and machinery for its non-existent textile and jute manufacturing industry. But no one had a clue as to how Pakistan was to manage its exports without a financial machinery and adequate port facilities in eastern Bengal. The more practical minded could see that the really urgent imperative was to set up a separate monetary system without further ado. So long as it remained tied to all-India monetary controls, Pakistan could not raise internal finances or avail itself of the option open to sovereign governments of printing currency to remain solvent.

Thrifty financial policies and one austerity measure after another were no match for the miracles needed to stretch the Rs. 200 million in the state treasury in order to meet the central government's own requirements as well as the demands imposed upon it by the refugee problem and the armed forces. As early as the first week of October 1947 the alarm had been sounded – Pakistan was quickly running out of cash. Archibald Rowlands, the financial adviser to the government of Pakistan, urged London to consider a long-term loan of £100 million to help tide Pakistan over its financial difficulties. But no one in London was prepared to extend credit to a country that seemed such a poor economic bet. The more so since Pakistan's finance minister, Ghulam Mohammad, was less concerned with the immediate cash-flow problems than with a long-term commitment from London to help finance the defence expenditure. Jinnah echoed the view; he was 'not in the least interested in the ways and means aspect but...with the defence aspect'. He was not

---

[44] British high commissioner [Karachi] to the secretary of state [CRO], telegram no. 50, 12 September 1947, L/F/7/2872, IOL.

'quite certain that he could ever get out of India his fair share of the existing military stores'. Irritated by threats from Sikh leaders to fight their way back into western Punjab, Jinnah took care instead to point to the problems of defending the north-west frontier; that at least was 'not only his interest but the interest of India and indeed of the Commonwealth as a whole'. Pakistan needed stores and equipment from Britain and would 'look elsewhere' if its demands were not met.[45]

Such a frank admission of priorities blunted the edge of Pakistan's case for a British financial rescue mission. In any case, Britain had more than its share of economic dilemmas in the post-war period. It had no financial resources to pull Pakistan out of its woes. And, as for its military reserves, they had been virtually depleted with drastic cut-backs in production expected for many years to come. Officials in the war office conceded that the government of India's attitude towards Pakistan was one of almost indecent hostility. The more important point was that the liquidation of Pakistan, now that they had helped put it on the map, would have serious repercussions for British strategic interests in South Asia and the Middle East.

But the Attlee government dismissed this as typical bureaucratic gibberish. It had no intention of losing Indian goodwill to strengthen Pakistani defences. So it was convenient to learn from Mountbatten that the government of India had every intention of making good its promises to despatch Pakistan's share of the military stores. A suggestion that Britain should press India to come to terms with Pakistan on the financial assets by refusing to make further releases of sterling balances[46] was shouted down by the chancellor of the exchequer, Stafford Cripps, in harmony with Attlee. Both were appalled at the ease with which some ministers accused India of foul play. As Cripps made it clear, there was no question of Britain 'us[ing] threats against India with the object of securing equitable treatment for Pakistan'.[47] Attlee concurred; it would be 'imprudent for His Majesty's Government to intervene precipitatively on the issue of the military stores' since this might gravely impair...relations with the Government of India'.[48]

With the gathering sinews of war in Kashmir, both dominions were less likely than ever to settle the disputes arising from partition.

[45] Note by A. Carter on conversations in Karachi between 1–3 October 1947, 8 October 1947, L/WS/1/1133, 147–9, IOL.
[46] This had been the opinion of P.J. Noel-Baker, the secretary of state for commonwealth relations, in a memorandum for the commonwealth affairs committee, dated 8 November 1947, L/W5/1/1694, 35–9, IOL.
[47] Minutes of the commonwealth affairs committee meeting, 14 November 1947, ibid., 53–6.
[48] Ibid.

Gandhi's sacrificial fasts notwithstanding, some subtle background diplomacy by London may also have had a hand in persuading the government of India to come to the negotiating table. In December 1947, after marathon sessions, representatives of the two sides at long last produced a formula to settle the issue of assets and liabilities.

In addition to the Rs. 200 million made available in August for its initial cash-flow requirements, Pakistan was given another Rs. 550 million as its full and final share of the rupee cash balances. The timetable for the actual transfer, however, was to be determined by India. Pakistan's share of the total assets and liabilities of undivided India was to be in the order of 17.5 per cent. A more complicated method was devised to determine Pakistan's share of the sterling balances.[49] All in all Pakistan ended up with some £147 million out of a total of £1,160 million in sterling balances held by the reserve bank. The entire amount was deposited in two separate accounts at the bank of England. Account no. I was to contain releases periodically made by Britain and could be drawn upon by Pakistan to finance its current expenditure. The rest of the sterling balances were to be kept in a separate blocked account.

Pakistan's share of the financial assets of undivided India fell short of what it had bargained for. It had claimed Rs. 1 billion of the estimated Rs. 4 billion in the cash balances, but received Rs. 750 million. As for the sterling balances, Pakistan's representatives had wanted 30 per cent of the £1,160 million sterling balances, about £348 million, on the grounds that they had 30 per cent of the defence forces of undivided India. Equipping and maintaining these forces would cost the central exchequer much more than 30 per cent of the total defence expenditure of undivided India.[50] And this was before the curtain dropped on Pakistan securing its share of the military stores. Moreover, it was difficult to deny that the Pakistan areas had contributed to the accumulation of the sterling balances. Yet they had hardly benefited from the spending undertaken by the government of India during the war years. Nearly all the new industries set up were in territories belonging to the union of India. So Pakistan had to undertake a programme of industrialisation as well as government spending aimed at raising the standard of living of its people. Since the government of India had flatly refused to consider parting with any of the existing machinery in its territory, Pakistan would have to incur heavy expenditure in the foreign markets for capital goods.[51]

[49] For details of the financial settlement see *Partition Proceedings*, 11, 97 and note dated 12 December 1947, L/F/7/2867, IOL.
[50] Expert committee on assets and liabilities, *Partition Proceedings*, 11, 12.
[51] Memorandum on sterling balances submitted by Pakistan's representatives to the expert committee on currency, coinage and exchange, ibid., III, 105–6.

None of these arguments did the trick. With 17.5 per cent of the total financial assets of undivided India, not all of which were available for its immediate use, Pakistan had a very nearly impossible task at hand. If it was to survive as an independent entity it had to create a new administrative structure for its central government, resettle millions of refugees, build new provincial governments in both western Punjab and eastern Bengal, take the first steps towards establishing an industrial infrastructure, modernise its defence forces, and to do so without anything remotely resembling a financial machinery. To set government priorities without upsetting a cart full of bad apples in the provinces required genius which in a state afflicted by all manner of troubles was unfortunately the scarcest of all resources.

3

Constructing the state

Creating a state out of territories which until recently had been part and parcel of the Indian union was no mean enterprise. The more so since the government of Pakistan's capacity for exercising central authority and securing the newly demarcated frontiers was severely constrained by the meagre resources made available to it at the time of partition. To make a bad case worse still, the unprecedented demographic changes and the accompanying socio-economic dislocations had shaken the existing administrative structure in the provinces as well as in most localities. With nothing remotely resembling a central administrative apparatus and the weaknesses inherent in the Muslim League's organisational machinery only the most tenuous attempts could be made to establish a hierarchy of command from Karachi into the provinces and localities of Pakistan. Once the Kashmir dispute with India reared its head, it became particularly urgent for the League leadership to impose central authority over Pakistan's constituent units.

But if defence against India provided added impetus for the consolidation of state authority in Pakistan, paradoxically enough, it also served to distort the balance of relations between the newly formed centre and the provinces. Nothing stood in the way of the reincorporation of the Pakistan areas into the Indian union except the notion of a central government whose structures of authority lacked both muscle and the necessary bottom. So in Pakistan's case defence against India was in part a defence against internal threats to central authority. This is why a preoccupation with afforcing the defence establishment – not unusual for a newly created state – assumed obsessive dimensions in the first few years of Pakistan's existence. An insecure central leadership of a state carved out of a continuing sovereign entity found it convenient to perceive all internal political opposition as somehow instigated by outside forces and, therefore, constituting a threat to the security of the state. In the process the very important distinction between internal and external security threats was all but blurred.

Yet the real paradox, and one that continues to plague Pakistan's

internal and external security perceptions, was the result of a rather
more fundamental dilemma. Pakistan's ability to pay for its external
defence was paralysed by a resource endowment which was insufficient
to meet even the most basic internal security needs. The initiation of
hostilities with India so soon after the establishment of the state entailed
a diversion of very scarce financial resources – inevitably extracted from
the provinces – into a defence procurement effort at a time when
political processes in Pakistan had yet to become clearly defined. But to
appreciate why its early managers were able to set priorities for the
centre with such little heed to the not so uncommon howls of complaints
in the provinces it is important to consider how the strategic and
economic consequences of partition, and Pakistan's relations with India
in particular, influenced the domestic and foreign policies of the new
state.

The strategic and economic consequences of partition

Even before its creation British military strategists studying the
implications of dividing the Indian army had painted a grim picture of
Pakistan's defence potential. A Pakistan consisting of the north-western
and north-eastern Muslim-majority areas would include two of the main
land frontiers of the Indian subcontinent. Such a strategically exposed
state would have to defend two geographically separate wings, keep the
tribes at bay as well as preserve internal law and order. Yet the existing
defence layout of British India was based almost entirely in the
Hindustan areas. Whatever the political arrangements for the subcontinent it was 'impossible to consider the strategic defence of Pakistan and
Hindustan separately'.[1] To defend itself Pakistan would have to
maintain an army and an air force of approximately the same size as
required to defend the whole of India. But the areas constituting
Pakistan had neither the industrial nor the military installations
necessary for their defence and would have to import practically all the
requirements of the defence forces for many years to come. In the unlikely
event of Pakistan managing to duplicate the military administrative
structure of undivided India, it would still remain vulnerable to an
attack by a major power. Its north-western provinces simply lacked
the 'depth necessary to enable the main bases to be located out of
effective range of enemy bombers'.[2] The defence of eastern Pakistan

---

[1] 'Defence Implications of a partition of INDIA into PAKISTAN and HINDUSTAN'
prepared by lt. general Arthur F. Smith [chief of the general staff in India], 1 April
1946, L/WS/1/1029, IOL.
[2] 'Appreciation of the defence problems of Pakistan', 1 February 1946, ibid.

posed still bigger problems; there would be difficulties in coordinating operations from the western wing where the general headquarters of the three services were expected to be located, not least because all the communication networks covering east Bengal were based in Calcutta. According to the British chief of the general staff in India, a division of the Indian army would 'practically mean disbanding units and rebuilding them' anew. It could take Pakistan anywhere from ten to twenty years to build armed forces comparable to those deployed in the defence of British India's north-western and north-eastern frontiers. There would be a serious shortage of experienced officers and trained personnel – a deficiency Pakistan could meet only by 'rely[ing] on treaties...[and] hired assistance from its friends'.[3] Yet 'even with powerful allies Western Pakistan could not be defended without the co-operation of Hindustan'. So the 'only sound military solution' was for both parts of India to share 'a common strategy, a common military administration, and a common higher direction'. Without some such arrangement, Pakistan would be a potential prey for a military attack from either Afghanistan, Iran or the Soviet Union. Given their geographical proximity 'neither Pakistan nor Hindustan...[could] remain indifferent to a threat...[to] either state'. While Pakistan was 'more immediately affected as *she l[ay]...as a buffer* between Hindustan and any likely invasion', it was imperative that New Delhi be 'vitally concerned that Pakistan should not be subdued',[4] especially by the Soviet Union. Even a united India could not hope to repel a Soviet attack without outside assistance.[5] As for Pakistan, it would need the combined help of Britain as well as Hindustan to stave off a Soviet invasion. It would be 'suicidal for Hindustan to refuse such assistance, because with Pakistan defeated and hostile bases prepared therein, the defence of Hindustan from the north-west would be an impossibility without armed forces as large and efficient as those which could be deployed against her'.[6]

There was for the time being no immediate danger of an invasion of the subcontinent, either from the north-west or the north-east. The more immediate concern was how Pakistan could afford to pay for its defence needs. Its share of the financial resources of undivided India, it was correctly surmised, would be hopelessly inadequate to maintain an effective defence establishment. Any attempt by Pakistan to construct military installations would be beyond its resource capacity; and it could

---

[3] 'Defence Implications of a partition of INDIA', 1 April 1946, ibid.
[4] Ibid.
[5] Ibid.
[6] 'Appreciation of the defence problems of Pakistan', 1 February 1946, ibid.

do so only at the risk of 'ruining itself'. While there was no shortage of unskilled manpower, the 'large numbers required' for its defence 'could...only be obtained by increasing the pay and privileges of the Army'. Alternatively, Pakistan would have to institute conscription; a policy the British, interestingly enough, felt would result in 'increased political and internal defence problems'. There would also be a serious 'problem of accommodat[ing] the PAKISTAN army in peace': it would entail 'a large building programme', not to mention special perks for military personnel. A separate defence establishment for Pakistan apart from being 'economically wasteful and quite impracticable'[7] seemed fraught with consequences for its political stability.

So there were good reasons to try and secure some sort of a common defence arrangement. A militarily and politically weak Pakistan might endanger Britain's long-term strategic interests in South Asia, and also in South-East Asia and the Middle East. These demanded continued uses of the subcontinent by the Western allies. Encouraging both India and Pakistan 'to play their full part in the defence of the Commonwealth' was an 'overriding concern' of the British chiefs of staff in London.[8] This is borne out by the untiring zeal with which the last viceroy pursued, and eventually executed,[9] London's aim of keeping both dominions inside the commonwealth. India and Pakistan could jointly make a valuable contribution in any future war against the Soviet Union by maintaining land forces large enough to secure subcontinental defences.[10] This required that they take steps to ensure the compatibility, efficiency and modernisation of their respective defence forces by accepting 'only British advice and assistance'. Significantly, the British chiefs of staff felt more confident about their ability to persuade Pakistan to toe the line; given its geographical location, many of Britain's strategic requirements could be met 'by an agreement with Pakistan alone'.[11]

Although the partition of India shook many of the old axioms of imperial defence, it kept open the possibility of weaning one or both dominions into the Western security network. The preferred course might have been to get both India and Pakistan to share a regional

---

[7] 'Defence Implications of a partition', 1 April 1946, ibid, IOL.
[8] Draft memorandum from the chiefs of staff to the ministry of defence, July 1946, *TP*, XI, 958–60.
[9] See A. Jalal, *The Sole Spokesman*, chapter 7.
[10] There was the need to control the western and the eastern entrances to the Indian ocean; the first to ensure the safe passage of oil supplies from Iran and Iraq, and the second to protect Singapore, the Malacca straits as well as Ceylon.
[11] Draft memorandum from the chiefs of staff to the ministry of defence, July 1946, *TP*, XI, 958–60.

defence arrangement, and perhaps even extend it to Ceylon and Burma.[12] Once that proved unworkable, the British turned to other less desirable, but nevertheless plausible ways of salvaging some part of their strategic doctrine in the region. Both states were dependent on Britain for the supply of military equipment and had solicited the services of British officers and technicians. Britain's strategic imperatives demanded that they 'maintain in peacetime defence organisations larger than they would need for their own purposes'. So the main question that had to be answered was 'what inducements, material, financial, or political' Britain could offer to 'persuade them to do what we wanted'.[13]

Britain was in no position to offer the kind of inducements contemplated by its more diehard elements. It was deeply in the red; the debt to the undivided government of India alone was over a billion pounds sterling. Post-war Britain's economic difficulties pointed inexorably to major readjustments in its strategic perceptions. But the new view of Britain's declining position as a global power had yet to be accepted by the old hands; they were ready to turn the new political arrangements in the subcontinent to their advantage. One way of securing British interests was to use the sterling balances owed to Pakistan and India as a bargaining counter. The beginnings of armed conflict between the two dominions, however unfortunate, was something of an opportunity. If Britain could continue to serve as their main arms supplier, it would not only find a way of scaling down the sterling balances but might also get the two states to maintain armed forces large enough for the defence of the commonwealth, if and when necessary.

Pakistan's predicament in the aftermath of partition made it a perfect candidate for Britain's strategic purposes, even if there were powerful elements in London staunchly opposed to favouring it over India. They could see that arms supplies to Pakistan were more likely to aggravate the Kashmir dispute than contribute usefully to commonwealth defence. It might strain Britain's relations with New Delhi while an uncertainly placed government in Karachi would be more of a liability than an asset. Yet these hard headed political arguments conflicted with the opinion of the military men. The chiefs of staff, influenced in no small measure by general Messervy – commander-in-chief of the Pakistan army – were coming to believe that it was 'probable that the long-term policy of the Government of India would be to seek the subjugation and incorporation of Pakistan into India'. From a military point of view, it was necessary to give 'every assistance . . . to the Pakistan

---

[12] See the 'Defence Implications of a partition', 1 April 1946, L/WS/1/1029, IOL.
[13] H. Wilson-Smith to Eric B.B. Speed [war office], 4 October 1947, ibid.

armed forces'.[14] So as ever, London adopted a policy of magisterial ambiguity. While carefully falling short of giving overt support to Pakistan in its disputes with India, it was agreed in principle to make good its requirements of the defence stores that were supposed to have been received from India. But this policy was based on the explicit understanding that Pakistan would have to pay cash for all the materials supplied.

All the worries about Pakistan's ability to shoulder its defence burden were quietly forgotten. This suited the government in Karachi perfectly. The decision to try and pluck Kashmir out of a sprawling Indian hedge, whether dictated by fears of economic strangulation or considerations of the state's strategic vulnerability, had committed Pakistan's early managers to refurbishing the army at whatever cost to the central exchequer. Pakistan's armed forces were short of basic maintenance requirements, as well as the war and mobilisation reserves needed to conduct internal and external security duties. A defence establishment without the requisite firepower is a potential source of disaffection in any state, let alone one that had to purchase the nuts and bolts before it could begin assembling its authority over territories separated by a thousand miles. With a mere 17.5 per cent of the financial assets of undivided India and a third of the defence forces, Pakistan was hardly well placed to square its economic and security needs. But it was the government's Kashmir policy which gave a cutting edge to the defence establishment's demands on the central exchequer. Pakistan's defence burden, though the concerns determining it were very different from what the British had anticipated, was nevertheless pointing to financial ruin and a degree of political instability the new state could ill afford.

Making a run on the international armaments markets without a real measure of the domestic coffers was pleasant business for army headquarters in Rawalpindi and for some top ranking officials in the ministry of defence in Karachi. But it was a trifle awkward for those in the ministry of finance who had also to account for other pressing needs like building a new central government apparatus, rehabilitating millions of refugees and setting up a handful of basic industrial units. Recognising that the erstwhile colonial masters had few resources of their own, Pakistan's representatives had been looking for allies who could offer some badly needed doses of financial assistance. The United States was the most obvious if not the best choice given its more narrowly defined interests in the region at the time. Within a month of

---

[14] This was the opinion of general Montgomery. (See minutes of the chiefs of staff meeting, 21 October 1947, L/WS/1/1133, 122, IOL.)

partition, Ghulam Mohammad, Pakistan's first finance minister, had asked Washington to lend a 'helping hand' to Pakistan, made much of its resource capacity and economic potential and used all the old arguments about the Soviet threat to the north-western frontier. He failed to convince the Americans, but left a clear impression that the finance minister was 'the most worried man in Karachi today'.[15] Not only was he faced with a large deficit and the prospect of heavy expenditure on defence but could only look forward to very slim revenues for some time to come. His view that it would be 'profitable to American capital'[16] to invest in Pakistan was heard with sympathy and promptly ignored with the same dismissive rigour as was to be displayed later by the merchant capitalists who were slowly beginning to migrate to the new state.

Just how desperately Pakistan needed financial assistance can be gauged by the two billion dollar loan requested from the United States in October 1947. Pakistani representatives in Washington frankly admitted that the new state's internal political situation depended upon its ties with Britain and the United States. So the 'Government of Pakistan...must naturally wish to line up its external and defense policy with the U.S.A.'.[17] What they wanted were cash advances from the United States to help finance Pakistan's administrative and defence expenses, as well as the industrial and agricultural development of the country. The 'bulk' of the loan was to be spent on capital and consumer goods, and military equipment purchased in America. So there would in fact be no net transfer of capital from the United States to Pakistan. Indeed 'very little of this amount would be transferred in cash to meet the defence services in Pakistan proper'.[18] In the event that the US could not cover the entire loan, Pakistan's representatives were ready to approach American oil companies. This is why the Pakistani charge d'affaires in Washington suggested that the Americans consider the

---

[15] Charles W. Lewis [American charge d'affaires, Karachi] to the secretary of state, 2 September 1947, NND.760050, RG 59, Box 6018, 845F.51/9–247, NA.

[16] See memorandum of conversation between Mir Laik Ali, M.A.O. Baig and officials at the US state department, 30 October 1947, ibid., 845F.51/10–3047.

[17] Ibid.

[18] Out of a total of $510 million estimated for defence expenditure, $305 million were to be used to purchase warlike materials from the United States. Significantly, $15 million out a total of $170 million allocated for the army was to be used as 'payment for specialized services and personnel', in the main salaries for some 1,600 British officers serving in Pakistan. A similar amount was to be spent for air force personnel, a service which was to have some $75 million of the total expenditure on defence. The remaining $60 million were for the Pakistan navy. (See appendix C of memorandum of conversation between Mir Laik Ali, M.A.O. Baig and American officials at the state department, 30 October 1947, ibid.)

proposal in 'an objective business fashion and not as a request for money on political grounds'.[19]

But the argument that Pakistan was a good business investment failed to sway the Americans. Uncertainties about Pakistan's ability to survive and a strong belief in the wisdom of a united India meant that the Americans were not minded to pay serious heed to Karachi's request. Within a week of the first meeting between Pakistani and American officials in Washington, the US charge d'affaires in Karachi reported that a growing 'feeling of disappointment with the practical outcome of Pakistan...[was] spreading in some quarters' and that it was 'not improbable that a movement for reunion with the Dominion of India may be instituted in the not too distant future'.[20] So the best policy for those who had so far kept their fingers out of this difficult region was to patiently wait upon events.

Those responsible for managing the affairs of the new state were left making desperate, and often contradictory attempts, to prevent the ship from sinking before it had struck course. On the one hand they wanted all and sundry to appreciate the very real financial difficulties facing Pakistan; on the other, even before acquiring independent sources of foreign exchange, they were bidding for arms and ammunition in the world markets. This was the logical outcome for a government anxious to incorporate Kashmir into Pakistan, but which had yet to establish authority over the areas that had fallen under its jurisdiction. If both pointed to building up the defence services of the state, the consequences of the policy were already hinting at some dangerous trends, trends which were soon to force the Muslim League government under Liaquat Ali Khan into a series of awkward compromises both domestically and internationally.

The Kashmir dispute

The Kashmir dispute has been a major bone of contention between Pakistani and Indian historians quite as much as between the two states. In the all too frequent exchanges of words and bullets a great deal of objective ground has been lost, figuratively as well as literally. To attempt to apportion blame simply to strike a sympathetic chord in one or the other camp would be an exercise in historiographical futility. To

---

[19] See memorandum of conversation between M.A.O. Baig [Pakistani charge d'affaires, Washington] and R.L. Thurston [assistant chief, SOA], 26 November 1947, ibid., 845F.51/11–2647, NA.

[20] Cited in M.S. Venkataramani, *The American Role in Pakistan, 1947–1958*, New Delhi 1982, 32.

steer a middle course might be an even more hazardous option, but it might at least help dispel some of the clouds that have dulled any understanding of the wide-ranging impact of the dispute on internal developments in Pakistan.

The accession of Chitral – the princely state where the Indian subcontinent meets China, Russia and Afghanistan and which since 1854 had maintained a relationship with Kashmir – to Pakistan sparked off the dispute. The broad lines had been drawn by the boundary commission's award in August 1947; in particular its decision to include Gurdaspur – a district with a bare Muslim majority – into the Indian union.[21] Gurdaspur district, with only one non-Muslim majority tehsil of Pathankot, provided the vital link between Kashmir and the union. This enabled New Delhi to despatch troops to the predominantly Muslim state after having secured, and not without some help from Mountbatten, the maharaja's controversial letter of accession.[22] But before the accession itself, the situation inside the state had begun deteriorating rapidly, forcing Hari Singh, the maharaja, to order his troops to crack down on Muslim dissidents demanding an end to Dogra rule. There were stories of persecutions and mass murders of Muslims in Poonch. A number of Kashmiri Muslim families from Poonch were settled in the Rawalpindi and Jhelum districts of the Punjab. In addition there was a colony of Afridi tribesmen in Poonch. Refugees fleeing from Kashmir related harrowing tales of massacres by Dogra troops of Muslim villagers. Some were no doubt exaggerated, but they helped stir up passions in both the Punjab and the North West Frontier. The tribesmen, attracted by opportunities of loot and plunder afforded by the British withdrawal, swung into action under the noble pretext of saving their Muslim brethren.

While it is not possible to establish what understandings, if any, were given to the tribesmen by the central government in Karachi, there is

---

[21] Pakistanis unfailingly point out that the government of India began constructing a bridge over the river Ravi in Pathankot days after the announcement of the boundary commission award. The insinuation, at times an open allegation, is that the Congress leadership had its eye on Kashmir long before the Muslim Leaguers began actively to encourage tribal incursions into the state.

[22] Lord Ismay, the principal aide to the last viceroy, abandoned Mountbatten's bandwagon a few days after Kashmir's accession to the union. He felt that the government of India had done the 'right thing in the wrong way'. Mountbatten should have taken the trouble of informing the government of Pakistan as soon as the first consignment of troops had been sent to Kashmir. The telegram eventually sent was '30 hours late'. (Memorandum of conversation between T. Eliot Weil [second secretary to the American embassy in New Delhi] and Ismay, 5 November 1947, NND.842909, RG 59, Box 5956, 845.00/11–1047, NA.) It is extremely doubtful whether a diplomatic gesture of the sort Ismay had in mind would have defused the problem.

now not the least doubt that the incursions were actively encouraged if not actually organised by government officials in the North West Frontier Province. The principal responsibility for the tribal campaign was in the hands of Khan Abdul Qayum Khan, the recently installed Muslim League chief minister, and himself a Kashmiri from Poonch. Under Qayum's direction, provincial officials ensured the supply of petrol – a scarce commodity in those days – provided grain rations as well as transportation for the tribal volunteers. According to one report, any 'firm measures to stop...the movement of tribesmen to Kashmir would probably have landed the N.W.F. and Pakistan Governments with trouble on the frontier on a scale...[for] which they had no...military strength to cope'.[23]

By assisting the comings and goings of armed tribesmen from the Kashmir border, the government inadvertently contributed to the already considerable law and order problems in western Punjab and the North West Frontier Province. Jinnah and Liaquat Ali Khan's contention that the tribal invasion was 'spontaneous and actuated by fraternal and religious sympathies'[24] does not explain why the 'provincial authorities...ha[d] been so forthcoming in the matter of petrol, transport and rations for the tribesmen'.[25] One has perforce to conclude that the government of Pakistan with the connivance of the Frontier ministry was actively promoting the sentiments that had encouraged the tribesmen to invade Kashmir. Admittedly, the Pakistani leadership refrained from officially committing the army in Kashmir. But they did so because of the severe shortage of arms and ammunition, not because this was the preferred course of action. If they had been in a position to do so, the Muslim League leaders, with Jinnah's blessings, would have thrown in the army behind the tribal effort. Pakistani officers, conveniently on leave from the army, were 'certainly fighting' alongside the 'Azad Forces' – a conglomerate of Kashmiri Muslims and Pathan tribesmen.[26]

There are no precise estimates of the actual strength of the forces fighting the Indian army. It was generally believed that Pakistan army regulars were no more than 5 per cent of the total strength of the Azad army. But as Russell K. Haight, an ex-officer of the American army, who had been fighting with the Azad forces, reported, the real importance of

---

[23] Extract from Peshawar despatch to the British high commissioner [Karachi], 27 November 1947, DO35/3172. PRO.

[24] British high commissioner [Karachi] to the commonwealth relations office, opdom no. 3, for the period ending 8 January 1948, L/WS/1/1599, IOL.

[25] See extract from Peshawar despatch to the British high commissioner [Karachi] 27 November 1947, DO35/3172, PRO.

[26] British high commissioner's opdom no. 3, 8 January 1948, L/WS/1/1599, IOL.

the Pakistani military personnel was far 'greater than their numbers' since they 'perform[ed] supply and organizational functions'. In his opinion, it would have been 'impossible for the Azad Kashmir Government[27] to maintain a fighting force...[if] not for the substantial assistance which it receive[d] from the Northwest Frontier Provincial Government'. The Azad forces relied heavily and 'openly...[on] supplies and equipment from the Pakistan Army depot'.[28] The commander-in-chief of the Azad Forces was a Pakistani army officer, colonel Mohammad Akbar, who went under the pseudonym of 'General Tariq' and was known to be in close contact with Qayum Khan and through him with Jinnah and the League leaders in Karachi.

All this refutes Pakistani denials of involvement in the actual fighting in Kashmir. More revealing, however, is the reluctance of the Pakistani army command to commit itself firmly in the Kashmir war. It instead wanted a cease fire and until that could be negotiated wished the tribesmen 'good luck'. Pakistani officers not involved in the fighting in Kashmir were of the view that the tribesmen were 'doing well against the Indian Army' and that so long as they stuck to the tactics deployed against British troops they would 'cause continual embarrassment and a steady toll of casualties'.[29] These attitudes mark the beginnings of a split within the Pakistani army command: between those who wanted a direct involvement in Kashmir and those who opposed such a course. Although the top brass, important exceptions notwithstanding, had few intentions of waging an all out war against India, this did not prevent them from pressing the government into making sorties in foreign armaments markets. Arms and ammunition are the necessary accoutrements for any army. In this case they were to be secured in order to bolster a defence establishment whose upper echelons were in two minds about the practicability of a military solution in Kashmir, but which was to become the main recipient of the state's financial resources precisely on account of that dispute.

The undeclared war in Kashmir cost the two dominions dear. But the drain on Pakistan's resources was clearly more acute, and the consequences for its internal political configuration more severe. Pakistani claims on Kashmir provided the government of India with an excuse to

---

[27] The Azad Kashmir government had been formed in Pulandari under Sardar Ibrahim Khan as soon as the maharaja of Kashmir acceded to the Indian union.

[28] See Howard Donovan [American charge d'affaires, New Delhi] to the secretary of state, 17 January 1948, NND.842909, RG 59, Box 5970, 845.20/1–1748. NA.

[29] Colonel W.W.A. Loring [military adviser to the British high commissioner in India] to the under secretary of state [war office], report no. 1, 26 January 1948, L/WS/1/1187, 1A. Between 23 September 1947 and 5 January 1948, Loring was commander of the armoured brigade and adviser to the armed corps in Pakistan.

increase its defence potential. On the pretext of balancing force levels, the Pakistani defence establishment – led by army headquarters – pressed the political leadership to proceed with the defence expansion. With no assurances yet of financial assistance from the West, Pakistan's central government had few alternatives except to expand the administrative machinery and begin digging more deeply and more extensively into provincial resources.

Central imperatives

With a serious shortage of cash and a range of intractable problems calling for immediate financial redress, the central government at Karachi was inexorably driven to perform a difficult, and at times impossible, tight-rope walking act. Building a stable state structure from such an unstable vantage point was awkward to say the very least. As it was, the League had little in the way of an organisational machinery linking the central leadership with those exercising power at the provincial and local levels in Pakistani society. While the provincial arenas continued to serve as the main centres of political activity, those who set about creating the new central apparatus were either politicians with no identifiable bases of support or civil servants well-versed in the traditions of British Indian administration. Not surprisingly, the view from the centre, more often than not, tended to diverge from the conflicting provincial perspectives which the socio-economic dislocations were helping to shape. Keeping the centre and the provinces from clashing in louder discord required a measure of coordination for which there was neither an effective political party organisation nor a well-established government apparatus.

The choice which presented itself to the Muslim League leadership at the centre was to either concentrate on refashioning a national political party out of the ramshackle organisation of the preindependence period, or to build the mechanisms of an effective state administration. The two, though not mutually irreconcilable, proved to be so in the very unusual circumstances facing Pakistan during its first few years of existence. The need to raise revenues required an administrative structure. In the absence of an existing central government apparatus, administrative reorganisation and expansion not only took precedence over real party building, but also served to thwart efforts – often well meaning – to give the state a political system that reflected its linguistic diversities and geographical peculiarities.

There are early hints of the emerging disjunction between political activity in the provinces and the formation of the state. Between 24 and

25 February 1948 the Pakistan League council – separated from the All-India Muslim League in December 1947[30] – adopted a new constitution based on the separation of government and party. In a clear reversal of his earlier position, Jinnah favoured linking the government with the party, arguing with much force that any separation would lead to endemic rivalries between the different offices.[31] But the Quaid-i-Azam's powers of persuasion were waning. Offering to waive the condition for Jinnah and inviting him to become party president did nothing to smooth the creases that had begun developing in the relationship between the leader and his lieutenants. Rejecting the offer, Jinnah blandly told his party that as governor-general he could not hold the highest office in a self-avowedly communal organisation.[32] This was the last time Jinnah attended a meeting of the Pakistan Muslim League, a point which needs underlining considering that this was the first time the organisation had met since its separation from the All-India League.

Jinnah's withdrawal from League affairs was to leave the one party capable of claiming a nationwide basis of support out in the cold. The separation of government and party officials confirmed the trend. In a state where political traditions had yet to be established firmly, and where real authority vested in the hands of the governor-general, the delinking of government and party officials worked to the disadvantage of the latter. The League members of the Pakistan cabinet were already preoccupied with purely administrative matters. Freed from official duties in the party, they now had less reason to attend to the organisation of the Muslim League. The task was left to Chaudhri Khaliquzzaman, the new president of the Pakistan Muslim League. But his status as a refugee from the United Provinces in India proved to be more of a liability than an asset for the national organisation.

So state formation proceeded independently of the Muslim League's performance. This suited those responsible for setting up the administrative machinery of the new state. But, since Pakistan was constitutionally a federation of provinces, the absence of a nationally based political party providing a two-way channel of communication between government and the different levels of society was to become a serious impediment to the integration of its diverse constituent units.

---

[30] On 14 December 1947, the All-India Muslim League met for the last time in Karachi. In view of the altered circumstances, it was decided to divide the party so that there were wholly separate organisations for Pakistan and India. This, of course, was consistent with the partition of India. Yet interestingly enough, Jinnah took care to leave the option open for a merger of the two parts. See Safdar Mahmood, *Pakistan: Muslim League Ka Dar-e-Hakumat, 1947–1954* [Urdu], Lahore 1982, 54–5.

[31] Ibid., 74–5.

[32] Ibid.

Since 14 August 1947, issuing central ordinances and governor-general's orders, a method of rule legitimised by the expedient adaptation of the government of India act of 1935 – that instrument of imperial rule – had been the one available means of confirming the presence of an executive authority over the Pakistan provinces. If Jinnah's position as governor-general lent a semblance of reality to the sovereignty of the new state, it was the structure of government which he helped to mastermind that provided the substance. On the face of it, the legislative assembly – which also served as the constitution-making body – was the sovereign authority. It could make or amend laws as well as restrict the governor-general's powers. But, very soon after Pakistan's creation, Jinnah secured his cabinet's approval to overrule their decisions and assumed similar levers of power *vis-à-vis* the legislative assembly.

There is an almost universal belief, especially among political scientists, that the perpetuation of the so-called 'viceregal system' by the founding father is at the root of the subsequent ills in the Pakistani political system.[33] It is true that Jinnah's dismissal of the Congress ministry in the Frontier was an all too early manifestation of authoritarian trends in Pakistan. But in the initial months of independence without strengthening executive authority at the centre it would have been impossible to underwrite the sovereignty bestowed upon the territories constituting Pakistan. Moreover, authority appropriated by a single individual cannot go very far in explaining the complex historical processes that have worked to shape the balance between elected and non-elected institutions in Pakistan.

A glance at the government structure at the centre indicates how executive authority was actually wielded over the Pakistan provinces. At the apex of government was the governor-general who in addition to being more than a constitutional figurehead was the president of the constituent assembly. The assembly which was also the national legislature initially consisted of sixty-nine members elected in 1946 by the provincial assemblies rather than by a direct vote of the electorate.[34] The mainstay of government after Jinnah was the Pakistan cabinet, responsible to the legislature and, in theory if not in practice, the supreme executive authority. Yet the 'magnificent seven' handpicked by Jinnah to serve in Pakistan's first cabinet were with few exceptions men without independent bases of support in the provinces. The relative balance of power between the cabinet – the bearer of political

---

[33] See for instance, Khalid B. Sayeed, *Pakistan, the Formative Phase* (second edition), Karachi 1968.

authority – and the administrative bureaucracy is a problem in even the most established of states. In Pakistan the structures of power were still in flux. There was nothing preordained about the shift in favour of the members of the Pakistan civil service, or the CSP as it came to be known. What paved the way for it was the lack of an effective organisational link between the politicians and the people at the base. Without concerted attempts to build a countervailing force to the administrative structure that was being assembled, the top civil servants were likely, sooner rather than later, to become the real wielders of authority in the new state.

Unlike the political leaders, the administrative bureaucracy had a better chance of putting together their own structures of command, control and coordination. Though not quite the pillar of the 'overdeveloped state' as some theorists of Pakistan have argued,[35] the administrative services showed a greater resilience than might have been expected after the dislocations wrought by partition. This was in part due to the ingenious device of creating the post of secretary-general during the first few years of Pakistan. It was occupied by a well-respected and experienced administrator, Chaudhri Mohammad Ali, who has described the office as the 'clearinghouse for information between the various ministries and also between the central government and the provinces'.[36] Assisting him was the cabinet secretariat consisting of a cabinet branch and the establishment division. The latter, dubbed as 'the custodian of the rights of all Central Government servants', was headed by a British deputy secretary – 'a key post in the administrative set

---

[34] After the accession of the princely states of Bahawalpur, Khairpur, the Baluchistan states union and the North West Frontier Province states to Pakistan, four more seats were added. To allow for refugee representation the constituent assembly was enlarged to include six additional seats – five for the Punjab and one for Sind. By 1948 the official strength of the constituent assembly–though this was subject to change owing to disqualifications, deaths and resignations – was:

East Bengal	44
Punjab	22
Sind	5
NWFP	3
Baluchistan	1
Baluchistan states	1
Bahawalpur	1
Khairpur	1
NWFP states	1
TOTAL	79

[35] See Hamza Alavi, 'The State in Postcolonial Societies: Pakistan and Bangladesh', in K. Gough and H.P. Sharma (eds.), *Imperialism and Revolution in South Asia*, New York 1973.

[36] Mohammad Ali, *The Emergence of Pakistan*, 245.

up'.[37] It was through him that the secretary-general supervised transfers and promotions, disciplined members of the central superior services in Pakistan, and maintained a line of contact with the chief secretaries in the provincial governments.

There was no comparable hierarchy of command within the Pakistan Muslim League despite the elaborate rules and regulations of the paper constitution. So the administrative bureaucracy was able, slowly but surely, to diddle the political leaders out of their expected roles as the principal decision-makers. But it would be a mistake to attribute the erosion of political leadership in Pakistan to the internal structuring of the two main civil institutions alone. The search for the answer must in part take place through an analysis of the broader socio-economic and political trends, and their impact on the evolving structure of the state.

No understanding of the magnitude of the task facing its early managers, whether politicians or administrators, is possible without a few bare statistics about the territories constituting Pakistan. With 23 per cent of the total land mass of the Indian subcontinent and nearly 18 per cent of the population – or more precisely 68.6 million out of 295.8 million in British India[38] – the new state had less than 10 per cent of the industrial base in the two dominions and just a little over 7 per cent of the employment facilities.[39] According to one estimate, in 1947 Pakistan's total industrial assets were worth only Rs. 580 million (approximately $112 million), of which the better part was owned by non-Muslims who had fled to India.[40] Potentially self-sufficient only in foodgrains, Pakistan was the quintessential agrarian economy with duties on exports of primary commodities constituting the main sources of revenue for the state. Given the fluctuations in world prices for primary commodities, it was both natural and logical for the state managers to want to turn to exporting manufactured products. But to do so they had first to build an industrial infrastructure.

So the large question was how to begin setting government's priorities without alienating social groups whose support was vital for the smooth functioning of the state. The advice rendered by Archibald Rowlands,

---

[37] Eric Franklin's manuscript, MSS.EUR.C.364, IOL. Franklin was the second deputy secretary of the establishment division.

[38] If only the population of British India is considered, Pakistan's share of the total would be slightly more – 23.2 per cent. The figures are taken from an 'Analysis Relating to the Partition of India', by the deputy economic advisor to the government of India's department of commerce; enclosed in Donovan [New Delhi] to the secretary of state, NND. 760050, RG 59, Box 6018, 845F.50/7-3147, NA.

[39] Stanley Maron (ed.), *A Survey of Pakistan Society*, Berkeley 1956, 2–3.

[40] Zafar Altaf, *Pakistani Entrepreneurs: their Development, Characteristics, and Attitudes*, London 1983, 1.

himself an imported commodity in the new dominion, was for 'ruthless economy'; a postponement of all schemes for social betterment and a series of new taxes.[41] Upon completing a three month stint of advising the governor-general on economic matters, Rowlands in a somewhat contrived display of 'robust optimism' told the bemused people of Pakistan that 'abstinence' had to be the watchword. What their state needed was an industrial base built around cotton, jute and hides, not social welfare schemes requiring large capital outlays.[42] In other words, the state had to strictly avoid any populist pretensions and settle for the more pragmatic policy of wooing those groups in society who were best equipped to help build a resource base, especially in the industrial sector.

In December, 1947, a Pakistan industries conference held out the promise of an industrial finance corporation which would provide credit to those interested in setting up industrial units. Applications for import licences were invited along with assurances that the government's policy in issuing these would be unabashedly liberal. But doubts about the availability of foreign exchange and disputes with India 'cast a dampening mist over the business situation'. So, although the central ministers had been 'actively engaged in exploring the possibilities of developing manufacturing industries',[43] most traders left the conference with a view to securing import licences for consumer goods rather than for the higher risk capital equipment they were being invited to obtain.

Quite apart from the trading community's general reluctance to invest in industrial enterprises requiring long-term commitments of capital, there were obvious attractions in making instant killings by importing consumer items in short supply. Recognising the trend, the government was forced to bend in a direction it might otherwise have wanted to resist. The commerce minister, I.I. Chundrigar, himself a businessman from Bombay, declared that private enterprise would be encouraged, public utilities and hydro-electric projects would be state owned and only heavy industries would be regulated. An elaborate five year plan was chalked out under which the state was to help private capital set up jute mills in east Bengal and cotton mills in west Pakistan.

---

[41] Including the restoration of the salt tax at a higher rate, a uniform and enhanced sales tax to be administered by the central board of revenue instead of the provinces and a countervailing excise on cotton textiles which were seen to be too 'heavily protected'. And although Rowlands, like many finance men after him, favoured the introduction of an agricultural income tax he was against the abolition of zamindari since this might lead to a reduction in state revenues. (Summary of Archibald Rowland's report to the government of Pakistan, DO/35/2746, PRO.)

[42] *Dawn* [Karachi], 4 December 1947.

[43] Monthly economic aerogram from the American embassy [Karachi] to the departments of state and commerce, 5 December 1947, NND.760050, RG 59, Box 6018, NA.

In early January 1948, the commerce ministry announced the liberalisation of its import licencing policy just when Pakistan's financial position seemed to favour measures aimed at conserving foreign exchange. An open general licence was introduced for certain categories of goods from the sterling area. Constrained by its membership of the sterling bloc Pakistan had to adopt a more cautious policy on purchases from the hard currency areas. In spite of this, Pakistani traders could try and obtain import licences for certain types of machinery from anywhere in the world. Yet, with all the rope the government could plausibly offer, few in the business circles were ready for the hanging. The announcement of a liberal import policy had coincided with the most serious outbreak of communal troubles in Karachi since the transfer of power. These had disrupted local trade and paralysed the banking structure in the city. Even a firm display of the state's law enforcement capacity did nothing to dispel 'future uncertainty', the single most important factor 'retard[ing] business commitments'.[44] With straightforward trading still the safest and quickest means to profit-making, the state's drive to create an industrial base proved to be a non-starter. It was only very slowly and painfully that the government inched its way into a position from which it could offer the kinds of inducements needed to channel trading profits into the construction of new industries.

Until then state revenues had unavoidably to be extracted from the agrarian sector. This meant taking steps to establish effective pricing and fiscal mechanisms to ensure the best returns from the commercial sector of the agrarian economy, particularly since customs and excise duties on raw cotton and raw jute together with a handful of other primary commodities accounted for nearly 80 per cent of central revenues. The state also had to maintain food production at a level commensurate with the subsistence needs of a rapidly growing population. Yet its ability to increase food production and establish an effective procurement and distributive machinery was circumscribed by the very importance of the agrarian sector. The first food conference held towards the end of 1947 had been strongly of the opinion that production could not be increased without a substantial reform of the agrarian structure. But economic power in the agrarian sector was the stranglehold of the very landed families who were in control of the provincial Muslim Leagues in west Pakistan and, with the important exception of emigre politicians from the Muslim-minority provinces in India, provided the bulk of the

---

[44] See monthly economic aerogram for January 1948, 50/2-648, dated 6 January 1948, ibid.

leadership at the centre. According to one estimate, 7 per cent of the landowners in west Pakistan owned 51 per cent of the land, while the upper crust of 1 per cent owned 30 per cent of the land.[45] With such concentration of economic and political power in the landed groups, the state was in no position to levy a tax on agricultural incomes, much less introduce far-reaching agrarian reforms. Any attempt to do so would almost certainly have sparked off an economic as well as a political crisis. The landlords would refuse to cooperate with the state's procurement efforts and, worse still, there might be a mass exodus of prominent rural notables from the Muslim League, the formation of opposition groups and a serious loss of support for the central government.

Fortunately, agriculture was a provincial subject. But for a central government which was gradually appropriating powers vested in the provinces by the government of India act of 1935, this was the least of the considerations. The centre's need to secure its bases of support was by far the most important reason why there could be no immediate restructuring of agrarian relations. Yet the need to intervene in the food market and in the commercial sector of the agrarian economy necessitated an expansion of the state's administrative capacities. One largely unforeseen consequence of this, and one that influenced the political process in no uncertain way, was that it pitched the administrative structure at both the central and the provincial levels against the very landed groups whose support the state was so anxious to preserve.

The mere creation of administrative capacity was no guarantee for effective state intervention in the economy. In the heady days of Pakistan's first few months of existence, an uncertain political leadership at the centre sought to strengthen the administrative arms of the state in the vain hope of bolstering its own position. The results were dramatically different. Far from enabling prime minister Liaquat Ali Khan's government to keep a better grip on the affairs of the state, the decision to stretch administrative capacities in order to intervene more decisively at all levels of society assumed a momentum which soon led to the erosion of political authority. But for the time being central authority needed teeth, even if it was the administrators rather than the political leaders who were to end up with the sharper set.

A Pakistan food and agricultural council was established to keep the centre up to date with the food situation in the country. The jute advisory committee was to decide on the jute acreage in east Bengal. Various special committees were set up to investigate the impediments to

---

[45] *Report of the Land Reforms Commission for West Pakistan*, Lahore 1959, appendix V.

industrial development in both western and eastern Pakistan. Above them all were the Pakistan development and advisory boards, the latter under the direct supervision of the prime minister. And, if this was not sufficient to enable the centre to intervene in economy and society, there was a special committee of the cabinet dealing exclusively with the economic situation in the country. The proliferation of these committees in turn called for a separate ministry of economic affairs. It was placed under the charge of the minister of finance, Ghulam Mohammad, because finance was after all the single most important problem confronting the economy.

The preparations for administrative interventions were matched by a corresponding increase in the state's law enforcement capacities. So although law and order was a provincial subject, the central government strengthened the central police force, ostensibly to root out the evil of corruption but in fact to keep watch and ward on all activities that seemed remotely threatening to the new state.[46] Appropriating provincial powers by issuing central decrees was relatively easier than their effective exercise. For one thing, the centre had problems in plenty with its own employees, in the civil service quite as much as in the police and the armed forces. As ever, it was the lack of finances that lay at the root of it all. Despite assurances by the Muslim League to honour the Indian pay commission's recommendations of April 1947, those on the government payroll had been forced to accept shrunken pay cheques owing to the financial stringencies facing the state. With a price spiral affecting most essential commodities and the rehabilitation of government employees still in the early stages, the service groups were not above voicing their discontent. The unrest was particularly strong among the junior echelons of the civil service and the police. And, as for the armed forces, they were even less amenable than their civilian counterparts to accepting the government's austerity measures unquestioningly. With trouble brewing within its own internal structures the state could hardly reach out effectively into society as a whole.

Setting up a Pakistan pay commission to lay down a new set of pay scales lent fuel to the fire. The railway workers union and the central government servants association, consisting of junior employees in the main, were the most vociferous defenders of workers' rights in a country

---

[46] A striking instance of the centre's encroachment on provincial autonomy was the promulgation by the governor-general of the west Punjab disturbed areas ordinance. This in effect gave the army overriding powers of arrest and search, powers that had been vested in the provincial police authorities. (See the west Punjab disturbed areas [special powers of armed forces and validation of certain acts] ordinance, in *Orders of the Governor-General, 1947–1950*, Karachi 1951.)

where organised labour had yet to find its voice. As one astute observer could see, the central government's failure to redress these grievances would soon place it in the awkward position of 'fac[ing]serious labour disturbances in [its] own ranks with further threat[s] to government stability'.[47] There were already signs of a 'definite conflict between certain ministers and [the] various provinces on matters [of] food procurement [and] taxes', and it was evident that irritations had compounded the 'center's problems and could lead to serious political repercussions within [the] country'.[48]

One way of avoiding a dangerous political backlash was for the centre to try and develop its own independent sources of finance. The financial experts led by Ghulam Mohammad came up with a series of innovative ideas about how to keep the state from an imminent bankruptcy. An example of this was the dispute over the Hyderabad securities. Worth some Rs. 20 crores, these had been obtained from the nizam in lieu of Pakistani securities by the finance minister himself. But the nizam's seemingly generous loan consisted of the government of India's securities and could not be transferred without the permission of the reserve bank. Unless New Delhi was willing to underwrite the transaction, which of course it was not, the securities had no real value. It is difficult to disagree with Jawaharlal Nehru that the loan was nothing more than a 'stupid and ineffectual piece of business'.[49] Pakistan's financial experts were not at all troubled. Since the Indian currency was backed by the blocked sterling balances, Pakistan could issue currency against the nizam's securities which might be 'regarded as equally blocked'.[50]

With such strained financial logic it is not difficult to see how the new state managed to claim solvency. It was towards the end of February 1948 that Pakistan's first budget was presented. By then it had received Rs. 50 crores as its share of the undivided government of India's cash balances,[51] Rs. 10 crores from the reserve bank as a ways and means advance, and about £20 million from its share of the blocked sterling balances. Other sources of revenue had also been tapped, largely

[47] P. H. Alling [American embassy, Karachi] to the secretary of state, telegram no. 181, 29 March 1948, NND.760050, RG 59, Box 6016, 845F.20/3-2948, NA.

[48] American military attache to the departments of state and army, no. 19, 10 February 1948, Declassified no. 785011, RG 319, Entry 57, Box 409, WNRC.

[49] Cited in the American embassy [Karachi] despatch no. 32, 9 January 1948, NND.760050, RG 59, Box 6018, 845F.51/1-1948, NA.

[50] See American embassy [New Delhi] to the secretary of state, 26 February 1948, ibid, 845F.51/2-2648.

[51] Despite protests by Karachi, New Delhi withheld Rs. 5 crores as part of the expenditure incurred by it on behalf of Pakistan since partition.

through the exercise of the governor-general's powers.[52] As a first step towards establishing an independent financial machinery for the new state, the central government laid the foundations of the gilt-edged market by floating four different types of loans. The principal subscribers were the Memon and Khoja merchant capitalists from Bombay and Kathiawar. The response to the floatation of government securities was ecstatic in comparison to the siren calls for investment in industry. But it would be a little hasty to conclude that business confidence in the future of the new state had somehow miraculously been restored. The real point was that buying government securities involved fewer risks, certainly fewer headaches, compared to the efforts needed to undertake the smallest of industrial ventures. And in any event, it was safer to invest in government securities than not at all. The banking structure had yet to be put back on its feet and there were enough law and order problems to worry even those accustomed to hoarding capital within the once safe environs of their homes.

So the central government was still a long way off from giving the people a sense of security in the future of the state. This was why the first budget was more an effort at bolstering morale than at presenting an accurate picture of Pakistan's economic prospects. On 28 February 1948, Ghulam Mohammad declared a balanced budget for Pakistan. It was only by presenting the revenue and the capital parts of the budget separately that the government was able to fly the kite of a balanced budget for a state whose expenditures were grossly in excess of its total revenues.[53] Not inappropriately dubbed the 'rich man's budget', Pakistan's first attempt at national budgeting was important in many other respects. As much as 70 per cent of the total revenues of the central government were allocated for defence and an apologetic finance minister had to confess that the 'expenditure for defence...[was] higher than would normally be justified for a young state like ours'. Yet, in view of the multiple dangers to the security of the state, he had been 'reluctantly constrained to spend on the Armed Forces money' which really should be channelled into the 'social, industrial, and economic development of the country'.[54] It was all very well for the finance minister to take refuge in this glimmer of conscience for the toiling

---

[52] A salt tax that was expected to yield some Rs. 2.5 crores annually was imposed. Railway fares were raised by 25 per cent. The export duty on raw cotton was increased from Rs. 20 to Rs. 40 per bale of 400 pounds, partly in response to the government of India's decision to decontrol the prices for both cotton yarn and cotton textiles.

[53] See finance minister's budget speech, *Budget of the Central Government of Pakistan, 1947–48 (15th August to 31 March) and 1948–49.*

[54] Ibid.

millions who had to await their turn to reap some of the benefits of independent statehood.

It certainly failed to assuage provincial sentiments, shocked by the centre's summary decision to temporarily withhold a share-out of income tax as well as the right to collect the sales tax, the single most elastic source of revenue for the provincial governments prior to partition. Slashing the revenue receipts of the provinces, keeping the reins drawn on development grants and monopolising the entire range of financial arrangements at a time when the provinces had yet to recover from massive social and economic dislocations was not the best way of winning adherence to the new central government. Vehement opposition by provincial representatives in the central legislature, led by the east Bengal contingent, against the centre's appropriation of the sales tax was shrugged aside confidently by the government benches persuaded by the righteousness of their cause. It was with equal ease that the finance minister secured safe passage for the tax amendment bill, designed to give extraordinary concessions to would-be industrialists and also to guard against tax evasion.[55] The assembly also gave the centre authority to continue wartime controls on the production and distribution of a number of commodities.[56]

With its powers to intervene in the economy greatly enhanced in principle if not in fact, all that the central government needed in order to bring the economy under its sway was the right to determine the course of industrial development in the country.[57] On 2 April 1948 when Pakistan's first industrial policy statement was announced, it was apparent that the centre was appropriating the driver's seat. Under the 1935 act industry had been a provincial subject. But the arrangement was 'inherently defective', since industrial development was inextricably linked to the fiscal policies of the central government. So, after token consultations with the provinces, industry was transferred to the concurrent list – the centre would do the planning and the provinces the implementation. About twenty-seven industries were to be directly under the centre's supervision. An industrial finance corporation was to assist the centre in establishing industries for which private capital was

---

[55] New industries were exempted from taxation of their profits up to nearly 5 per cent of the capital for the first five years apart from getting a 15 per cent depreciation exemption on machinery and construction. But, at the same time, the state's tax collecting machinery was streamlined and income tax officers were given greater powers than before.

[56] Namely cotton, wool, paper, foodstuffs, petroleum, machinery, coal, steel, iron and mica–all of which were in short supply.

[57] In addition to industries, the centre took over from the provinces the authority to regulate and develop mines as well as oil-fields.

not forthcoming; these would then be transferred to the private sector. The industrial policy statement categorically welcomed participation by non-Pakistanis so long as Pakistani nationals were included. But, significantly enough, the government was prepared to leave the entire field to foreign capital in the event that indigenous capital continued to resist investments in industry.[58]

The centre's industrial policy was to place it at greater odds with the provinces. For one thing, the focus on industry as opposed to agriculture was less likely to have even benefits for the provinces. For another, the centre's ability to attract capital, indigenous and foreign, was just as uncertain as it had always been. Gearing the central government's machinery to a task which by its very nature could not be accomplished overnight exposed the central government to charges of neglecting the immediate problems afflicting the provinces. And in any event the centre's grandiose schemes for the industrial development of the country were doomed by the lack of interest on the part of the principal commercial groups. The American ambassador was horrified to find the complete lack of interest in industrial matters on the part of an audience – a 'cross-section of the business people and intelligentsia of Karachi' – which had 'on other occasions when purely political matters were being discussed ... displayed the greatest interest'.[59]

Hardly surprising if we consider the dominant political and economic trends in the country. All the provinces had registered huge budget deficits for the year 1948–9. The imposition of unpopular taxation measures to help finance these provincial deficits in turn generated dissent. There were grievances in plenty with which to clobber the provincial and the central governments. Cloth and foodgrains were in short supply, and so were a number of other essential commodities. In the Dera Ismail Khan and Bannu districts of the North West Frontier Province 'a complete breakdown of food supplies' had been reported despite the fact that these had been 'pouring in regularly'.[60] In east Bengal rice was selling at staggering prices. Certain areas of Sind were equally badly affected and the provincial government was not minded to pay much heed to the centre's directive to send emergency food relief to Baluchistan where a locust invasion had all but destroyed the winter crop. Widespread hoarding, black-marketeering and smuggling into

---

[58] See 'Industrial Policy Statement', 2 April 1948; it was presented to the constituent assembly on 17 May 1948 and considered on 25 May 1948. *Constituent Assembly Debates* (henceforth *CAD*).

[59] Alling [American embassy, Karachi] to the secretary of state, 24 May 1948, NND.760050, RG 59, Box 6019, 845F.60/5-2448, NA.

[60] *CAD*, II, 6 March 1948.

India by enterprising traders and landlords of western Punjab had made a mockery of the centre's procurement drive.

With something very near anarchy reigning in the provinces, the central government felt less confident than ever about its ability to keep the country pulling in the same direction. It was a frightened and uncertain central government which had been equipping itself with wide-ranging emergency powers to parry threats from the provinces. As early as November 1947, the governor-general had issued a directive establishing a Pakistan national guard – to consist of some 75,000 volunteers – whose chief responsibility was to maintain law and order and so relieve the regular army for external security duties along the Kashmir border. The creation of a central police force and additional recruitments into the provincial police establishments – irrespective of the severe shortage of finances – suggests that the government was of the definite opinion that the maintenance of law and order had to proceed, whatever the cost in political and economic terms. If in the process it incurred the wrath of its provincial underlings, they could soon be disciplined by a single loud crack of the whip.

So an element of coercion was injected into the relations between the centre and the provinces very early on in Pakistan's history. But, if the centre was to monopolise the instruments of violence, it had to look for some way of creating pockets of support in an ocean of discontent, indifference and gloom. Both Jinnah and Liaquat made impassioned speeches to 'restore confidence [in] provincial governments'. Not because they were trying to secure the political futures of their provincial lieutenants but because they had to 'decrease [the] confusion and chaos [in the] country'. Yet it was apparent that piecemeal solutions to the multiple problems facing the state, whether refugee rehabilitation, food supplies, housing, defence or finance, would simply not do. What was needed were 'prompt aid and strong well administered programs' inspired and directed by the centre. Otherwise the swelling ranks of the 'have nots' would be fertile ground for political agitators, the religious ideologues quite as much as the recently established Communist party of Pakistan. More alarming was the view that although 'superficially all appear[ed] well', the 'large cancer underneath neither destroyed nor dormant' was 'growing toward an eruption'.[61]

The centre's recipe for avoiding this disaster was to hammer out a grand strategy to reorganise the Pakistan Muslim League along populist lines. The League's constitution was revised to make provision for the

---

[61] Hoskot [American military attache, Karachi] to the departments of state and army, 19 April 1948, NND.785011, RG 319, Entry 57, Box 409, NA.

setting up of peasant and labour boards, seemingly to democratise the national party but actually to prevent them coming under the sway of communists and socialists.[62] However these ambitious plans to co-opt the downtrodden remained high-flying in conception only. There were low-lying confusions about the real purpose of strengthening the League. Khaliquzzaman told League workers in Lahore that they could serve the party only by resisting all temptations to seek government jobs and ministerial posts. But he did not explain how he proposed to constitute ministries if not from the party's ranks. The League president's views contributed to 'an increasing feeling that Parliamentary democracy...[was] not suited to conditions in Pakistan', giving added impetus to demands for 'Islamic democracy and Shariat rule'.[63] Just as Jinnah had feared, the gulf between the party and government had begun to widen. This might have caused fewer anxieties if not for the dismal state of the League organisation, or what there was of it. There were 'increasing fissiparous tendencies' within the party 'both at the provincial level and lower down the scale'. There were all too clear 'indicat[ions of] a general weakening of party discipline', attributable to the 'stress and strains of a universal scramble for the profits of office'.[64]

There was something incredulous about Khaliquzzaman's claim that the League's popularity was growing by leaps and bounds. The final date for enrolments had been 21 June 1948. Arguing that it was the limited availability of membership forms, a result of the general shortage of paper in the country, and not lack of enthusiasm for the party that had restricted the recruitment drive, Khaliquzzaman was encouraged to find that 2.5 million had been collared in west Punjab; about 500,000 in east Bengal and 120,000 in Baluchistan. But despite his best efforts he had not been able to conjure up figures for Sind and the NWFP. And, as for his optimistic view that League organisers in all the provinces were 'busy making preparations for the primary elections',[65] the less said of it the better.

With the Muslim League as disorganised as ever and new factions sprouting daily, the central leadership quietly abandoned whatever hopes it might have had of getting the backing of a popular party. Populism as many of them knew all too well was a double-edged sword. It seemed eminently more sensible to bring the Muslim League and its president to heel and instead rely on the civil administration and the

---

[62] British high commissioner to the CRO, opdom no. 22, 11–17 March 1948, L/WS/1/1599, IOL.

[63] British high commissioner's opdom no. 38, 6–12 May 1948, ibid.

[64] British high commissioner's opdom no. 42, 20–6 May 1948, ibid.

[65] British high commissioner's opdom no. 50, 17–23 June 1948 and no. 52, 24–30 June 1948, ibid.

police even if the provincial and the central parts of these two services did not always see eye to eye. The policy of posting central government servants to key positions in the provinces did not always ensure Karachi's rule; it simply kept open that possibility. Of course too much dependence on the administrative arms of the state was not without its costs. Forced to accept cuts in their salaries as part of the centre's juggling to finance the defence effort, the civil service and the police were hardly the loyal and conscientious servants of the new state. Nor were they any less incompetent and corrupt than the politicians. So the quality of administration declined precipitously.

An acute dissatisfaction in most sections of society left the central government as the most obvious target of attack. The provinces 'exhibit[ed] growing independence'.[66] There was an open 'disrespect for the Centre'[67] in western Punjab; the Sindhis had long been fighting a losing battle to retain Karachi as their provincial capital; the east Bengalis were outraged by the directives issued by a centre ignorant of the stark realities in their province; the Baluchis had no regard for their self-proclaimed leaders in Karachi; and, as for the Pathans, they were befuddled by a provincial ministry in which two chosen individuals shared all the portfolios. Within a year of Pakistan's creation, unbeknown to itself, the central government had mobilised all manner of opposition to its policies. Political agitators and ideologues of all complexions had mushroomed in all the provinces, hastening Pakistan's drift towards becoming a 'police state'.[68] Labour troubles in Karachi, west Punjab and eastern Bengal, agrarian unrest in the NWFP were all dubbed, for the sake of simplicity, as part of a grand Communist design. It was hard to spot any silver linings to the clouds. Unable to see the way forward, some groups cynically 'long[ed] for the British to return',[69] others looked towards America, and the crucial question in Pakistan during the scorching summer of 1948, while Mohammad Ali Jinnah was alive, was whether the central government's political authority had been weakened irreparably.

The answer to that all important question rested squarely on the central government's ability to reconcile its defence imperatives with policies aimed at redressing provincial grievances. It was not easy, especially since Pakistani army intelligence was nervously churning out reports about the rapid increase in India's war potential.[70] This alone

[66] British high commissioner's monthly appreciation for June 1948, ibid.
[67] High commissioner's fortnightly report, 5 July 1948, L/WS/1/1204. IOL.
[68] High commissioner's monthly appreciation for June 1948, L/WS/1/1599, IOL.
[69] High commissioner's fortnightly report, 5 July 1948, L/WS/1/1204, IOL.
[70] See for instance 'The Expansion of the Indian Armed Forces since 15 August 1947', prepared by general headquarters, Pakistan, intelligence unit, L/WS/1/1188. IOL.

would have been sufficient pressure on the political leadership. Accompanied by Pakistan's claims on both Kashmir and Hyderabad it proved to be deadly. New Delhi's lightning attack on Hyderabad, coinciding as it did with Jinnah's death on 11 September 1948, was the last straw. Within a matter of hours the Pakistan cabinet had sanctioned an immediate expansion of the armed forces.

By that time Pakistan had placed firm orders for defence stores worth nearly £8 million from Britain alone.[71] But cut-backs in British armament production slowed down deliveries. To the further dismay of military headquarters similar orders could not be placed in the United States. In March 1948, following clashes on the Kashmir border, Washington had imposed an arms embargo on both Pakistan and India. Although private individuals and government officials had been sounding off arms suppliers in every conceivable nook and cranny of the world, the shortage of foreign exchange – dollars in particular – remained a serious constraint. So the military authorities decided to take matters into their own hands; they were ready to forge their own links with potential suppliers.

The American military attache was delighted to find 'a very strong feeling of friendship and admiration for all things American on the part of the majority of Pakistani officers and men'. Top ranking army officers were willing to hand over 'information of a highly classified nature...without hesitation' apart from providing 'every facility...[to] the M[ilitary] A[ttache] in his activities'.[72] Much as the Pakistani army officers had hoped, the military attache was increasingly critical of American policy on arms supplies to Pakistan:

Our present policy of procrastination and promises that we will do so-and-so when such-and-such conditions exist is not enough and is not winning the battle. If we persist in this passive obstructionist policy dire necessity on the part of Pakistan may force her to deal with other powers and drive her into an orbit of influence [namely the Soviet] that is prejudicial to our interests.[73]

These views were taken seriously in Washington. On 2 May 1948, without lifting the arms embargo, the Americans agreed to give Pakistan a $10 million credit to purchase surplus US property in the subcontinent. Ostensibly, the credit was for refugee rehabilitation. But the agreement did not actually stipulate against the credit being used to purchase arms and equipment. Indeed, most of it was used to obtain

---

[71] Extract from J. Mark [treasury], 18 June 1948, T229/164, PRO.
[72] Hoskot to the chief of staff [general intelligence department], 8 May 1948, Declassified 785011 RG 319, Entry 57, Box 409, Pakistan File, WNRC.
[73] Ibid.

discarded and usually defective arms and ammunition, not the most effective foil to the Indian army.

Clearly then, even before the central cabinet had acquiesced to giving the go ahead for the defence expansion, army headquarters in complicity with officials in the ministries of defence and foreign affairs had worked out various arrangements to obtain warlike materials from foreign governments as well as arms dealers, both at home and abroad. In a number of cases, the arms bought for Pakistan by private individuals rarely made their way to the Kashmir front. Arms racketeering, a notoriously venal business, provided Pakistan with some of its earliest entrepreneurs – many with the closest of connections in the civil bureaucracy and the army. Of course, these patriots concerned with securing the defences of the state were not alone in profiting from the war in Kashmir. So too did many others, especially those in the trade for clothing, food and petrol, to mention only a few. An investigative effort at identifying these men and their families, however, would detract from rather than add to an historical understanding of the real implications of the Kashmir war on political processes in Pakistan.

More to the point, the central government was simply giving official sanction to a process that was already well under way. By doing so, it could at least press Britain to make more generous releases of the sterling balances and allow a larger amount to be spent in dollars. As Mohammad Shoaib, the financial advisor to the government of Pakistan confessed, his minister was 'under heavy pressure to spend dollars' since Britain had not been able to supply all the requirements of the Pakistani defence forces. Pakistan was ready to purchase from hard currency countries and 'in the armament "black market"'.[74] Shoaib's 'predominant interest' was the procurement of defence stores, leaving British treasury officials with the distinct 'impression...that Pakistan intends to spend as heavily as she can on arms, and...will pledge her available foreign exchange up to the hilt'.[75]

Certainly, the defence authorities in Pakistan would have happily spent the entire sterling balances in a single year. Their requirement for ammunition alone was estimated to cost $47 million.[76] An absurd figure which no one at the British treasury was ready to swallow, however powerful the arguments in favour of strengthening Pakistan's defences against India. Increased dollar expenditure was a drain on the sterling

[74] Pakistan consultative committee, progress report, 2 December 1948, T236/1331, PRO.
[75] Note by Mark, December 1948, ibid.
[76] Pakistan consultative committee, note of discussion, 9 December 1948, T236/2618, PRO.

area. Losing the Pakistan market for British military equipment was not a prospect that could be viewed with equanimity by the treasury or the ministry of defence in London. It was heartening to learn from the high commissioner's man in Rawalpindi that the British still had 'far more real control of this Army [Pakistan's]' than over the Indian army.[77] A cautious handling of the sterling releases was the one card the British could still play to retain influence over the Pakistani defence establishment.

Sensing British and American eagerness to beef up the Pakistani army, the central leadership fell into line with alacrity. By the end of 1948, the entire central apparatus was in gear for the defence expansion. Yet enthusiastic calls for unity and discipline from the centre, unmatched by real political party organisation and material rewards, even when heard in good faith went largely unheeded in practice. There was 'some doubt...[whether] the Pakistan provinces...[were] taking matters as seriously as the Centre'.[78] With worries of their own, Pakistan's constituent units – the provinces as well as the recently acceded princely states – were neither willing nor able to march in step with the martial beats being drummed at the centre.

Provincial concerns

WEST PUNJAB

Consisting of nineteen districts of the old British Indian province, western Punjab had been a stranglehold of landed oligarchs. Assiduously cultivated by the imperial rulers, members of the Punjabi Muslim landed gentry dominated the cross-communal Unionist ministries that had ruled the province uninterruptedly since the 1920s. At the last moment a majority, more out of expedience than conviction, shifted allegiance to the Muslim League. With the shakiest of commitments to the Muslim League, these landlord-politicians were not the most effective channel of communication between the national party and the rural populace. But in due course these hard headed sons of the soil – absentee landlords in the main – came to play a decisive role in shaping relations between state and society in Pakistan.

Initially they were distracted by the unexpected opportunities afforded by the socio-economic dislocations of 1947. Within the first few

---

[77] See A.H. Reed to S.J.L. Olver [British high commission, Karachi], 26 October 1948, L/WS/1/1188, 3A, IOL.

[78] British high commissioner's fortnightly report, 8 November 1948, L/WS/1/1204, IOL.

months of partition over 5.5 million Muslims entered western Punjab
and about 3.8 million non-Muslims, from both urban and rural areas,
fled to India. The influx of refugees, from eastern Punjab in the main,
strained the provincial administrative structure – already weakened by
the loss of non-Muslim personnel – to breaking point. By contrast, the
exodus of Hindus and Sikhs, though it left western Punjab's economy in
shambles, did not fundamentally alter social relations in the countryside. If anything the transfer of populations saw the landed notables
tightening their grip over rural society still further.

This was to have large consequences for the politics of the province as
well as its relations with the new central government. So it is important
to see how the landlords were able to benefit, politically and economically, from the dislocations. Statistics relating to the early years of
Pakistan are notoriously suspect; but 350,000 to 420,000 acres of arable
land are thought to have been abandoned by the non-Muslims. In
theory, though not necessarily in practice, the vacated land was to be
used solely for the purpose of resettling Muslim refugees. According to
provincial government sources about 4 million Muslim refugees were
temporarily resettled on approximately 350,000 acres, each family
receiving between five to eight acres of irrigated and twelve and a half
acres of non-irrigated land.[79] The remainder of the land continued to be
occupied by Muslim tenants of Hindu and Sikh landlords. Much as
might be expected, there was considerable friction between the indigenous tenants and the newcomers, discounting the possibility of an
agrarian populist movement in the foreseeable future. And of course
those already in possession of substantial tracts of land were not above
trying to augment their holdings. They did so by paying off local and
provincial administrators and the police. The departure of non-Muslim
moneylenders and traders who had once dominated the commercial
sector of agrarian society gave the more enterprising members of the
Muslim landed gentry an opportunity to enter both the credit and the
produce markets, thus fortifying their hold over tenants as well as rural
society at large.

The urban areas offered quite as many opportunities to those with
access to government patronage. An intense scramble for allotments of
houses, shops and small industrial units vacated by non-Muslims saw

[79] *The Punjab: A Review of the First Five Years (August 1947 to August 1952)*, Lahore
1952, p. 47. In 1958, the then central rehabilitation minister, Moula Bux Soomro
maintained that 6,000,000 acres were abandoned by non-Muslims in western Punjab
as opposed to 4,500,000 acres by Muslims in eastern Punjab. (*Dawn*, 6 January 1958,
cited in Talukder Maniruzzaman, 'Group Interests in Pakistan Politics', *Pacific
Affairs*, 39, Spring–Summer 1966, 92.)

indigenous groups flouting official regulations and taking illegal possession. Those linked with provincial civil servants and the equally venal but more powerful police establishment were rarely penalised. Refugees benefiting from the government's allotment policy were with few exceptions people who had money or contacts with those in power.

With so much up for grabs in both the rural and the urban areas, jostling for position within the Punjab Muslim League – a less than healthy appendage of the All-India Muslim League and destined to remain so in the aftermath of partition – seemed the most certain means of cashing in. The changing configuration of forces in the provincial party was mirrored by ministerial intrigues. Nawab Iftikhar Hussain of Mamdot, the League chief minister, and Mian Mumtaz Daultana, the finance minister, were old rivals. Now that a League ministry was at long last in office, Mamdot and Daultana – both scions of influential landed families – instead of working to steer the Punjabi ship out of muddied waters politely agreed to do each other down. Mamdot a favourite of the more conservative elements, was not well thought of by the central leaders and the British governor of the province, Francis Mudie. Daultana, the more competent of the two, was better liked by Jinnah and Liaquat, but had 'progressive' views which did not go down well with western Punjab's oligarchs and even fiercer religious ideologues.

The provincial administration, far from helping steady the state of affairs, was simply another arena for 'rabid factionalism'; 'bribery...[was] rampant in every department'.[80] It was a well-known secret that Mamdot was under the thumb of three top civil servants and the editor of a local Urdu newspaper – the *Nawa-i-Waqt*.[81] Pitted against them were Daultana's supporters in the provincial League and the civil service. So the party, the assembly and the administration were all split down the middle. Consequently, policies announced with great fanfare rarely reached the stage of implementation. Of the bills floated in the assembly, those specifically aimed at restricting individual liberties were the ones which made it to the statute books. As for resettling those huddled in refugee camps in sub-human conditions, the provincial government, its patience exhausted and its resources depleted, tried blunting the edge of criticism by lambasting the centre.

By the summer of 1948 the situation had deteriorated beyond belief.

[80] These were some of the findings of a report on the Punjab administration prepared by Malik Qadir Baksh, a lawyer by profession, in October 1951. (See *Dawn*, 4 November 1951.) There is no reason to believe that things were any better during the years immediately following partition.
[81] *Dawn*, 3 February 1951.

Jinnah, not for the first time, tried slotting in Daultana as chief minister. But the alarms and excursions of Punjabi politics defeated the Quaid, sparking criticism in some quarters against this 'unwarranted interference of the Centre'.[82] While Mamdot survived the assault, Daultana along with Shaukat Hayat – the revenue minister and a member of yet another important landed family – tendered their resignations. Mamdot promptly brought in four of his henchmen into the ministry and began actively courting the increasingly vocal Islamic lobby. His job creation scheme and pandering to religious pieties had its rewards; the Mamdot ministry remained in office 'amid growing scandal and odium'.[83] Public opinion was less surprised by the 'cynical corruption of Mamdot and his supporters' than at the way 'the wishes of the Central Government...[were being] flouted'.[84] But these were the political innocents, unduly impressed by Karachi's ability to issue ordinances, and unable to appreciate where the balance of power lay in the still relatively fluid relations between the new centre and its provinces. As Mamdot's new finance minister had made amply clear, the centre would simply have to cough up resources irrespective of the defence procurement effort. There was a 'complete lack of coordination between the Central and Provincial Governments' he complained; the Punjab as well as the other provinces had 'practically no revenues and yet were continually forced to make disbursements and incur obligations'.[85] This was a stern warning to Karachi of a possible provincial campaign under Punjabi direction for a more equitable share of financial resources. To avert such a disaster, the centre reluctantly agreed to dole out some money for refugee rehabilitation, apart from extending a development grant and a credit of Rs. 50 million to the Punjab government.

The Punjab could muster a sufficiently potent form of provincial chauvinism to laugh the centre out of existence. Exploiting its many factions was one way the central government could try and harness Punjabi energies. But, with many horses in the running, the centre wisely decided to wait on events and rope in the winner. In November 1948, when Daultana managed to become president of the provincial League, the centre saw a chance of turfing out Mamdot and his reprehensible coterie. On 24 January 1949, the governor-general – Khwaja Nazimuddin – ordered the governor to dissolve the legislature and takeover the provincial administration under section 92a of the amended

[82] British high commissioner's opdom no. 42, 20–6 May 1948, L/WS/1/1599, IOL.
[83] High commissioner's monthly appreciation for June 1948, ibid.
[84] High commissioner's opdom no. 45, 3–9 June 1948, ibid.
[85] Economic aerogram [American embassy, Karachi], 1 September 1948, NND. 760050, RG 59, Box 6018, NA.

government of India act of 1935. The initial sighs of relief in the province
soon gave way to grief, especially among those who had hoped to
replace Mamdot and his lot. Daultana, sensing that the tide had turned,
now joined with the provincial League council to condemn the centre's
intervention as undemocratic and retrograde. This marked the beginning of a bitter Punjabi campaign against Liaquat Ali Khan and Mudie
while Daultana, the central ministry's man on the spot, sat uncomfortably on the fence.

What gave special impetus to Punjabi bitterness towards the
centre were the results of elections for office-bearers to the Pakistan
Muslim League. On 19 February 1949, at the annual session of the
Pakistan League council, bloc voting by representatives from the
NWFP, Bengal and Baluchistan assured that no Punjabi was elected to
an office in the national party. A theatrical walk-out by delegates from
west Punjab, preceded by noisy exchanges of abuse, set the tone for the
relationship between the provincial and central Leagues. But, more
importantly, it accentuated the estrangement between the province and
the centre. Agitated by the turn of events, Daultana quietly relinquished
his post as president of the provincial League and instead brought in
Maulana Abdul Bari who apart from being a non-entity was more
acceptable to Mamdot's supporters. Yet these attempts to bring
about a united front against the centre soon foundered on the Punjabi
disease for intrigue and faction-building. Bari saw wisdom in joining
forces with Mamdot's supporters. This temporarily left Daultana in the
lurch.

By the spring of 1949, the Punjabi press had pulled out all the stops in
its campaign against the British governor and Karachi. As the editor of
the *Nawa-i-Waqt* explained in plain language, Punjabi pride could not
suffer an Englishman in the role of its sole representative. The dismissal
of the Mamdot ministry and the provincial assembly was a blatant
indication that the centre, dominated by Urdu-speaking refugee politicians, considered all Punjabi representatives to be dishonest and
corrupt. In the constituent assembly, Punjab alone among the provinces
had less representation than its population warranted. To add insult to
injury, no attempt had been made to fill its vacant seats. Moreover,
Punjabis were being denied places in the central government as well as in
the Pakistan Muslim League and the central civil service. Non-Punjabi
civil servants, from the United Provinces in particular, were being
posted to important positions in the province and Punjabi traders had
been short-changed in the issuing of import and export licences. All this
was seen as proof apparent of a concerted attempt by the centre to

weaken the Punjab as a political and economic force.[86] Here was a mixture of Punjabi particularism tinged with paranoia, a lethal combination which in due course was to hit back at the centre with a vengeance.

EAST BENGAL

The agrarian backwater of the undivided province, eastern Bengal had an overall majority in the new state. But far from being allowed the dominant political voice in Karachi, let alone influence, recognition of eastern Bengal's importance stemmed from its role as the principal source of revenue for the centre. So, while there were good economic reasons to woo the distant eastern wing, few of the central leaders showed much appreciation of or sensitivity towards a people conscious of their own distinctive traditions and uncertain about their position in Pakistan. There is overwhelming evidence to suggest that the seeds of Bengali alienation were sown by a series of ill-conceived central government policies in the first few years, indeed months, of partition.

Of course not all of the factors contributing to eastern Bengal's troubles can be laid squarely at the central government's door. Quite as important were the peculiarities of its socio-economic and political structures: a predominantly rural population, malnourished, debt-ridden and unlettered; an articulate and politically active, but by no means wholly Muslim, class of urban professionals; an economy whose life-line flowed through the industrial hinterlands of western Bengal, especially Calcutta, and a political leadership split along lines of community, class and faction. In contrast to the Punjab, the exodus of Hindu landlords, traders and creditors who dominated the rural scene came in fits and starts. So, although the Bengal Muslim League was committed to introducing tenancy reforms and abolishing the permanent settlement of 1793, the Muslim peasantry had no immediate cause to rejoice. As for the Muslim urban professionals who had provided the backbone of the League's movement, independence brought limited opportunities. Of the positions vacated by Hindu service groups, only a few were filled by Bengali Muslims.[87] The rest were parcelled out to Punjabi and UP servicemen. Beyond the administrative apparatus,

---

[86] See *Nawa-i-Waqt* (Lahore), editorial, 21 April 1949.

[87] Bengali Muslims were traditionally underrepresented in the civil service of the undivided province. According to one estimate, out of 239 permanent Bengali civil service officers, 60 per cent were non-Muslims; of some 505 permanent junior civil servants, 59 per cent were non-Muslims. Yet nearly 76 per cent of all civil servants in Bengal came from the eastern districts. (Charles O. Thompson, [American consul, Calcutta] to the secretary of state, 15 July 1947, NND.842909, RG 59, Box 5955, 845.00/7–1547, NA.)

Hindus dominated the professions, whether legal, educational or medical. As for opportunities in trade and commerce, urban Bengali Muslims had little appetite for such activities, but were nevertheless irked to find non-Bengali Muslims replacing the hated Hindu Marwaris.

Despite the many possibilities of political alignments offered by this complex matrix of communal and class divisions, factional infights were the bane of politics in eastern Bengal, Muslim as well as Hindu. But factional rivalries were not the main factor determining the course of developments in the province. In eastern Bengal, more than in any other province, the administrative apparatus studded with Punjabi and other non-Bengali officials had a decisive bearing on the provincial ministry's tenure in office. The first League ministry under Nazimuddin was anything but popular. It managed to stay in office because it had the centre's blessings and, by extension, that of the provincial administration and also because the most vocal opposition to its rule came from the east Bengal Congress which besides being divided into three different groups[88] was a mainly Hindu organisation.

Visits by central ministers did nothing to defuse the increasingly strident protests against both the ministry and the provincial administration. A severe food shortage, labour troubles, and the provincial government's failure to curb smuggling across the border with western Bengal, wounded some and elicited screams from many more. There was a chorus of charges. The cruellest, because it was true, was that the ministry was unrepresentative; the chief minister and two ministers in a cabinet of seven had failed to secure a nomination, much less get elected to the provincial assembly. The provincial cabinet was averse to calling a session of the assembly, ostensibly because the central government had not sanctioned the redrawing of new constituencies, but really because it was afraid of 'losing any no-confidence motions'.[89]

A ministry uncertain of the confidence vested in it by the assembly or for that matter the local League was hardly the best link between the central government and the populace at the base. That the relationship between Dacca – the provincial capital – and Karachi was more in the form of a one way communication was made strikingly evident by the eruption of the language controversy. At the beginning of 1948 Jinnah, at his most insensitive, declared categorically that Urdu would be the national language of Pakistan. This outraged the Bengali majority, advertising a possibility which so far had been carefully concealed, namely that the two wings of Pakistan instead of coming together in a

---

[88] These were the Gana Samity, the Pakistan National Congress and the Pakistan Scheduled Caste Federation.
[89] British high commissioner's opdom no. 6, 21 January 1948, L/WS/1/1599, IOL.

spiritual embrace might have to be forced into an unhappy union. Student protests, though quashed by armed police, brought the ailing leader to eastern Bengal – the first time since the creation of Pakistan. Jinnah, not the most persuasive proponent of Urdu, told his restive Bengali audiences in clipped English that they would have all the advantages of equal citizenship, including recruitment to the Pakistan army. But he would not tolerate 'quislings' and 'fifth columnists'. And, while the final decision would be that of the people, in his opinion the official language of the state could only be Urdu. By his resolute insistence that the first loyalty had to be to a centre which had so far done nothing to win popular support, the Quaid-i-Azam missed the pulse of the Bengalis by an arm's length.

The language controversy was the most obvious and direct source of tension between the centre and the people of east Bengal. But, by picking an unpopular pack of provincial lieutenants, the centre seriously undermined its ability to contain the popular forces that the socio-economic conditions in the province were helping unleash. Soaring prices for foodgrains and most other essential commodities were a breeding ground for many discontents. As economic conditions went from bad to worse, so too did the law and order problems. Unable to accept the logic of its own ineptitude, the provincial government raised the spectre of a Red scare working alongside the Indian to undermine the security of the state. The public safety act was deployed to clap opponents into jail and the Hindu minority became a convenient scapegoat for all that was wrong in the province. But the Red-Indian threat frightened the provincial authorities more than it did the starving multitudes.

In July 1948, a strike by 200 armed policemen in Dacca was alleged to have been 'fomented by the local Communist Party'.[90] The striking policemen were simply agitating against delays in receipts of pay. The army had to be called in to stamp out the revolt. There were exchanges of fire; the incident revealed the weaknesses of the provincial security apparatus. So anxieties about securing the province, both against India and the enemies at home, became even more pronounced. But, with the Kashmir dispute and the defence of west Pakistan engaging as much as 98 per cent of the army, there was for the time being at least no prospect of the centre despatching troops to the eastern wing, much less doling out money to strengthen the internal security forces. According to the commander-in-chief of the Pakistan army, general Gracey, the 'battle for East Bengal would be fought in the West Punjab'.[91]

[90] British high commissioner's opdom no. 58, 15–21 July 1948, L/WS/1/1599, IOL.
[91] Walker to Redman, 24 September 1948, L/WS/1/1187, IOL.

The absurdity of the proposition was not lost on the men in charge in east Bengal. The new chief minister, Nurul Amin,[92] along with the Punjabi provincial chief secretary, Aziz Ahmed, paid a flying visit to Karachi, 'ostensibly to discuss certain economic matters but in reality to perfect plans for defence'. The local commander of the Pakistan army, major general Mohammad Ayub Khan, shared their opinion and was 'one of those principally responsible for spreading apprehension that Pakistan [was] likely to be attacked in the near future by India'.[93] But Karachi had enough troubles defending west Pakistan and could only hope against hope that the eastern wing would somehow withstand the threat from India. The attitude is all the more interesting considering Sardar Vallabhbhai Patel's provocative statements about the mistreatment of Hindu minorities in east Bengal. Patel, not a man to mince words, thought Pakistan should pay for its intolerance by ceding territory to allow for the resettlement of Hindus fleeing to India.[94]

Such statements by Indian leaders and the realisation that a mere 2 per cent of the Pakistan army was deployed in the eastern wing enraged most intelligent Bengalis. It was clearly unrealistic to expect them to be enthused by the centre's defence procurement drive. Kashmir simply did not stir the hearts of the majority of eastern Bengal's Muslims. The question of the national language, jobs in the civil and military service, the solution of the food problem, a reduction in the high cost of living, however, were issues the Bengalis understood and identified with passionately. As an astute observer of the situation put it:

The continued administration of East Bengal...by a provincial government composed of Punjabis and by a central government...located in Karachi ⋯ may not be impossible, but...[it may] prove increasingly difficult...to avoid a crisis of fundamental political and economic importance for Pakistan.[95]

By choosing to forestall the crisis instead of striking at its roots, by making a habit of bringing unrepresentative Bengalis to Karachi, by exploiting Islam to counter provincial dissidence,[96] and by relying on outright coercion when all else failed, the centre merely helped to worsen its relations with the eastern wing. So the crisis far from being averted continued to cast a menacing shadow on political developments.

---

[92] Nazimuddin by now was governor-general of Pakistan.

[93] This information was given to the American consul general in Calcutta by N.K. Gupta, professor of history at Dacca university and at the time in charge of the British information service in Dacca. (See Charles H. Davy to the secretary of state, 7 October 1948, NND.842909, RG 59, Box 5959, 845.00/10–748, NA.)

[94] Cited in British high commissioner's opdom no. 89, 5–11 November 1948, L/WS/1/1599, IOL.

[95] Franklin W. Wolf [counsellor for economic affairs, Karachi] to the secretary of state, 19 November 1948, NND.760050, RG 59, Box 6018, 845F.50/11–1948, NA.

SIND

In Sind, more than elsewhere, the political clout of the rural notables dominating the provincial arena was in direct proportion to the size of their landholdings. It was also the province with the highest concentration of land ownership in the new state. With an almost perfect symmetry of economic and political power, Sind's predominantly Muslim landlords were well-placed to perpetuate a parasitical and tyrannical form of domination. About 8 per cent had holdings over 100 acres which accounted for approximately 55 per cent of the total area, while those in possession of 500 acres or more constituted less than 1 per cent of all the owners and controlled 29 per cent of the land. As much as two-thirds of the peasantry were *haris* – share-croppers with no occupancy rights – or worse still, landless labourers.

Forced to pay a series of illegal exactions (*awabs*), the *haris* had in addition to perform various unpaid services (*begar*) for the landlord. There was a tacit agreement among the rural lords not to employ or lease land to tenants who had failed to honour past obligations. If the prospect of starvation was an ineffective deterrent to peasant recalcitrance, the existence of the landlord's 'police' force was sufficient to scotch the first stirrings of rebellion among the rural population. The power of the 'feudal' lords or *waderas* was all the more significant since the vast majority of the people of Sind depended on agriculture for their livelihood. The absence of any major agrarian reforms prior to the creation of Pakistan preserved a status quo that was repressive and restrictive in the extreme.

The coming of independence changed nothing. As in west Punjab, the exodus of Hindu landlords proved a boon for the rural notables of Sind. According to one estimate, of the 1,345,000 acres abandoned by Hindus as many as 800,000 acres were seized by Sindhi landlords.[97] If their stake in the economy was now greater, so were the prospects of manipulating a provincial administration no longer under the control of the colonial rulers. So Sindhi landlord-politicians celebrated freedom by engaging in an unedifying spectacle of intrigue and counter-intrigue. But in all

---

[96] In January 1949, a 'long succession of students' strikes and demonstration' ended in the celebration of 'anti-repression' day. (High commissioner's opdom no. 3, part II, 14–20 January 1949, L/WS/1/1600, IOL.) Alarmed by the apparent growth of 'Communism' among the students, the Muslim League tried introducing the 'Islamic way of life'. The vernacular press was 'virtually unanimous in recommending a fully Islamic constitution as the best safeguard against Communist encroachment'. Significantly, Nazimuddin after touring the province thought that Communism though active was 'not gaining ground there'. (High commissioner's opdom no. 7, part II, 11–17, February 1949, L/WS/1/1600, IOL.)

[97] Yu. V. Gankovsky and L.R. Gordon-Polonskaya, *A History of Pakistan (1947–1958)*, Lahore, 138.

fairness to Sindhi politics, the province did pay a considerable price for the establishment of the new centre. The decision to house the central government in Sind and the influx of refugees in their hundreds of thousands served to magnify some of the least palatable aspects of political and social life in the province – venality, particularism and the all too familiar face of factionalism. The search for office space and residential accommodation for the central government and its employees was the shot from the starter's pistol. It hit the lower and middle ranks of the provincial administration the hardest. There were complaints against 'corruption and high-handedness' in the rent control and housing departments. The relatively prosperous Hindu community, and the most obvious target of attack, was 'subject[ed] to immediate eviction by gangs of toughs, without any protection from the police or redress from the local authorities'.[98] The flight of Hindu capital and the collapse of the existing commercial networks exacerbated the Sind government's financial difficulties. It entailed a dramatic loss of revenue from excise and increased the burden of the provincial deficit which, according to the provincial authorities, reflected the cost of providing the central government with headquarters and paying for the upkeep of the refugees. So Sindhi outrage at the central government's decision to takeover the administration of Karachi – a main source of revenue for the province – had as much to do with hard headed financial calculations as with provincial particularism.

The separation of Karachi from the rest of the province was to become the symbol of Sindhi antagonism towards the new centre. Whatever their own differences, Sindhi politicians in an unprecedented display of unity were ready to take up cudgels against the central government. Sensing the hostility of Sindhi public opinion on the matter, the central government batted for time, secure in the knowledge that the stresses and strains within the ministry, the assembly and the provincial League would make way for a compromise on Karachi sooner or later. Surveying the field, it decided to widen the divide between Khuhro, the chief minister, and Pir Ilahi Baksh. Ghulam Hussain Hidayatullah, himself a veteran political intriguer, but now elevated to the position of governor, was given the responsibility of getting Khuhro out of office. On 27 April 1948, Hidayatullah – acting on Jinnah's advice – dismissed Khuhro for 'mal-administration, gross misconduct...and corruption'.[99] This prepared the way for an Ilahi Baksh ministry, but only after he had promised to play the centre's game.

---

[98] British high commissioner to the CRO, 30 December 1947, L/WS/1/1599, IOL.
[99] High commissioner's opdom no. 33, 22–8 April 1948, ibid.

Of course the temporary disappearance of the irrepressible Khuhro did not solve the problem of Karachi. When the issue was debated in the constituent assembly, Hashim Gazdar, yet another Sindhi politician of long-standing, pointed to the deepening discontent in his province 'over this centralisation of everything, over this dictatorship all over the Provinces'. The Sindhis were not opposed to Karachi becoming the capital; but were dead set against its separation from the province. After all, they were the ones who had given refuge to the central government – 'this child who had not legs [sic] to stand on, no chair to sit and no papers to write'.[100] But the child had now turned into a veritable demon. Impassioned speeches by the Sindhi contingent failed to sway delegates from the other provinces. A resolution endorsing the centre's decision was duly adopted; the stipulation that adequate compensation be paid to the provincial government was cold comfort for the patriots of Sind.

Pir Ilahi Baksh did his level best to avert a Sindhi backlash against the centre. But the provincial Muslim League, though divided on a score of other issues, adopted a unanimous resolution condemning the centre's decision. However, on 23 July 1948, without any payment of compensation to the provincial government, Karachi was formally declared as the federal capital of Pakistan and placed under the centre's administration. The wave of anger that swept through the province helped to further embitter relations between the Sindhi and non-Sindhi speakers, both in the urban and the rural areas.

This made it all the more difficult to prevent the disintegration of the political and administrative systems that was already well underway. It took a judicial verdict to eventually dislodge Ilahi Baksh from office. But the centre's replacement, Yusuf Haroon, was an industrial magnate and somewhat of an oddity in a province where political power was vested squarely in the landed classes who dominated the provincial legislature. It was not long before Khuhro had returned to the political scene[101] to try and pitch-fork Haroon out of office. But, as one commentator bemoaned, 'the political storms in Sind are totally unrelated to the problems of the Province.[102] He was right. Yet this was hardly a sound omen for relations between the centre and the province.

---

[100] See *CAD*, 111, 22 May 1948, 78–82.
[101] In February 1949, Khuhro had been charged with a 'criminal breach of trust' and sentenced to two years imprisonment under PRODA – the public and representative offices disqualification order, 1949. (See *The Pakistan Times* (Lahore), 26 February 1949.) But Khuhro managed to overturn the court decision and by December of the same year was back in the saddle as president of the Sind Muslim League.
[102] *The Pakistan Times*, editorial, 22 December 1949.

THE NORTH WEST FRONTIER PROVINCE

Strategically located, the North West Frontier Province occupied a special position in the new state, both administratively and politically. Yet at the time of partition the province had a Congress ministry in office, and this despite the fact of its overwhelmingly Muslim majority. Although the province voted to join Pakistan in the 1947 referendum, the central government had more than a handful of irritations on the Frontier. Afghanistan claimed parts of the province, there was talk of a 'Pakhtunistan' or 'Pathanistan' outside the pale of Pakistan, not to mention the urgent need to pacify the tribes in the adjoining areas. So the incorporation of the NWFP firmly into Pakistan was one of the main items on the centre's agenda.

Within eight days of partition, Jinnah had dismissed Dr Khan Sahib's Congress ministry. Instead a League ministry under Khan Abdul Qayum Khan was sworn into office. The centre's high-handedness did not go unnoticed.[103] Yet only the most ardent supporters of Congress raised cries of protest. Once it became clear that the centre had no intention of enlarging the provincial ministry – conveniently restricted to Qayum and one other minister – others too began questioning Karachi's line. And with good reason. The chief minister's sole colleague rested peacefully in his own village and had 'little idea of the transaction of public business'. Qayum's superhuman efforts to run the government single-handedly were laudable. But in the process 'power...[was] acquired by a group of officials who...[were] free to pursue their own policies' which, naturally, were 'designed more for their own than for the public good'.[104] This did not worry Karachi. It was better to let officials wield authority in a province which was the centre-piece of the central government's Kashmir policy.

As a result, the quality of provincial administration, never very high to begin with, stooped to new lows. The British governor of the province, George Cunningham, an old hand at Frontier affairs, 'attributed the general deterioration of the administration...to the Kashmir affair more than to any other single cause'. Not only were the officials utterly distracted from their duties, but were aiding and abetting

---

[103] It might have been more politic to let Dr Khan Sahib face a motion of no-confidence in the provincial assembly. But this was a dangerous course since Congress had a majority in the assembly. If both the provincial ministry and the assembly had in fact lost the confidence of the Pathans, as the Muslim Leaguers maintained, it is not clear why both were not dismissed. The provincial assembly elected in 1945–6 continued to serve as the representative body until 1951.

[104] C. B. Duke [deputy high commissioner, Peshawar] to the high commissioner, 27 November 1947, DO35/3172, PRO.

the chief minister in his efforts to fight the centre's war in Kashmir through 'deceitful and secret methods'. Consequently, 'all discipline and mutual confidence in the services between officers and men and between senior and subordinate officers...[had been] hopelessly undermined'.[105] Particularly disconcerting to the governor was the knowledge that junior police officers had been authorised to assist tribal incursions into Kashmir over the head of the inspector general.[106]

So in the NWFP, at least, there was an alliance of convenience between the provincial ministry, or what there was of it, and the administrative services. There were historical precedents for this. The main support for the Muslim League's demand for Pakistan was provided by the big landlords [Khans] – the local collaborators of the British – and their allies in officialdom. Religious leaders – pirs and mullahs – professionals and students did rally under the League's umbrella with effect. Yet the alliance between the big Khans and the officials was perhaps the more important factor in the referendum which sealed the future of the province. The social base of support for the Congress, on the other hand, came from the smaller landlords or Khans who were denied access to official favours and staunchly opposed colonial rule. The Khudai Khidmatgar [literally, servants of God] or Red Shirt movement organised by Dr Khan Sahib's younger brother, Khan Abdul Ghaffar Khan, was an attempt by the smaller landlords to mobilise support among the peasants to challenge the authority of the big Khans.[107]

Seen in this context, the politics of the NWFP in the immediate aftermath of independence become more easily explicable. Qayum Khan, a lawyer by profession, had been a Congressman until the summer of 1945. Though he joined the Muslim League, his links with the local Congress party as well as the Khudai Khidmatgars, however stretched, were by no means broken. By giving a free reign to the alliance between the big landlords and the local officials, by pressuring Congress members of the assembly to join the Muslim League and by hedging his bets on the long-term policies of his government, Qayum managed not only to survive in the quagmire of Pathan politics but also helped convert the NWFP from a Congress stronghold into an essentially 'League' province.

---

[105] Extract from the Peshawar deputy high commissioner's report, 10 December 1947, ibid.

[106] Ibid.

[107] For a detailed account of NWFP politics in the pre-independence period see Erland Jansson, *India, Pakistan or Pakhtunistan: The Nationalist Movements in the North West Frontier Province, 1937–47*, Uppsala, 1981.

The key to Qayum's skilful manipulation of Frontier politics was his remarkable ability to withstand the worst consequences of his own policies. The alliance between the big Khans and the local officials had a particularly devastating effect in the rural areas. Together with the shortage of food and cloth in the province it sparked off a blaze of agrarian unrest in the Hazara and Peshawar districts. As one commentator noted, there was 'excellent revolutionary material' in the situation and it could 'consume the present upper class and [the] existing order of society entirely'.[108] Qayum lost no time introducing some agrarian reforms, despite opposition from the big landlords in the assembly. This won him the backing of old Congress members, but brought about a split within the provincial League. Yet as a party the League was irrelevant in the Frontier. Even the defection of seven League members in the assembly did not endanger Qayum's position which appeared 'more strongly entrenched now than before' due to the agrarian policy.[109]

Qayum's rivals in the League saw that their prospects were limited so long as they remained subjected to the chief minister's whip. This was one reason why the first opposition party in Pakistan was set up in the NWFP. It was led by the pir of Manki Sharif, an important late-comer to the League, and an ardent advocate of 'Shariat rule'. Qayum responded by slapping the public safety ordinance on the province. It elicited wails of protest but helped steady the ministry, allowing Qayum to suppress all opposition to his iron rule on the Frontier. He succeeded in pacifying the tribes, taking the sting out of the 'Pakhtunistan' demand, taming the provincial assembly and bringing the local League firmly under his wing. All this made it relatively easier for the centre to believe that the Pathans were behind it. From Karachi's point of view, the only real danger now was the possibility that the man who stepped into Qayum's boots would have to tread extremely delicately to keep the NWFP in line.

BALUCHISTAN

The incorporation of this strategically vital but socio-economically and politically least well-developed region into the rest of Pakistan was a challenge as well as an ordeal for the central government. A challenge because Baluchistan constituted nearly 40 per cent of the land mass of western Pakistan and shared borders with Iran and Afghanistan. And an ordeal because Baluchistan's predominantly tribal social system had remained impervious to the administrative penetration which accom-

---

[108] Duke to the high commissioner, 23 February 1948, DO35/3172, PRO.
[109] CRO fortnightly note no. 5, 23 April 1948, L/WS/1/1204, 13, IOL.

panied the centralisation of colonial rule in most other parts of the subcontinent. When power was transferred, Baluchistan lacked the administrative unity of Pakistan's other constituent units. It consisted of territories administered by the British, a vast expanse of area under the control of the tribal sardars, as well as four princely states: Kalat, Kharan, Las Bela and Makran. Moreover, unlike the other provinces, Baluchistan was administered by an agent to the governor-general and the chief commissioner rather than by a representative government under the supervision of a governor.

The Muslim League's negligible presence in the area prior to the creation of Pakistan was in part a reflection of the retarded nature of Baluchistan's political development. But it had quite as much to do with the importance of other political groups espousing a specifically Baluch nationalism as opposed to an Indian or a Pakistani one. Baluch antipathy to central rule predated the establishment of the new state; it was to become even more potent after it. The most striking manifest-ation of it came in the form of the Khan of Kalat's categorical refusal to accede to Pakistan unconditionally. Not ready to be ruled by the rudder, the Khan had to be ruled by the rock. The army was deployed to secure the accession of Kalat along with the other three princely states. But, far from establishing the centre's writ in Baluchistan, the use of coercive power simply lent weight to the view, common among some Baluch sardars, that independence rather than subjugation to the Pakistani state was the only logical option.

A combination of factors prevented an explosion in Baluchistan during the initial years. For one, Baluchistan was not culturally and linguistically homogeneous. Only one-third of the population were Baluchi speakers; Brahuis and Pathans accounted for the two other main linguistic communities in the region. So, although there is no denying the reality of a specifically Baluch nationalism, it would be inaccurate to assume that the feelings were shared by the people of the region as a whole. This gave the central government an opening, one which it willingly exploited while trying to extend its hold over a region that had consistently defied rule by outside authorities.

II

Defence and the national economy

With an uncertain handle on politics in the provinces and a commitment to shouldering a defence burden far in excess of its financial resources, the central government faced the dire prospect of giving way under the

impact of some of its own policies. Deteriorating economic conditions – rampant inflation, the shortage of foodgrains and essential
commodities, widespread hoarding, smuggling and black-marketeering – were all powerful indicators of the potential for social unrest and
the grave political consequences for the centre and the provinces alike.
In part a product of the structural constraints Pakistan inherited at
the time of its creation, the poor health of the economy owed as much
to the financial policies of a central government anxious to make
political capital out of its various quarrels with India.

Designed to augment central revenues and finance defence expansion,
the policies underlined the inadequacies of the administrative machinery
and resulted in a growing contradiction between the state's external
security perceptions and the need to ensure internal stability. The
limitations of the revenue base of the central government indicate why
political stability was so easily endangered by the concerns that were
coming to shape Pakistan's external security perceptions. During 1949-
50, indirect taxes – customs and excise duties, the sales tax and salt
duty – contributed most of the centre's revenues; customs receipts alone
accounted for 40 per cent. Defence was not only the largest single item
in capital expenditure, but swallowed as much as 68 per cent of the
centre's revenues. Since direct taxes on incomes constituted a mere 10
per cent of central revenues,[110] defence expenditure had to be met in
large part through indirect taxation and the drawing down of the
sterling balances owed by Britain.

Between July 1948 and July 1949, excluding India with whom it had
an estimated trade surplus of approximately £11 to £15 million,
Pakistan's net deficit with the rest of the world was in the order of £34
million.[111] So there was no choice but to draw heavily on the sterling
balance account.[112] In the summer of 1949, while negotiating the new
financial agreement with treasury officials in London, Karachi's representatives admitted being 'perturbed' by the 'rate at which Pakistan was
running down her sterling balances'. But they pointed to the 'peculiar
circumstances' facing the new dominion,[113] and made no secret of the

[110] See *Budget of the Central Government of Pakistan for the year 1949–50.*
[111] See Ghulam Mohammad to Douglas Jay [economic secretary, treasury], 5 August
1949, T236/2621, PRO.
[112] In June 1948, there were £37 million in its current account with the bank of England.
But by July 1949, the account stood at £8.4 million, below the required working
balance of £12 million. On this basis Pakistan was expected to deplete the sterling
reserves half way through the ten year period it had agreed upon with Britain. (Note
by Mark, 16 July 1949, ibid.)
[113] See note of conversation between M.T. Flatt and Mumtaz Hassan, 8 June 1949,
T236/2620, PRO.

Constructing the state 95

fact that the deficit was 'largely due to expenditure on government account on arms and other commodities'.[114] According to estimates supplied by the Pakistani officials, Britain would have to release £35 million for 1949-50 and allow £29.5 million to be spent in dollars.[115] That most of the dollar component was to be syphoned off for purchases of arms and ammunition was implicit. British treasury officials had reason to 'suspect strongly' that Pakistan was spending the dollars to 'purchase...armaments from third countries' or, alternatively, was 'potting up dollars at ...[Britain's] expense'.[116] MacFarquhar, the secretary to the Pakistan commerce ministry, tipped members of the British board of trade about Karachi's plans of keeping an 'unallocated reserve of jute up her sleeve for the express purpose of trading it for defence stores'.[117] But there were other reasons why Britain could not make light of these tactics. Efforts by Pakistan to buy arms in the hard currency area through surreptitious methods entailed losses for the British defence industry, which despite cut-backs in production had by no means abandoned its interest in markets, both old and new. Moreover, there was the danger of a drain on the sterling area if Pakistan could not be weaned away from spending dollars. In desperation to procure defence stores, Pakistan could plausibly 'indulge in all sorts of undesirable commercial manoeuvres in international markets with the aim of acquiring cheap sterling' in order to 'pay higher prices for arms'.[118] The only way to take the sting out of Pakistani attempts at blackmailing the metropolis, weakened but no less wiser, was to make seemingly generous releases of sterling and then supply her with at least part of her defence requirements. After all, 'the only way of mopping up her sterling...[was] by substantial exports of arms...'.[119] At the end of exhaustive talks Pakistan received more sterling releases as a reward for accepting a cut in its dollar allowances.

But the restriction on its dollar expenditure was inconvenient for a

[114] Minutes of third joint meeting on Pakistan's financial negotiations, 28 May 1949, T236/2169, PRO.
[115] Note of conversation between Flatt and Mumtaz Hassan, 8 June 1949, T236/2620, PRO.
[116] The bank of England had detected a gap in Pakistan's dollar expenditure for the year 1948-9. The figures for Pakistan's trade with the United States and Canada failed to account for some $10 million. (Note of meeting held between the bank of England and treasury officials with Pakistani representatives, 9 June 1949, ibid.)
[117] I.A.H. Moore [board of trade] to Mark, 10 March 1949, DEFE7/155, PRO. Since the autumn of 1949 production in Dundee had fallen sharply, resulting in a shortage of jute products. So the threat to withhold supplies of raw jute to Britain was no mere bluff. Raw cotton imports from Pakistan, though expensive, allowed Britain to spend fewer dollars and ease off the pressure on the sterling.
[118] Mark to C. Walworth, 5 April 1949, ibid.
[119] See CRO to British high commissioner, draft telegram, 3 or 4 April 1949, ibid.

state anxious to industrialise and militarise at the same time. Some of the items on the government's shopping list were not only more easily available in the non-sterling area but also cost considerably less.[120] This was why officials in the ministries of finance and commerce were busy working out strategies to increase Pakistan's availability of dollars. They had begun learning the ropes of the international financial system even if in the process they neglected to refine the art of domestic economic management. In June 1949, the announcement of an unexpectedly liberal import policy was a poignant indication of the central government's determination not to let other peoples' troubles dull its sense of Pakistan's interests.[121] Whatever the impact on the sterling area, Pakistan was eager to push ahead with its plans to industrialise. And as for the search for defence stores these as usual would be obtained wherever, whenever and however possible.

On 15 September 1949, London's decision to devalue the sterling might conceivably have deflected Pakistan from both objectives. The devaluation of the Indian rupee one day later seemed to have left Pakistan with no alternative except to follow course. In a remarkable show of its capacity for intransigence at a time when the dice appeared to be loaded against it, Pakistan refused to devalue its rupee, sending shock waves through much of the sterling area and beyond. There are those who believe that the decision not to devalue was Pakistan's coming of age, a long-delayed assertion of its sovereignty and independence *vis-à-vis* both India and Britain. Others see in it nothing more than a piece of fractured economic logic, and – to quote the prime minister of India – one befitting 'a gang of brigands, cut-throats and robbers'.[122] The explanation must surely lie somewhere in between these two extremes.

The decision not to devalue was the brainchild of the Bengali minister of commerce, Fazlur Rahman. Mindful of the shortage of various

---

[120] In June 1948, Britain had undertaken to supply Pakistan with capital equipment over a three year period for an amount not exceeding £20 million. But a year later it had become evident that the total value of capital goods Britain could supply over the period would be no more than £8.5 million. (See letter from the engineering industries division, ministry of supply, to Mark, 10 June 1949, T236/2620, PRO.) There were greater hurdles in supplies of defence equipment to Pakistan – some genuine, others dictated by political considerations.

[121] The open general licence for sterling and soft currency areas was extended for another year; the list of items for which licences could be obtained for imports from hard currency areas was increased. Controls on licences for industrial goods were relaxed while those on imports of luxury goods were made stricter.

[122] See Graffley-Smith to the secretary of state [CRO], a review of events, September–December 1949, 21 February, 1950, F0371/84198, PRO.

commodities in east Bengal, especially rice,[123] Rahman was looking for a way to decrease the price of imports. According to the calculations of the commerce minister and other like-minded officials, Pakistan's decision not to devalue the rupee would not have an adverse effect on the demand for raw jute, or for that matter on its other export commodities. This assumption, if correct, would mean that other countries in the sterling area would pay more for Pakistan's exports. By the same token Pakistan's imports from the sterling area would become cheaper, while those from the hard currency area would cost no more. It was evident that the 'latter factor...[was] probably of importance to the Pakistani Government in connection with their purchases of arms for dollars'.[124]

By refusing to follow India's example and devaluing the Pakistani rupee, the central government could look forward to getting 44 per cent more for exports of raw jute quite apart from a 40 per cent increase in the value of its existing trade surplus. Subtler still was the calculation that larger quantities of coal, cotton textiles, vegetable oils, steel and tobacco from India might enable Pakistan to avoid a trade surplus which under the circumstances had no practical value. Furthermore, imports intended for Indian markets might conceivably filter through the largely unpoliced frontiers, allowing Pakistani consumers to at long last partake of the simple joys of relatively cheaper imports. If all this could be made to work, Indian sterling resources would effectively be paying for imports into Pakistan and so easing the existing payments difficulties between the two dominions.[125]

Three months before the devaluation decision, New Delhi had stopped all transfers of Pakistan's share of the assets of undivided India. These were thought to be in the order of Rs. 490 million, consisting of note issues, gold coin and bullion, sterling securities, government of India's securities and rupee coins.[126] If Pakistani officials were trying to force India's hand by refusing to devalue the rupee, they wholly miscalculated the strength of the reaction. New Delhi slapped export

---

[123] Despite awesome problems with the government's procurement and distribution machinery, a good wheat harvest in west Pakistan had solved the food problem in that part of the country. The situation was dramatically different in east Bengal where floods in the summer of 1949 had practically wiped out the rice crop. Rice imports were, therefore, unavoidable. The real difficulty was the declining purchasing power of people; jute prices had plummetted by well over 30 per cent during the first half of 1949 while rice prices were soaring.

[124] Note by the CRO on 'Pakistan's Decision Not to Devalue Her Rupee'; considered by the cabinet committee for commonwealth economic affairs, 24 September 1949, T236/2170, PRO.

[125] Ibid.

[126] Wolf [Karachi] to the secretary of state, despatch no. 98, 12 July 1950, NND.842909, RG 59, Box 5548, 890D.131/7–1250, NA.

duties on various commodities required by Pakistan and suspended the supply of coal, crucial for the few industries in operation in the new state. India's refusal to accept the value of the Pakistani rupee and, in particular, its 'ruthless administrative boycott',[127] brought interdominion trade to a standstill. This hurt the jute industry in India, but it hurt jute producers in east Bengal even more. The cessation of all imports from India was to bear down heavily on the average consumer in Pakistan since substitutes from other countries tended to cost more, not less.

The central government had now to face the consequences, both in the short and the long term, of its cavalier decision. The policy was an astute play on national sentiments. Immensely popular insofar as it was seen as a sign of Pakistan's ability to withstand bullying by India, it had the effect of 'creat[ing] doubt, uncertainty and confusion' in the commercial sector, much of which suffered 'a partial, if not complete paralysis' with many firms reporting financial losses.[128] The governor of the state bank, Zahid Hussain, was disturbed by the huge deposits in the recently revived private sector.[129] There was now a very real danger of large capital transfers out of Pakistan, a trend the government machinery was incapable of checking. Assuming the role of prime borrower and issuing treasury notes was one way of preventing a run on the banks. But this merely pushed up the internal debt and was not a policy that could be pursued with abandon.

By the beginning of 1950, an increasingly longer set of odds threatened the central government's seemingly calculated gamble with non-devaluation. Despite a revision of the import policy and the setting up of an export promotion committee, Pakistan continued to experience a worsening balance of trade and consequent pressures on its foreign exchange reserves. Contrary to all expectations, the average consumer was much worse off after the non-devaluation. Prices for practically all consumer goods were 'as high, if not higher'. Those elbowed out of agricultural land and left to seek employment in the urban areas found it impossible to 'sustain life on even a reasonable level'. The government's own employees were in a hapless predicament – the 'costs each month

---

[127] Grafftey-Smith to the secretary of state [CRO], review of events during September-December 1949, 21 February 1950, FO371/84198, PRO.
[128] Economic aerogram from H. Doolittle to the secretary of state, 1 October 1949, NND.760050, RG 59, Box 6018, 845F.50/10–149, NA.
[129] Under the monetary laws in operation, the size of such bank deposits could not exceed Rs. 50 million. But in September 1949 they were in the order of Rs. 222.1 million. (Zahid Hussain's speech at the first meeting of the shareholders of the state bank, 29 September 1949; cited in Wolf to the secretary of state, 30 September 1949, NND.760050, RG 59, Box 6019, 845F.516/9–3049, NA.)

for the bare necessities of diet and clothing...[were] almost invariably in excess of wages received'.[130] Low wage levels and a web of price spirals loudly hinted at the potential for political unrest, much of it already in the making.

Cognizant of the dangers, yet unable still to accept their full implications, some officials in Karachi admitted 'confidentially that...[the] administrative machinery...[was] not effective'.[131] Traders nimble enough to survive the maze of bureaucratic red tape whetted the appetites of ravenous government officials. Textile importers could expect to make profits up to the tune of 70 per cent. Alternatively, the licences could be sold for as much as 55 per cent of the nominal value of the goods that were to be imported and at even higher prices in established commercial circles.[132] The Pakistan chambers of commerce and industry as well as individual businessmen were among the most zealous crusaders against a devaluation of the rupee. Anxieties about defence, now greater due to the intensification of economic and political tensions between the two dominions, was another reason why Karachi could not afford to give serious thought to the devaluation of the Pakistani rupee. The budget for 1950–1 showed a deficit of Rs. 380 million ($115 million); this was equivalent to 35 per cent of total government expenditure. The outlays on defence alone were more than one and a half times the total deficit,[133] absorbing 66.8 per cent of the estimated revenues of the central government. Taking account of the expenditure on the armed forces charged to capital account (68.5 per cent of total capital expenditure), the total cost of defence amounted to approximately 100 per cent of current revenues.[134] A series of indirect taxes, mainly import duties, were expected to help finance the budget deficit. But at the same time the central government abolished the capital gains tax, reduced the super tax and cut duties on various capital goods. As for the provinces, there was no prospect of their getting any substantial development grants in the near future.

By July 1950, Zahid Hussain at least was convinced that the non-devaluation policy was 'proving ruinous to Pakistan'. He was alarmed

---

[130] Wolf's despatch no. 133, 2 February 1950, NND.842909, RG 59, Box 5542, 890D.00/2–250, NA.

[131] Ibid.

[132] Acting British high commissioner's opdom no. 3, part II, 8 February 1950, FO371/84199, PRO.

[133] 'International Economic Position of Pakistan', memorandum to the national advisory council staff committee, staff document no. 414, 1 May 1950, NND.842430, RG 59, Box 7, File-Pak. Pol.1950–1, NA.

[134] See *Budget of the Central Government of Pakistan, 1950–51*, and Wolf's despatch no. 276, 15 March 1950, NND.842909, RG 59, Box 5547, NA.

by the heavy budget deficits, the rapidly growing internal debt, a wholly unsatisfactory tax situation and Pakistan's failure to find alternative markets for its exports, especially those of raw jute. Depressed and disheartened by the 'selfishness of a few who were making unconscionable profits', Zahid Hussain 'expressed grave fear of developing social unrest' and thought 'Pakistan might be forced to turn to some modified form of state socialism or statism.'[135] Prices for jute and wheat slumped while those of essential commodities rose appreciably. The producers of two of the main agricultural commodities bore the worst brunt of the non-devaluation decision. But average consumers in the urban areas were also left smarting under the effects of higher prices. Only the favoured few did well out of the general social duress.

The outbreak of the Korean war, admittedly, stemmed Pakistan's drift towards an imminent financial and political collapse. But its salutary effect on an economy visibly reeling under the combined impact of partition and the non-devaluation decision has tended to be exaggerated. The impact on Pakistan's financial position – external as well as internal – was far too fleeting and uneven to make a dent on the national economy. All that really happened was that exporters of raw jute and raw cotton could now tap alternative markets for products which had been absorbed mainly by India, and to a lesser extent by Britain. Through the usual device of imposing heavy export duties, the government of Pakistan was able to divert a large proportion of the windfall in higher commodity prices to the exchequer where it was used to finance capital expenditure on defence. In February 1951, New Delhi's decision to accept the value of the Pakistani rupee, prematurely hailed as the triumph of sound economy over politics,[136] seemed to have exonerated the central government. The Pakistani rupee was not devalued until 1955. But, far from postponing the day of reckoning, the central government finally out of the cul-de-sac found itself driving imperceptibly towards a head on collision with the provinces.

The emergence of institutional imbalances

Central policies aimed principally at extracting and only marginally at reallocating limited financial resources naturally had a bearing on the shifting political configurations in the provinces. This was to leave lingering effects on relations between state and society since the structures governing them were still very much in the incipient stages of

---

[135] Minutes of interview between Zahid Hussain and Wolf, despatch no. 50, 8 July 1950, NND.842909, RG 59, Box 5548, 890D.131/7–850, NA.
[136] See *Dawn*, 27 February 1951.

development. The socio-economic and political realities in the constituent units on the one hand, and the imperatives of the centre on the other, were the most pronounced domestic tunes in the tortured medley that accompanied the balancing of forces within the emerging structure of the Pakistani state. Equally important were the international tunes, especially since none of the state institutions had a clear edge during the initial years of independence. Yet it was in these years that the basis was laid for the institutional imbalances that have shaped Pakistan's history.

In a state where regional diversities and economic inequalities undercut the supposed solidarities of a common religion, the need for a well-organised political party commanding support in all the constituent units was undeniable. Yet the Muslim League was in organisational disarray; a victim of calculated neglect. The need to broaden the state's resource base had justified focusing on the expansion of administrative capacities instead of building up the Muslim League. But, once the implications of the central government's financial policies – whether the preoccupation with bolstering defences against India or concerns about creating an industrial infrastructure – began taking a toll of politics in the provinces, the lack of some sort of a representative party soon showed up as the Achilles' heel of the new state. The evolving structure of the Pakistani state was tending more and more towards distorting rather than reflecting complex social dynamics. By the time its early managers saw attractions in nurturing the League, much ground had been lost. Mounting economic grievances made it difficult to secure support for the Muslim League in urban and rural areas alike. This in turn made politics at the central as well as the provincial levels far more uncertain and precarious.

Various factors militated against the League developing into an important pillar of the state. The decision to separate the party from the government had formalised the rift between the party and the central and provincial ministries. In the short run those in power were able to use the administrative machinery to curb the activities of the political organisation. But in the long run this meant losing the only vehicle of popular support for those in government. The League president was reduced to being 'a pawn in manoeuvres between the Provinces and the Centre'.[137] By March 1949, the central government had such a 'firm hold on the proceedings' of the League council that it was 'not likely to permit any party programme beyond the vaguest generalities'.[138] So it

---

[137] British high commissioner's opdom no. 96, 26 November-2 December 1948, L/WS/1/1599, IOL.

[138] Grafftey-Smith to Noel Baker, 29 March 1949, L/WS/1/1039, IOL.

was futile for the local party bosses to keep their ears fixed to the ground or to push for any policies unacceptable to the central government.

Leaving all initiative to the central government, the League lapsed into its favourite pastime – factional intrigues. A few cosmetic changes here or there did precious little to alter the League's image as an impotent appendage of the central government.[139] Sporadic efforts were made to resuscitate the League at the district and tehsil levels. But these owed nothing to the central high command and little to the provincial Leagues. It was not unusual to find more than one group purporting to be the 'authentic' League organisation at the local as well as the provincial levels. Many of the opposition parties that sprang into action during these years were splinter groups from the League. The high command had difficulties distinguishing between its lieutenants and opponents which, given the choice, was perhaps just as well.

Ignorance, however, has its limitations. There was convincing evidence of landlords ejecting tenants in west Pakistan. To defuse the tensions in the rural areas and win a few laurels, the central government instructed the Pakistan League to set up a committee to investigate possible changes in tenancy legislation. But this was merely stoking discontent among the bigger landlord supporters of the League. Even before the report of the Pakistan Muslim League's agrarian reform committee had become public, the bigger landlords had taken recourse to religion – a time-honoured ploy of the well-off among the Faithful. Defections came thick and fast, strengthening the hands of the pro-Shariat lobby. The unity of the League, difficult to forge and never easy to sustain, had been shaken.

In July 1949, when the Muslim League's agrarian reform committee publicised its findings, the opposition to it was more formidable than its prescriptions.[140] The central government had to beat a hasty retreat. Having relied all along on support from the principal beneficiaries of the status quo rather than building its own bases of support, there was nothing astonishing about the central government's reluctance to follow

---

[139] In April 1949, amidst great fanfare, the Pakistan League was moved from its makeshift office in a small private home in Karachi and given all the paraphernalia of a central secretariat – with a foreign relations section and a publicity wing – overseeing the work of the provincial secretariats. But its budget for 1949–50 showed an estimated income of Rs. 35,000 while expenditure was expected to be in the order of Rs. 79,000. There were some Rs. 72 lakhs in the All-India Muslim League's central kitty at the time of partition. But this had been lying in various bank accounts pending a division between the Leagues in the two dominions. (*Nawa-i-Waqt*, 27 April 1949.) So there was not much in the way of money with which to stiffen the sagging morale of League workers.

[140] See *Report of the Agrarian Committee appointed by the Working Committee of the Pakistan Muslim League*, published by S. Shamsul Hasan, assistant secretary of the Pakistan Muslim League, 1949.

through on its foray into agrarian reform policy. Its handling of party affairs had undermined the one policy specifically designed to consolidate support in the rural areas. For all its efforts at centralised decision-making, Karachi agreed to let the provincial Leagues carp and criticise the reform committee's report and produce their own tenancy legislations. It might have been more sensible to read the writing on the wall, hold internal party elections and rope in the populist elements. This would have preempted other organisations from taking advantage of the simmerings of discontent. Above all, it would have served as an effective check on the bigger landlords whose overweening ambitions were widening the gulf between the League and the people below. The Pakistan Muslim League's working committee, however, chose the path of masterly inactivity and postponed all elections within the party. The ostensible excuse was the 'hopeless confusion' of League organisations, particularly in the Punjab, east Bengal, Sind and Karachi.[141] This was followed up by a resolution prohibiting League members from joining rival political organisations.[142] From now on all criticism of the Muslim League was dubbed high treason.

Far from steadying the League's fortunes, these policies evoked further discontent. Some League members were disheartened by the high command's attempts to keep fences mended with the old guard, consisting of bigger landlords in the main. The disillusioned now looked towards other groups. One alternative was Shaheed Suhrawardy's All-Pakistan Awami League. An advocate of civil liberties and progressive economic policies, Suhrawardy claimed that his party was not in opposition to the League, but merely seeking to reform its retrograde policies. Similar claims were made by other opposition groups – ranging from the extreme right to the far left. Unconvinced, the central and provincial ministries reacted by clamping down on these would-be reformers. Throwing critics into gaol on charges of sedition was an insurance against the emergence of any effective opposition to the League. In the absence of attempts at revitalising the League or a move towards general elections, this was tantamount to torpedoing the development of a political process in the state. As one observer noted, the 'mystique' of the Muslim League though tarnished by the activities of 'corrupt and unscrupulous personalities' had not faded altogether.[143] Even a party devoid of purpose and principles could, if given half a

---

[141] High commissioner's review of events, September to December 1949, FO371/84198, PRO.

[142] The decision was taken by the working committee of the All-Pakistan Muslim League which met in Karachi between 25 and 27 December 1949.

[143] High commissioner's review of events, September to December 1949, FO371/84198, PRO.

chance, serve as a respirator to a political process threatened with asphyxiation.

Internal wranglings and jockeying for position, in any case, had been part and parcel of the League tradition. So the erosion of the political process in Pakistan cannot be attributed simply to provincial politicians using the League as an arena for advancing personal interests or fighting out family vendettas. It offers one thread only in an explanation of the failure of a party system to strike roots in Pakistan. Constructing a central authority where none existed was an important factor, perhaps the most important one. No less important was the impact of the central government's financial policies on the socio-economic conditions in the provinces.

The central government's decision not to devalue the rupee is a good illustration of how financial policies recoiled on politics in general, and the League in particular. In the months preceding the non-devaluation, an exceptionally good harvest followed by the lifting of controls saw wheat prices hitting a record low in the Punjab. Ordinarily the wheat surplus would have been absorbed by the Indian market. But the war of the rupee ruled out that possibility.[144] Before the outbreak of the Korean war changed the picture, wheat was selling in Lahore for less than half the price in Indian Punjab.[145] But consumers in Lahore were paying much higher prices for imported goods than in either Karachi or New Delhi. Lower food prices, however welcome, were insufficient compensation for the urban consumers in the Punjab. As for the wheat producers, their incomes were falling while prices for essential commodities were rising. For the first time since 1939 there was some danger to the agricultural prosperity of the Punjab. Rural discontent may have posed a serious threat to the stability of the province if not for the miraculous boom in the international price of raw cotton. But, as ever, it was the traders and not the actual producers who made windfall profits. During the early summer of 1950, there were instances of agrarian unrest in many districts of the Punjab. And, while the reasons were more complex than the fate of wheat prices alone, the correlation is significant nonetheless.

[144] Rationing was abandoned and a floor price fixed. The government entered the market with the backing of the newly established National bank to buy up the surplus wheat. The expectation was to sell the wheat in the international market; the foreign exchange could come in handy for the purposes the central government had in mind. Yet, once its efforts to find outlets for the surplus came to naught, the government lost its initial enthusiasm. Consequently prices dropped further still.

[145] R.L.D. Jasper [deputy high commissioner, Lahore] to high commissioner, despatch no. 20/50, review of events in the Punjab, December 1949 to June 1950, DO35/3186, PRO.

The provincial government's Punjab protection and restoration of tenancy rights act was the source of the trouble. Announced in May 1950, it promised security of tenure under certain conditions and nullified all ejectments since the appearance of the League's agrarian reforms report in July 1949. The landlords retaliated by systematically ejecting tenants before the act could be implemented. The tenants, many of whom were refugees from east Punjab, had been agitating for reforms far more wide-reaching than those on offer. Their demands were orchestrated by the Punjab Kisan committee. But the Kisan committee was thought to be a Communist front. So although the tenants had sound reasons for fighting to keep what had been given to them in principle, if not as yet in fact, it was easy for their oppressors to point to the Red threat and secure support from the government machinery. Governments are adept at giving with one hand and taking back with the other. Landlord pressures on the Muslim League and the provincial government ensured that nothing much came of the tenancy protection act. The 'stubborn pursuit of the status quo by the landlords' had won the day. But only at the risk of giving the populist elements cause to strike while the iron was hot. The view that the situation in some districts had assumed 'semi-revolutionary proportions' may have been an exaggeration. Yet it was unquestionably the case that 'unrest among the urban as well as the rural people' was manifesting itself increasingly as 'dis[i]llusionment with the League'.[146]

East Bengal had even more reason for disillusionment with the Muslim League. The provincial economy had been hard hit by the suspension of trade between Pakistan and India. The plight of the Punjabi wheat producers was light compared to the sufferings of the east Bengali jute growers. The drastic fall in the price of raw jute, despite the high demand for the commodity just across the border in west Bengal, was a strong indictment of Karachi's priorities. The central government's panacea was to takeover the jute trade. It set up a jute board, fixed a floor price, and ventured forth to save the producer from Hindu middlemen. The board was under the supervision of Ghulam Farooq – the non-Bengali secretary of industry – and included such business luminaries as M.A. Ispahani, the elder brother of Karachi's ambassador in Washington and the 'largest Pakistani jute dealer'.[147] The activities of the jute board are a macabre tale of exploitation and

---

[146] A.R. Preston [American consul general, Lahore], despatch no. 137, 1 June 1950, NND.842909, RG 59, Box 5549, 890D.16/6-150, NA.

[147] Memorandum prepared by J. Russell Andrus [first secretary of the American consulate, Dacca], 30 May 1950; enclosure to Dacca despatch no. 51, 2 June 1950, NND.842430, RG 84, Box 7, File 500-Pak. 1950–1, NA.

misuse of high office. Under its auspices jute producers were selling at lower than the official minimum price to favoured speculators like Ispahani who then sold to the jute board at a profit. The 'high handed operations'[148] of the members of the jute board gave 'impetus to East Bengali provincialism'; there was a universal feeling that 'the central government's policy...[was] bearing most heavily on the province' and that 'West Pakistan [was] prepared to fight the "cold war" with India "to the last Bengali"'.[149]

During February and March 1950, the worst communal disturbances in the two halves of Bengal since partition lent credence to this view. Most informed sources were unanimous in their opinion that the real cause of the riots was economic and not communal. The jute board in complicity with the nawab of Dacca was thought to have engineered the riots in order 'to squeeze out the Marwari [Hindu] traders'; they found convenient shock troops in the form of the so-called Ansars, the local version of the Pakistan national guard.[150] In west Bengal, it was the Hindu Mahasabha that wanted to make political capital out of Indo-Pakistan disputes, and so there Muslims were the victims. Yet another exchange of populations followed naturally. The gravity of the situation was highlighted by a massive deployment of Indian troops along the largely unprotected east Bengal border. In April 1950, the signing of a minorities agreement between Liaquat and Nehru eased tensions.[151] But Karachi's own relations with east Bengal were very far from easy.[152]

Malik Firoz Khan Noon, a member of a renowned Punjabi landowning family, was made governor of the province. Noon's appointment was good news for the jute board, but bad for the chief minister. As the appointees of the central government, the jute board and the governor had no qualms about flouting the authority of the provincial ministry. The biggest offender was M.A. Ispahani whose Muslim Commercial bank was 'playing an active commercial role' in the jute trade. His 'flagrant misuse' of influence over the jute board, the National bank as well as Karachi was the main cause for the 'widespread grumbling'

---

[148] High commissioner's review of events, September–December 1949, FO371/84198, PRO.
[149] High commissioner's opdom no. 3, part I, 7 February 1950, ibid.
[150] Charles D. Withers' [American consul, Dacca] despatch no. 24, 9 April 1950, NND.842430, RG 84, Box 8, File 570.1, NA.
[151] The communal troubles were not confined to the Bengals alone. There were riots in the UP, resulting in yet another stream of refugees into Pakistan. But it was the mounting military tensions that compelled Liaquat to go to New Delhi in person and sign an agreement whose historic importance has unfortunately been forgotten in the flurry of recriminations between the two dominions.
[152] One result of the border tensions in the spring of 1950 was the central government's decision to finally buttress east Bengal's defences.

among the lesser men in the trade.[153] While the producers of raw jute were effectively fleeced and many smaller traders weeded out, Ispahani's profits between September 1949 and June 1950 alone amounted to Rs. 20 million.[154]

Meanwhile Amin was finding it increasingly difficult to keep his house in order. The provincial budget for 1950–1 showed a deficit of one crore and seventy-three lakhs of rupees.[155] The centre and the provincial government had been quibbling over their respective share of the export duty on jute. Until that could be settled, the only way to finance the provincial deficit was to impose another series of unpopular taxes on an extremely weary population. Amin tried allaying provincial feelings by launching one of the strongest public diatribes by a League chief minister against the central government's financial policies. He accused the centre of 'trying to deprive the Provinces of their sources of taxation and flattering itself' by producing 'superfluous or super-surplus budgets year after year'. This was nothing short of an invidious 'policy of strangulation'; an attempt by the centre to 'build its castle on the carcasses of the Provinces'.[156]

In private, Amin was equally bitter but more revealing. He had been virtually cast aside by the jute board, that 'foreign government' which was running the affairs of the province. By now the board had effective control over every aspect of economic life in the province – transportation, communications, as well as the price of rice – due to its monopoly over decisions dealing with the jute acreage. Amin's demand that the ministry ought to be consulted on matters to do with jute met with the retort that 'the government of East Bengal had nothing to do with it'.[157] The central government's financial policies, shamelessly reminiscent of those adopted by the colonial state, succeeded in destroying the last vestiges of Bengali sentiments for the Muslim League. Recognising the trends, the provincial League tried distancing itself from the centre and became a major proponent of complete provincial autonomy. But the League's associations with the centre, however strained, meant that other groups, it did not matter which, could by voicing the same slogan improve their chances at the hustings. So in the Punjab and Bengal, the two provinces that could tilt the

[153] Memorandum by Andrus, 30 May 1950; enclosure to Dacca despatch no. 51, 2 June 1950, NND.842430, RG 84, Box 7, File 500-Pak.1950–1, NA.
[154] Withers to American embassy [Karachi], despatch no. 51, 2 June 1950, ibid.
[155] *Nawa-i-Waqt*, 27 February 1950.
[156] See *CAD*, 21 March 1952, 52–3.
[157] Withers to Avra Warren, despatch no. 7, 29 May 1950, NND.842430, RG 84, Box 7, File 350-Pak. Pol. 1950, NA.

political balance in the new state, the League was on the ropes licking its wounds. This was portentous for the stability of Liaquat Ali Khan's government, especially since the League was in equally tumultuous waters in the smaller provinces. In Sind, where landlord politics were beyond hope of redemption, the League was an euphemism for any faction that temporarily managed to outwit its rivals. The province also had socio-economic difficulties of its own, most of them aggravated by the influx of refugees. With the Sind Hari committee urging tenants to force the issue of agrarian reform by resisting the strong arm tactics of their landlords, unsettled conditions prevailed in many rural districts. Filibusting by landlord-politicians ensured that the Sind assembly could produce only the most watered down version of tenancy reforms. So the agrarian question continued to hang fire. Labour unrest in the urban areas completed the grim scenario. Sind's oppressive agrarian social structure and the presence of hundreds of thousands of Urdu-speaking refugees in the urban areas made it an attractive target for ideologues with leanings towards the left.

In the North West Frontier Province, there was no immediate danger of left-wing ideologues rousing the Pathans against the keepers of the status quo. But neither was there much prospect of a League organisation availing itself of Qayum Khan's reforms and building a solid phalanx of support for the central government. Qayum's carrot and stick methods did work wonders on the Frontier. Yet Karachi's hold over the province depended on the chief minister and not the other way around. In any case, Qayum was believed to have set his sights on Liaquat's job at the centre. In Baluchistan, the local League had still to make its first dent; the better part of its energies were expended in factional fights or in fending off the Tribal Federation.

Unsure of its staying capacity, Liaquat's government – operating under emergency powers – fell into deeper embrace with the higher echelons of the administrative bureaucracy. The experience was neither short, nor sweet. Administrators are rarely amenable to being overruled by politicians with brittle bases of support. Ghulam Mohammad is a good example. He had long ago 'acquire[d] illusions [of] grandeur' and 'visualize[d] him[self as] Jinnah's successor'. Holding the twin portfolios of finance and economics, he had 'unlimited power' and had readily and ably exploited the widespread dissensions among 'high League leaders and politicians [to] acquire many followers'.[158] Though not as fortunate as Ghulam Mohammad, other senior civil servants were just as capable of building networks of support by disbursing patronage through the usual devices: jobs, licences, contracts or requisition orders for factories

[158] Alling to the departments of state and army, no. 262, 8 May 1948, Declassified 785011, RG 319, Entry 57, Box 409, WNRC.

and houses. Nepotism and corruption, religiously condemned, were among the fastest growing concerns in the 'land of the pure'. Administrators were as culpable as the politicians. But, as permanent officials answerable only to the governor-general, they had far greater freedom of manoeuvre than politicians whose tenure in office depended on the ability to ward off opponents.[159] In short, the administrators had all the trappings of a social class, one capable of deploying the state apparatus to further its own interests.

The best that could be expected from the relative autonomy of administrators in a state that was in the process of formation was a measure of coordination within the government machinery. At worst they could be relied upon to misuse high office. No doubt some coordination of government activities was achieved. But successes in that direction were qualified by a considerable flexing of muscle between politicians and administrators, the latter taking refuge in a superiority syndrome and their better knowledge of the processes of government. Politicians, if they were not altogether detested, were viewed with condescension and suspicion, not the best augury for a healthy interaction between the political and the administrative arms of the state.[160] More to the point, between 1947 and 1950, Pakistan was very far from possessing the kind of government machinery that might have vindicated the autonomy of its administrators, or the centralisation policies so diligently pursued by Karachi. The shortage of skilled personnel had seen inexperienced, sometimes undeserving, individuals pushed up the ladder in the administrative hierarchy. The policy of 'progressive expansion',[161] proudly proclaimed by Liaquat Ali Khan himself, in some cases had the effect of a regressive contraction of the central government's real authority. It was difficult to monitor the operations of individual administrators, many of whom were not above twisting official rules. Moreover, despite the existence of a quota system[162] to ensure representation from all the provinces, non-

---

[159] Cases of corruption against civil servants were not uncommon. But these generally attracted far less attention than the trials of politicians under PRODA.
[160] Various writers on the administrative services in Pakistan have commented on this phenomenon. (See for instance, Munir Ahmed, *The Civil Servant in Pakistan*, Oxford 1963.)
[161] *CAD*, V, 2 March 1949, 261–2.
[162] In 1949 the quota for federal government employees was:

East Bengal	42%
West Punjab	24%
NWFP/Sind and Baluchistan	17%
Karachi	2%
Non-Pakistanis	15%

(*Nawa-i-Waqt*, editorial, 10 November 1949.)

Punjabis – with the exception of migrants from the United Provinces – were underrepresented. The posting of members of the central superior services to the provinces, though consistent with the centralisation policy, was to become a major source of tension, not only between the central and the provincial governments, but also between the provinces themselves.

So the centralisation drive left the state at a double disadvantage. While it created sources of internal tension within the government structure – between members of the provincial and the central services – it also opened up the possibility of power struggles between administrators and politicians at the central, provincial as well as the local levels. Some politicians, for instance the rural notables with formidable resources and local influence, could bend the government machinery to their advantage. Those in the provincial, and especially in the central arenas, were much less capable of undercutting the administrative services, certainly not without a countervailing force in the form of an organised political party. The result, exceptions at the local levels granted, was a decisive shift in the balance of power from the political to the administrative arms of the state.

The passing of initiative from the political leadership to the administrative bureaucracy was to manifest itself subtly but surely. At the centre, the prime minister was left gasping for breath in the face of a pincer movement – increasing social disorder in the provinces and deadlier intrigues within the central government. Liaquat's attempts at plugging the leaks in the ship illustrate the difficulties of trying to reverse the ill-effects of policies formulated during the initial years of constructing the state. Without some solution to the Kashmir problem Liaquat was incapable of weathering the mildest of political storms. So, although clearing the inner decks was a pressing need, Liaquat began his countermanoeuvres by concentrating on the international rather than the domestic front. Deeply dispirited by his failure to turn the commonwealth connection to Pakistan's advantage, Liaquat had been trawling for support from all possible quarters. Washington's measured response to Pakistan's stance on Kashmir, if it had not been tempered by behind the scene diplomatic gestures, might well have resulted in a visit by Liaquat to the Soviet Union in 1949.[163] The strength of the old imperial

---

[163] On 8 June 1949, Choudhry Zafrullah, the foreign minister, announced the prime minister's acceptance of Stalin's invitation to visit Moscow. This upset the commonwealth relations office in London which began sounding off the state department for an extension of a similar invitation to Liaquat. It would, the British officials believed, 'take a good deal of the sting of any visit...Liaquat Ali Khan actually makes to Moscow...'. (H.A.F. Rumbold [CRO] to R.H. Scott [FO], 13 June 1949, DO35/2981, PRO.)

connection at the official level, however, had proven stronger than the public jubilation in Pakistan over the prime minister's proposed trip to Moscow. Pakistani officials in the foreign and defence ministries acting in close consort with the commonwealth relations office and the state department made sure that Liaquat not only postponed his visit to Moscow but boarded a plane to the United States instead.

By May 1950, Liaquat was in the United States trying to muster support for his faltering government. He did not get anything concrete out of his hosts, no assurances on Kashmir; certainly no promises of economic and military aid for Pakistan. The trip was significant because it gave the prime minister a chance to further vent his thinking on Pakistan's defence problems. As early as June 1949 Liaquat had floated the idea of a territorial guarantee for both Pakistan and India underwritten by Britain and the United States. In April 1950, he had reiterated the line, arguing that it was the 'best, if not the only way of exorcising mutual fear and releasing massive proportions of the budgets of both Dominions now spent for less sterile and more constructive expenditure'.[164] Hammering the point harder in the presence of a bemused American audience, Liaquat asserted that he would have 'no further need to maintain an army', let alone a large one, if the United States was ready to 'guarantee Pakistan's frontiers'.[165]

Liaquat had raised the issue of a territorial guarantee at an opportune moment. The new American ambassador to Pakistan, Avra Warren, was believed to be 'obsessed with the need to fight Communism'.[166] This was good news for the pro-American elements in Pakistani officialdom led by Ghulam Mohammad. So the prime minister was putting out feelers to the Americans. His apparent readiness to consider sending Pakistani troops to fight in Korea confirms the point further. A territorial guarantee would release financial resources for various development schemes and perhaps pave the way for a reconciliation of the centre with the provinces. Liaquat had potentially hit upon a solution to Pakistan's problems. The practicability of the idea was, of course, a different matter. But it is significant to note the importance Pakistanis attached to a territorial guarantee. Even if offered by the

---

[164] Liaquat's interview with C.L. Sulzberger, *New York Times*, 18 April 1950.

[165] P.S. Stephens [British embassy, Washington] to J.D. Lloyd [FO], 1 June 1950, DO35/2981, PRO.

[166] There were indications that the Americans were thinking of formalising their right to use air facilities in Karachi – first granted during the second world war – by signing a treaty with the government of Pakistan. Ikramullah, the pro-British foreign secretary, thought such 'a formal treaty would surely be playing into the hands of the Russians'. (See record of conversation between Garner and Ikramullah, 2 May 1950, ibid.)

Soviet Union, it would have been 'welcomed with fierce joy throughout the country'.[167]

Liaquat's efforts were not restricted to high-sounding ideas alone. In April 1950, he had shown his mettle for statesmanship by signing the minorities agreement with Nehru. While in Delhi, he had 'frankly' told both Nehru and Patel that 'unless...troubles between the two Dominions could be settled by the present Leaders who understood each other and had worked together there was little hope of avoiding conflict by any possible successors'.[168] Although the agreement did not solve the many outstanding disputes between the two dominions, it was a first step in the right direction. However, India's refusal to withdraw its troops from the borders eroded the credibility of an agreement that might have opened a new chapter in Indo-Pakistan relations.

With nothing substantive in hand after his American debut, and no success at all on the Kashmir issue, Liaquat was ineluctably drawn deeper into the domestic quagmire. He had returned to a country buzzing with labour troubles, agrarian problems, refugee discontents and, as ever, political intrigues. The new twist to an already complicated situation was the heightened activity of pro-Communist fronts – the peace committees, the civil liberties union, the Pakistan trade union federation and various student groups. They were all believed to be operating under the direct inspiration of the Soviet embassy – established in March 1950 – which provided finance as well as pro- paganda material. The 'peace' campaign may have been 'a sounding board for Soviet propaganda'.[169] But it was sweeping the country like wild fire and actually had a 'very great appeal to the people of Pakistan whose one wish...[was] to be allowed to remain outside the entanglements of the "cold war"'.[170]

Whatever the prime minister's assessment of the situation, the admi- nistrative and military authorities were ready to pick up the gauntlet. Since the ceasefire in Kashmir, the joint services intelligence had been fabricating increasingly bizarre reports about the fledgling local Communist party and its purported plans to destabilise the state. An early attempt to get attention from London and Washington was 'a most hair-raising leaflet...which talked...of subterranean armies of

---

[167] See article by Patrick O'Donovan, 'Pakistan May Cut its Links with Crown', *Sunday Observer* (London), 14 August 1949.

[168] Attlee's note on talk with Liaquat Ali Khan, 1 May 1950, DO35/2981. PRO.

[169] British high commissioner's opdom no. 15, part II, 10 July-23 July 1950, FO371/84201, PRO.

[170] Acting high commissioner to Attlee, review of events, April–June 1950, ibid.

shock troops, planned attacks on "nerve centers" shadow governments and so on'.[171] By the summer of 1949, the director of military intelligence, brigadier Shahid Hamid, had started dreaming up phantoms and spent the better part of his waking hours 'seeking funds and authority to establish a large secret civilian intelligence agency'.[172] The brigadier had touched a sensitive nerve among senior bureaucrats. The finance minister himself showed a keen interest in the matter and began exploring the possibility of receiving help from American intelligence to build an 'Islamic barrier against the Soviets'.[173] Long before the Soviets had squarely entered the picture, a move had been 'afoot in Karachi for the coordination of American and British propaganda and assistance to the Government'.[174] But it was the discovery in July 1950 of 'Communist maps and pamphlets'[175] circulating as reading material in an army unit stationed in Lahore that really jolted the central leadership and army headquarters. The British high commission and the American embassy also began exploring ways of assisting the Pakistani security apparatus to counter Soviet propaganda effectively.

So, despite the trend in popular opinion, an insecure and divided political leadership was unable to prevent Pakistan becoming an arena where the minor propaganda battles in the 'cold war' were to be fought. Liaquat for all his failings was not a man who could give short shrift to the popular pulse. But he was under extreme pressure from his own cabinet and the bureaucracy. There was 'a sharp division' in the cabinet on whether or not to despatch Pakistani troops to Korea. Some like Liaquat thought the 'price of their support' should be a positive American assurance to help equip...[the] Pakistan army...'. Opposing them was Ghulam Mohammad who insolently told the prime minister to 'Govern or get out' and went on to liken the highest executive body of the state to 'a stable with mules'. This inspired the American ambassador into making a remarkably apt assessment of Liaquat who was: 'without any Cabinet strength but saddled with liabilities of which the public, whether organized in the various Muslim Leagues or outside

---

[171] The leaflet was entitled 'Organization Plan of the C[ommunist] P[arty] in Pakistan'. See Reed to H.S. Stephenson [deputy high commissioner, Lahore], 20 March 1949, L/WS/1/1188, 38A, IOL.

[172] American embassy to the secretary of state, 5 August 1949, Declassified 785012, RG 319, Entry 57, Box 443, WNRC.

[173] Ghulam Mohammad's meeting with George McGhee. 9 December 1949, cited in Venkataramani, *The American Role in Pakistan,* 104.

[174] Withers to Warren, 25 August 1950, NND. 842430, RG 84, Box 7, File 350-Pak. Pol. 1950, NA.

[175] British high commissioner's opdom no. 15, part II, 10 July-23 July 1950, FO371/84201, PRO.

these organizations, are increasingly critical on account of growing economic burdens'.[176]

Liaquat nevertheless showed his steadfastness of purpose by getting parliament to pass a resolution which fell far short of what the Americans would have liked. It condemned North Korean aggression; but offered 5,000 tons of wheat instead of ground troops. To dispel any doubts that the national parliament was toeing the American line, the resolution declared itself 'against Pakistan aligning herself inextricably with any power bloc'.[177]

Sharply at odds with members of his own cabinet and unable to keep tabs on the doings of bureaucrats and military officers, the prime minister was making a last ditch attempt to rebuild bridges with popular opinion in the provinces. On 28 September, in yet another piece of bad timing by the centre, the basic principles committee submitted its interim report on the future constitution. The recommendations were roundly attacked by a broad spectrum of opinion: by the ideologues of religious rectitude because it contained no specific mention of an 'Islamic state'; and by the regionalists in east Bengal because Urdu was proposed as the official language of the state. Among the other divisive issues was the question of provincial representation at the national level and the balance of power between the centre and the provinces. Seeing that his stay in office now depended upon popular support, Liaquat tried resuscitating the Muslim League. On 8 October, he got himself elected president.[178] An amendment of the League constitution legalised the remarriage of party and government. A belated gesture; but it gave Liaquat the sanction he needed to intervene more decisively in the provincial Leagues which were displaying an alarming 'tendency...[of] reject[ing] the authority of the Centre'.[179] But it was not easy to heal the intricate breaches within the League all at once, much less transform it overnight into an effective organisational machinery. Nothing short of a miracle was needed to claw back for the party advantages which had gradually been appropriated by the civil bureaucracy and the military establishment.

The infusion of international factors was to make it more difficult for the prime minister to regain political initiative and mend relations between the centre and the provinces. His attempts to reform the League

---

[176] Warren to Acheson, 30 August 1950, telegram 219, NND.842430, RG 84, Box 7, File 350-Pak. Pol. 1950, NA.
[177] On 11 October 1950, the resolution was adopted by a vote of forty to two. The dissenting votes were cast by Mian Iftikharuddin and Shaukat Hayat.
[178] In August 1950 Khaliquzzaman had been forced to step down.
[179] British high commissioner's opdom no. 20, part II, 18 September–1 October 1950, FO371/84203, PRO.

here or revive it there proved to be of less consequence than the activities of civil bureaucrats and military officials working alongside British and American diplomats. Consequently, the state structure took a more definite shape under the influence of a bureaucratic-military-diplomatic axis rather than that of a handful of political leaders who occasionally managed to rise above their personal interests to lend an ear to the mutterings of the people below.

The volatile situation in east Bengal received prompt attention from the axis. The activities of the local Awami League were jointly monitored in Dacca by the provincial home department, the American consul general and the British deputy high commissioner. Aziz Ahmed, the chief secretary to the provincial government, had been looking for British 'cooperation in supplying the Government material to combat Communist influence'. There was no obvious link between Suhrawardy's Awami League and the various pro-Communist groups in the province. But the American consul general was 'convinced' that the local Communists were 'taking advantage of the Awami League' which was 'becoming popular'. It was his 'belief that counter measures...[would] have to be taken' since the 'coalition' was 'gaining in strength' and posing 'a very distinct threat' to American interests. Some government officials in east Bengal were 'expressing anti-Western and pro-Russian sentiments'. Clearly 'something...[had to] be done immediately' and the state department had to 'make up its collective mind' about setting the United States Information Services into action in the province.[180] It was convenient that the governor, Firoz Khan Noon, was 'very pro-American' and had 'close and most pleasant relations w[ith] the US Consul'.[181] An even better bet for a successful USIS thrust into east Bengal was the assistance sought by Pakistani army intelligence 'in fighting Communist influence among the troops'. But Pakistani intelligence wanted to use 'very subtle' propaganda techniques, since so far there was no firm evidence of Communist influence among the troops. By December 1950, as a preventive measure, army officers in east Bengal were hearing 'indoctrination lecture[s]'.[182]

Yet interestingly enough, until the end of December 1950, the 'anti-Communist drive' in both wings of Pakistan, however 'sporadic in actual operation', was being carried out 'without central authority'. The

[180] Withers to Warren, 25 August 1950, NND.842430, RG 84, Box 7, File 350-Pak. Pol.1950, NA.

[181] Withers' memorandum of conversation with Noon, Dacca despatch no. 73, 8 November 1950, ibid.

[182] Withers' despatch no. 91, 16 December 1950, ibid.

'original targets' of the USIS in Pakistan were, naturally enough, the 'high government officials and ranking military officers'; the entire programme was 'designed to hit these priority groups [the] hardest'.[183] By contrast, the main 'targets' of Soviet propaganda were individuals and groups with populist pretensions. The USIS programme, as conceived, was not really an anti-Communist drive; its main contribution was to convert a government machinery already thriving on coercion into an effective bastion of anti-populism.

But the power of critical thinking was still greater than all the propaganda and coercion the state could muster. Towards the end of 1950, the United Nations security council's decision to postpone discussion on Kashmir unleashed a storm of protest in Pakistan. Ignoring censorship regulations and reaching the highest level of vituperation against the United Nations and the British commonwealth, the Pakistani press openly called upon the government to look for more dependable friends in the international arena. Some 'responsible officials' admitted that the 'present Government...[was] dangerously threatened by the prolonged deadlock over Kashmir', but saw 'no possible replacement of comparable calibre'. The high commissioner lamented that in the existing political climate Britain could not 'hope for assistance from Pakistan in the field of anti-Communist publicity'; India, not the Soviet Union, was the enemy.[184]

In western Punjab, the province which supplied the bulk of the Pakistan army, and in the Peshawar and Kohat districts of the NWFP which provided the rest, there were influential social networks fiercely attached to Kashmir. Yet it was in Lahore – the capital of the Punjab and the political nerve centre of the country – that some of the most virulent opponents of the commonwealth were bunched. So in the Punjab more than anywhere else 'the dangers of Russian influence in the long term...were very great'. There was already a discernible 'move towards Russia among the educated middle class'. Soviet newspapers were doing the rounds in the coffee houses of Lahore and had started filtering into some of the city's best educational institutions.[185] What perturbed the British and the Americans the most was the ricochetting of these trends on the Pakistan army, in particular the officer corps many of whom came from middle-class families. The army had hardly remained impervious to the discontents sweeping the country. There

---

[183] Document VIII, 28 December 1950, NND.42424, RG 84, Box 1, SOA , NA.

[184] High commissioner's opdom no. 26, 11 December–21 December 1950, FO371/84204, PRO

[185] Jasper to the high commissioner, Lahore despatch no. 5/51, review for July–December 1950, DO35/3186, PRO.

were grumblings over conditions of pay, promotions, housing and, inevitably, the military stalemate in Kashmir. Among the first stirrings of disaffection in the army was the call for the removal of all British officers. Although all unit commanders on the Kashmir front were Pakistani, military reversals were generally attributed to stone-walling by senior British officers. Britain's failure to make good its promises of supplying arms and ammunition to Pakistan was seen as an attempt to help India achieve a *fait accompli* in Kashmir. But plumping for the departure of British officers was also a matter of expediency, especially for those who had an eye on promotion, greater privileges and better access to the levers of power. These anti-British sentiments dovetailed neatly with popular demands for the nationalisation of the defence as well as the administrative services. Provincial Muslim Leagues passed resolutions to that effect without official sanction from the party high command. The overlapping of discontents in the defence services and the society at large was ominous for the stability of the state.

As early as September 1948, Liaquat had tried humouring army officers with a light discourse on 'Pip fever, or why we can't all start as Brigadiers'.[186] Rapid promotions of junior officers barely crawling out of the training institutes, combined with the meteoric rise of middle-ranking officers to positions of brigadier and major general, had excited ambitions of all manner and description. The loftiest of these tended to look beyond the horizons of the military establishment. To keep the lid on the demands to nationalise the Pakistani army was a little uncomfortable since Kashmir continued to dominate the newspaper headlines. An unstable military establishment, the British and Americans feared, might sound the death-knell for Pakistan. British discomfit was understandably greater. With an eye on the political gyrations in the Middle East in general, and unrelenting nationalist pressure on the Anglo-Iranian oil company in particular, the British had good reason to want to keep the Pakistan army under their direct influence. But, if a nationalisation was unavoidable, they were as ever ready to cut their losses. All that was needed was a core of indigenous officers who could be relied upon to serve imperial and Pakistani security interests both at the same time. This is why Kashmir was a cold sore for Britain's post-war strategic designs. It was not only a main factor hastening the departure of some 400 to 435 British officers in the Pakistan army,[187] but a major barrier to pulling it firmly behind Britain's policing efforts in the Near and Far East.

---

[186] High commissioner's opdom no. 5, 28 January-3 February 1949, L/WS/1/1600, IOL.
[187] See *Nawa-i-Waqt*, 13 November 1949 and 24 May 1950.

So it made sense to harp on the imperative of streamlining the Pakistan army. This helped to slow the pace of the nationalisation process and gave British officers more time to train and appoint dependable Pakistanis to key positions in the army. It had been the considered opinion of the nationalisation committee that the process should not be completed before 1953. But Liaquat had told general Gracey, Pakistan's second British commander-in-chief, that 'he might be forced by outside pressure to speed up the progress of nationalisation so that it was completed by 1950', though it would still be essential to retain some British officers as advisers.[188] According to British sources, Liaquat's willingness to bend with the wind was regretted by 'most thinking and sensible Pakistanis' but was welcomed with glee by 'many others out for their own ends'.[189] With the question of nationalisation now a settled matter, the British began considering how best to delegate responsibility within the army. A series of promotions and transfers ensured the emergence of a reasonably satisfactory constellation of officers at general headquarters in Rawalpindi. Those suspected of anti-British sentiments were kept at arms length, if not removed from high positions altogether. A promising result of these changes was that most senior Pakistani army officers in Rawalpindi agreed with the British and American recipe for a resolution of the Kashmir deadlock: a partition based on territories then under the control of Indian and Pakistani troops. A wise solution from the military point of view, but a sticky one politically. Liaquat certainly would have nothing to do with it. Senior civil officials in the ministry of Kashmir affairs had made it known that 'it would not be politically possible for Liaquat to agree to partition [in Kashmir] at this stage'. By contrast 'senior Army officers', basking in the glory of their recent promotions and consequently more inclined to prefer the course of moderation, were 'clearly beginning to take the view that a partition on the Chenab[river] would be a reasonable solution which Pakistan would do well to accept as part of a general bargain'.[190]

This indicated the soundness of promotion decisions at the higher levels. Younger Pakistani officers were becoming increasingly 'warlike in their talk' and needed to be 'counseled to take it easy by older officers

[188] Reed to Olver, 14 June 1949, L/WS/1/1188, 48B, IOL.
[189] Brigadier J.F. Walker [British military adviser, Pakistan] to major general Redman [director of operations, war office] 18 June 1949, ibid. Some Pakistanis felt that nationalisation should make slow haste. They were concerned about the dangers which a predominantly Punjabi army might pose – in the event of a military intervention – for the integration of the newly created state.
[190] Jasper's 'Note on a visit to Rawalpindi' 4 May-6 May 1950, dated the 10 May 1950, DO134/11, PRO.

and [the] British CINC'.[191] To make them more effective in their dealings with the junior ranks, senior Pakistani officers were sent off for further training at the Imperial Defence college in London. In spite of the nationalisation programme, all British officers on duty at the staff college in Quetta had their service contracts extended until the end of December 1951. And at GHQ itself, a special team under major general Hutton was given charge of training and 'indoctrinating brigade and higher commanders'.[192] With such meticulous planning, things had to go the British way.

All that remained now was to select the first string of command for a fully nationalised Pakistan army without unduly arousing jealousies. The most coveted position was, of course, that of commander-in-chief. There had been a number of contenders for the job. Two officers tipped for the position died in a mysterious plane crash in late 1949. But there were still many who were disappointed when out of the blue general Ayub took over the mantle in January 1951. With a less than distinguished career as the highest ranking Pakistani officer in the ill-fated Punjab boundary force, Ayub had been despatched off to east Bengal and only recently brought back to Rawalpindi as adjutant general. There is a curious absence of any documentation on how the first Pakistani commander-in-chief was selected. But, undoubtedly, general Gracey had a hand in the decision. Even the Americans seemed reassured; Ayub was 'believed to be pro-American'.[193]

Ayub's unexpected elevation to the post of commander-in-chief was followed by interesting developments. In early March 1951, the newly appointed chief of the general staff, major general Akbar Khan, known for his 'heroic' efforts in Kashmir, was arrested along with a handful of other senior officers for allegedly planning a *coup d'etat*. Akbar and his cohorts had all fought in Kashmir, and had strong views on the problem. They apparently planned to sack the central government, replace it by a military dictatorship winking at Moscow instead of London, and to complete the grand slam with a decisive victory in Kashmir. They had rallied support amongst the junior ranks in the army by arguing that Pakistan needed a military government to wrest Kashmir from Indian control. The 'conspirators' had the support of some senior officers in the air force, and well-wishers in the higher echelons of the civil service. They had apparently been egged on by certain members of

[191] American military attache [Karachi] to CSGID [Washington], no. CLN 30, 14 April 1950, Declassified 785013, RG 319, Entry 57, Box 477, WNRC.
[192] American military attache to CSGID no. DWH.13, 21 July 1950, ibid.
[193] American military attache to CSGID no. DWH 23, ibid.

the Arain *biraderi* [clan] in the Punjab who were believed to have Communist leanings.[194]

The central government knew what was brewing six months before it moved to make the arrests.[195] It was during these same six months that British, American and Pakistani intelligence began their joint operations against pro-Soviet propaganda, both within and outside the armed forces. So the 'plot', if it was a plot, could not have been too serious. There were justified reasons for 'some doubts whether a political movement of a potentially subversive character had reached the stage of criminal conspiracy'.[196] George McGhee, the American assistant secretary of state, was 'doubtful about Communist inspiration [in]...the recent plot' and believed that its 'root lay in the ambition of senior officers concerned'.[197] Internal rivalries within the army were certainly an important factor. It was not a small matter that major general Akbar Khan was a popular war hero and apparently 'regarded himself as the divinely appointed successor to the Quaid-i-Azam'.[198] Someone claiming to be Jinnah's successor was a threat to anyone in a position of power in Pakistan. The more so if he was also the most persuasive proponent of the extreme view in the army which wanted a military solution in Kashmir. Akbar had been promoted in the hope that the 'prospect of eventually becoming Commander-in-Chief' might lead him to 'change his ideas'.[199] Ayub Khan along with the secretary of defence, Iskander Mirza, represented the moderate opinion favoured by the British. So apart from the rivalry between Akbar and Ayub, the 'Rawalpindi Conspiracy' as the affair came to be known, was a tussle between two divergent perspectives on the Kashmir dispute within the Pakistani defence establishment.

It was evidence garnered by Ayub and Mirza which confirmed the existence of a 'serious plot' to overthrow the central government.[200] Both men concluded that Akbar and his fellow travellers could not be allowed to mobilise the rank and file on the Kashmir dispute. General Gracey, who had perhaps come to imbibe some of the social mores of the state he was serving in, had been disturbed by Akbar's tendency to 'give

[194] Jasper to high commissioner, telegram no. 34, 11 March 1951, FO371/92866, PRO.
[195] High commissioner to the foreign office, telegram no. 257, 10 March 1951; ibid.
[196] R.R. Burnett [office of the high commissioner] to Garner [CRO], 19 March 1951, FO371/92867, PRO.
[197] Record of conversation between foreign office officials and George McGhee, 3 April 1951, ibid.
[198] This was the information of the governor of Sind. (See Burnett to Garner, 19 March 1951, ibid.)
[199] High commissioner to CRO, telegram no. 202, 10 March 1951, FO371/92866, PRO.
[200] Mohammad Ayub Khan, *Friends Not Masters: A Political Autobiography*, Karachi 1967, 36.

alcoholic parties into which pretty girls were introduced as decoys and, at a suitable stage of the proceedings, officer guests were sounded on subversive topics'.[201] But these subjects were being discussed in the bazaars and mohallas of Pakistan. They ranged from wanting to sever Pakistan's connection with the commonwealth to 'toy[ing] with the idea of reorienting Pakistan's foreign policy towards Russia', not for any well thought out ideological reasons, but because people were actually coming to believe that 'Russia would be a better ally...against India'.[202] This, as the deputy inspector general of police in the Punjab had suggested, was a result of the 'wave of defeatism...sweeping the Punjab'; people felt that Kashmir was the 'difference between survival or defeat at the hands of India', and some had taken to 'predicting that Pakistan...[could] not escape Communism'.[203] Here is a clue to the complex influences that served as background to the 'Rawalpindi Conspiracy', a tragic watershed in Pakistan's history. Tragic because it provided the ostensible justification for insulating the army from the nascent nationalism combing some parts of the land and because it marked a break in critical thinking from which the people of Pakistan one generation later have still not recovered. Nearly four decades after the event, access to the proceedings of the tribunal set up to try eleven military officers and four civilians remains closed.

But it is clear that the roots of the 'Rawalpindi Conspiracy' go much deeper than the Kashmir dispute itself, though the connection is undeniable. Efforts to indoctrinate an army free of Communist ideologues hints at the presence of other tendencies which, depending on the angle of vision, were either major irritants or obstacles to the strategic plans under consideration by general headquarters. Some Pakistani officers imbued with a sense of patriotism, misguided perhaps but patriotism nonetheless, wanted the government to formulate its foreign and defence policies independently of British and American strategic interests. This was contrary to the logic of the 'cold war' which demanded the containment of Soviet and Chinese influences, present and future. 'Anti-Colonialism, sensitive and impatient nationalism', or just plain 'anti-Westernism', were seen by the Americans as a threat to their 'national objectives' in South Asia. Nothing short of 'a sustained campaign of psychological warfare' had to be waged to combat 'anti-Western attitudes' and their replacement by 'pro-Western, anti-Soviet

---

[201] Burnett to Garner, 19 March 1951, FO371/92867, PRO.
[202] Ibid.
[203] The deputy inspector general was Anwar Ali. Preston's Lahore despatch no. 96, 4 January 1951, NND.842430, RG 84, Box 42, File 350-Pak. Pol. 1951, NA.

attitudes'.[204] Put bluntly, indubitable patriotism could not be permitted to stalk the armed forces of a state whose 'vital strategic location' made it the 'only logical base' from which to launch an attack on the southern and eastern areas of the USSR. Even in the absence of Western bases in Pakistan, it was essential to assure 'the control or cooperation of...Pakistan' and 'deny...bases in this area to the USSR' since otherwise the 'entire East-West lines of communication' would be gravely 'endanger[ed]'.[205] This was the American policy of containment par excellence. It was also one of the best restatements of the time-honoured imperial defence policy which British officers serving in the Pakistan army had been following to rule.

More than principles were at stake. As early as February 1949, major general Tottenham, then serving as divisional commander in the Pakistan army had received directions from general Gracey 'for moving a Pak[istan] Division into the Iranian Oil Fields to "lend a hand" in case the British or Americans needed it'.[206] Pakistan's defences in Baluchistan along the Khojak pass were also to be fortified in readiness of a British decision to resort to a military solution in the dispute over the nationalisation and control of the Anglo-Iranian oil company. This had brought Ayub into direct confrontation with brigadier Latif, the station commander in Quetta and one of those accused in the 'Conspiracy', who felt that it would be in 'Pakistan's interest to be neutral in any future war'.[207] General Gracey had apparently masterminded a wargame – aptly entitled 'Exercise Stalin' – in which the Pakistan army was to fight against the Soviet Union.[208] It is difficult to be dismissive of the view expressed by the secretary of the Rawalpindi case trial committee that the whole affair was a flagrant misuse of the government

---

204 'Examination of Tendencies Towards Anti-Westernism', prepared by SOA [Washington] in December 1950 for conference of American ambassadors in Ceylon, NND.842423, RG 84, Box 1, Doc. III–B, NA.
205 'US Strategic Interests in Area', submitted by the US embassy [Karachi], 28 December 1950 for the conference of American ambassadors in Ceylon; ibid., Doc. V.(A).
206 Towards the beginning of 1950, a 'top secret' letter from the American embassy in Karachi to the Pakistani inter-services intelligence directorate had asked for detailed information on: (1) airfields in Pakistan, (2) the actual spread of its railway system, (3) classification of major bridges, and (4) facilities for stationing standard divisions in the Western border areas of West Pakistan. (Secretary, Rawalpindi case trial committee to Louis Saillart[general secretary] and Serge Rostovsky [secretary] World Federation of Trade Unions-Vienna, 7 September 1951; intercepted by the American Legation in Vienna – 2 October 1951, NND.842430, RG 84, Box. 42, File 350-Pak. Pol. 1951, NA.)
207 Ibid.
208 Ibid. The rehearsal which was to have been carried out in 1950 was postponed until October 1951, coincidentally the month Pakistan's first prime minister was assassinated.

machinery; the 'so-called "Conspiracy" is nothing more than a frame-up engineered by British and American Intelligence working through their stooges in the Pak[istan] Government and Armed Forces in order to "clean up" the army of outstanding patriotic officers...'.[209]

The background to the incident, and its grim aftermath, provide incontrovertible evidence of how international strategic considerations together with internal rivalries in the defence establishment had begun impinging upon incipient political and social processes in the newly independent state. The purge of senior military officers for plotting to align Pakistan with the Soviet bloc became the pretext for a systematic crack down on individuals and groups espousing anti-imperialist sentiments. By accusing budding patriots of pro-Communist leanings and government critics of sabotage, the security authorities adopted the postures of holy warriors entrusted with responsibility to metamorphosise the 'land of the pure' into a veritable intellectual wasteland.

In the gradual erosion of critical thinking in Pakistan, the 'Rawalpindi Conspiracy' stands out as an important landmark. General Akbar was an old friend of Faiz Ahmad Faiz[210] – the pro-Moscow editor of *The Pakistan Times* and one of the leading intellectuals in Pakistani society. Faiz's arrest on charges of conspiring to overthrow the government gave the central intelligence department an excuse to hound and hunt down prominent writers, trade unionists and members of the Mazdoor-Kisan and Communist parties of Pakistan.[211] Significantly, the police considered the 'intellectual group [namely the Progressive Writers Association] as a much greater threat to security than the labour group'.[212] But in crisis ridden societies, intellectuals can hardly match the threats posed by unstable military establishments.

The 'Rawalpindi Conspiracy' dispels any notion of the Pakistan military possessing a superior edge over an inefficient civil service and a hopelessly disorganised political party. The inescapable conclusion is that some four years after the establishment of the state, no single

---

[209] Ibid.

[210] Interestingly enough, Hooker A. Doolittle, one of the first American consul generals in Karachi, had been of the view that Faiz and Mian Iftikharuddin – another outspoken critic of the central government with leanings to the left – 'were liberals, the former by conviction, the latter through dilettantism'. But 'neither was a thorough going Communist'. (Doolittle to the secretary of state, 14 December 1948, NND.842430, RG 59, Box 424, 845F.911/12-1448, NA.)

[211] By July 1951, the central intelligence department was 'confident that no important Communists...[were] at large in Pakistan and that any threats from the organization ha[d] ceased for an indefinite period'. (John C. Craig [American vice consul, Lahore], despatch no. 28, 26 July 1951, NND.842430, RG 84, Box 42, File 350-Pak. Pol.1951, NA.)

[212] Craig's despatch no.150, 16 May 1951, ibid.

institution was either stable or solid enough to command a clear monopoly of power – not the military, not even the well-oiled civil bureaucracy and certainly not the main political party. While an alliance between certain members of the defence and civil establishment had begun pushing the pendulum of power away from the political leadership, it was the skilful manipulation of international connections that eventually cleared the ground for the development of the institutional imbalances that have plagued Pakistan's history. This can best be seen by the methods used to restore the credibility of the Pakistani armed forces. And more strikingly, by the artless attempts to secure international support to strengthen bureaucratic controls over the domestic economy while at the same time confirming the dominance of the armed forces in the still very fluid positioning of forces within the state apparatus.

After March 1951, there was no longer any question of Ayub's preeminence in the armed forces. But the arrest and trial of senior military officers had showed up the Pakistan army for what it was – an institution which was quite as brittle as any other in the new state. Akbar was 'well known and liked by the younger officers and tribesmen [in Azad Kashmir] who resented the way he was being treated'. The summary dismissal of senior military men was seen to have 'lowered the prestige of the officer class'.[213] Civilian confidence in the army had been badly shaken, and national paranoia about Pakistan's ability to defend itself took on its darkest taint since independence. Army morale is unlikely to have been restored by the mere assurance that no further arrests would be made. General headquarters in Rawalpindi slammed on a sterner discipline and banned the circulation of most thought provoking literature. The 'severe shock to Army spirit and discipline' was still evident in the summer of 1951 when Pakistan faced a massive troop build up on the Indian border.[214] Lt. general McCay, one of Ayub's advisers, noted that 'whereas previously there was a blind devotion to orders by the soldiers, they now stop to consider whether the officer's order is a correct one'.[215]

[213] Burnett to Garner, 19 March 1951, FO371/92867, PRO.
[214] A 'close[r] liaison' between the British high commission and the Pakistani civil and military establishment was one of the obvious results. The deputy high commissioner was delighted to find that the 'danger' of Communism was 'now fully realised'. He was certain that 'the increase in the distribution of special [anti-Communist] pamphlets by the Army and civil authorities' together with the decline in the circulation of pro-Soviet newspapers like *The Pakistan Times* would lead to 'some improvement in the attitude to[wards] Russia', (Lahore despatch, no. 17/51, 2 August 1951, DO35/3186, PRO.)
[215] Gibson [Lahore] to the department of state, despatch no.64, 20 October 1952, NND.842430, RG 84, Box 42, File 350-Pak.Pol. July-December 1952, NA.

It was for all these reasons that Ayub took immediate steps to reorganise the Pakistan army. He joined forces with Mirza, and this alliance proved instrumental in shifting the balance of advantage in favour of general headquarters in Rawalpindi. Ayub found it cumbersome to get clearance from Karachi – 'a hotbed of intrigues'[216] – for military decisions he took sitting 800 miles away. The telephone network in Pakistan was not the most efficient or the safest way of communicating.[217] As for travelling in poorly maintained military aircraft to Karachi, that was an experience one could do without. Ayub had ideas – if that was possible – of how to go about building and defending the state Jinnah had founded. But, for the time being he had to put his own house in order and began nagging and nudging defence establishments in the United States and Britain to buttress the Pakistani army.

Fortuitously, the American state department was also in the process of reviewing its policies towards the Middle East and South Asia. Between 26 February and 2 March 1951 at a conference of American ambassadors in Nuwara Eliya, Ceylon, a fascinating thesis dominated the proceedings. Pakistan, according to proponents,[218] was a 'better bet than India' for the United States.[219] Nehru was seen to be angling for Indian hegemony over a neutral bloc consisting of countries in South East Asia and the Middle East. Neutralism contradicted the fundamentals of 'collective security', an euphemism to describe American strategic interests since the coming of the 'cold war' to Asia in 1949. So it was proposed that the United States should be 'more active in opposing Nehru's efforts and gear itself to exposing the 'fallacious basis' of Indian foreign policy which ignored the dangers posed by international Communism.[220]

The conference concluded that Washington should 'deal with ... [Nehru] firmly and patiently' and 'go ahead with Pakistan as a friendly country'.[221] Pakistan's geographical proximity to the Persian

---

[216] Ayub Khan, *Friends Not Masters*, 39.

[217] Mian Iftikharuddin's point of information in the national assembly is a superb comment on the quality of telephone communications in the country: 'We all know there is a buzzing sound in the telephones in Karachi and the connections are always wrong.... Is it a fact...as is rumoured in the bazaar, that the buzzing sound is the snoring sound of the Minister in charge [then Sardar Abdur Rab Nishtar] and that there is not much wrong with the telephone?'. (*CAD*, V, 4 March 1949, 359.)

[218] In particular, Avra Warren, the ambassador to Pakistan.

[219] Jasper to Grafftey-Smith, 27 March 1951, DO35/3008, PRO.

[220] See 'United Nations Problems', A.W. Warren File, March 1951, NND.842424, RG 84, Box 5, NA.

[221] This was the opinion of Loy Henderson, the American ambassador in India. Minutes of meeting on 'Foreign Policy', February 1951, South Asian conference in Ceylon, NND.842424, RG 84, Box 6, NA.

Gulf oil fields could be turned to the advantage of the Western allies. Britain's influence in the Middle East was on the wane and the Americans wanted to preempt any Russian efforts, planned or unplanned, to steal a march in that strategically vital area. Egypt, Iran, Iraq and Syria were all fertile ground for penetration by the world's policing agencies. American ambassadors serving in the Middle East were of the view that 'the Persian/Iraq sector could not be defended without help from Pakistan'.[222] So both the United States and Britain should 'bring about an early build-up of Pakistani ground forces...by the provision of military equipment...'. Karachi too had illusions of assuming a position of leadership in the Muslim world; this was a trend some American officials wanted to see reinforced even at the high price of offering a unilateral territorial guarantee to Pakistan.[223]

Officials in the foreign office scoffed at the idea of the state department considering the possibility of giving Pakistan a territorial guarantee. It would offend both India and Afghanistan without adding a jot or a tittle to the defence of the Middle East. The British embassy in Washington was advised to 'bring home to the Americans...the probable cost...in terms of Indian goodwill in paying the price demanded by Pakistan'.[224] Americans could be 'very rash and stupid about these things'.[225] But their 'immature oscillations'[226] in South Asia could not be allowed to undermine Britain's interests in the region. The secretary of commonwealth relations quipped: 'Let's talk with the Americans – but for heaven's sake don't let's be rushed into any paper guarantees. India's friendship is very important and must not be jeopardised'.[227]

This marked the beginning of a polite British and American rivalry in South Asia. The state department shied away from giving Karachi a territorial guarantee,[228] but could not resist the temptation of finding alternative ways of associating Pakistan with the defence of the Middle East. Britain's steadily deteriorating position in Iran as well as Egypt,

---

[222] Draft note by Cockram [CRO]. April 1951, DO35/3008, PRO.
[223] See *Foreign Relations of the United States*, 1951, VI, II, Asia and the Pacific, Washington, DC 1977, 1666–9 (henceforth *Foreign Relations*).
[224] S. Holmes to the secretary of state [CRO], 5 September 1951, DO35/3008, PRO.
[225] Gordon-Walker's minute, no date, ibid.
[226] Jasper to Grafftey-Smith, 27 March 1951, ibid.
[227] Gordon-Walker's minute, no date, ibid. According to a joint document prepared by the ministries of foreign affairs and defence, 'we have...had a good deal of co-operation from India over Korea and other Far Eastern questions, and whatever the Americans may say or think it has been *very valuable to have India more or less with us*'. ('India and Pakistan in relation to Middle East Defence', April 1951, ibid. [emphasis added])
[228] Memorandum of conversation between Burrows and Belcher [British embassy] and Mathews and Leach [SOA], 2 May 1951, NND.842430, RG 84, Box 42, File 350-Pak. Pol.1951, NA.

together with improvements in the military situation in Korea, gave the state department time to focus attention on the Middle East. By 30 June 1951, the secretary of state was fully satisfied with 'Pakistan's present orientation to the West', 'its active cooperation with the countries of the Middle East', and 'its orientation towards Turkey'. It followed that the United States 'should consult more intimately with the Government of Pakistan on questions of common interest in the Middle East'. American embassies in the Middle East were instructed to use 'every appropriate occasion' to bring Pakistan closer to the Middle East. But they had to be 'gradual, patient and tactful', since Egypt and Turkey might 'resent a Pakistani campaign to gain leadership among Muslim countries', especially if American backing for the effort was too obvious.[229]

On 1 July 1951, the state department's policy statement on Pakistan followed along the same lines. But it made explicit what had always been implicit, namely that the kingpin of US interests in Pakistan was its army. Provided it had the necessary equipment, the army could 'send troops to Iran's assistance' and 'fulfill one of the traditional functions of British-Indian troops in past wars'. Fortunately, the government of Pakistan did 'not suffer' from 'violent anti-Westernism'. The central and the provincial governments were bending over backwards to cooperate with the 'Western democracies' to counter Communist influences. It appeared that Pakistan could be 'persuaded to afford military bases to the US and the UK in the Indian Ocean area'. Apart from Communism, the other main threat to American interests in Pakistan was from 'reactionary groups of landholders and uneducated religious leaders' who were opposed to the 'present Western-minded government' and 'favour[ed] a return to primitive Islamic principles'. So the best course of action for the United States was to back the existing government.[230]

The state department's optimism stemmed from conversations with higher civil servants and military officers, not all of whom represented the official policy of Liaquat Ali Khan's government. As early as April 1951, George McGhee, the American state department's expert on Pakistan, had warned that the central leaders were so precariously placed that they had to be able to 'satisfy public opinion that Pakistan's security was thoroughly assured in order to counter propaganda against aligning herself with the "Anglo-American" imperialists'.[231] Even a top

[229] Dean Acheson to certain American diplomatic and consular offices, telegram no. 3837, 30 June 1951, NND.842430, RG 84, Box 1, File 310-South Asia, NA.
[230] 'Policy Statement – Pakistan', department of state, 1 July 1951, NND.842430, RG 84, Box 42, File 350-Pak. Pol.1951, NA.
[231] 'India and Pakistan in relation to Middle East Defence', prepared by the ministry of defence with suggestions from the foreign office, April 1951, DO35/3008, PRO.

bureaucrat and America's most powerful ally inside the central cabinet made the occasional disconcerting statements. Ghulam Mohammad belittled the state department's most recent offer of $12.5 million in grant aid to Pakistan; India, the favourite, was to get a loan of $190 million for foodgrains alone. This had led to a 'widespread attitude' in Pakistan which was very 'similar to that of a prospective bride who observes her suitor spending very large sums on a mistress, i.e. India, while she herself can look forward to not more than a token mainten-ance in the event of marriage'. Boldly hinting that beggars can also be choosers, Ghulam Mohammad indicated that he wanted 'generous financial and technical aid', but not if it entailed passing over the 'control of the Pak[istan] economy' to the United States.[232]

This was shrugged aside as sheer bravado. To sell the idea of military and economic aid for Pakistan to Congress and the American people, the state department needed concrete evidence of Karachi's commit-ment to Western security interests. By August 1951, McGhee certainly had come around to the view that 'the declining prestige of the UK in...[South Asia], as well as throughout the Middle East' made it 'more and more expedient [for the United States] to approach the Pakistan Government independently' while preserving, if possible, the facade of 'efforts to cooperate with the British'. He had been deeply gratified by 'the spot reporting from Karachi'; it showed 'what close working relations' the American embassy had 'developed with the key officials of the government'.[233] Warren for his part was delighted to report that the 'top command' in Karachi was at long last 'doing a little hard thinking, and debating among themselves, on high foreign policy strategy'.[234] Indian military pressure and the publication of the report by the United Nations mediator, Dr Graham, had provided the necessary stimulus. Graham's report recommended a demilitarisation of both Indian and Pakistani controlled Kashmir, to be followed by a plebiscite. There were some signs of the central cabinet's willingness to accept the report. Yet this had required considerable arm twisting by Ghulam Mohammad, Choudhry Zafrullah – the foreign minister – and Mushtaq Gurmani – the minister of Kashmir affairs. Significantly, all three were civil servants. They joined forces, 'demanded a showdown' with Liaquat, and what was more 'got it'.[235]

Liaquat's hesitation had less to do with the substance of Graham's

---

[232] Warren to the secretary of state, telegram no. 62, 19 July 1951, NND.842430, RG 84, Box 12, File 320-Pak. Pol.1951, NA.

[233] George McGhee to Warren, 11 August 1951, ibid.

[234] Warren to McGhee, 30 August 1951, ibid.

[235] Ibid.

proposals. He more than anyone else needed to be let off the Kashmir hook; but not if it meant crashing through the tattered net of Pakistani unity. By the summer of 1951, a massive concentration of Indian troops along the borders of western Pakistan and the recrudescence of tensions with Afghanistan had left him clutching more desperately than ever at the popular pulse. Fed on unrealistic assessments of the state's military capabilities and disappointed by the report's failure to deliver the whole of Kashmir to Pakistan, vocal opinion openly called upon the central government to abandon the policy of moderation and brace itself for a war with India. A seasoned but unlucky politician, Liaquat saw that currying favour with the people was the most effective counter to external bullying and pressures within the cabinet. To Liaquat's credit, he did not avoid recourse to diplomatic channels. The clinched fist was balanced by conciliatory statements about a possible rapprochement with New Delhi.

Unalleviated Indo-Pakistan border tensions and the impending security council vote on Graham's report were some of the considerations guiding Liaquat's go slow policy on Pakistan's participation in the defence of the Middle East. But his cabinet colleagues, backed by an increasingly impatient military high command and a handful of civil officials, wanted to make the best of British and American anxieties over the worsening situation in both Iran and Egypt. To keep peace in the top floor of a decaying house, Liaquat had put his name to identical letters, one for the British prime minister and the other for the American secretary of state, making a strong plea for an immediate delivery of defence equipment. The letters were delivered personally by the foreign secretary, Ikramullah. Drafted under Ghulam Mohammad's watchful eye,[236] they made a special play of Pakistan's commitment to the defence of the 'free world'.[237]

Seeing it as a routine bid by Pakistan to acquire defence equipment, Attlee stalled for time. Coming at a time when Indian troops were amassed on Pakistan's borders, Ikramullah could only manage a faint smile while remonstrating with London about its policies which were preventing 'United Kingdom's satellites' from 'doing their part' in the 'defence of freedom'.[238] When Attlee finally got down to drafting a response, he regretted Britain's inability to meet the request for arms,

---

[236] See Memorandum by Acheson on conversation with Ikramullah and Ispahani, 22 October 1951, *Foreign Relations*, 1951, VI, II, 2225–6.

[237] Liaquat to Attlee, 25 August 1951, DEFE7/157, PRO.

[238] Minute by P. Leisching [CRO] on meeting with Ikramullah, 18 September 1951, DO35/3008, PRO.

but quickly peppered it with the proviso that:

If, at some future date we are able to agree upon some arrangement by which Pakistan undertakes to provide forces to assist in the defence of the Middle East in wartime, we should naturally be prepared to reconsider the supply of equipment in the light of this new situation.[239]

By mid-September Ikramullah had communicated to Karachi the gist of London's response. The delivery of military items by Britain depended 'on the degree to which the country asking for equipment was *committed politically to participation in any war which might occur*'.[240] This kept up the pressure on Karachi. But, with the United States ready to step into Britain's shoes, London had reason for consternation. Any move by Pakistan to switch to American equipment meant 'los[ing] an important export market and a means of keeping up UK war potential'.[241] Moreover, Britain had genuine troubles in the Middle East and could use the Pakistan army in case of an emergency. In Egypt, the government of prime minister Mustafa el-Nahas Pasha had enforced a blockade of the Suez canal against ships bound for Israel and refused flatly to renegotiate the treaty of 1936 which had given Britain the right to maintain troops in the country. In Iran, the tortuous dispute over the fate of the Anglo-Iranian oil company was now well and truly on the boil with Mossadeq riding a crest of nationalist fervour. In a terrible squeeze in the Middle East, Britain was not prepared to concede Pakistan; its support might blunt the edge of the nationalist wave sweeping through the Muslim world.

To expect Pakistan, the would-be leader of the Muslim world, to back the erstwhile colonial masters against its co-religionists was a cruel irony. Yet there were powerful men in Pakistan who wanted to save the crumbling empire rather than issue an unequivocal call in support of their Muslim brethren in Iran and Egypt. For them the bond of Islam was weaker than the old imperial connection. But these were subtle facts few Pakistanis could discern. Declarations of support for Egypt and Iran kept abreast with furious demands that the government adopt a more resolute posture on Kashmir. The unmistakable force of popular

---

[239] Draft of Attlee's letter to Liaquat, 12 October 1951, DEFE7/157, PRO. It is doubtful whether Liaquat saw the reply. And as for the matching enquiry to the American secretary of state, that was not delivered until 18 October, two days after Liaquat's assassination. (See Memorandum of conversation by Acheson and McGhee, 18 October 1951, *Foreign Relations*, 1951, VI, II, 2220–1.

[240] Record of meeting between Ikramullah and Leisching, 18 September 1951, DEFE7/157, PRO [emphasis added].

[241] 'Supply of Equipment to India and Pakistan', draft memorandum by the ministry of defence', 10 October 1951, DEFE7/150, PRO.

opinion on foreign policy issues eventually broke the cracked shell concealing the severe differences of opinion within Liaquat's cabinet. Reassured by the leap in his popularity, Liaquat decided to rid himself of the main troublemakers. According to 'reliable information' the impending cabinet reshuffle was to affect some heavyweights,[242] but no one had a real measure of what the prime minister precisely had in mind. All that was clear was that no deputy prime minister would be appointed and 'if something happened to L[iaquat] A[li] K[han], the G[overnor] G[eneral], Nazimuddin would] take over until some-one...[was] chosen'.[243] There was no reason to believe that anything could happen to the prime minister; the pressure of events, however, proved otherwise.

A flurry of alarming reports from the Middle East, uncertainties about impending ministerial changes and the popular mood in the country, persuaded Ayub and Mirza to by-pass Liaquat. Pakistan needed arms. If the only way of acquiring them was by strapping it to the defence of the Middle East, then it was a gamble worth taking. Prior to leaving for the meeting of the commonwealth military staff in London, they broached the subject with the American ambassador and expressed their 'interest...in the idea of Pakistan being associated with the defence of the Middle East' with the bait that they thought it 'essential that the Middle East Commander should be an American'. Yet it remained to be seen whether this represented the 'official view of the Pakistan Government'.[244] Governments rent by internal divisions can rarely put forth credible official policies. Both the British and the Americans knew of the differences inside Liaquat's cabinet. Ghulam Mohammad certainly was at one with Ayub and Mirza on the question of Pakistan joining an Anglo-American inspired Middle East defence organisation. Zafrullah was 'very frightened' of a Soviet thrust into Iran and 'did not think [Indo-Pakistan] tension[s]...would last for more than nine months or a year'.[245]

That did not make the choice any easier for Liaquat. To go against the grain of developments in the Middle East at this point in time was an

---

[242] The information reaching the Americans mentioned the names of Khwaja Shahabuddin, then the minister of interior among others. (J. Bowling to Warren, office memorandum, 17 September 1951, NND.842430, RG 84, Box 12, File 320-Pak. Pol. 1951, NA.) Yet as is well known in Pakistan, Mushtaq Gurmani the minister for Kashmir affairs – was one of those expected to be axed.

[243] Interestingly enough, the American ambassador thought Zafrullah would be the next prime minister of Pakistan. (ibid.)

[244] O. Franks [British ambassador in Washington] to CRO, telegram no. 3238, 8 October 1951, DO 35/3008, PRO.

[245] Extract from record of conversation between the secretary of state [CRO] and Zafrullah Khan, 30 August 1951, ibid.

incalculable risk which he at least was in no position to take. In early October 1951, Raja Ghazanfar Ali Khan, Pakistan's ambassador to Iran, had received instructions from the prime minister to discuss with Mossadeq the possibility of a joint Pakistan-Iran-Egyptian policy on the Middle East.[246] On 11 October, the secretary of the Arab League, Azzam Pasha, formally called upon all Arabs and Muslims to give their unflinching support to Egypt. Iran had already set a fine example; Iraq was ready to follow course. The British empire, struck by successive lightning attacks, seemed to be in veritable danger of being exterminated in the Muslim world. In Pakistan, the popular urge to follow the trend was irrepressible. The delay in the security council's discussion on Kashmir further inflamed passions. The press, several provincial Muslim League leaders and student groups in Karachi wanted to cash in on Muslim fervour and pitch in a bid for Kashmir. The general outcry against the government's 'wait and see' foreign policy was too loud for any political leader to ignore. If public statements are anything to go by, Liaquat was ready to come out strongly in support of the Egyptian stance. Bitter about the delay in the presentation of the Graham report to the security council, Liaquat spoke of a 'double-cross',[247] adding sarcastically that 'Pakistanis are convinced that action happens in short order where American interest is engaged'.[248] This was a dark hint as to where he was coming to stand on foreign policy. So on 12 October when Warren approached Liaquat about Pakistan's contribution to Middle East defence, he must have anticipated the reaction. The prime minister was 'exceedingly "cagey"' and most reluctant to commit himself in any way'; he instead pointed out that the 'Kashmir question was the primary one'.[249]

Liaquat was assassinated within just a little over one hundred hours. So it is not possible to establish how hard a battle he would have fought to stick to his theme of a territorial guarantee for both India and Pakistan before climbing on all fours on to the Western strategic bandwagon. All that is known is that at the time of his murder the prime minister was being pulled in at least three different directions. The old way of the British, the not so different way of the Americans, and the

[246] See Syed Nur Ahmad, *From Martial Law to Martial Law, Politics in the Punjab 1919–1958*, Mahmud Ali (trans.); Craig Baxter (ed.), Colorado 1986, 310.

[247] Warren to the secretary of state, 10 October 1951, *Foreign Relations*, 1951, VI, II, 1879.

[248] Warren Austin [American representative to the UN] to Acheson, 12 October 1951, ibid., 1881.

[249] British high commissioner to CRO, telegram no. 1775, 23 October 1951. FO371/92876, PRO.

uncertain way of the Muslim world. While the first had been consistently unrewarding, the second proving equally unsatisfactory, the third at least gave him a line to the people and his own party – the last resort for a politician who had all but exhausted his fund of patience with supposed friends, both at home and abroad.

It was on 16 October 1951 while addressing a League meeting at Paltan Maidan in Rawalpindi that Pakistan's first prime minister fell victim to an assassin's bullets. Liaquat was speaking extempore. So no one really knows what he intended to say; the shooting started seconds after his opening remarks. But Kashmir was not the only item on the prime minister's agenda; the Graham report had been submitted to the security council on the previous day. According to Begum Liaquat Ali Khan, her husband was to have made one of the most important speeches in his life.[250] Whether or not that was the case, Liaquat could hardly have avoided any mention of the Middle East. If his attitudes in the days just prior to the assassination are taken as indicators, the prime minister was going to make a play for the Muslim gallery, stating – implicitly if not explicitly – that his government had given up on its old ways and was now ready and able to keep the Anglo-American bloc at a healthy distance. This would have fortified the prime minister's hand while the UN security council deliberated over Kashmir; it was also the best insurance for a smooth cabinet reshuffle.

An inkling of the general drift of the prime minister's thinking still falls short of providing the answer to the question that continues to mesmerise those with courage enough to raise it. Who really killed Liaquat? There have been various theories; but each has faltered on account of patchy evidence due to the deliberate suppression of information. Despite a series of officially sponsored investigations, the people of Pakistan are farther away than ever from knowing the real motives behind the assassination.

But motives, however well concealed, reveal themselves in the very act itself. The murder of Liaquat Ali Khan removed the one politician with the will and the ability to lend an ear to popular opinion and turn it to positive advantage. If Liaquat's decision to strike a note of caution on foreign and defence policies stymied the ambitions of domestic claimants to power, it was an equally inconvenient piece of timing for those whose stocks in the international arena were falling. Allusions to a connection between domestic and international actors in the engineering of the disaster are not new. But with the passage of time an increasing amount of evidence, even if circumstantial, points to the need for a

---

[250] *Dawn*, 20 October 1951.

serious reconsideration of such a possibility. That, however, is a job for a team of detectives.

Insofar as the task of the historian is to tap the collective memory, and perhaps also the collective conscience, a few points are clearly in order. It was as early as February 1950 that Pakistani intelligence first filed a report on a planned attempt on Liaquat's life. Orders were issued stipulating that no 'suspicious characters' be allowed within thirty to forty yards of the prime minister. Yet the fatal bullets were fired a mere eighteen feet from the dais.[251] The assassin, Said Akbar, was an Afghan national, who had been a British intelligence agent in the preindependence period. Akbar at the time was on the payroll of Pakistani intelligence and under the strictest of surveillance. When he fired the shots, Akbar was sitting in a row of policemen with over two thousand rupees in his pocket. He was killed instantly by the police. These are clues of the highest value in understanding why neither the police nor the intelligence investigations came up with convincing enough explanations for the assassination.

Here one has to pause and consider the various possibilities. The assassin's national origins led to the immediate conclusion of an Afghan or an Indian hand. That would imply an infiltration of Pakistani intelligence by the state's two principal enemies; a difficult proposition to sustain. As the evidence suggests, the Pakistani security apparatus had maintained a close contact with British intelligence ever since partition; its reliance on American intelligence was a more recent development. Key positions within the provincial police services were still occupied by British officers. If segments of the Pakistani intelligence had a hand in the plot, it is not improbable that the two main foreign intelligence networks were in the know even if they themselves did not partake in the actual planning of the incident. There is even less reason to doubt the existence of a link between Pakistani intelligence and highly placed men within the state apparatus.

There have been outright allegations from opposite ends of the spectrum implicating the British in Liaquat's assassination. Begum Liaquat represents one end. According to a news item in a Calcutta based Communist daily, Avra Warren himself in a report to the state department 'believe[d] that the clue to the mystery of the assassination...[could] be traced to the conspiracy of British diplomats in that country'. The American ambassador is alleged to have maintained that the British had used anti-US elements for their own ends by

---

[251] *The Assassination of Liaquat Ali Khan: Report of the Commission of Enquiry* (second edition), Karachi 1952, 33.

'forg[ing] a powerful front against Liaquat in the political and official circles'.[252] Whatever the truth of these allegations, the state department was not wholly dismissive of the news item. In a telegram to the American consul in Calcutta, it indicated that it was 'interested in learning what news service or reporter purportedly cabled the item from Washington'. The hint of a leak, not unusual in Washington,[253] is implicit.

Whatever the final verdict on Liaquat's assassination, the full extent of the tragedy is writ large on the subsequent course of Pakistan's history. By the time Pakistan's first prime minister became the target of an evidently hired assassin, the institutional balance had begun gravitating away from the political centre in Karachi to military headquarters in Rawalpindi. It was to take a few years and the unfolding of yet more painful domestic political and economic crises before the central government itself was forced to make the shift. The swapping of horses on the international front was another reason for the delay. Liaquat's murder helped postpone Britain's final exit. Yet those preparing to make a triumphant entry were coming in with the view that the United States 'should be no more annoyed if a given policy or course of action backfires than the scientist whose test tube explodes in his face. We should merely chalk it up to clinical experience and be the wiser, and start off again'.[254] Making others wiser could leave Pakistan a great deal weaker. The real tragedy of the Pakistani state lies in its very early rejection of the people's intuitive ability to distinguish between would-be masters and friends.

[252] Ghulam Mohammad, Khaliquzzaman and H.S. Suhrawardy were also mentioned. See *Swadhinta* [Calcutta] 30 October 1951; cited in American consul [Calcutta] to the department of state, despatch no.226, 7 November 1951, NND.842905, RG 59, Box 4145, 790D.00/1-2251, NA.

[253] Department of state to American consul [Calcutta], 4 December 1951, ibid.

[254] A.M. Warren, 'Appraisal of Foreign Policies of SOA countries', NND.842424, RG 84, Box 5, A.M. Warren File, NA.

4

Wielding state power: Politicians, bureaucrats and generals

Pakistan survived the assassination of its first prime minister. But the ensuing power struggles and tensions within the state apparatus and the constituent units suggest just how deeply the political process had been scarred. Between October 1951 and October 1954, politicians, bureaucrats and generals jockeyed for position amidst a complex interplay of domestic, regional and international compulsions. As this three-cornered game sapped political energies the exercise of state power became increasingly far removed from any notion of responsible government. Those holding executive authority and answerable to parliament were able less and less to influence government policies while real power came to rest with state officials unencumbered by such constitutional niceties as accountability to the people. The inversion of 'parliamentary government' was to have large implications for relations between state and society. So it is essential to examine how authority derived from positions within the civil administration and the armed forces, rather than from bases of support in society, came to be the key to the wielding of state power in Pakistan.

Fencing for the centre

Expediency triumphed over the fundamentals of parliamentary government when the governor-general, Khwaja Nazimuddin, was saddled with the office of prime minister. Under the constitution, the central cabinet stood dissolved by virtue of the prime minister's death. Normal constitutional procedure demanded that the governor-general select a new team of ministers. Instead the incumbents prevailed upon the governor-general to takeover as prime minister. This set a precedent for the future: principles of succession so uncertain as to be non-existent and, more certainly, the irrelevance of parliament or the people in the matter.

The new governor-general was none other than Ghulam Mohammad, the civil bureaucrat of Punjabi origin whose impatience with politicians and parliamentarians had earned him notoriety in daring and initiative – fine ingredients for tenacious governance, but not the best guarantee for fledgling democratic processes. With the exception of Chaudhri Mohammad Ali, who relinquished the office of secretary-general to become finance minister, and Sardar Abdur Rab Nishtar, who gave up being governor of the Punjab to take a place at the centre, the new cabinet was the old gang of ministers under the leadership of a man whose reputation for weakness was tempered only by that for religious piety.

So, while it was easy to stick to many of the policies pursued by Liaquat's government, facing up to the changes contemplated by him called for a measure of courage that was difficult to muster. This is borne out by the contradictory postures of Nazimuddin's government on the foreign policy front. Coming under the same domestic pressures, the new government – whatever the predilections of some of its members – was quite as reluctant to hook up Pakistan with Western-inspired security arrangements for the Middle East. But neither was it ready to cry itself hoarse in support of the popular-nationalist trends in the region. Before the cabinet was sworn into office on 24 October, the foreign secretary was in Washington reiterating Pakistan's willingness to play a part in the defence of the Middle East in exchange for firm backing on Kashmir. 'Pakistan wanted action', Ikramullah blurted out despondently; its people were 'becoming more difficult to restrain'; the United States had to 'make up...[its] mind'; at least give Pakistan the arms it needed, otherwise the central government might be forced to 'turn away from the West'. After all, 'what...[was] the meaning of Liaquat's death? Only this, that others of us will be killed. Pakistan will have to fight.'[1] Nothing much came of this heart-rending performance. Certainly, the British now had more reason to doubt Pakistan's sincerity about joining a Middle East defence command. The high commissioner's impression was that the Pakistanis were clamouring 'to secure supplies of equipment and training facilities for troops' in order to place themselves in a 'stronger negotiating position over Kashmir'.[2] There was also a possibility of Pakistan claiming a 'more substantial voice in Middle East policy'; even the most pliable of governments in Karachi would be 'most reluctant to...pressure...other Muslim states'.[3]

Yet the British needed to keep trimming the wings of their former colony just in case it went flying off into the American camp. Some elements in Nazimuddin's government clearly favoured a tilt towards

---

[1] Memorandum of conversation by Thomas W. Simons of the office of South Asian affairs, 18 October 1951, *Foreign Relations*, 1951, VI, II, 2223.

[2] Laithwaite to CRO, telegram no. 1175, 13 October 1951, FO371/92876, PRO.

[3] Laithwaite to Leisching, 8 November 1951, DO35/3008, PRO.

Washington. The prime minister's stolid loyalty to the British crown was reassuring. While his predecessor had been considering an alliance with Egypt and Iran, Nazimuddin skated around a parliamentary motion to debate Pakistan's policy on the evacuation of British troops from Suez. So there were sound reasons for believing that the government of Pakistan 'wishe[d] to stay in with us [the British]'. It might get 'a warmer response if she...[went] straight to the Americans', but that was 'not a feeling...[the British] want[ed] to encourage'. However powerful the arguments against letting Pakistan use the issue of Middle Eastern defence as a trump it would, according to the high commissioner, 'be a grave decision...to conclude against taking advantage of readiness on her part of help, even if...accompanied by conditions some of which are undesirable from our point of view'.[4]

The opinion of the man on the spot did not go down too well in London. But the Pakistani waiting game was beginning to have the desired effect in Foggy Bottom. Some American officials in the state department were concerned lest feelings of 'neglect' force Karachi to pull down the shutters on the West and make it more obstinate about 'co-operat[ing] at a later date when danger was imminent'. An invitation from the Western allies asking the Pakistan army to participate in the Middle East command might create a 'favourable impression' and prove that 'they were being taken seriously'. Whatever the reaction in London and New Delhi, officials in the state department were ready to make an 'early approach'; they had been 'impressed with the smoothness' of the succession in Pakistan and saw no reason for 'anxiety...[about] the political stability of the country'.[5]

The apparent stability was simply the lull preceding the storm. Within weeks of forming his first ministry the prime minister had to repeat the drill over again. His brother, Shahabuddin, was dropped from the cabinet and the ministry of the interior placed under the charge of another redoubtable Punjabi – Mushtaq Gurmani.[6] The prime minister's fragile grip was not hidden from the mandarins or the generals in army headquarters; they after all had a hand in placing him in that august office. Recognising the priority army headquarters attached to supplies

---

[4] Ibid.

[5] O. Franks [British ambassador in Washington] to the foreign office, telegram no. 1150, 9 November 1951, ibid. The official who communicated the views was Donald Kennedy, the new American hand on Pakistan – he still had a lot to learn.

[6] Shahabuddin, with Qayum Khan's approval, was given the governorship of the NWFP. Dr Mahmud Hussain took the Kashmir affairs portfolio and was given full cabinet rank. Dr. I.H. Qureshi, the minister of state for refugees, also became a cabinet minister with charge of the information ministry which was now separated from the ministry of the interior.

of military equipment, Washington issued a cautious ultimatum to the political leadership in Karachi: they would have to 'make up their minds' about the extent of their commitment to the Western allies.[7] The air of confidence in the message betrays a prior exchange between Washington and Rawalpindi. In December 1951, general Ayub was actively soliciting membership in the Middle East command.[8] Wary of the trends in popular opinion at home as well as in the Middle East, he now wanted Turkey instead of Britain to sponsor Pakistan. The high commissioner, who maintained a direct line with the prime minister, thought the gesture was 'an indiscretion or a *ballon d'essai* on Ayub's part, perhaps prompted by elements...such as Iskander Mirza...but not by the Government'.[9]

By now there were two centres of power in Pakistan – Karachi and Rawalpindi. The latter was gaining ground. Mindful of the need to keep his own patch well-watered, Ayub was taking a personal interest in army grievances over salary, allowances, housing and pensions. He was also showing greater concern for Punjabi ex-servicemen. Addressing a gathering of 'over ten thousand' in the province, he announced the setting up of a cloth mill as part of the post-war rehabilitation scheme for ex-servicemen.[10] Here were the makings of one of the most important political constituencies in the country. The political leadership was under subtle but sure challenge from the men in uniform on both the domestic and the foreign policy fronts.

It was not uncommon to hear 'suggestions of a military dictatorship' in social circles in Karachi. Yet, as even the British high commissioner could see, 'the Army...[was] certainly no more competent...to throw up a strong Government'.[11] But the intermeshing of domestic crises with external pressures was preparing the ground for the ascension of the military, and more specifically the army, to the commanding heights in the state. So to explain the emergence of the military as the dominant institution within the Pakistani state it is important first of all to examine how domestic constraints led to compromises in the international arena.

There was nothing preordained about the collapse of political

---

[7] Memorandum of conversation between Zafrullah and Acheson, Paris, 17 November 1951, NND.842430, RG 84, Box 12, File 320-Pak. Pol. 1951, NA.

[8] Ayub had sent a 'personal message' to the Turkish chief of general staff expressing Pakistan's anxiety [sic-his own?] to join the proposed Middle East command. (K. Helm [British ambassador in Turkey] to foreign office, 17 December 1951, FO371/92876, PRO.)

[9] British high commissioner to the CRO, telegram no. 37, 11 January 1952, ibid.

[10] *Dawn*, 4 December 1951.

[11] Laithwaite to the secretary of state [CRO], 'Review of events', September 1951-April 1952, DO35/3185, PRO.

structures in Pakistan. Those who are content to attribute the dominance of the Pakistan army to weaknesses in political organisation or to a poorly developed political culture are justifying a phenomenon without fully understanding its origins. Undeniably, the League was never more than a tottering political machinery. But to argue that the lack of organisation alone ensured its descent into oblivion is to take refuge in narrow determinism. Vagaries of political alignments, competition for the spoils of office and factional in-fighting form part of even the most sophisticated political systems. What then are the reasons for the collapse of governments based on political parties – weak or strong – and their replacement by military dictatorships? The Pakistani experience – one among many examples of military rule in the developing world – is a particularly intriguing one. Contrary to popular belief, the political process in Pakistan went off the rails long before the military takeover in October 1958. Liaquat's failure to frame a constitution and hold elections, however deplorable, was a consequence of the massive dislocations following partition and the very real fears of those entrusted with the task of constructing the state. But the first four and a half years of Pakistan's existence had at worst tarnished the political process. It was during Nazimuddin's tenure in office that the decisive blows were dealt. This can best be seen by the central government's responses to the manifold economic, social and political problems confronting the state.

Within months of assuming office, the new prime minister was struggling to stabilise an economy that was deteriorating quite as rapidly as the political conditions in the provinces. A man whom fate had flung into a political ring that was more of a minefield than an arena where games were played according to a set of rules, Nazimuddin had neither skill nor vision to withstand the tests. As a result, decision-making fell increasingly to the bureaucracy and, in the last resort, the governor-general. The implications for a political system based on the Westminster model – in theory if not in actual practice – are easy to gauge. A notable feature of the new mode of policy-making was the lack of any connection between public opinion – whose significance should not be discounted in countries with low literacy levels – and the decisions and stances of the government. The tendency was most evident in the realm of foreign policy; but was no less true for policies purportedly aimed at fashioning a semblance of domestic stability.

Admittedly, even the most responsive of governments are liable to find their hands tied by trends in the international markets – whether a drop in the prices of export commodities or a sharp increase in the cost of imports. But, while popular governments might be expected to modify their economic policies and provide cushioning for the average citizen, those committed to preserving the prerogatives of privileged interest groups can be relied upon to search for different remedies. The central government in Karachi, whatever its pretensions, was not of the popular ilk. Far from improving the fortunes of the Nazimuddin ministry, the general tenor of the centre's economic policies hastened its demise.

By late 1951, the national economy was slipping badly. The temporary relief offered by the Korean war had lost its midas like touch; the value of Pakistani exports fell by more than 20 per cent, while the prices of imports shot up by nearly 38 per cent on levels reached during FY 1950–1.[12] With worsening terms of trade, foreign exchange reserves dropped to an all time low. As the self-proclaimed wizards in the ministry of finance learnt to their dismay, it took longer to thumb through files merely to identify old policies than it did to discover their irrelevance in the face of shocks administered by the international economy. So, although the Korean war boom was over, Karachi, in a prodigal mood hardly befitting the size of its coffers, persisted with an unusually liberal import policy. Announced in July 1951, that policy had given trading groups, old as well as new, some real incentives to import. As much as 85 per cent of the total imports could gain entry into the domestic market without a licence. But, unless exports could also fetch high prices, this was a sure recipe for bankruptcy. Significantly, until late in the summer of 1952, no measures were taken to restrict imports and stem the run on the foreign exchange reserves.

The government's reluctance to alter its trade policy had something to do with the inertia typical of bureaucracies. But it had a great deal to do with the desire not to discourage the favoured few who were making handsome profits on imports and at long last showing signs of wanting to invest in large-scale industrial enterprises, textiles in particular. A determination to become self-sufficient in cotton textiles and jute manufactures demanded the continuation of a liberal import policy. It would encourage traders with idle funds to purchase industrial machinery despite prohibitive prices in the international markets. As late-starters, Pakistani traders and merchant capitalists interested in industry suffered from a competitive disadvantage in capital costs. A government committed to rapid industrialisation had to be able to offer a range of sweeteners. The industrial finance corporation was one of them; with limited financial resources it could assist private entrepreneurs with resources of their own in setting up industries. So the fastest route to capital accumulation was to let the more enterprising traders make

---

[12] *Economy of Pakistan: 1948–68*, Islamabad 1968, 102.

profits on imports, in some instances at rates of 100 per cent to 200 per cent. In other words, reckless policies of import liberalisation were in fact calculated steps towards industrialisation – a term that was almost synonymous with the goal of extricating Pakistan from dependence on India. That such a policy might exhaust the foreign exchange reserves and spark off a wave of political unrest may have worried the more far-sighted civil servants in the capital. But they could always console themselves with hopes of foreign grants and loans and, failing these apparently acceptable forms of dependence, with confidence in the law enforcement capacities of the state.

Allowing the economy to slide was not the only distinguishing feature of the new order. The prime minister had a soft spot for religious ideologues. It was during the one and a half years of palpably weak government following Liaquat's death that the state faced its most formidable challenge from the proponents of a strictly Islamic order.[13] With an abundance of political and economic grievances waiting to be exploited, there was no better moment than now to raise the green banner of Islam against the enemies within. But, like the so-called secular politicians, the religious groups were quite as divided on the question which has been the bane of politics in Pakistan, namely who was to lead and who was to follow. The question was a particularly prickly one since there were groups with no previous record as champions of religion who now wanted to use Islam to squeeze their way into the political arena. Allama Mashriqi, the eccentric leader of the para-military Khaksar movement in prepartition India, rose from the ashes to organise an Indo-Pakistan Islam League. It had some support among petty shopkeepers, lower ranking government servants as well as the upper ranks of industrial labour. Mashriqi was thought to be receiving 'undetermined sums of money from some unidentified source'.[14] Another group with equally spurious religious credentials, but soon to spearhead a movement against the heterodox Ahmediya community, was the Majlis-i-Ahrar whose main claim to fame had been a special talent to make and break fences with both League and Congress in rapid succession.

A bigger threat to the League, because it was organised and had a well-defined religious ideology, was Abul Ala Maududi's Jamat-i-Islami. Its

---

[13] This is not to suggest that the discontent voiced by these religious groups was unknown prior to Nazimuddin's assumption of office as prime minister. Indeed, some of the earliest opposition to the ruling party came from precisely these circles. But whereas earlier they were snubbed or ignored, they could now take advantage of Nazimuddin's well-advertised religiosity.

[14] American embassy [Karachi] to the department of state, despatch no. 409, 4 October 1951, NND.842430, RG 84, Box 42, File 350-Pak. Pol. 1951, NA.

main bases of support were in the Punjab where it had contested the provincial elections of March 1951 by forging an alliance with Mamdot's Jinnah Awami League. It won only one seat in the provincial assembly despite expending large sums of money for the effort. In 1951 the Jamat claimed a membership of 661 with some 1,000 staunch sympathisers.[15] Yet these figures and its electoral failure are, and always have been, a misleading measure of the very real influence it enjoyed among a small but loyal constituency – consisting in the main of small shopkeepers, and the lower echelons of both the civil service and the army. Within less than a month of Liaquat's assassination, in what was a concerted demonstration of strength, the Jamat held its second annual meeting in Karachi. Between 30,000 to 50,000 delegates and well-wishers from all over the country attended. The speakers berated the League for its unIslamic policies, castigated women for mixing with members of the opposite sex, and lambasted the state in general for its lack of morality and poor quality of administration. This was just the prologue. The Jamat's objective was nothing less than a 'complete renaissance'; Islam had to be established 'de novo – as the system of Government' so that it could 'dominate thoughts and ideologies, education, politics, and [the] economy'.[16]

Other religious groups may not have been as well-organised as the Jamat but were no less determined to spring into the political limelight. Some like the Jamiat-ul-Ulema-i-Islam had ambitions of linking up with Islamic parties in the Muslim world. In February 1952, there was much ado about a conference attended by such religious luminaries as the grand mufti of Jerusalem and members of the central cabinet including the prime minister himself. The net result of these activities, which had the tacit if not the official authorisation of the government, was the establishment of a branch of the Muslim Brotherhood [Akhwan-ul-Muslimeen] in Pakistan.[17] This may have been part of Karachi's bid for leadership of the Muslim world. But these flirtations with religion were to backfire in the domestic arena before they could deliver the goods internationally.

The ministry's political record did nothing to stem the rot. At a time when the economy was entering its most difficult period since partition and the religious groups were girding their loins for a showdown, extreme prudence on matters touching the political sensibilities of the

---

[15] Withers to the department of state, despatch no. 660, 28 November 1951, NND.842430, RG 84, Box 12, File 320-Pak. Pol. 1951, NA.

[16] *Civil and Military Gazette* (Lahore), 11 November 1951; *Dawn*, 12 November 1951 and NND.842430, RG 84, Box 12, File 320-Pak. Pol. 1951, NA.

[17] *Dawn*, 22 January 1952.

people was essential. Anyone could see that after Liaquat's assassination and the 'evident weakening of central authority', the 'provin-
cialists...[were] entering a period of increasing strength and influence'.
The 'centrifugal trend of provincialism...[was] becom[ing] stronger';
people almost 'instinctively' thought of themselves 'as Bengalis, Punjabis, Sindhis, or citizens of other provinces, rather than as Pakistanis'.[18] The most common manifestations of this were: demands for
better representation in the civil, diplomatic and the armed services;
intra-provincial quibbling on revenue allocations; the language issue
and refugee demands for separate representation. Unfortunately, those
in office in Karachi were sorely lacking the tact needed to square these
diverse interests even though the passage of time gave them a better
chance than the previous ministry to resolve some of the more biting
issues like the allocation of finances between the centre and the
provinces. In January 1952, after nearly two and a half years of
agonising negotiations with central and provincial representatives,
Jeremy Raisman[19] – published his report on how the federal government and the provinces were to share out the national finances. The mere
fact that such a report was able to see the light of day was in itself a
positive development. Predictably enough, the Raisman award – as the
report came to be known – did not entirely satisfy all the provinces, the
Punjab and Sind in particular.[20] But it did give sanction to greater
financial autonomy for the provinces apart from increasing their overall
share of revenues. So the possibility of improved relations between the
centre and the province was not inconceivable. To understand why
relations between the centre and the constituent units remained on the
downward slope, a return to the maelstroms of provincial politics is
unavoidable.

THE PUNJAB

The Punjab exercised the greatest weight in Pakistani politics. Despite
the opportunities its political divisiveness presented to an artful
manipulator at the centre, it was difficult for a national government to

[18] American embassy [Karachi] to the department of state, despatch no. 1093, 27 February
1952, NND.842430, RG 84, Box 41, File 350-Pak. Pol. 1951-June 1952, NA.
[19] In the summer of 1949 Jeremy Raisman – the senior research officer of the Australian
treasury – was asked by the government of Pakistan to examine financial arrangements between the centre and the provinces.
[20] Both the Punjab and Sind claimed a share of the export duty on cotton on the grounds that
east Bengal was to have 62.5 per cent of the export duty on raw jute. Raisman rejected this
as well as the joint demand of all the provinces that proceeds from the sales tax should be
distributed among the constituent units, not shared out between them and the federal
government. (See *Financial Enquiry Regarding Allocation of Revenues Between the
Central and Provincial Governments*, report by Jeremy Raisman, Karachi 1952.)

remain in office without keeping its bridges with the Punjab in good repair. Yet as Nazimuddin's predecessor had learnt to his cost, it was not always easy to formulate policies for the Punjab without alienating some influential quarter or other. The best that could be expected from any central government was to choose the faction most capable of stomping its provincial rivals and, having done so, to give it unqualified support.

By nailing the centre's colours firmly on Daultana's bandwagon, the late prime minister had hoped to give the provincial League the progressive bent it had lacked so conspicuously under Mamdot's leadership. In January Mamdot's ministry had been dismissed by governor Mudie and section 92a imposed on the province; in July of the same year Mudie himself was forced to resign. Until March 1950 the centre administered the province with help from the new governor, Abdur Rab Nishtar, and a highly controversial advisory quartet – which besides enjoying a reputation for corruption was believed to be in Mamdot's camp. As for the provincial League, it was as ever languishing in the shadows of its all too brief moments of glory. Yet the opposition was in a worse predicament. Despite an array of opposition groups – whether Mamdot's Jinnah Muslim League, Main Iftikharuddin and Shaukat Hayat's Azad Pakistan party, Maududi's Jamat-i-Islami or the Majlis-i-Ahrar, to name but a few – none had the stature or the capability of toppling the Punjab League. Here the provincial League – and its new president Daultana in particular – had much for which to thank the centre. Not only had Karachi 'shown no willingness to allow opposition groups to develop freely at the expense of the Muslim League',[21] it was ready to resort to coercion if the ruling party's position in the province was even remotely endangered.

Just how much importance the centre attached to the Punjab can be seen in Liaquat's decision to move the entire central government to Lahore during the run up to the provincial assembly elections. Held in March 1951, the elections were based on adult franchise – the first time ever in the history of the areas constituting Pakistan. The Punjab was also the first province to elect a new provincial assembly. Out of a population of some 19 million, 9 million were registered; of these less than 2 million qualified as literates. It is doubtful whether many voters understood the meaning, much less the irony, in the League's apparently simple election slogan: a vote for the League was a vote for stability. The League's own stability was severely tested by the number of applications for party tickets. As many as 800 to 900 hopefuls wanted to contest

---

[21] This was the observation of the British high commissioner. (See opdom no. 15, part II, 10–23 July 1950, FO37/84201, PRO.)

elections on a League ticket. And, while the enthusiasm must have been heartening for both the provincial and the central League parliamentary boards, it was impossible to square it with the electoral arithmetic. Around 153 constituencies were to return 197 members to the assembly, including forty-four representatives of the 5.5 million, or more, refugees settled in the province.[22] In Punjabi politics, the denial of party tickets is typically followed by realignments with other groups or, if the disappointed individuals have resources of their own, a decision to go it alone. So in selecting a contingent for the elections, the League unavoidably risked disturbing its own uncertain inner balance before it could begin posturing as the harbinger of stability.

Once again it was the political ineptitude of its opponents that came to the League's rescue. Mamdot's uneasy coalition with Suhrawardy's All-Pakistan Awami Muslim League and Maududi's Jamat-i-Islami could hardly produce an electoral programme that was convincing and imaginative. Though he had managed to get himself acquitted of corruption charges under PRODA,[23] Mamdot was in 'the dubious company of dismissed officials' charged with dealings in which he himself had had a hand.[24] All that Mamdot had going for him was the symbolic support of Jinnah's sister – Fatima – some powerful backing from Hamid Nizami, the editor of the *Nawa-i-Waqt*, and a manifesto dipped in Islamic slogans which appealed to the conservative anti-reform landlord lobby.

The provincial League, its factional bickerings notwithstanding, was better poised for victory. Not only did it have the support of the government – a vital resource – but a manifesto tinged with such popular panaceas as tenancy reforms, labour legislation, better educ-

---

[22] Five seats were reserved for women, including one for a refugee representative; four seats were for Christians and Anglo-Pakistanis; and two university and general constituency seats. The districtwise allocation of seats was:

Lahore	19	Rawalpindi	8	Dera Ghazi Khan	8
Sialkot	13	Attock	7	Muzafargarh	8
Gujranwala	10	Mianwali	6		
Gujrat	13	Montgomery	17	TOTAL	186
Sheikhupura	10	Lyallpur	20		
Shahpur	12	Jhang	9		
Jhelum	6	Multan	20		

[23] Among the charges against Mamdot was his misuse of public office to secure prime land in the Montgomery district. The deputy commissioner of the district, Hasan Akhtar, and the commissioner of the Rawalpindi district, Khwaja Abdur Rahim, were both dismissed from the civil service for aiding and abetting corruption under Mamdot's ministry. They now acted as the main advisors to Mamdot.

[24] Joyce R. Herrman [American vice consul] to the department of state, Lahore despatch no. 111, 25 January 1951, NND.842430, RG 84, Box 42, File 350-Pak. Pol. 1951, NA.

ation and health facilities, road and agricultural improvements, etc. Masterminded by Daultana, the manifesto was the most progressive political programme the Punjab had seen. Yet instead of applause Daultana had to face accusations of having produced too 'able and detailed a programme'. A whispering campaign aimed at deflating Daultana predicted that, irrespective of the election result, within a year the province would end up under Mushtaq Gurmani, Mamdot or even that old Unionist stalwart, Khizar Hayat Tiwana. Frightened by these portents, Daultana quietly amended the final manifesto and introduced various safeguards against possible pressure by the landlords.[25]

Himself a landlord from Multan district, Daultana was well aware of the hurdles he would have to overcome before implementing the League's election promises. In a province reeling under a variety of socio-economic problems, it was easy to identify the spheres where reforms were most urgently needed. The movement of populations had imposed rather more strains on Punjabi cities and towns than on the rural hamlets.[26] The shortage of housing, the high cost of rents as well as utilities and food, unemployment and undisguised favouritism in the allotment of property were the reasons for widespread opposition among urban and town refugees to anyone or anything associated with the central government. The League was expected to be mauled by the opposition in key urban centres. In the countryside the Azad Pakistan party and the Kisan committees had been stoking agrarian discontent. To leave the initiative in the countryside to these groups, when the League's popularity in the urban areas stood at an all time low, was to court defeat. Though the stark inequalities of Punjabi agrarian society demanded a spate of radical reforms – of an estimated 13 million landowners, over 9 million owned less than five acres of land – Daultana took care to restrict the League's promises to tenancy reforms alone. Such a policy was bound to appeal to an approximately 3.5 million refugee farmers who had no security of tenure. Many of them had

---

[25] Jasper to the high commissioner, Lahore despatch no. 5/51, 9 February 1951, DO35/3186, PRO.

[26] During 1941–51 the population of Lahore alone had increased by 25 per cent, largely due to refugee inflows from Amritsar, Jullundur and Ludhiana. According to the 1951 census, the urban population of western Punjab was 3.4 million, or 18 per cent of the total population of the undivided province. At the time of the provincial elections, the proportion of refugees living in the cities of the Punjab was approximately:

Lahore	43%	Multan	49%
Jhang-Maghiana	64%	Rawalpindi	37%
Gujranwala	50%	Sialkot	32%
Lyallpur	69%		
Sargodha	69%		

(See *Census of Pakistan*, 1951, 75.)

received small pieces of land immediately after partition; but by the summer of 1950 a systematic campaign by the bigger landlords, frequently with the help of local and district police, had left hundreds with the difficult choice of becoming tenants or being displaced altogether.

The contradictions in the League's plans to champion the cause of the rural downtrodden became apparent even before the elections. Impeccable rhetoric is easier to weave than a string of committed members to the assembly. Not one to get bogged down in debates over principles, Daultana had abiding faith in political expediency. So, having made his bid as a social reformer, he turned to the more hard headed calculations of a political operator. The majority of the party tickets were issued to members of the landed gentry – the *nawabzadas* of Gujrat, the *sayids* of Jhang and the *sardars* of Muzafargarh and Dera Ghazi Khan – some of them unlettered men of the Unionist persuasion.[27] To expect them to ratify agrarian policies which whittled down their age-old privileges was mere wishful thinking. For the time being, however, Daultana had succeeded in outmanoeuvring the opposition. With over four lakhs of rupees in election funds – one lakh contributed by the central Muslim League[28] – support from the Jamiat-ul-Ulema-i-Islam, the Ahrars and, above all, the government machinery, the League had more than was needed to cross the victory line. It won 153 seats, later increased to 166, and 52 per cent of the total vote cast. Mamdot's Jinnah Awami League had to rest content with a mere thirty-two seats.[29] To everyone's amazement, and an indication that the opposition's charges of election fraud were not baseless, the League had somehow managed to win fifteen of the twenty-three urban seats.[30]

---

[27] See *Nawa-i-Waqt*, 27 February 1951, for a complete list of candidates from the various constituencies.

[28] *Nawa-i-Waqt*, 14 February 1951.

[29] On 30 March 1951, when the initial election results became known, the different political parties had won the following number of seats and per cent of votes:

Party	no. of seats	% of votes
Muslim League	140	52 (not including eight unopposed candidates)
Jinnah Awami Muslim League	32	18.3
Independents	17	23.7
Azad Pakistan party	1	2.0
Jamat-i-Islami	1	4.4
Islam League	—	0.4
Communist party	—	0.1

(See *Dawn*, 30–31 March, 1–3 April 1951.)

[30] *Dawn*, 1 April 1951.

The League's resounding success might seem to have placed Daultana in an invincible position. He was elected chief minister and the leader of the League's parliamentary party unopposed. But his cabinet consisted wholly of landlords, large and small, of whom only one was a refugee.[31] To Daultana's credit, he was able to swing the ministry and the provincial administration behind his plans for the expansion of small-scale industries and social services. In the opinion of one observer, Daultana's ministry was not 'financially corrupt'; nepotism, while present, was 'not greater' than before and it was unlikely that a 'better Ministry w[ould]...appear in West Pakistan in this generation'.[32] The assessment may have been overly optimistic; it was certainly premature. Daultana's ministry had yet to face up to the bigger tests that were in the offing. There was a disquieting delay in bringing the issue of tenancy reforms before the provincial assembly. Daultana was hedging his bets. Yet continued dithering on tenancy reforms was having catastrophic effects on the League's popularity in the rural areas where landlords in anticipation of the new legislation had begun evicting tenants.

Towards the end of September, the provincial League assembly party produced a compromise formula heavily weighted in favour of the larger landlords. Tenants were to have security of tenure that was heritable as well as 60 per cent of the produce;[33] occupancy tenants were granted proprietary rights; all *jagirs* other than those for military personnel or religious and charitable institutions were abolished; cesses and special services to landlords were scrapped; the Punjab protection and restoration of tenancy act, 1950,[34] was permanently placed on the statute book; and any infringement of the new tenancy act was punishable by law.[35] Yet as some League leaders had to confess, the proposed reforms offered no economic relief whatsoever to the tenants. At best, they gave them a 'new social dignity',[36] albeit a severely circumscribed one. Under the proposed act it was illegal for tenants to participate in agrarian

---

[31] Sufi Abdul Hamid, the token refugee representative, was thought to be a 'nonentity and a tiresome one at that'. The other ministers were Mohammad Hassan Chatta [revenue], Sardar Abdul Hamid Dasti, Ghulam Mohammad Leghari, Piracha [an ex-civil servant with experience in refugee and revenue matters] and Gardezi [industries]. (Jasper to Burnett, Lahore despatch no. 17/51, DO35/3186, PRO.)

[32] Ibid.

[33] Daultana had publicly called for a 2:1 ratio, but accepted the 3:2 ratio demanded by the larger landlords. He also agreed to set up a special committee to consider the acreage landlords could claim as *khud khast*, or self-cultivated. The limit in the League's formula was 25 acres; the landlords wanted it increased to fifty acres of irrigated and 100 acres of unirrigated land. They got their concession which received legal sanction under the Punjab tenancy (amendment) bill of 1952.

[34] The act had been put into effect for a period of two years.

[35] See *The Pakistan Times* and *Dawn*, 29 September 1951.

[36] Craig to the department of state, Lahore despatch no. 65, 9 October 1951, NND.842909, RG 59, Box 5549, 890D.16/10-951, NA.

agitations like no-rent campaigns. Moreover, the seemingly generous concession to the tenants of a 60 per cent share of the produce was a regressive measure; in some parts of the Punjab, tenants were entitled to three-fourths of the crop. The League could not have contrived a shabbier window dressing for its electoral promises.

Even these modest reforms met with bitter opposition. Stone-walling by twenty-five members of the League's parliamentary party, led by Malik Mubarik Ali Shah and Naubahar Shah, postponed debate on the bill for three months. Liaquat's assassination, conveniently following in the wake of the provincial League's reform proposals, strengthened their case. They could now count on solid support from Mushtaq Gurmani, the central minister of the interior and a long-standing rival of Daultana. Gurmani, while careful not to oppose the League's adopted policy openly, favoured reforms that placed greater emphasis on efficiency than change. The line was 'intended to embarass[sic] Mumtaz Daultana personally' and became another source of the underlying tensions between the provincial ministry and the new government in Karachi.[37] It was only by threatening to resign that Daultana managed to convince the League parliamentary party to pass the tenancy reform bill. But it was a hollow victory. The larger landlords retaliated by refusing to bring wheat to the *mandis* or by smuggling it across the borders to India. The ministry's attempt to institute rationing was a fiasco. By the middle of 1952, speculation and hoarding had played havoc with the provincial distribution machinery. In spite of repeated requests for emergency food supplies, the centre was unwilling to pay for provincial mismanagement. So the politics of a province – once the 'bread basket' of India – had left it facing a man-made famine. The Punjabi landlords could not have struck back more cruelly. By the fall of 1952, wheat was selling for Rs. 35 per maund in some parts of the province. Realising that the 'temper of the people could not countenance further dallying', the provincial government decided to requisition wheat. But to no avail since the biggest hoarders were almost without fail the 'political bigwigs of the Muslim League'.[38] More alarming still were reports about how '*zamindars*, politically hostile to the Daultana ministry's recent agrarian enactments' were having their lands sown under cash crops, like oilseeds, instead of wheat.[39] The prospects for the *rabi* crop and the political stability of the province were bleak indeed.

---

[37] Jasper to Burnett, Lahore despatch no. 17/51, DO35/3186, PRO.
[38] Leon B. Poullada [American consul general], Lahore despatch no. 81, 18 November 1952, NND.842430, RG 84, Box 42, File 350-Pak. Pol. July–December 1952, NA.
[39] *Dawn*, 19 November 1952.

The shortage of food was not the only crisis looming on the horizon. Fringe groups, religious or lay, had been waiting for an opportune moment to swing into action. Soaring grain prices and, in some cases, the complete absence of wheat, together with longer standing grievances – whether of the Punjabi small traders against the centre's alleged discrimination in the allotment of licences or of the lower ranking provincial civil servants against the pay scales recommended by the Punjab pay commission[40] – presented a perfect scenario. It was the Ahrars who took the lead; because they were the most adept of the religious opportunists and because their electoral deal with the Daultana ministry provided a cover for activities, however dangerous and reprehensible. Whatever else they may have been, the Ahrars were not innovators. Short of ideas on how to go about acquiring political prominence, they stuck to themes which had a proven appeal to the religious orthodoxies of the people. In a campaign that was to lay the foundations of religious intolerance in Pakistan, the Ahrars reverted to their favourite hobby-horse – reviling the Ahmediya community for its unorthodox approach to Islam and demanding that they be declared a minority.

The Ahmediyas or Mirzais were a closely knit sect of some 200,000 who had deviated from one of the fundamental precepts of Islam by according their spiritual leader, Mirza Ghulam Ahmed (1835-1908), a status comparable to the Prophet Mohammad. And, while the Ahmediya view on the finality of Mohammad's prophethood was blasphemous for orthodox Muslims,[41] it had been around long enough for them to be treated as simply another sect under the broad umbrella of Islam. Anti-Ahmediya sentiments, where they existed, had material and political rather than purely religious moorings. The Ahmediyas, by and large, were better off than the vast majority of the Faithful; they held prominent positions in government service and also in the professions. The foreign minister, Zafrullah Khan was the most influential member of the sect and, naturally, the main target of the Ahrar onslaught.

Anyone with the ability to think could see that the Ahrars were merely seeking to restore a public image marred by their outspoken opposition

---

[40] The Punjab pay commission's report was announced on the eve of the provincial elections. (*Nawa-i-Waqt,* 9 March 1951.) Street protests by lower ranking civil servants against the report's provisions may have petered out, but the economic conditions in the province gave them no cause to temper their grievances.

[41] A group of Mirza Ghulam Ahmed's followers based in Lahore did not subscribe to the claim of his prophethood. Known as the Lahori party, they were nevertheless targets of the Ahrar attack.

to the Pakistan demand.[42] Those with a longer memory span may not have failed to notice the striking similarity between the Ahrars' description of Jinnah as 'Kafir-e-Azam' [leader of the infidels] and of the Ahmediyas as Kafirs [infidels]. But few in the Punjab had the courage to think and even fewer who could remember. For the simple minded, there was profound wisdom in the Ahrar allegation that Kashmir had been denied to Pakistan because Zafrullah, like many other Ahmediyas, was in league with the British. The more calculating had sensed advantages in giving the Ahrars their head; Zafrullah's removal along with that of other Ahmediyas holding key government positions could mean job opportunities at the centre.

With a mixture of ambivalence and active connivance from the educated sections of society, the field was left wide open for an agitation that was to result in the downfall of not one but two governments. By the summer of 1952 when the food shortage was increasingly beginning to be felt, illiterate or at best half-educated audiences throughout the province were held spellbound by the fiery and flawless oratory of Ahrar leaders like Ata Ullah Shah Bokhari, Qazi Ehsan Ahmed Shujabadi, Mohammad Ali Jullunduri and Sahibzada Faiz-ul-Hasan. The gist of the speeches was much the same; it was the level of indecency and obscenity that distinguished one orator from the other. Their fulminations left the Ahmediyas in a virtual state of siege: their properties were burned and looted; excited crowds murdered members of the sect and mock funerals of Zafrullah topped the list of local entertainments. It is not just the unmentionably poor taste of the perpetrators that is galling. But the knowledge that no decisive steps were taken to quash the Ahrar menace. And this despite a vivid realisation on the part of top officials in the Punjab police that the agitation with its criminal overtones was a potential forerunner to anarchy. The blame, because the failure to proscribe such activities cannot escape blame, must rest squarely with the Punjab ministry in the first instance and on the central government in the final analysis.

There is something deeply peculiar about the widespread impact of a movement led by a group of discredited men with a following of no more than 1,064.[43] With all the rope historical circumspection can possibly

---

[42] Describing them as 'political charlatans and jingoes', Anwar Ali, the deputy inspector general of the police in Punjab, was convinced that the Ahrars were trying to 'retrieve their lost prestige'. (See Anwar Ali's letter of 4 April 1952, cited in the *Report of the Court of Inquiry constituted under Punjab Act 11 of 1954 to Enquire into the Punjab Disturbances of 1953*, Lahore 1954, 50 – henceforth *the Munir Report*.) As early as May 1950, Anwar Ali had recommended that the Ahrars be declared an illegal organisation. (Ibid., 57.)

[43] *The Munir Report*, 52.

allow to the Daultana ministry and the provincial Muslim League, the available evidence is too overwhelming to absolve them of responsibility in the agitation.[44] In his most enigmatic political phase ever, Daultana not only protected but encouraged a movement that cut against the very grain of his progressive views. The reasons for this intriguing *volte face* are complex and unedifying. The Ahrar agitation was seen by Daultana as an opportunity to browbeat the central government into submitting to the Punjab's economic and, by late 1952, constitutional demands. If successful, Daultana could hope to replace Nazimuddin or Zafrullah at the centre, thus fortifying his position within the province. These Machiavellian calculations were implicit in the dramatic policy turns taken by the Punjab chief minister against the advice of his principal henchmen in the provincial administration. In July 1952, Daultana finally gave in to pressure from Qurban Ali Khan, the inspector general of the Punjab police, to impose section 144 in certain districts in the province. While this prevented the Ahrars from holding meetings, it also encouraged them to close ranks with other religious and like-minded groups. On 13 July, an All-Parties Muslim Convention in Lahore endorsed Ahrar demands. Far from being unsettled by these developments, Daultana saw them as evidence of support for his pro-Ahrar policy. So on 21 July, upon receiving limp assurances from Ahrar leaders disavowing violence, Daultana lifted section 144, prefacing it with a public statement that since the finality of prophethood was an article of faith for all Muslims the issue of declaring Ahmediyas a minority should be taken up by the constituent assembly.[45] Within less than a week the council of the Punjab Muslim League had adopted a resolution by a vote of 264 against eight in support of the anti-Ahmediya agitation. In what is proof of Daultana's hand in the phrasing of the resolution, the final decision was left to the 'mature judgement of the leadership of the Pakistan Muslim League and the Constituent Assembly'.[46]

Such unequivocal backing from the provincial arm of the ruling party encouraged the Ahrars to spread the poison of sectarianism more deeply and widely. With support from fourteen religious groups, including the Jamat-i-Islam, the Jamiat-ul-Ulema-i-Pakistan and the Jamiat-ul-Ulema-i-Islam,[47] the Ahrars had become the vanguard of a movement that was no longer confined to the Punjab or to the Ahmediya question alone. By now Karachi too was affected by anti-Ahmediya riots. But the

[44] Ibid., passim.
[45] British high commissioner to CRO, opdom no. 14, 8–21 July 1952, DO35/3185, PRO.
[46] Ibid., part II, 28 July 1952.
[47] Ibid., 78.

sympathisers of the agitation were far from agreed on its precise objective. For the religious groups this was an opportunity to force the central government to bend to their demands for an 'Islamic constitution'; for Daultana and his associates, a thinly disguised ploy to detract attention from a worsening food situation, not to mention an excuse to extract a more acceptable constitutional deal for the Punjab; and for Nazimuddin and his inner coterie, a highly dangerous tactic to muffle all opposition by appearing to come down on the side of religion.

It was confusion galore. As a frustrated police official in the Punjab put it in graphic terms, the agitators were exploiting the food situation 'vigorously', 'abus[ing], malign[ing] and defam[ing] the government'; people returning from Karachi related stories of the secretariat officers having 'lost faith in the future' and going about business as if 'a collapse...[was] imminent'. Things were no better in the Punjab; bitter charges against the government, central and provincial, could be heard in almost any quarter; League members and government servants were 'no exception and indulge[d] liberally in such talks'. The situation was 'desperate'; someone had to 'save...the nation from chaos and anarchy'.[48] But, before the miracle could occur, one or the other government had to fall. That was an issue which depended critically on the nature of the other links in the province-centre chain.

EAST BENGAL

East Bengal was easily the most brittle link in the centre-province chain. Politics in the province were marked by unbending hostility towards the central government. The list of Bengali disaffections with Karachi is a long and telling one. It had all started with Jinnah's pronouncement of Urdu as the national language. Provincial sentiments were wounded further by the centre's decision to appoint Nurul Amin as chief minister over the head of the provincial League. The nakedly colonial policies of the west Pakistani dominated jute board killed the little love still remaining between the centre and the province. The decision not to devalue the Pakistani rupee buried the last remnants of good will; it quickened the pace of the jute grower's immiseration just when food, if available, was selling at astronomical prices. In May 1949, voters of Mymensingh district registered their protest by defeating the League candidate in a by-election.[49] The rest of Bengal paid the price for the insolence; they were deprived of the vote for the next five years.[50]

---

[48] Anwar Ali's Lahore daily diary, 15 December 1952, cited in ibid., 116–17.

[49] The successful candidate was Shamsul Huq, later the secretary of the Awami League. (*Nawa-i-Waqt*, 4 May 1949.)

[50] Vacancies in the provincial assembly were allowed to remain unfilled. By August 1953, as many as thirty-four out of 171 seats were vacant, (See Keith B. Callard, *Pakistan: a Political Study*, London 1957, 56.)

This helped keep Amin's ministry in office; it did not prevent the growth of opposition groups both within and outside the League. True to South Asian political traditions, the groupings revolved around key personalities, not principles or programmes. Amin's main opponent in the League was Hamid-ul-Huq Choudhry, the commerce minister, who had to resign in December 1949 to fight charges under PRODA. The fiercest opposition to the chief minister, however, revolved around three grandees of Bengali politics – Shaheed Suhrawardy and Maulana Abdul Hamid Bhashani of the Awami League, and Fazlul Huq who kicked off the final quarter of his chequered political career by joining the People's Muslim League.[51]

Among the common allegations against the ministry was its failure to alleviate the food shortage, its totalitarian tendencies, and its weak stance on the language question. Political opinion deemed Amin unfit for the job. But the centre was not convinced; an alternative ministry with a line to the people could prove difficult to discipline. The provincial League's unpopularity was the best guarantee for Amin's continued subservience to the centre. In east Bengal, the centre had come to depend on a clique of non-Bengali civil servants who could be relied upon to work in its interests better than the most loyal of Bengali politicians. It was rare to find the centre's agents cooperating with the provincial ministry; they were more frequently trying to undermine its position. Agha Hilaly, a senior civil servant, actually wished Suhrawardy 'luck' since, in his opinion, the League 'needed opposition in order to progress rather than stagnate'.[52]

Of course Amin did try his level best to do something worthwhile. In August 1949, he had announced the provisions of the east Bengal estate acquisition and land tenancy bill which abolished the permanent settlement of 1793, gave tenants permanent security of tenure, established a direct link between government and the cultivator by doing away with intermediary rent collectors and set a thirty-three acre limit on personal holdings.[53] In February 1950, the provincial assembly passed the bill despite opposition from the Congress benches. But Amin's one opportunity to win public approbation was blocked by the central government. The bill needed the governor-general's consent; this was withheld for over a year since it could jeopardise Pakistan's chances

---

[51] Formed in June 1949, it consisted of various dissident groups within the League. Some of them were to later join Huq's Krishak Sramik party. There were other smaller opposition groups as well. But identifying the main one is a hazardous enterprise; in the imbroglio of Bengali politics there was no such thing as a permanent grouping; alliances were made, broken and remade with little difficulty.

[52] Memorandum by Hewes [American consulate, Dacca] to Warren, 11 May 1950, NND.842430, RG 84, Box 7, File 350-Pak. Pol. 1950, NA.

[53] *Dawn*, 11 August 1949 and J. Russell Andrus and Azizali F. Mohammad, *The Economy of Pakistan*, Oxford 1958, 120–2.

of attracting foreign investments.[54] Such patent subversion of provincial interests would have put off the most ardent supporter of the
centre. Though occasionally given to trenchant criticism of the central
government's policies,[55] a recognition of his impotence dissuaded Amin
from breaking with Karachi.

This was to cost him dear. In December, 1949, the Bengal League had
adopted a resolution demanding full provincial autonomy in all matters
except defence and foreign affairs as well as increased representation in
the constituent assembly. Karachi saw this as a red-rag and began
exploring ways of curbing the Bengal League. A section 92a administration was ruled out because the province had a British governor,
Frederick Bourne. The first step was to appoint a man who would carry
out the centre's dictates without suffering any pangs of conscience. The
mantle had fallen on Malik Firoz Khan Noon. His presence gave a fillip
to the jute board's scandalous activities and worked wonders for the
morale of the non-Bengali civil servants. With Amin and his team of
ministers rapidly becoming redundant, the affairs of the province were
run more and more along the lines of a section 92a administration. Like
'most West Pakistanis', Noon had 'absolutely no use for the Bengalis';
he made no bones about the fact that 'in his dealings
with[Bengalis]...he...treat[ed] them like "willful children"'.[56] These
admissions by Karachi's governor, he could just as well have been
London's, lend credence to the oft-repeated Bengali allegations against
Punjabi colonialism.

In October 1950, the appearance of the basic principles committee's report convinced educated Bengalis of all persuasions that the
centre was determined 'to reduce East Bengal to the status of a municipality' and 'subordinate its majority population to the will of West
Pakistan'.[57] The opposition to the report was not restricted to the
Awami League; the Bengal Muslim League was among its most virulent
critics. The ambiguities of their domestic politics notwithstanding, the
Bengali view of the future constitution was unequivocal: it had to be
federal in form with maximum autonomy for the provinces. Irked by the
unusual display of Bengali solidarity, the central government scrapped
the report and guided the BPC back to the drawing-board.

---

[54] Memorandum of Withers' conversation with Firoz Khan Noon, Dacca despatch no.
73, 8 November 1950, NND.842430, RG 84, Box 7, File 350-Pak. Pol. 1950, NA.

[55] See Amin's speech to the national assembly above, p. 107.

[56] Memorandum of Withers' conversation with Firoz Khan Noon, Dacca despatch no.
73, 8 November 1950, NND.842430, RG 84, Box 7, File-350-Pak. Pol. 1950, NA.

[57] Withers to Warren, Dacca despatch no. 68, 20 October 1950, ibid.

Towards the end of 1950, the outbreak of communal riots in both parts of Bengal knocked the policy-makers in Karachi out of complacency. Effective sabre-rattling by the Calcutta press in tandem with Patel's ultimatums helped serve notice to the Pakistani establishment that east Bengal might be lost long before the battle to save it could begin in west Punjab. By the beginning of 1951, irrespective of the preoccupations with Kashmir, the central government was despatching military forces in 'growing' numbers to the eastern wing.[58] But this newfound concern for its external security was not matched by steps to ameliorate the socio-economic conditions in the province. A more visible presence of the armed forces was intended by Karachi as a deterrent to would-be internal saboteurs.

By now Suhrawardy and Bhashani were drawing more crowds at their public meetings than the most charming of League personalities. The politically charged atmosphere of university campuses was equally portentous. Many of the university professors were Hindu and realised that their own futures depended upon the students learning the simple, but now endangered, truths about academic and political freedom. There were also signs of students and intellectuals gravitating towards the local Communist party whose headquarters were rumoured to be in Calcutta. An overworked and paranoid provincial home department desperately tried countering the trend; it arrested hundreds of Communists and approached the British and American information services for assistance. The fear of police reprisals kept student activists from holding meetings under the red banner. But their resentments now found expression in political pamphleteering and, in due course, gave birth to the famous 'two economy' thesis which argued that east and west Pakistan should be treated as entirely separate economies.

The discontent occasionally forced Karachi to make half-hearted gestures to Bengali public opinion. But these were invariably cosmetic in nature. There was much talk about giving Bengalis better representation on the jute board. Yet the centre's flat refusal to relinquish control over the jute trade made Bengali presence on the board quite meaningless. Bringing Bengalis to the central cabinet was an equally ineffective tactic, especially since the chosen ones did not have to bother testing their claims to be representative.[59] The Raisman award admittedly did give

---

[58] Memorandum prepared by the American consulate, Dacca, for the SOA conference in Nuwara Eliya, Ceylon, dated 17 January 1951, NND.842430, RG 84, Box 1, File 310-South Asia, NA.

[59] Towards the end of April 1951 the centre, destined never to get the right end of the stick in east Bengal, decided to increase Bengali representation in the Pakistan cabinet. Dr A.M. Malik, the minorities minister at the centre, was replaced by Azizuddin Ahmed and Ghyasuddin Pathan.

east Bengal a decent deal. But even with proceeds from export duties on jute and income tax, the provincial government was perpetually in the red. The only alternative to political upheaval – a very real possibility if the people were to pay more taxes to finance the provincial deficit – was for the centre to funnel resources. Aggregate figures of grants and development funds from the centre to east Bengal as such are not unimpressive. But with few exceptions, projects financed by the centre were among the finest textbook cases of abysmal planning, widespread corruption and gross mismanagement. This needs special emphasising since the 'primary reason' for the centre assuming a more interventionary role in east Bengal than elsewhere was the fear that leaving it to its own devices would result in complete 'chaos and disintegration in the Province'.[60]

The Bengal League could have done with a fraction of Karachi's concerns about the provincial economy. If anything, it was the League and not the province that was threatened by disintegration. There were internal disputes in practically all the branches, such as they were. Mindful of the consequences of stirring up a hornet's nest, party elections had been called off repeatedly. Amin, now the president of the provincial League, was busy quarrelling with Yusuf Ali Choudhury, the general secretary. An example of the provincial League's lack of touch with the people was a resolution calling for the adoption of Arabic as the state language.[61] This was a travesty of provincial sentiments on the language issue; it implied that Urdu, not the imposition of a foreign language, was unacceptable to the Leaguers. Another resolution, more in tune with provincial realities, demanded the nationalisation of the jute industry. The resolution was undoubtedly a popular measure. But it was rejected out of hand by the central government. Ironically enough, the main opposition to the proposal came from Fazlur Rahman, the Bengali minister of commerce at the centre. Rahman's long-standing political enmity with Yusuf Ali Choudhury – 'the prime mover behind the nationalization proposal' had given Karachi a stalking-horse.[62] The Bengal League ignored the rebuff. The proposal for the nationalisation of the jute industry was vital for its 'political self-preservation'.[63]

Just how close the League was to political extinction became apparent

[60] Memorandum prepared by the American consulate, Dacca, for the SOA conference in Nuwara Eliya, Ceylon, dated 17 January 1951, NND.842430, RG 84, Box 1, File 310-South Asia, NA.

[61] Enclosure to Withers' Dacca despatch, 26 January 1951, NND.842430, RG 84, Box 42, File 350-Pak. Pol. 1951, NA.

[62] American consulate [Dacca] to the department of state, despatch no. 45, December 13, 1951, NND.842909, RG 59, Box 5559, 890D.19/2-2951, NA.

[63] Ibid.

with the revival of the language controversy. In one of those typical paradoxes of Pakistani politics, the die was cast by Nazimuddin himself. On 27 January 1952 while addressing an audience in Dacca, Nazimuddin declared that Urdu would be the national language of Pakistan. The screams of protest were promptly followed by an organised agitation led by the *Pakistan Observer*, various student groups, Suhrawardy's Awami League and other left-wing groups. On 21 February, students called a general strike in Dacca, defying a ban on public meetings and processions. In the ensuing pandemonium, the district magistrate took a fatal decision. He ordered the police to open fire; they did so mercilessly, killing four students and injuring many more. The army was called in. Students, university professors, Communist sympathisers, Awami League and Congress members of the assembly were rounded up. Although organised repression brought the situation under control, the central government was now universally detested. The local League tried washing its hands of the incident; within twenty-four hours of the killing it passed a resolution exhorting the constituent assembly to declare Bengali as a state language. But the provincial League had missed the bus; defections from its ranks assumed torrential proportions. Amin's margin of support in the assembly began 'melting away rapidly'; the embittered chief minister thought the centre had 'hung him out as a punching bag on the language issue'.[64] The lament was justified; the Dacca killings had sealed the League's fate in east Bengal.

SIND

In Sind, politics was a term dignifying power struggles between rival landlord factions. While true of all politics in Pakistan, the state of the art in Sind was in a class by itself. Those in the fray took their business seriously; here politics was a matter of life and death, literally and figuratively. But this is what made politics in Sind so exciting. Despite the trappings of parliamentary government, Sind remained the personal bailiwick of individuals belonging to landed families with genealogies predating the British. Since no one in Sind was ready to suffer the inconvenience of sharing power, the pretenders to the provincial throne had to be especially adept at jostling for position.

The most talented politician in the province was Mohammad Ayub Khuhro, a landlord from Larkana district, with a penchant for turning the roughest tumbles to his advantage. In February 1949, Khuhro had

[64] American consul general to the department of state, 1 March 1952, NND.842430, RG 84, Box 41, File 350-Pak. Pol. 1952, NA.

been booked under PRODA for corruption and maladministration. But within a year he had outwitted the court and was back on centre stage. With Khuhro in action, Sindhi politics moved at breath-taking pace. Yusuf Haroon, the chief minister, was the first victim. Khuhro, once again president of the Sind League, engineered a no-confidence motion against Haroon. The motion nearly succeeded since most of the assembly members were indebted to Khuhro – the uncrowned 'King of Sind'.[65] Ten days of 'devious manoeuvres' which, according to one observer, were almost 'comic had they not so tragically disclosed the corruption of Sind politics' gave the chief minister a temporary reprieve.[66] But only after he had agreed to let Khuhro choose three of the ministers in a reconstituted cabinet.[67]

With a commanding influence over the provincial ministry as well as the assembly and a suffocating hold over the local League, Khuhro 'completely dominate[d] Sind politics'.[68] This put paid to hopes of a genuine agrarian reform in the province. Before Khuhro's dramatic reentry, Haroon had been pressing for tenancy reforms. The stumbling-block was Mir Ghulam Ali Khan Talpur, the revenue minister, and 'an opponent of all land reform'[69]. But Haroon had Liaquat's backing; agrarian reforms were vital for the League's electoral prospects in the province. Parts of rural Sind were in the throes of an agrarian agitation organised by the Hari committee with tacit support from the Awami League and smaller left-wing groups. On 4 April, the provincial assembly passed a garbled resolution and proclaimed it as the Sind tenancy bill. Khuhro hurriedly pushed through an amendment postponing the operation of the act for a year. This was intended to give Sindhi landlords time to ensure that when the bill came into effect it would be minus the teeth the assembly had so grudgingly conceded. For instance, tenants in possession of land for over three years were to get occupancy rights. Yet there was nothing to prevent landlords from evicting tenants after the second year.[70] The Sind Hari committee naturally savaged the bill; it was irrelevant to the needs of the rural dispossessed. The landlords countered by unleashing a reign of terror. Larkana – Khuhro's domain – and Nawabshah were among the worst

[65] See Mahmood, *Pakistan: Muslim League Ka Dar-e-Hakumat*, 197.
[66] British high commissioner's opdom no. 2, part II, 7–20 January 1950, FO371/84198, PRO.
[67] Mahmood, *Pakistan:Muslim League Ka Dar-e-Hakumat*, 193–4.
[68] High commissioner's review of events, January–March 1950, FO371/84201, PRO.
[69] High commissioner's opdom no. 45, part II, 11–23 December 1949, FO371/84198, PRO.
[70] American embassy to the department of state, Karachi despatch no. 368, 5 April 1950, NND.842909, RG 59, Box 5549, NA.

affected areas. Private armies could perpetrate heinous crimes, including murder, secure in the knowledge of being protected if not rewarded for helping restore rural Sind to its traditional quiescence.[71] Moreover, where the landlords' mercenaries had failed to mop up the trouble, state authorities armed with the tenancy bill could now succeed. As in west Punjab, its provisions had actually legalised evictions by landlords. That the anti-reform lobby had won hands down was painfully evident.

In May 1950, Haroon resigned as chief minister. Qazi Fazlullah, Khuhro's henchman, formed the new cabinet. With the Sind ministry at his beck and call, Khuhro widened the base of his machinations. The centre was the obvious target; Khuhro was 'believed to have ambitions to enter the Central Government'.[72] And, while no one at the centre wanted to see him in their midst, it was dangerous to spurn Khuhro altogether. So he was given a seat on the Pakistan Muslim League's working committee; he lost no time meddling with its affairs. One of his principal preoccupations now was to settle scores with Abdus Sattar Pirzada, the Sindhi central minister for food.[73] Khuhro's incursions at the centre, though inconvenient, had to be tolerated. Although incorrigible, he was 'an essential and permanent cog in the Muslim League machine'. In the aftermath of the agrarian reform bill, G.M. Syed's Awami League and Hyder Bux Jatoi's Hari committee had intensified their rural campaigns. The central government was incapable of battling with these groups without the assistance of Khuhro's personal machine – the Sind provincial League. In the opinion of an astute observer, 'the administration and the M[uslim] L[eague] could not have a more efficient hatchet man than Mr. Khuhro'.[74] This may have been true in the short-term, but fanning Khuhro's ambitions amounted to eschewing any direct contact with the people of Sind. By March 1951, Khuhro had regained the office of chief minister. He immediately dismissed all speculations about his stance on agrarian reforms; the plight of the haris, he asserted, was a figment of journalistic imaginings.[75] Unfortu-

---

[71] *Nawa-i-Waqt*, 8 June 1950.

[72] Acting high commissioner to Attlee, review of events, April–June 1950, FO371/84202 PRO.

[73] The ostensible reason for Khuhro's tirades against Pirzada – a member of another important Sindhi landlord family – was that the central ministry of food and agriculture's wheat procurement policies were short-changing Sind's cultivators who had to sell their crop at low prices while middlemen made handsome profits. But no one was impressed to see Khuhro posing as the champion of the poor cultivators; his enmity with Pirzada was well known.

[74] Warwick Perkins [charge d'affaires, Karachi] to the department of state, 18 September 1950, NND.842430, RG 84, Box 7, File 350-Pak. Pol. 1950, NA.

[75] *Dawn*, 28–30 March 1951, cited in M. Rafique Afzal, *Political Parties in Pakistan: 1947–1958*, Islamabad 1976, 76.

nately for Khuhro, the governor of Sind, Justice Din Mohammad, was in sympathy with the supporters of agrarian reform. But Khuhro's skilful manipulations ensured that no steps were taken to improve upon, much less implement, the tenancy reform bill.

By December 1951, Khuhro was pitched against three members of his own cabinet – Ghulam Ali Talpur, Ghulam Nabi Pathan and his former aide, Qazi Fazlullah – who had Pirzada's backing at the centre. Half a dozen petitioners and some sixty charges under PRODA put Khuhro back into the dock, but not before his supporters had also booked the rebels.[76] The governor had no alternative except to demand the cabinet's resignation. A week of frantic activity saw the province lapsing into its worst political crisis ever. There were now two Sind Leagues, one loyal to Khuhro and the other to Talpur. On 29 December 1951, the province was placed under section 92a; the provincial assembly was dissolved and fresh elections scheduled. No one who had witnessed the political scene in Sind was minded to challenge the centre's intervention. But there were 'a great many...[who] thought that Nazimuddin, by hesitation and delay, was principally responsible for the disintegration of the Muslim League organisation in Sind' as well as the 'practical collapse of the provincial administration'.[77] These were serious charges, especially since the centre's clean up of Sindhi politics had left Khuhro in control of the dominant section of the provincial League.

There was an even darker side to the centre's mishandling of Sindhi affairs. It had three shades. First, the provincial governor had carried out a coup by capturing and resettling the pir of Pagara's Hur bandits, the most consistent offenders of the law in rural Sind. He had come to terms with Ali Mohammad Rashidi, an uncle of the seventh pir of Pagara. But Rashidi's group was out of favour with the central government. Another reason for the centre's displeasure with Din Mohammad were his 'close relations' with the leaders of the Hari committee which was seen to have reduced the League's prestige, if that was possible. Provincial elections were on the anvil; Karachi concluded that under the existing governor they would be 'too free'.[78] Finally, the governor had publicly accused the Sind League for the food shortage; its leading lights, he disclosed, were among the biggest hoarders of grain.[79] Unable to go along with these gubernatorial assessments, the centre

---

[76] Ibid., 77 and Mahmood, *Pakistan: Muslim League Ka Dar-e-Hakumat*, 198–9.

[77] American embassy [Karachi] to the department of state, despatch no.1175, 12 March 1952, NND.842430, RG 84, Box 41, File 350-Pak. Pol. 1951-June 1952, NA.

[78] Withers to the department of state, despatch no. 519, 20 November 1952, NND.842430, RG 84, Box 42, File 350-Pak. Pol. July–December 1952, NA.

[79] Afzal, *Political Parties in Pakistan*, 78.

asked for his resignation. He complied. And so the province was left to the tender mercies of a gang of wily men who had reduced Sindhi politics to a mess of unspeakable mixtures.

NORTH WEST FRONTIER PROVINCE

In 1947 the incorporation of the North West Frontier Province and the adjoining tribal areas posed formidable problems for the central government. Yet within a matter of years Khan Abdul Qayum Khan's ruthless dictatorship had refashioned the NWFP into the most orderly of the Pakistan provinces.[80] By suppressing political opposition and establishing his sway over the provincial League, Qayum had carved a comfortable niche for himself in Frontier affairs. His draconian rule had the centre's sanction for as long as it took to wean Pathans away from the Congress. But Qayum's very success in burying the Congress in the Frontier became something of a threat to the central government. The paradox illuminates one of the finer points in the relationship between the provinces and the centre. Karachi's strength *vis-à-vis* the constituent units depended upon its playing the role of broker among warring provincial factions. But in the NWFP the chief minister had gagged all opposition and Karachi, if not irrelevant, was merely a junior partner in the enterprise that determined the highs and lows in Pathan politics.

By 1950, Qayum had deployed the public safety act to ban as many as twenty organisations hostile to his government.[81] A believer of the carrot quite as much as the stick, Qayum introduced tenancy reforms which though imperfect were by all accounts the closest a provincial government came to restructuring agrarian society. It was as early as April 1949 that the broad provisions of the NWFP tenancy act were made public. It aimed at abolishing all *jagirs* except those given to religious institutions and military personnel; some tenants were to have ownership rights while others were given the option of buying the land within a prescribed period of time.[82] A more innovative measure, and evidence of Qayum's skills as a political operator, was the decision to

[80] By deciding not to extend its writ over the tribal areas and by continuing with the colonial policy of paying annual subsidies to the *sardars* the central government was able to secure the implicit, if not the explicit, allegiance of the tribesmen.

[81] *CAD*, I, no. 7, 27 March 1951, 572–3.

[82] *Nawa-i-Waqt*, 25 April 1949 and *Khyber Mail* (Peshawar), 20 May 1949. But as usual, it took an appreciable length of time before the legislation could begin to have the desired effects. In January 1950, the provincial assembly passed the legislation, pending the governor-general's approval. Bureaucratic delays ensured that the NWFP tenancy act (1950) was not implemented until January 1951 and even then there were various lacunas that remained to be either filled or clarified. (See Henry W. Spielman [agricultural attache] to the department of state, Karachi despatch no. 1172, 14 February 1951, NND.842909, RG 59, Box 5549, 890D.16/2- 1451, NA.)

takeover the administration of *Waqf* properties. These were charitable trusts under the management of religious leaders – namely *imams* or *khatibs* – and were supposedly run in accordance with Islamic tenets. But they were notorious for maladministration and misuse of funds. One way to put the fear of Allah in the hearts and minds of the spiritual leaders was to uphold the supremacy of temporal authority. Qayum created a provincial *Waqf* department and placed the *imams* and *khatibs* on the government's payroll.[83] A theological college was established and in future its graduates alone could qualify for appointment by the government.[84] So at a stroke of the pen Qayum had brought institutionalised religion under his control; it was an impeccable *tour d'force*.

But as his opponents correctly pointed out, Qayum's policies were intended to consolidate his personal position, not that of the League. In the Frontier, it was Qayum who was popular; the League as ever was irrelevant. By building roads, establishing schools and launching a new university in Peshawar, by pumping funds into hydro-electric works and the Mardan sugar mills, Qayum had 'won the confidence of the middle-class and the peasantry'. Yet curiously enough, the League was 'encountering a strong undercurrent of criticism', much of it directed against the central government. It was not uncommon to hear social circles in Peshawar voice the opinion that Qayum was the best candidate for the job of prime minister at the centre.[85]

This was why other hopefuls for the office wanted to prick Qayum's bubble. By April 1951, he was facing a determined challenge from within the League. The dissidents, bigger landlords in the main, were led by Khan Mohammad Ibrahim of Jhagra – a member of the central League's working committee as well as the secretary of the central League parliamentary board – whose main bases of support were in the districts of Bannu and Kohat. Jhagra had the backing of another Pathan of national standing – Yusuf Khattak, the general secretary of the Pakistan Muslim League. So the possibility of collusion by the central government in unsettling Qayum cannot be ruled out. Yet Karachi had to make the difficult choice of openly backing the opponents of a man

[83] The NWFP charitable institutions act was criticised profusely by the Punjab press. In the cynical view of the *Civil and Military Gazette* (16 May 1950) an officially appointed *imam* would now have even less of a reason 'to conform to Islamic standards'; his 'main concern...[would] be to keep his pay-master in good humour'. (See Warren to the department of state, despatch no. 193, 27 July 1950, NND.842909, RG 59, Box 5555, 890D.413/7-2750, NA.)

[84] John W. Bowling to the department of state, Karachi despatch, Z/1836, 14 June 1951, NND.842909, RG 59, Box 4145, 790D.00/1-2251, NA.

[85] Report by George J. Candreva [American cultural officer], NND.842430, RG 84, Box 7, File 350-Pak. Pol. 1950, NA.

whom it would have liked to cut down to size but who had the leading edge in provincial politics. Liaquat at least avoided an open breach with Qayum.[86] But the unity of the Frontier League, already strained by defections of prominent landlords opposed to agrarian reforms and expulsions engineered by Qayum himself, had been badly damaged. There was considerable muscle flexing between the Qayum and Jhagra factions. At Khattak's behest, the Pakistan Muslim League was firmly behind Jhagra and his conservative landlord group even though officially, if not constitutionally, they had been expelled from the provincial League. As the run-up to elections for the provincial assembly revealed more forcefully, the NWFP was in the unique position of witnessing an electoral battle between the local and the central Leagues.

Scheduled for November 1951, the elections were held on the basis of adult franchise. An estimated 47 per cent of the total population in the province made the electoral rolls.[87] The contest for the eighty-five assembly seats was between the League, its dissidents, the Jinnah Awami League[88] and a string of independents. A seven-member provincial parliamentary board headed by Qayum reviewed 400 applications for League tickets. Of the eighty-four selected, none belonged to the Jhagra faction. Cries of foul play and formal appeals to the central parliamentary board led to the resurrection of eighteen candidates, including Jhagra.[89] It was Qayum's turn to carp and complain. He surrendered the League tickets to Jhagra and his men, but surreptitiously began plotting their defeat. He was in a position to do so. Although the provincial assembly had been dissolved in the spring of 1951, Qayum had contrived a way to remain in office. With the provincial government machinery at his disposal, he could ignore the party high command's decisions. Men loyal to Qayum were set up to fight as independents against Jhagra and his supporters. Jhagra and Khattak, sensing doom, withdrew from the elections in a huff; so did 112 other opposition candidates, including the president of the local Jinnah Awami League, the pir of Manki Sharif.[90]

---

[86] In April 1951, Jhagra opposed Qayum's candidacy for the provincial League president. After failing to work out a compromise, Liaquat wisely chose to back the old horse. And so Qayum romped home by eighteen more votes than Jhagra. (See Afzal, *Political Parties in Pakistan*, 70–1 and Mahmood, *Pakistan:Muslim League Ka Dar-e-Hakumat*, 215–18.)

[87] *Dawn*, 9 November 1951.

[88] With the understandable exception of Qayum and his minister, Mian Jaffar Shah, the most prominent Leaguers from the preindependence days were in the Jinnah Awami League – for instance, the pir of Manki Sharif, the pir of Zakori Sharif, Samin Jan and Khan Bakhat Jamal.

[89] *Dawn*, 6 December 1951.

[90] Afzal, *Political Parties in Pakistan*, 72.

Having restricted the opposition to the sidelines, Qayum had little difficulty in bulldozing the Frontier according to his design.

The provincial League or, more accurately, the Qayum League won sixty-seven of the eighty-five seats. Thirteen independents, including the nine whom Qayum had supported in the elections, and the solitary non-Muslim closed ranks with the League. A band of four waving the Jinnah Awami League's flag was all the opposition Qayum had to face in the assembly.[91] On 14 December 1951 he was unanimously elected leader of the League's parliamentary party. With a five-member provincial cabinet in his pocket, Qayum was perfectly equipped to wipe out any remnants of opposition to his brand of politics in the Frontier. He had also checked the centre. The election results had loudly demonstrated the political bankruptcy of tactics aimed at undermining the frontier prince. Like it or not, Karachi had to do a deal with Qayum. Intra-provincial rivalries – between the NWFP and the Punjab on the one hand and Bengal and the Punjab on the other – were powerful reasons for Qayum and Nazimuddin to resist doing each other down. Yet personal understandings based on exploiting provincial jealousies were not a good omen for the stability of the state.

BALUCHISTAN

Unlike the other provinces Baluchistan was administered directly by the central government. Instead of an elected executive responsible to a provincial assembly, an advisory council consisting of fifteen – ten Leaguers and five tribal *sardars* – was nominated by the governor-general. A special agent to the governor-general in turn kept watch and ward over its activities. Yet, despite these differences, politics in Baluchistan were not distinctive from those in the rest of the country. A survey of the political scene in Baluchistan explodes any notion of factionalism being a feature peculiar to full responsible government.

The struggle for power was between the local League and the Baluchistan Tribal Federation. The League's influence in the province was strictly limited to the urban centres, Quetta in particular. The Tribal Federation, led by Sardar Mohammad Khan Jogezai, claimed to represent 90 per cent of Baluchistan's population. Yet the logic of controlled politics had given the League a disproportionate represent-ation on the advisory council. The chief advisor to the governor-general was Qazi Mohammad Isa who was also the president of the provincial League. Described as 'a bumptious young demagogue', Isa claimed to

[91] Ibid.

be committed to drastically revising the 'barbarous' customary tribal laws.[92] This was not the best way of endearing himself or his advisory council to the tribal leaders. With the advisory council the butt of criticism and the local Leaguers making a mockery of party discipline, the central government was horrified to find that everyone in Baluchistan favoured full autonomy for the province. In November 1951, the constituent assembly's special committee on Baluchistan made the same recommendation.[93] But no one, least of all an overworked prime minister, was sure how to go about bringing Baluchistan on par with the other provinces in the federation. So the report was shelved. It was more difficult to ignore the power struggles within the Baluchistan League. Even the centre's own inspection committee reported that the League had no standing whatsoever in Baluchistan. In February 1952, without consulting his provincial lieutenants, Nazimuddin dissolved the Baluchistan League. A three member *ad hoc* committee was left to ponder over how to establish the League in a province whose demands for autonomy were as sophisticated as its politics were unstructured.[94]

THE BALANCE SHEET

Many of the strains ruffling the political surface during Nazimuddin's eighteen months in office are traceable to the initial years of constructing the state. But with few exceptions the adverse effects of policies formulated in a period of unremitting duress were magnified under the new government. Its record in the provinces was remarkably undistinguished. The balance sheet would be incomplete without assessing the impact provincial politics had on the centre, and on the Pakistan Muslim League in particular. After all, without a political organisation providing comparable institutional support such as was available to the other contenders for power at the centre, politicians were unlikely to withstand a pincer movement by bureaucrats and generals.

Nazimuddin did try riveting control over the Pakistan Muslim League. In November 1951, he was elected president, a position he retained the following year when the League's constitution was amended to give greater representation to east Bengal. This belated attempt to appease the eastern wing was unpopular with Leaguers in the western wing. Sindhi and Baluchi representation in the League council

---

[92] British high commissioner's opdom no. 24, part II, 10–17 June 1949, L/WS/1/1600, PRO.

[93] *Dawn*, 18 November 1951; for full text of the *Report of the Committee on Constitutional and Administrative Reforms in Baluchistan* see *CAD*, I, 1951.

[94] Mahmood, *Pakistan: Muslim League Ka Dar-e-Hakumat*, 262–3.

was reduced.[95] The Punjabis too were put off; they accepted the new arrangements only after striking a bargain with their Bengali rivals – a Punjabi was slotted in as general secretary for three years since another amendment extended the tenure of office bearers. Yusuf Haroon was elected vice-president, but soon fell out with Nazimuddin. With a fragile unity at the top and multiple disunities at the base, the Pakistan Muslim League was not the politicians' best bet against bureaucrats and generals.

There were no official estimates of its membership.[96] Sporadic recruitment drives did result in the distribution of membership forms. But these were bought up by politicians in the heat of a battle for some office or the other. Except for election campaigns there was no active participation by the members; internal party elections were rare and mainly an occasion to settle old scores or to find grounds for new quarrels. To avoid displaying the tears in its seams, the high command wisely avoided meetings of the Muslim League convention – the largest representative body consisting of members of the central and the provincial League councils.

A party which was more a source of embarrassment than a solid pillar of support was better neglected than nurtured, or so it seemed. Liaquat who had better political sense than Nazimuddin at least dabbled with the League's organisational aspects. Apart from making ceremonial appearances or acting judge in the interminable party squabbles, the new prime minister made no pretence of being a machine politician. He was not a domineering personality or an orator; he was certainly not a political charmer or even a good administrator. Resting in a luxury launcher near the Sundarbans is what he was qualified to do best. Consequently, the bureaucrats were running the country in everyway

---

[95] Between 11–13 October 1952, the All-Pakistan Muslim League held its annual meeting in Dacca – a less than subtle attempt to pacify Bengali opinion in the aftermath of the language riots. The principle of parity was accepted and the party constitution amended. Since it was not advisable to further risk alienating the western wing, the membership of the League council was increased by nearly 33 per cent, from 440 to a grand total of 654. The allocation of seats was:

East Bengal	327	Punjab		184
NWFP and tribal areas	58	Baluchistan		11
Sind and Khairpur	45	Bahawalpur		18
Karachi	11		TOTAL	654

[96] Paradoxically enough, it was the American embassy which came up with an estimate of the Muslim League membership: Karachi – 150,000; NWFP – 400,000; Punjab – 4,000,000; East Bengal – 2,500,000; Sind – 600,000; Baluchistan – 200,000; Bahawalpur and other states – 200,000. (American embassy [Karachi], despatch no. 489, 24 October 1951, NND.842905, RG 59, Box 4145, 790D.00/1-2251, NA) These figures, however, overstate the reality.

except in name. But, since even Nazimuddin was not above wanting to impress his rights as chief political patron, clashes between his favoured few and the administrative services were all too frequent. The net result was a sharper decline on almost every front just when the national economy was faltering dangerously and the authority of the state was under challenge from the religious ideologues.

The food shortage in itself would have been sufficient to rock the central government. By the end of the summer in 1952, an unusually dry monsoon season followed by India's refusal to part with scarce river water, not to mention the cussed resistance of landlords in western Punjab, Sind and the NWFP to sell grain in the open market, had left the Pakistan government with a food problem of mammoth proportions. Food imports were unavoidable; an excruciating burden for a central government which had allocated 50 per cent of its revenue expenditure in FY 1952-53 to the defence services. The choice between feeding the people and steeling the army could not have presented itself at a more inauspicious moment.

Since the Korean war boom turned to bust export earnings from jute and cotton had fallen below the threshold of safety. In June 1952, officials in the ministries of finance and commerce, panic-stricken upon discovering the level of Pakistan's foreign exchange reserves, had to concede that a liberal import policy was an anomaly for a country with an adverse balance of payments. By November 1952, all imports became subject to licencing. But, while this halted the run on the foreign exchange reserves, it also saw a dramatic drop in the central government's revenue receipts already hard hit by cuts in export duties on cotton and jute. A wheat loan of $15 million from the United States and a series of deals with the socialist bloc pulled Pakistan through to the end of 1952. But the shortage for 1953 had still to be reckoned with. The serious dip in the foreign exchange reserves[97] – there were some £13 million remaining in the blocked sterling account[98] – and continued difficulties with the balance of payments placed the central government on the horns of a dilemma. There was talk of a 'warlike' drive against landlords hoarding grain in west Pakistan[99] and impassioned campaigns urging people to grow more food. Yet as Karachi knew all too

---

[97] Foreign exchange reserves dropped from Rs. 151.3 crores in mid-1951 to Rs. 60.6 crores at the end of 1952. *Economy of Pakistan: 1948–68*, 167.

[98] Memorandum of conversation between Mumtaz Hassan, secretary of finance, and John N. Plakies on 27 October 1952; enclosed in Karachi despatch no. 497, 13 November 1952, NND.842909, RG 59, Box 5548, 890D. 10/11-1352, NA.

[99] See American consul general [Lahore] to the department of state, 11 June 1952, NND.842909, RG, Box 5545, 890D.03/6-1152, NA.

well the only real alternative to a political explosion was to make urgent pleas to Washington for an outright wheat grant.

Bouts of generosity from a country which was coming to define its national security interests in the broadest of terms were not unusual. But Washington had no reason to beef up a central government headed by a politician who apart from being pro-British was thought to be an 'unimaginative' man in a job that was simply 'too big for him'. It was the considered view of the American embassy in Karachi that, unless someone or something could ease its manifold crises, there was 'no prospect' of Pakistan being 'drawn into closer formal relationships with the Western powers'. A weak ministry was unlikely to do anything that might 'stir up the "anti-imperialistic" sentiment which in different ways and degrees, consciously or unconsciously, still strongly influence[d] the thinking of most Pakistanis'.[100] So the American response to Pakistan's appeals for a one million ton wheat grant could only be one of extreme caution. To sell such a package to Congress and American public opinion the state department would have to argue the Pakistani case with conviction which, until circumstances changed, it was not minded to do. Washington could see that Pakistan's domestic troubles would eventually force it into compromises in the international arena. As for the anti-imperialist sentiments in Pakistan, it was better to interpret them as directed at Britain rather than the United States. With a thinly veiled Anglo-American rivalry providing the external stimulus to its delicately poised internal political balance, Pakistan moved towards forging its 'special relationship' with Washington. Yet, without accounting for the subtle manoeuvres which dimmed Britain's resolve to resist American pressures, not to mention the matching shifts in its institutional balance of power, it is not possible to grasp the implications of the relationship for Pakistan, both in the short and the long-term.

Encouraged by the Pakistani military high command's enthusiasm about joining the Middle East defence organisation, the Americans had kept up pressure on London, reminding it of its responsibilities in South Asia and chiding it for failing to discharge them. By early 1952, the state department had come to the conclusion that 'it was high time' for Britain to review its policy in the region which in its view was 'too rigidly conditioned by preoccupation with India to allow other considerations to have their proper weight'. In short, London should stop 'putting the brakes on a constructive policy towards Pakistan'.[101] No one at the

---

[100] Perkins to the department of state, Karachi despatch no. 334, 27 September 1952, NND.842430, RG 84, Box 42, File 350-Pak. Pol. July-December 1952, NA.

[101] Burrows [British embassy, Washington] to J.D. Murray [FO], 2 February 1952, DO35/3008, PRO.

foreign office was impressed by the American assessment; 'impatience at this juncture about Pakistan and the Middle East seem[ed]...ill-conceived and potentially dangerous'.[102] Reports from Karachi, however, were reassuring for the Americans. In April 1952, a 'secret meeting of high government officials' quickly came to the conclusion that Pakistan was in a 'desperate position' and should 'declare itself openly for the United States'; it was the only 'hope' for a 'young nation'. Zafrullah, Chaudhri Mohammad Ali, Nishtar and I.H. Qureshi were thought to favour a change in foreign policy. Most important of all, the governor-general, 'the strongest man in Pakistan' wanted closer ties with Washington.[103] Nazimuddin was the stick in the mud. Yet his pro-British leanings were in contrast to popular demands to sever Pakistan's links with the commonwealth. Mian Iftikharuddin, the most vocal and consistent critic of the government in the national legislature, expressed these feelings succinctly; before partition the central government was in Delhi, now 'the Central Government is in London, this Government in Karachi is really a Provincial Government and the Provinces have assumed the status of District Boards'.[104] Missing the deeper meaning in these assertions. Washington thought Pakistanis were ready to make a switch in the international arena to rid themselves of an abject dependence on London.

But the shift in Pakistan's foreign policy owed nothing to popular opinion. Quite the opposite. Relentless demands for military equipment by the defence establishment generated pressures for warmer relations with the United States; financial stringency and a deepening food crisis made them irresistible. By the summer of 1952, Pakistan's representatives in Washington were holding the military's shopping lists in one hand and the begging bowl in the other. American officials were startled to discover that Pakistan was proposing to spend $45 million on armaments over three years while its representatives were lobbying for a wheat grant.[105] The surprise gave way to horror when Pakistani representatives glibly asked for a long-term military credit from the American government. The British, more accustomed to the negotiating style of Pakistan's military missions, had no cause for surprise. Outlandish requests for arms and ammunition were not backed up by firm orders; explorations on availability of supplies were followed by

---

[102] Murray to Burrows, 28 February 1952, ibid.

[103] Memorandum of conversation between Fareed S. Jafri[editor of the *Civil and Military Gazette*] and Hugh Crumpler, 1 April 1952, NND, 842430, RG 84, Box 12, File 320-Pak. Pol. 1952, NA.

[104] *CAD*, I, no. 4, 19 March 1952, 228.

[105] British embassy [Washington] to the foreign office, telegram no. 1443, 28 July 1952, DEFE7/152, PRO.

enquiries about credit. Long before the Americans, the British concluded that Pakistan was being 'driven by economic pressures to cut rearmament...programmes'.[106] London derided Pakistani threats to buy in the American market. One treasury official barely disguised his delight at showing up the almost childlike quality of the blackmail:

> whereas Pakistan until recently threatened that she would go into the dollar market unless she got her own terms from us, she is hardly able to use this threat today; her No. 1 Sterling Account has been run down to a bare cover for existing commitments.[107]

Although at one with the Americans on the imperative of keeping the 'Pakistani armed forces...in good heart',[108] the British had the 'greatest objection to giving credit terms to Pakistan'.[109] So there was no prospect of either Washington or London modifying its policy of not offering arms on credit. This is why army headquarters in Rawalpindi had to push Karachi to take a firm decision to join the Middle East defence command; it was now the only hope of making good Pakistan's military requirements. Since the British were not persuaded by Pakistan's sincerity to help the Western allies defend the Middle East, Karachi had to be pressed into contriving a tilt towards the seemingly more gullible Americans.

It was difficult for Nazimuddin and his few remaining allies at the centre to resist being dictated to by army headquarters while also trying to grapple with a host of economic and political problems. Senior bureaucrats who ought to have been concentrating their minds on ways to solve the problems agreed whole-heartedly with the generals' line: Pakistan had to choose between sinking or swimming in the international arena. Mounting pressure for a shift on the foreign policy front within the state apparatus is an important clue to why Karachi failed even to do its inefficient best to alleviate the various crises facing the country. No government, weak or strong, can be expected to tackle problems without a modicum of cooperation from the administrative services. But the prime minister was officiating over a cabinet fiercely divided on external as well as internal issues. These disagreements were reproduced in the administrative realm and, in due course, very nearly

---

[106] British high commissioner to CRO, 13 September 1952, ibid.

[107] I.P. Bancroft [treasury] to M. Gresswell [defence], 11 February 1953, FO371/106935, PRO.

[108] Foreign office to British embassy [Washington], telegram no. 3419, 22 August 1952, DEFE7/152, PRO.

[109] At a time when the British economy was being stretched to the limits in order to finance the rearmament programme, it was indeed 'odd' to take on 'the further burden of pre-financing Pakistan's defence preparations'. (Bancroft to Gresswell, 11 February 1953, FO371/106935, PRO.)

succeeded in bringing about a governmental paralysis. A deft handling of the political, if not the economic, problems might conceivably have afforded the prime minister an opportunity to take the sting out of the revolt by the senior echelons of the administrative and military services. But his political ineptitude, his inimitable talent for making wrong decisions at critical moments, and the lack of an organised party which could act as a countervailing influence to the ambitions of bureaucrats and generals proved to be major handicaps. So the duel to determine Pakistan's external policy and, by the way, its internal balance of power was fought out between two sides of strikingly unequal qualifications.

If the food shortage and the financial crisis eroded whatever credibility he could claim to possess, Nazimuddin's fatal stumble was on an issue dearest to his heart – the role of Islam in the state. It raised the thorny question of the powers to be assigned to the religious guardians in the constitution. Whereas earlier the matter had been carefully swept under the carpet, the anti-Ahmediya agitation and the prime minister's predilections had given it a potent new direction. Any constitutional formula that could satisfy the religious leaders would put at risk the plans which the bureaucratic-military combine was charting out for Pakistan's future. Senior civil and military officials, with their secular orientation, had a fundamental aversion to cutting in the most retrograde section of society into the power structure; it was difficult enough trying to minimise the politicians' role. But the prime minister in one of his typically wrong-headed judgements – the religious appeal was not nearly as pervasive as it appeared to be – thought his chance of surviving the storm was to ride the Islamic tiger. He prevailed upon the basic principles committee to welcome in its midst a team of ulema, the Talimaat Islami [Islami studies] board, who would advise and guide it on religious matters. He also began toying with the idea of giving in to the demands of the anti-Ahmediya campaigners, a line of thinking which invited a strong rebuke from the governor-general indignant about the prime minister's reluctance to openly support Zafrullah.[110]

With the prime minister at blows with his cabinet associates on ideological issues it is hardly surprising that the administration was hamstrung by the anti-Ahmediya controversy. Elated by their apparent hold over the populace, to say nothing of the psychological advantage they gained from the tacit support of Daultana's ministry in the Punjab, the religious ideologues were fighting a running battle with the central

---

[110] Laithwaite to Leisching, 9 August 1952, DO35/3185, PRO. Zafrullah was understandably disappointed about the failure of his cabinet colleagues to issue a public condemnation of the attacks against his person and community. (See Laithwaite's note, 23 July 1952, ibid.)

government. Statements by some central ministers that Pakistan would wobble under 'the most wild and pernicious tyranny' if a company of narrow-minded religious bigots were allowed to capture political power and that 'we will never allow it to happen' suggests that the campaign had begun to bite.[111] Towards the end of December 1952, the appearance of the basic principles committee's report, better known as the 'Nazimuddin report', left the guardians with a considerable say in the affairs of government. A board of five ulema was to advise the head of state whether or not any legislation was repugnant to Islam; the provision practically amounted to creating a third legislature in a political system that had yet to come to grips with the concept of an upper and a lower house. The concession to the ulemas brought immediate charges of surrender to mullahism; others interpreted the report as a 'curiously anachronistic and ill-conceived document' and as evidence of the political leaders' willingness to 'mortgage the future of th[e] nation'.[112] The religious leaders for their part were unhappy at being restricted to the position of advisers; they wanted the quintet of Islamic sages to help the supreme court establish the religious orthodoxy of all legislation.[113]

Having fallen off the tiger, Nazimuddin now faced the prospect of being torn to pieces by provincial reactions to the BPC report. Only sixteen of the twenty-nine original members of the committee had signed the final report. The principle of parity between the two wings had been accepted, albeit through a circuitous method. In the upper house, nine separate units represented west Pakistan; in the lower house – which had the real authority – east Pakistan had a majority; parity between the two wings was possible only when the two houses met jointly.[114] So the report, though it did not address the issue of the national language, was the central government's attempt to make amends with east Bengal. Naturally enough, the report was 'not popular in the Punjab'; the Punjabis were worried that the Bengali-Pathan alliance would result

---

[111] This was the opinion of Dr Mahmud Hussain, the minister for Kashmir affairs. (Cited in British high commissioner's opdom no. 24, part II, 25 November-8 December 1952, DO35/5283, PRO.)

[112] *Dawn*, cited in British high commissioner's opdom no. 25, part I, 9–22 December 1952, ibid.

[113] In January 1953, the ulema met for ten days to study the BPC's report. The exercise left them exhausted and divided; their suggestions elicited thunderous criticism and it was apparent that in insisting on a bigger slice of the pie they had weakened their own position. (British high commissioner's opdom no. 3, part II, 20 January–2 February 1953, ibid.)

[114] Talukder Maniruzzaman, *The Politics of Development: the Case of Pakistan, 1947–1958*, Dacca 1971, 45–6.

in their being denied 'a fair share of control of the country'.[115] Daultana had signed the report to register his preference for a unitary instead of a federal form of government. Echoing his stance, the Punjab Muslim League called for a postponement of all discussion on the BPC's report.[116] By contrast, the Bengali reaction was generally favourable; in the NWFP the entire cabinet went off on tour to apprise the people of the significance of the proposed constitution – Qayum praised his Bengali allies for their spirit of 'sacrifice and magnanimity in accepting less than...[their] entitlement'.[117] The Sindhis and Baluchis shared some of the Punjabi fears, but were categorically opposed to the idea of a unitary government. Punjabi opposition, however, set the stage for another prolonged constitutional stalemate. This was precisely what the bureaucratic-military axis had wanted and just about the last thing Nazimuddin needed.

A federal constitution with a Bengali majority in the lower house was anathema to the civil bureaucracy and the defence establishment, and not simply because a majority of them belonged to the Punjab. Bureaucrats and generals were by no means battling to save the Punjabi politicians from the Bengali-Pathan axis. On the contrary; politicians, irrespective of their provincial affiliations, were seen to be a danger to the larger imperative of streamlining the state and inserting it into the international system. So it was not provincial but institutional interests that demanded a unitary instead of a federal form of government. The refusal by senior bureaucrats and military officers to accept the implications of a Bengali majority had placed state-building on a collision course with the political process.

One day, after the appearance of the BPC report, general Ayub told the American consul general in Lahore that, while there was no question of the military taking over the government, 'the Pakistan Army ...[would] not allow the political leaders' or the people of Pakistan to 'get out of hand'. Loudly hinting that scrounging the globe for equipment was not his idea of military professionalism, Ayub confessed that protecting the country from internal catastrophes and external threats was 'a large responsibility' for the army which, he was happy to report, was 'friendly to the United States'. He had told 'leading politicians' that they had to 'make up their minds to go *whole-heartedly with the West*'. So long as Pakistan had been in a 'strong financial

---

[115] British high commissioner's opdom no. 1, part I, 23 December 1952–5 January 1953, DO35/5283, PRO.

[116] Maniruzzaman, *The Politics of Development*, 46.

[117] Cited in British high commissioner's opdom no. 1, part I, 23 December 1952–5 January 1953, DO35/5283, PRO.

position' the 'political leaders...wanted to stay neutral'. But financial stringencies were forcing them to 'realize the position of the country'.[118] The commander-in-chief's opinions were endorsed by the acting foreign secretary, Akhtar Hussain. Pakistan would 'jump at [the] chance' of joining the Middle East defence organisation since it would help the government 'attract support [from] reactionary religious elements'. His 'only sour note' was the doubt about what the central government under Nazimuddin would do; it so rarely 'kn[ew] the score'. But he predicted that the influence of the foreign office and ministry of defence 'would be decisive'.[119] As the high commissioner confirmed, there was a 'rapidly growing dissatisfaction with and disillusionment in the present Government' among Pakistanis of practically 'all professions'. Public opinion in general was 'clearly weary of shilly-shallying and indecision, and would welcome a strong hand and a unified Cabinet'. For the time being, however, the internecine warfare in the central cabinet together with the bickerings of the administrative and defence services had left the people 'thoroughly unsettled'; no one was quite sure where they were 'going or why'.[120]

Things were moving precisely the way the Americans had hoped and expected they would. The American embassy in Karachi had taken on the appearance of the central secretariat; 'several...officials and in-fluential non-officials' were seeking interviews, expressing fears about the weaknesses of the central government and arguing 'without exception' that Pakistan's entry into the Middle East defence organis-ation was the 'one method of reestablishing...[the] dwindling influence...[of the] Gov[ernment]'.[121] Those maintaining this view included Iskander Mirza, Akhtar Hussain, Amjad Ali, Yusuf Haroon and Chaudhri Salahuddin.[122] Army officers with 'personal connections in high defense circles' had taken an 'identical line'.[123] Excited by the

---

[118] Memorandum of conversation between general Ayub and Raleigh A. Gibson [American consul general, Lahore], despatch no. 105, 23 December 1952, NND.842430, RG 84, Box 42, File 350-Pak. Pol. July–December 1952, NA.

[119] John K. Emmerson [American embassy, Karachi] to the secretary of state, telegram no. 941, 22 December 1952, NND.842430, RG 84, Box 12, File 320-Pak-Egypt, NA.

[120] British high commissioner's opdom no. 3, part I, 20 January-2 February 1953, DO35/5283, PRO.

[121] Emmerson to the secretary of state, telegram no. 1207, 11 February 1953, NND.842430, RG 84, Box 42, File 350-Pak. Pol. General Affairs 1953, NA.

[122] Amjad Ali, occasionally in the role of the roving ambassador, was a member of an influential Punjabi industrialist family while Haroon hailed from one of the richest Memon business families in Karachi – the alliance between big business and the bureaucratic-military axis was already well-established. Salahuddin was the general secretary of the Pakistan Muslim League.

[123] Emmerson to the secretary of state telegram no. 1207, 11 February 1953, NND.842430, RG 84, Box 42, File 350-Pak. Pol.General Affairs 1953, NA.

ferment in government circles, the American embassy urged Washington to immediately approach Karachi on the question of Middle Eastern defence. It would be 'unfortunate' to leave the initiative to Britain; the Pakistanis 'resented [the] UK carrying [the] ball on such matters' and were 'exhibiting [the] friendliest [of] feelings'.[124] According to Akhtar Hussain, there was 'damn all' left in the Pakistan treasury. The acting foreign secretary, whose opinion extended 'throughout civil servants and defense officials both civilian and military', revealed that the 'leaders of Pakistan were on the verge of openly aligning themselves with the West' and piously hoped that American 'guidance' would be forthcoming.[125]

The guidance, if given, could only have been an unequivocal one. There was no doubt that a change at the centre was a prerequisite; a government pulling in different directions could not expect anyone, least of all Washington, to treat its offer of military support seriously. Having contributed in no uncertain a manner to the central government's lack of credibility in American eyes, the bureaucratic-military axis had now to consider ways of restoring confidence in the Pakistan government. In early March 1953, the eruption of anti-Ahmediya riots in the Punjab provided an opening. On 6 March, after failing to get sanction from Karachi, general Azam, the area commander, had 'taken over ...[apparently] entirely on his own', imposing martial law in Lahore and ensuring the dismissal of Daultana's ministry.[126] Ayub's men had proven true to his words – the army would not let politicians or religious ideologues turn the country over to anarchy. The message to Washington was more than implicit; the army was Pakistan's main, perhaps the only, hope. It had to be strengthened; left to unruly politicians Pakistan would crumble in no time. The deputy commander-in-chief of the Pakistan army, lieutenant general Nazir Ali, confessed that he was 'more worried... over the action of politicians than he was of the Indian army'. The view was parroted by Americans stationed in Pakistan; the food shortage was 'a good thing' since it made it 'more difficult for political leaders to arouse the public on the Kashmir problem'. But the people of Pakistan were extremely 'volatile' and unpredictable, 'if led by political leaders' they could 'change the picture and bring up problems'.[127] Officials at the state department took serious

[124] Ibid.
[125] Memorandum of conversation between Emmerson and Akhtar Hussain, 14 February 1953, and Emmerson to the secretary of state, telegram no. 1207, 11 February 1953, ibid.
[126] British high commissioner to the CRO, telegram no. 417, 7 March 1953, DO35/5326, PRO.
[127] Gibson to the department of state, Lahore despatch no. 28, 29 August 1952, NND.842430, RG 84, Box 4, File 320-Pak-India, NA.

note of these insights; they were familiar with Hobbes' *Leviathan* and
had been monitoring the Pakistani variant of the state of nature with
disturbed curiosity.

The central government's budget for 1953-4 aimed at alarming them
further still. It had been prepared by a 'very few men, lacking either the
bureaucratic or statistical support necessary to produce a finished
job'.[128] For the first time since the creation of the state the outlay for
defence had been slashed by one-third; but army headquarters had
already requested a supplementary appropriation following the imposition of martial law in Lahore. The government made a big play of its
commitment to economic development; yet allocations to ministries
most concerned with development – namely those of industries and
agriculture – had been cut by 25 per cent to 30 per cent. The ministry of
the interior, headed by the ubiquitous Mushtaq Gurmani, escaped the
austerity measures[129] since the new fiscal year was expected to witness
more, not less, political turmoil. Allowing for periodic adjustments, the
budgetary prescriptions were likely to result in a much lower level of
imports – and a sharp increase in prices of consumer goods[130] – higher
taxes, unemployment and a decrease in the standard of living. Interestingly enough, the budget made no allocations for food imports;
according to the finance minister, foreign grants and loans would have
to take care of Pakistan's food requirements. The Americans agreed. The
budget was a 'potent source of unrest'; it could 'jeopardize the
Government's ability to carry out its fiscal policies'. Forced retrench-
ment would strain the already ineffective mechanisms for price controls
and rationing; 'violent public reaction...[was] almost certain'. Without
a wheat loan, or its equivalent in foreign aid, Pakistan would have to
undergo 'the most serious economic and political stress'.[131]

Just as its authors had hoped, the very unpopularity of the budget
gave the bureaucratic-military axis the opening they had been searching
all along. An emergency food conference was called in Karachi to
discuss the worsening situation in the country. In the presence of an
uncharacteristically taciturn governor-general, senior civil servants
joined the commander-in-chief in levelling abuses at the prime minister.

[128] 'Analysis of the Proposed 1953-54 Budget of the Government of Pakistan and of the
Attendant Import Restrictions and Foreign Exchange Controls', prepared by Rufus
Burr Smith [American counselor for economic affairs], 3 April 1953, NND.842909,
RG 59, Box 5548, 890D.10/4-353, NA.
[129] See *Central Budget, 1953–54*, Karachi 1958.
[130] Since January 1953 the general wholesale price index had increased by 20 per cent.
[131] 'Analysis of the Proposed 1953–54 Budget of the Government of Pakistan and of the
Attendant Import Restrictions and Foreign Exchange Controls', prepared by Smith,
3 April 1953, NND.842909, RG 59, Box 5548, 890D.10/4-353, NA.

Sensing his end, Nazimuddin considered requesting London for the governor-general's recall.[132] Apart from being a sick man, Ghulam Mohammad was patently in league with the bureaucrats and the commander-in-chief. The prime minister still enjoyed the confidence of parliament and could conceivably turn the tables on his enemies. But Nazimuddin was not blessed with the intelligence and fleet-footedness required of top class intriguers. On 17 April 1953, he was summoned by the governor-general along with his cabinet and ordered to resign. Nazimuddin declined and had to be dismissed. Crestfallen by such a poor reward for his services, Nazimuddin tried appealing to Buckingham palace only to discover that the overseas telegraph service was out of operation. Even the British high commissioner thought it politic not to transmit the prime minister's telegram to the Queen. The governor-general had acted under section ten of the adapted government of India act. Despite the constitutional gloss, he had in fact carried out a bureaucratic-military coup.

There has been a long speculative debate on the rights and wrongs of the governor-general's action. He was certainly preempting his own dismissal. But the force of the documentary evidence makes it transparent that Nazimuddin's dismissal was 'planned and accomplished through [the] combined efforts of [the] Army leadership...particularly...Iskander Mirza and...General Ayub...and [the] Governer-General himself'.[133] Ayub confessed that 'he had worked hard to have something along this line accomplished'.[134] Mirza for his part disclosed that the army had been positioned at 'key points' in the country on the day of the dismissal. The prime minister's house was under armed guard and his telephone lines disconnected. The inescapable conclusion was that the army, in spite of its public denials about wanting a military dictatorship, 'might have been prepared to go even to that length if no alternative had presented itself'. But the governor-general's willingness to go along with the defence establishment's game plan had 'brought about one of the most popular coups in history'.[135]

It nevertheless has remained the least well known of such coups. The governor-general's sleight of hand saved the army from intervening prematurely. The new prime minister, Mohammad Ali Bogra, was

---

[132] See note of conversation between Malik Khizar Hayat Khan Tiwana and R.H. Belcher in Washington, 3 August 1953, DO35/5201, PRO.

[133] Emmerson to the secretary of state, 20 April 1953, NND.842430, RG 84, Box 42, File 350-Pak. Pol. General Affairs 1953, NA.

[134] Memorandum of conversation between general Ayub and Gibson in Lahore, 28 April 1953, ibid.

[135] Emmerson to the department of state, Karachi despatch no. 968, 23 April 1953, ibid.

Pakistan's ambassador in Washington. A confirmed political non-entity
from east Bengal, Bogra was pathetically pro-American – the type
whom Americans often find a trifle embarrassing. Brought back to
Karachi, ostensibly for a briefing on how to sway the Americans on the
issue of a wheat loan, Bogra was caught unawares by the offer to become
prime minister. He accepted with measured reluctance; the new cabinet
included all except those branded the most corrupt or rabidly religious
of Nazimuddin's ministers.[136] Bogra's appointment and the purge of
the 'pro-Mullah' group was intended to demonstrate to Washington
that Pakistan meant business. In return for his elevation to high office,
Bogra had to perform two functions on behalf of the bureaucratic-military axis. Internationally, he had to use his connections in
Washington to secure a hefty wheat grant and prepare the ground for a
substantial military aid package. At home, he had to claim to speak for
Bengal, albeit along lines chalked out for him. It was an unenviable
position for anyone to be in. But if it was any consolation for Bogra, the
Americans were delighted to see him in the job. Pakistan had 'turned its
back on the mullah-dominated theocratic state' and would 'look more
to the United States than in the past'. The change of government offered
'great opportunities' which through 'tactful guidance' and 'firm
example' could 'do much to develop the stability of this area [Pakistan]
so important to the foreign policy of the United States'.[137] A Pakistani
bureaucrat or military officer could not have put it better. Pakistan had
indeed turned a corner. The bureaucratic-military axis had wrested the
balance of advantage. For politicians it was no longer just a painful
tumble downhill but a steep fall all the way into a bottomless pit.

Domestic scuffles and international compromise

After the spring of 1953 the bureaucratic-military alliance was brooking
no further interference from politicians, certainly not on foreign policy
issues. Yet, unable to deny politicians altogether, they had selected as
prime minister a man who had no real bases of support. It was a
temporary solution, to be abandoned as soon as politicians began
squeezing through the few remaining loop-holes to claim a say in
decision-making. So bureaucrats and generals, if they could maintain
their unity of purpose, had still to establish an unchallenged dominance
over the state apparatus.

[136] Abdus Sattar Pirzada, Abdur Rab Nishtar, Mahmud Hussain and Fazlur Rahman
were among those dethroned.
[137] Emmerson to the department of state, 23 April 1953, despatch no. 968, NND.842430,
RG 84, Box 42, File 350-Pak. Pol. General Affairs 1953, NA.

The wind was blowing in their direction. Domestically, the circle of support was widening. Businessmen anxious to see a relaxation of import controls and a healthier climate of investment blamed Pakistan's economic ills on venal politicians, a view that found sympathy among professional groups shocked by the recent outburst of religiously inspired violence in the Punjab and pleasantly surprised by the swift reversion to normalcy under martial law. Informed opinion understandably had no stomach for seedy politics. But no one was prepared to issue a *carte blanche* to bureaucrats and generals, much less authority to restrict civil liberties or to drive Pakistan into American arms.

Yet one of the first items on Bogra's agenda was to negotiate a million ton wheat grant from the United States. Washington preferred giving a loan instead of an outright wheat grant; that would have placed Pakistan further in the red by some $110 million. Syed Amjad Ali, Karachi's roving ambassador and a man who knew the art of haggling, began by emphasising 'Pakistan's desire for the goodwill of the United States'; then proceeded to explain why it could not repay the loan without reducing the size of its army.[138] John Foster Dulles, the American secretary of state, who was delighted at the prospect of the Pakistan army helping raise security umbrellas against Communism in the Middle East and South East Asia, was quick to the rescue. The government of Pakistan was 'most friendly to us' and 'needed immediate assurance of our aid'; he 'strongly recommended' that the 'aid be in the form of a dollar grant'.[139] The arrival of the wheat aid was greeted by an enthusiastic procession of camels carrying placards of 'Thank You America'; the reaction of the people was notably muted. Bogra had delivered the goods; army headquarters was confident it could get him to repeat the performance with a substantial military aid package.

Since September 1952, when the original concept of a Middle Eastern command was revised to a Middle Eastern defence organisation, or MEDO, many of the earlier arguments against Pakistan's participation had lost their force. Under the new arrangement, the participants were to be concerned primarily with planning. So contributing troops while Kashmir remained in Indian hands was no longer an issue. Worries about Indian reactions to pulling Pakistan into Middle Eastern defence could be laid to rest by reopening dialogue with New Delhi. On

[138] Memorandum of conversation between officials of the state department, Amjad Ali and M. Shafqat [Pakistani charge d'affaires], 28 April 1953, NND.842909, RG 59, Box 5545, 890D.03/4-2853, NA.

[139] John Foster Dulles' comments on memorandum prepared by the Near Eastern affairs office on 'The Food Situation in Pakistan', ibid.

Washington's advice,[140]and army headquarters' approval, Pakistan was to have another chance shooting at India across the negotiating table. Whatever the outcome, Bogra would incur the blame, not the army. The exchanges between Bogra and Nehru in Karachi aroused great expectations; but achieved little. In mid-August, Bogra reciprocated Nehru's gesture and visited the Indian capital. A joint communique was issued and promptly added to the Kashmir archives at the two foreign ministries. But not before it had received a thorough brushing down in Pakistan. There was 'considerable opposition in the Cabinet' which met seven times to muse over the Bogra-Nehru proposals. The president of the Pakistan chambers of commerce and industry, M.A. Rangoonwala, led the businessmen's choir against the Delhi proposals. The 'feeling of frustration over Kashmir ha[d] returned in full measure' and Bogra's prestige had suffered appreciably.[141] Just how much is suggested by Dulles' request to the Karachi embassy for a 'continuing evaluation [of the] Prime Minister's position'.[142]

That position had never been particularly secure. Despite an initial spurt of enthusiasm for the change in government, the 'new broom ha[d] scarcely swept clean'; the 'bureaucracy move[d] with [the] same exasperating obstructionist slowness'. By testing the new prime minister unfairly, the bureaucratic-military axis and its allies outside the state apparatus wanted to demonstrate the inadequacies of the parliamentary system. Unlike his predecessor Bogra would not be allowed to slip with abandon. He would have to go and the 'resulting change of government regardless of who became Prim[e Minister], would almost certainly represent [a] trend toward authoritarian rule and [a] distinct defeat for [the] democratic process'.[143] There was nothing democratic about the political process. With the gun permanently positioned against his temple, Bogra in many respects was a more tragic figure than Nazimuddin. He was a civilian presiding over a country where the military had assumed power without formally acknowledging it. While politicians discredited themselves with intrigue and counter-intrigue, the defence establishment pretended to keep watch from the anteroom where the controls were located. The need for the pretence is obvious enough. Since a military arrangement with the United States was unpopular domestically it was better negotiated under the auspices of a

[140] John Foster Dulles' in particular. See Venkataramani, *The American Role in Pakistan*, 211.

[141] Withers to the department of state, Karachi despatch no. 148, 29 August 1953, NND.842430, RG 84, Box 12, File 320-Pak. India, Ali-Nehru talks, NA.

[142] Dulles to Karachi embassy, telegram no. 175, 1 September 1953, ibid.

[143] Emmerson to the secretary of state, telegram no. 55, 15 July 1953, NND.842430, RG 84, Box 36, File 360-Govt.General, NA.

civilian government. Moreover, it was infinitely more prudent to build up the defence services before exposing them to the mixed treats of running Pakistan.[144] Not for the first time, Iskander Mirza told the American ambassador that though the military had 'no political ambitions' – a standard line – it would have to 'step in' if the government failed to 'produce results'.[145] Ayub was no less explicit; while ready to give the new prime minister a chance he was 'not close to him' and had his share of 'trouble with him in East Bengal'.[146] Others were less circumspect. Mushtaq Gurmani – the 'heart of the Punjabi group'[147] in the central government – and Sardar Bahadur Khan – the minister of communications and the commander-in-chief's brother – were manoeuvring for Bogra's removal. So too was Khan Abdul Qayum Khan, the ex-Premier of the NWFP who had been given a place at the centre to wean him away from Nazimuddin and his band of supporters in the constituent assembly. Two of the most important civil servants in the country – Aziz Ahmed and Ghulam Ahmed, the cabinet and interior secretaries respectively – were also doggedly opposed to Bogra.[148]

All eyes were on Bogra's handling of the constitutional deadlock, an issue so vital to Pakistan's domestic politics it could dampen initiatives on the foreign policy front. The Punjab Muslim League's rejection of the parity formula proposed by the BPC report had rekindled the debate on the future constitutional set up. The Punjabi construct – with some dissenting voices – was for a unitary form of government; east Bengal's retort, backed by political factions in the smaller provinces was a confederal arrangement between the two wings. The notion of a confederation was implicit in the Lahore resolution of 1940. So, although its proponents could not be charged with treason, it was a knife close to the state bureaucracy and army's jugular. The arguments

---

[144] After the free officers coup in Egypt, and military takeovers led by younger officers in Syria and Lebanon, Ayub had reason to worry about 'talk of the Pakistan Army taking over the Government'. He instructed his divisional commanders to put a stop to such speculations in army messes. His point that the Pakistan army 'did not have trained men in Government affairs' was less important. (See Gibson to the department of state, Lahore despatch no. 105, 23 December 1952, NND.842430, RG 84, Box 42, File 350-Pak. Pol. July–December 1952, NA.)

[145] Horace A. Hildreth [American ambassador] to Dulles, telegram no. 200, 5 September 1953, NND.842430, RG 84, Box 36, File 360-Govt.General, NA.

[146] Memorandum of conversation between Ayub and Gibson, 21 April 1953; enclosure to Lahore despatch no. 179, 28 April 1953, NND.842430, RG 84, Box 42, File 350-Pak. Pol. General Affairs 1953, NA.

[147] Note of conversation between Khizar Hayat Khan and Belcher in Washington, 3 August 1953, DO35/5201, PRO.

[148] Hildreth to Dulles, telegram no. 200, 5 September 1953, NND.842430, RG 84, Box 36, File 360-Govt. General, NA.

against confederation, namely that it would weaken the state, apart from being administratively cumbersome, were reminiscent of those used by the Congress high command in that fateful summer of 1946.

Elections to the east Bengal assembly, scheduled for early 1954, made Bogra's task doubly difficult. Without constitutional concessions the east Bengal League was set to receive a drubbing from a rainbow opposition determined to present a united front against the central government. The loss of the eastern wing would seriously upset the balance at the centre. On 7 October 1953, Bogra made the first move to give the League a fighting chance at the east Bengal hustings. His compromise formula provided for a lower house of 300 elected on the basis of population and an upper house of fifty in which the units were to have equal representation. The principle of parity was made more palatable to the Punjabis. West Pakistan was to be represented in the upper house by five instead of nine units – Punjab; NWFP and the tribal areas; Sind and Khairpur; Bahawalpur, Baluchistan, Baluchistan states union; and Karachi. The real difference between the Bogra formula and the BPC report was the provision that all vital motions – such as votes of confidence or no-confidence and the election of the president – would be decided by a majority vote of the two houses meeting jointly.[149] The majority had to include at least 30 per cent of the total number of representatives from each wing. The failure of the two houses to agree could result in their dissolution by the president. The 30 per cent safeguard was intended to allay west Pakistani, and more particularly Punjabi, anxieties about being outvoted by the eastern wing. It cut both ways, however. The same number of east Bengal representatives could veto controversial bills on industrial, defence and foreign policy – just what the bureaucratic-military alliance feared the most.

The provision for Islamic boards was another sore point in the BPC report. Bogra began by toeing the Jinnah line: religion had no place in politics; the religious clauses in the BPC had to be 'got rid of'.[150] But he changed his mind upon learning from Nurul Amin that Islam was the League's one hope of warding off defeat in east Bengal. To up the ante for the Bengal League, the debate on the Islamic aspects of the constitution was revived in the constituent assembly. Fifty-four of the sixty-eight members of the assembly were Leaguers. So it was not too difficult to make a big deal about the role of Islam in the state without conceding anything to the ulema. The debate left everyone exhausted.

[149] Inamur Rahman, *Public Opinion and Political Development in Pakistan*, Karachi 1982, 55–6.
[150] Record of conversation between the secretary of state [CRO] and Bogra, 26 May 1953, DO35/5203, PRO.

Confusion was heaped upon confusion. At its simplest, the state was to be known as the Islamic republic of Pakistan and the head of state had to be a Muslim. At its most complex, the supreme court rather than the Islamic boards had now to determine whether or not laws were repugnant to Islam. The judges of the supreme court had no expertise in Islamic law and would have to rely on expert opinion. The more so since according to another amendment judicial decisions acceptable to one Islamic sect could not be imposed on another. This left the religious guardians with considerable influence over the highest judicial body in the state. To prevent them from interfering in the affairs of government, budgetary and financial matters were kept immune from the repugnancy clause.[151]

The visions of the future emanating from the constituent assembly were worrying for Mirza and a few like-minded individuals who began considering how to put an end to the charade of constitution-making. Bogra had clearly exceeded his brief. And, while the forthcoming elections in east Bengal made a break with the prime minister impracticable, his constitutional formula could not be allowed to stick. It was the biggest threat so far to the intricate patchwork of state-building so carefully put together by the mandarins and the praetorian guard.

More to the point, the compromise formula was cobbled together just when the strengths and not the weaknesses of the Pakistani state needed emphasising. Since September 1953, Ayub and Ghulam Mohammad had been in Washington negotiating the terms of an American military aid package. After nearly six years of monitoring its political see-sawing the state department and the pentagon had turned their attention to Ayub – the 'strongest individual in Pakistan' and the 'person to talk to'.[152] He had the backing of the army which was in a 'firm position'[153] as well as Iskander Mirza's – the key to any successful intrigue in Pakistan. The governor-general may have been old, sick and senile, but clearly preferred Ayub and Mirza over the politicians. So, while not discounting the political developments altogether, Washington was ready to go ahead with a token military aid package for Pakistan. This was why Mirza was anxious to reassure Washington of the central

[151] See American embassy [Karachi] to the department of state, despatch no. 416, January 1954, NND.842430, RG 84, Box 36, File 360.1, NA.
[152] Ayub was also awarded the American legion of merit which, significantly, the Americans had first considered doing in 1951 but postponed after the 'Rawalpindi Conspiracy'. (Hildreth to Dulles, telegram no. 230, 15 September 1953, NND.842430, RG 84, Box 40, File 320-Pak-US, NA.)
[153] Emmerson to Dulles, Karachi despatch no. 1582, 20 April 1953, NND.842430, RG 84, Box 42, File 350-Pak. Pol. General Affairs 1953, NA.

government's resilience in the face of political pressures. The constituent
assembly's recommendations on the Islamic aspects of the constitution
could conceivably put off the Americans. Mirza and Wajid Ali – a
member of one of the leading Punjabi industrial families and the
elder brother of Amjad Ali, Pakistan's new ambassador in
Washington – decided to preempt the reaction. In 'several conversations' with the American ambassador they pointed to the need for
'drastic measures' to 'save Pakistan from becoming [a] fanatical
theocracy'. What they had in mind was a change of government,
naturally with the governor-general's approval. The new government
would be 'committed to military cooperation and closest relations with
[the] United States' and Bogra might even continue as prime minister.[154] Both men were angling for a 'constitutional dictatorship'. The
governor-general would dissolve the constituent assembly and establish
governor's rule in all the provinces except east Bengal which would be
placed under direct military rule. The change to a 'stable, progressive
[and] effective' government would be 'smooth', 'constitutional' and
ultimately popular. All this was to be sprung on the people of Pakistan
before the elections in east Bengal but after the governor-general's
return and the visit by the American vice-president, Richard Nixon.
Somewhat shaken by these 'extraordinary revelations', the American
ambassador was relieved to learn that Mirza and Wajid merely wanted
'general sympathy'; not direct 'United States involvement'.[155]

The overlap between domestic and international factors is striking.
Far from being an innocent victim of plots hatched by foreign
governments, Pakistan was in effect hostage to a handful of individuals
nested in the highest positions of power and influence within state and
society who were willing and able to use international connections to
mould internal developments.

The American ambassador was urged to recommend that in their
meetings with the governor-general both Eisenhower and Dulles should
hint at the United States' deep 'disappoint[ment] if Pakistan developed
[a] reactionary government and constitution accentuating [the] importance [of] religious zealots . . .'. Since Pakistan and Turkey were about
to join hands in an American inspired military agreement, the 'infor-
mants' also wanted Washington's ambassador in Ankara 'to make
discreet suggestions to Turkish officials'. The only signs of nervousness
on Iskander and Wajid's part was a special plea that the information
'under no circumstances' be 'leaked to any Pakistani official', including

---

[154] Hildreth to Dulles, telegram no. 341, 2 November 1953, NND.842905, RG 59, Box
4147, 790D.00/11-253, NA.
[155] Ibid.

Ghulam Mohammad, Amjad Ali and Bogra. The success of the plan 'depend[ed] on presenting it suddenly' to the governor-general with the prime minister's cooperation, who until the last minute would be kept in the dark, so as to 'preclude building up of alternatives and objections'.[156]

Although the plans did not get off the ground in time to forestall elections in east Bengal, an opposition victory could present a perfect opportunity to implement the plan. So a safe enough plan of action while Pakistan braced itself for the most decisive move ever in the international arena. But from the American point of view, Bogra's future seemed a little too uncertain in Mirza's scheme of things – the atmosphere in Karachi was thick with rumours of a change of government and 'press dope stories prohesying [a] military grab for power'.[157] The American embassy was strongly of the view that propping up Bogra's government would be 'a beneficial thing...[for] US-Pakistan relations'.[158] Bogra was known to be excessively enthusiastic about America, often 'embarrass[ing] Pakistan by his open friendliness to the United States'; it seemed politic to get the prime minister's personal estimation of his chances of survival.[159] In December, the American ambassador had a series of 'frank' exchanges with Bogra. The prime minister was adamant 'to stick to the ship' and seemed reasonably confident of his ability to do so. When pressed a little harder on the possibility of a military takeover, Bogra grovelled and confessed that such a 'demand had been made on him' but he had 'resisted and refused'. 'Now', he said, 'we will see what happens.'[160] In an uncharacteristically philosophical word of warning, Bogra had hinted what he feared might happen; he told the American ambassador:

Take whatever time you need [to confirm the military aid] but for God's sake if you once make an affirmative decision, stick to it because we will have burned our bridges behind us although we are not afraid...it would be a tragic thing for us...if there were to be any reneging regardless of pressure.[161]

The prime minister had laid his finger on the disquieting set of contingencies facing Pakistan prior to the arrival of American military

---

[156] Ibid.

[157] Hildreth to Dulles, telegram no. 476, 30 December 1953, ibid.

[158] Hildreth to the department of state, Karachi despatch no. 346, 2 December 1953, NND.842430, RG 84, Box 42, File 350-Pak. Pol. General Affairs 1953, NA.

[159] Hildreth to Dulles, telegram no. 476, 30 December 1953, NND.842905, RG 59, Box 4147, NA.

[160] Ibid.

[161] Hildreth to the department of state, Karachi despatch no. 346, 2 December 1953, NND.842430, RG 84, Box 42, File 350-Pak. Pol. General Affairs 1953, NA.

aid. Domestically, the defence establishment was on the alert, determined not to allow stray political incidents sabotage the final round of negotiations for a gift it had coveted for so long. Internationally, the pressures were mounting – not only from New Delhi but from Moscow and Beijing as well. It was easy to ignore Indian reactions.[162] But charges from the other two giants that American aid to Pakistan was a threat to their security could not be dismissed lightly. So all in all, Pakistan was about to pay a heavy price for an aid package which, contrary to Ayub's expectations, was not to exceed the $25 million mark.

On 19 February 1954, Pakistan and Turkey signed the military agreement, a precursor to still more ill-fated international treaties. London sighed at this American attempt to poach on its territory, produced elaborate arguments against the move, but at the eleventh hour relented. Britain's policy of maintaining 'broad parity' in arms supplies to India and Pakistan was producing unintended results. Pakistan's financial embarrassments had tilted the military balance in South Asia in India's favour. So 'American assistance to Pakistan...[seemed] the answer after all'.[163] Having silenced London, Washington had no qualms about announcing its decision to send a survey mission to determine Pakistan's military needs.

At Dulles' insistence Eisenhower's announcement was timed to 'help Prime Minister Mohammad Ali's Moslem League in the elections in East Bengal'.[164] The polls were postponed by three weeks to enable the League to make political capital out of American military aid. It was a typical misreading of popular opinion and, in any case, the party's image was beyond repair. The United Front – an alliance of convenience rather than an expression of unity between more than half a dozen independent parties[165] – fought the elections on a twenty-one point programme. First and foremost was the demand for the adoption of

---

[162] Indian reaction to the American decision proved counter-productive. It was clear to see that Indians had 'overplay[ed] their hand as to make it now virtually impossible for the Americans to back out even if they had otherwise so wished'. (R. Makins [British embassy, Washington] to the foreign office, telegram no. 2757, 21 December 1953, FO371/106937, PRO.)

[163] Official minute [signature illegible], 19 November 1953, FO371/106935, PRO.

[164] The report was filed by Sidney H. Seltzberg, the *New York Times* correspondent in June 1954. (Cited in Afzal, *Political Parties in Pakistan*, 127, fn. 110.)

[165] The United Front consisted of the east Pakistan Awami Muslim League led by the pro-Beijing Maulana Bhashani and Shaheed Suhrawardy; Fazlul Huq's Krishak Sramik party; the left-leaning Ganatantri Dal; the right-wing Nizam-i-Islam; Abul Hashim's Khilafat-i-Rabbani; the east Bengal Communist party and a smattering of left-wing student groups. Riddled with ideological differences, the United Front held together only in opposition to the Muslim League.

Bengali as a national language, followed by a call for the nationalisation of jute and an autonomy so wide as to restrict the centre's authority to three subjects only – defence, foreign affairs and currency. But the demands which gave the central leadership and the defence establishment many sleepless nights were the repeal of the safety acts, the shifting of naval headquarters to the eastern wing and the establishment of an armaments factory.[166] By the time the votes were counted the ranks of insomniacs had swollen in Karachi, Rawalpindi and Dacca. While no one had been sanguine about the League's prospects, they had not expected a rout. The United Front polled 65.6 per cent of the popular vote and secured 223 seats in an assembly of 309; the League was reduced to a mere ten seats and to add insult to injury Nurul Amin himself was roundly defeated by a twenty-eight year old student leader. In sixty constituencies League candidates lost their security deposits and managed to make a decent showing in only fifty electoral fights.[167] The League had met its nemesis in east Bengal; on 3 April 1954, Fazlul Huq formed the first non-League ministry in Pakistan.

The League may have been redundant to the actual running of the state, but its defeat in a province containing the majority of Pakistan's population was a hammer blow to the centre. The United Front's electoral programme was a red herring across the bureaucratic-military alliance's path. So there could be no question of the League and the United Front sharing power at the centre. The Front's unanimous demand for the dissolution of the constituent assembly on the grounds that it was no longer representative of Bengali opinion was shrugged aside; a significant reaction since before the elections the Bengali contingent, led by Nazimuddin and Fazlur Rahman, topped the bureaucratic-military alliance's hit list. Instead of accommodating the sea-change and turfing out the old Bengali gang, the central government concentrated attention on compiling allegations against the United Front ministry's garrulous chief minister. A man for whom slips of the tongue were what turns of the phrases are for the seasoned writer, Huq found himself being charged with treason of all manner and sort – complicity with India, secessionism and pro-Communist inklings.

The latter charge was the least plausible, but it proved decisive in Huq's undoing. His ministry could not have taken office at a more unpropitious moment. The provincial economy was in a parlous

---

[166] See Afzal, *Political Parties in Pakistan*, appendix I for complete text of the twenty-one point programme.

[167] American consul general to the department of state, Dacca despatch no. 106, 30 March 1954, NND.842905, RG 59, Box 4147, 790D.00/3-2554, NA.

condition. In the last week of March 1954, a gruesome riot at the Karnafuli paper mills had left thirteen dead and thirty-five injured.[168] Throughout the ministry's brief tenure in office the province was gripped by industrial violence, including trouble in the Dacca central jail which resulted in fifty injuries – nineteen of whom were victims of insouciant police firing. The climax was reached with the outbreak of riots at the Adamjee jute mills, infamous for its sub-human working conditions and so a powder keg of discontents; some 400 people were killed and many more wounded.[169] The army had to be called in. Laying the blame on the provincial government's Communist friends was a favourite excuse. But, while anything is possible in South Asian politics, the United Front ministry's eagerness to dig its own grave is something of a historical conundrum.

The 'Red scare', however faded the colouring, was the best pretext for the centre's intervention. So the connivance of a predominantly non-Bengali bureaucracy in helping stir Bengali discontents cannot be ruled out.[170] In Karachi, Mirza pulled out the plans from his inner pocket and over sips of tea with the ailing governor-general managed to get his way. It was not too difficult. There was a law and order problem in east Bengal even if the proposed remedy was liable to fall short of providing the cure. The United Front's reaction to American aid was the last straw; 162 members of the newly elected Bengal provincial assembly expressed 'grave concern' about the possible undermining of Pakistan's 'freedom and sovereignty'. While the negotiators were putting the finishing touches to the mutual aid pact, the United Front observed an 'anti-US-Pakistan Military Pact Day'.[171] On 19 March 1954, Pakistani and American representatives signed the agreement. Within two weeks the governor-general had dismissed Huq's ministry, though not the provincial assembly, and appointed Mirza as the governor who would administer the province under section 92a.

This was act one of 'plan Mirza'. Bayonets were sufficient to discipline east Bengal; they could not resolve Pakistan's constitutional problems. During the summer of 1954, the sky was covered with constitutional kites of all coloured combinations. Those reduced to watching the

---

[168] A few days later the leader of the mob was given a place in Huq's ministry. (K.K. Aziz, *Party Politics in Pakistan: 1947–1958*, Islamabad 1976, 17–8.)

[169] Rahman, *Public Opinion and Political Development in Pakistan*, 212.

[170] According to one view, the United Front's electoral success owed much to 'bureaucrats, especially West Pakistani District Magistrates' who were reacting with a vengeance to the pressures placed upon them by members of the old assembly and also the Bengal League's working committee. (See Aziz, *Party Politics in Pakistan*, and Leonard Binder, *Religion and Politics in Pakistan*, Berkeley 1971, 347.)

[171] Afzal, *Political Parties in Pakistan*, 131–2.

spectacle from the sidelines – the members of the United Front in particular – registered their protest by reiterating the demand for the dissolution of the constituent assembly. Bogra, conveying the opinions in the control room, declared that the constituent assembly would be dissolved only after completing its assignment.[172] Yet the assignment was not being conducted to the satisfaction of the principal power brokers at the centre. Even without the United Front things were going east Bengal's way. Bogra's constitutional formula had given Bengali the status of a national language. It had not accounted for a demand voiced by Punjabi political figures like Firoz Khan Noon but which, more importantly, had always been the main aim of the bureaucratic-military alliance – the merger of west Pakistan into a single administrative unit. Lumping the smaller provinces with the Punjab would decrease the chances of their negotiating joint fronts with east Bengal, the only guarantee for central autonomy in decision-making. Interestingly enough, the proposal was not acceptable to all Punjabi politicians. This suggests yet again that the centre's interests were not always those of the Punjab's or that the bureaucratic-military alliance was necessarily working from a provincial perspective.

On 3 September 1954, the Muslim League's assembly party voted overwhelmingly to reject the proposal for the unification of west Pakistan.[173] An alternative scheme for a zonal federation with safeguards for the smaller provinces against Punjabi domination was also floated. But, to the dismay of its proponents in the Punjab, the Bengali members of the constituent assembly – suddenly in a hurry to get on with constitution-making – ensured that it was meted the same treatment as the one unit proposal. A fluid grouping of the non-Punjabi provinces had succeeded in impressing its imprimatur on the proceedings of the constituent assembly. This, rather than a commonality of interest, left the Punjab with little choice but to rally behind the centre. Punjabi demands for the dissolution of the constituent assembly were now quite as strident as those voiced by the United Front in east Bengal.

A series of unsavoury steps saw the bureaucratic-military alliance and its Punjabi 'allies' at swords' point with other members of the constituent assembly. There were rumours of Mirza working in consort with the governor-general to book several prominent members of the east Bengal Muslim League under PRODA. To parry the threat, three different groups in the east Bengal League led by Nurul Amin, Nazimuddin and Fazlur Rahman respectively, lured Bogra into sup-

---

[172] Rahman, *Public Opinion and Political Development in Pakistan*, 143.
[173] Ibid, 74.

porting a series of constitutional amendments aimed at whittling down the governor-general's powers.[174] On 20 September 1954, just before Bogra went off on a tour of Britain and the United States, the constituent assembly ratified his constitutional formula. Later in the day, with only the sponsors and supporters of the bill present, the assembly repealed PRODA but not the existing disqualifications. On 21 September, sections nine and ten of the government of India act of 1935 were amended. While the former effectively placed the politicians' above the law, the latter prevented the governor-general from dismissing the cabinet which was to be wholly responsible to the national assembly. The Bengali members of the assembly, backed by such 'have-nots' of the League like Nishtar, Yusuf Haroon, Qayum Khan and Abdus Sattar Pirzada, had carried out a veritable coup.[175] They could now conceivably regain control of the centre and use it to recover lost ground in east Bengal. As a result of the constitutional amendments, the Punjabi group – loosely defined – was seen to have 'lost influence, and clearly regard[ed] the blow at the Governor-General as a blow at itself'.[176] Unwilling to countenance a shift in the balance of power at the centre, Punjabi and Sindhi politicians like Daultana and Khuhro as well as members of the Karachi business community joined forces with the higher civil service and the army to rally around the governor-general.[177] Ghulam Mohammad consulted the chief justice of the supreme court, summoned Bogra home and, after threatening the unrepentant prime minister with martial law and worse, on 24 October 1954 dismissed the constituent assembly.[178]

The decision was challenged in the courts by the east Bengali president of the constituent assembly, Maulvi Tamizuddin Khan. While the courts began their long and tedious deliberations, the bureaucratic-military alliance and their cohorts in political and business circles in west

---

[174] J.D. Murray [acting British high commissioner] to A.F. Morley[CRO], 30 September 1954, DO35/5153, PRO.

[175] Murray to Morley, 24 September, ibid., PRO.

[176] As the British high commissioner astutely noted, 'one result' of the constitutional changes was to 'bring a step nearer the possibility that the Army and the higher Civil Service...may one day come to the conclusion that the politicians have made such a mess that it is necessary for non-political forces to take over – e.g. in Egypt'. (Ibid.)

[177] Daultana and Khuhro admittedly, had to be won over by the governor-general's promise to withdraw PRODA proceedings against them.

[178] On 23 October when Bogra arrived at Karachi airport he was hustled into a car by a couple of Pakistani generals and taken straight to the governor-general's house. In what is further evidence of the army's close involvement with the dismissal of the constituent assembly, before the governor-general's 'proclamation was published troops were moved in from their barracks a few miles outside Karachi to the Transit Camp in the town' in readiness for disorders 'beyond the power of the police to control'. (Murray to secretary of state [CRO], 10 December 1954, DO35/5406, PRO.)

Pakistan congratulated themselves for having successfully established a 'constitutional dictatorship'. It would now be infinitely easier to keep the lid on domestic troubles and marshal support for their cause internationally. East Bengal was under Mirza's reliable jackboot; Punjab had been brought into line and the smaller provinces were unlikely to pose any serious threat without one or the other of the two main component units of the state. Things were going quite as well, if not better, on the foreign policy front. American military aid had begun arriving in driblets; Pakistan had joined the South East Asian treaty organisation [SEATO] and was impatiently waiting to put its name to a similar treaty covering the Middle East. The interplay of domestic, regional and international factors had brought about a decisive shift in the institutional balance of power; bureaucrats and generals had triumphed over politicians and the complex dynamics of Pakistan's political process were no longer relevant to the actual building and consolidation of the state.

5

Breaking down the political system, 1954–1958

The seven years prior to the dismissal of the constituent assembly had firmly underlined the uneasy fit between the internal dynamics of the Pakistani political system and the preferred bureaucratic and military blueprint for the state structure. By October 1958, the disjunction between the political process and state-building was to lead to direct intervention by the army. The responsibility for the military takeover is commonly laid at the door of Pakistani politicians. It is true that, during 1954 and 1958, the quality of politics – never very high to begin with – went from bad to worse. Yet to attribute the first military coup to the doings of politicians in the main is to credit them with a result which, upon sifting the evidence, grossly overstates their ability to influence events in the climacteric last four years of 'parliamentary government'.

During the run-up to the military coup the new and significant development was not a sudden deterioration of politics as such but the frequency and ease with which an already dominant bureaucratic-military axis was able to deploy central authority to ride roughshod over provincial interests. Factional in-fighting among politicians far from impeding the exercise of state authority by the centre appeared, at each step, to be facilitating its consolidation under bureaucratic and military direction. So the disarray in Pakistan's political arenas was an opportunity for the bureaucratic and military axis to advance their own institutional interests by virtually equating these with the imperatives of the state. An intriguing question, therefore, is whether the collapse of the political process was precipitated by internecine warfare among the politicians, or whether it was further distorted and eventually broken down by civil and military officials looking to stretch the ambit of central authority in order to give a long-delayed impetus to their ambitious plans to industrialise and militarise Pakistan, while at the same time nurturing their own recently forged links in the international arena.

Such an investigation demands a closer analysis of the main constitutional issues, especially the crisis following the dissolution of the first constituent assembly. Pakistan's constitutional problems, when placed in the context of centre-province relations, highlight the extent to which the evolution of the political process was influenced by the shifting institutional balance of power within the state structure. Elucidating the politics of the constitutional deadlock and its resolution in this way brings the dialectic between the political process and state consolidation into sharper focus. A careful study of this key dialectic in Pakistan's history offers quite a different perspective on the causes of the military intervention from the one which sees the failure of 'parliamentary government' solely in terms of the confusion and chaos within its political arenas.

The constitutional imbroglio

After dissolving the constituent assembly the governor-general opted for a 'cabinet of talents'. Bogra was retained as prime minister because of his American connections. Real power, however, was concentrated in the hands of an 'inner ring' consisting of three men who already occupied key positions within the state structure. General Ayub Khan, the commander-in-chief, was given the defence portfolio; major general Iskander Mirza, the former defence secretary, took over as minister of interior and Chaudhri Mohammad Ali, a man who commanded the support and loyalty of the administrative services, was asked to continue as finance minister. Among the new entrants were M.A.H. Ispahani, Pakistan's former ambassador to Washington and a representative of business interests in Karachi, and Dr Khan Sahib, the Congress chief minister of the NWFP just before partition.[1] These may have been the men of 'talents', but many of them had never been elected to public office – a serious flaw in the eyes of those who had hailed the dismissal of an unrepresentative constitution-making body as a prelude to general elections and a truly representative government.

It was not long before the governor-general and his closest aides dampened such expectations. Getting rid of the constituent assembly was realpolitik at its best, not a step towards restoring 'democratic freedom'. The immediate preoccupation of the ministerial group at the centre was to expedite the amalgamation of west Pakistan into a single administrative unit, to be accompanied by the creation of one ministry and assembly for all the provinces and states. A reorganisation along these lines would enable the centre to place more effective controls on politicians in the western wing and neutralise Bengali demands for

---

[1] The other cabinet ministers included Dr A.M. Malik, Ghyasuddin Pathan, A.H. Sarkar, Abid Hussain, Ghulam Ali Talpur, Mumtaz Ali Khan, and H. I. Rahimtoola. By December 1954, as part of the attempt to make one unit more palatable to the eastern wing, H. S. Suhrawardy – the leader of the Awami League – was given the law portfolio at the centre; see above, pp. 200–1.

greater provincial autonomy. All this was to be achieved by foisting a constitution on the country; it would be prepared by bureaucrats, approved by the commander-in-chief, and given legal sanction by the governor-general. There was no time to consult the people, certainly none for the election of fresh recruits to a new constituent assembly. The 'proper course', in Mirza's private opinion, 'was to continue to ignore the politicians and to allow them to destroy each other.'[2]

Such candid statements of intent by members of the new cabinet led the more astute to ponder whether the dissolution of the constituent assembly was in fact a constitutional *coup d'etat* aimed at establishing a 'veiled military dictatorship'. A flurry of denials merely confirmed the suspicions. The prime minister tried debunking theories that the army was the 'dominant power behind the scenes in Pakistan'.[3] Yet, as even outside observers of Pakistan could see, for the past eighteen months or so it was effectively being ruled by police, civil and military officials. The governor-general had finally acted because the army was 'tired of bad rule' and because the 'British trained civil service resented interference of politicians it despised'.[4]

Recollecting the events, general Ayub maintained that he declined the governor-general's offer to takeover the reins of government and force a constitution on the people. Yet in the same breath, Ayub practically claimed authorship of the 'one unit' scheme. A detailed memorandum in his political autobiography, intended to bear testimony to that fact, outlines the general's belief that a 'controlled form of democracy' was the only appropriate system of government for Pakistan.[5] The general's thinking was in keeping with the views expressed by Mirza at the time. This needs some emphasising since it was Mirza, 'an *enfant terrible*' with a habit of 'putting into uncomfortably blunt language what others...hestitate[d] to say openly',[6] who disclosed that the army had 'responded' warmly to the 'governor-general's appeal for support' and would '*get out of politics* as soon as a proper election...[could] be held'. But he promptly rejected the practicability of holding elections; Pakistan was 'not ripe for...democracy';[7] it needed a system of

---

[2] Mirza was responding to a query about the prospects of restoring parliamentary government in east Bengal. (G. P. Hampshire [deputy high commissioner, Dacca] to Murray, 22 November 1954, DO35/5406, PRO.)

[3] *Dawn*, 16 November 1954.

[4] This was the view of Philip Deane of the London *Observer*, cited in *Dawn*, 2 November 1954.

[5] See Ayub Khan, 'A Short Appreciation of Present and Future Problems of Pakistan' in *Friends Not Masters*, 186–91.

[6] Murray to secretary of state [CRO], 20 December 1954, DO35/5406, PRO.

[7] *Dawn*, 13 November 1954 [emphasis added].

'controlled democracy' with real power for the head of state so that if the 'train...[went] off the rails' or, more accurately, was derailed, 'somebody' could put it back on the tracks once again.[8]

Here was a line with which the people of Pakistan were to become all too familiar in later years when military takeovers no longer needed the guise of constitutional autocracy. That in 1954 the civil bureaucracy and the army high command felt constrained to keep up the pretence hints at some lingering weaknesses in state authority. Maintaining the facade of constitutionalism for what in effect was a bureaucratic *coup d'etat* underwritten by the military high command betrays a grudging recognition that the political system, though ineffectual in the actual formulation of government policies, could still present challenges against any restructuring of the state which cut against the grain of Pakistan's federal configuration.

The writ petition before the Sind high court questioning the governor-general's authority to sack the constituent assembly and appoint an unrepresentative central ministry makes the point. Filed on 7 November 1954, by Maulvi Tamizuddin Khan, the petition was a test of the judiciary's independence from the executive. Anyone could see that the case should be settled before formalising the new constitutional set up. Pretending to ignore the writ petition the central managers instead kept public opinion agape by an astonishing series of political manoeuvres in preparation for the unification of west Pakistan. But the link between the court case and the campaign for lumping west Pakistan's districts into a unitary system of administration could not be wished away. And indeed, the outcome of the Tamizuddin case was to have a vital bearing not only on the constitutional framework adopted in 1956 but on the very role that came to be assigned to the political process within the Pakistani state system.

The idea of merging west Pakistani provinces and states was as old as the state itself. Initially articulated in 1948, it was justified on grounds of administrative efficiency, greater economy and as a foil against provincialism. In March 1949, it was aired in the constituent assembly by Firoz Khan Noon, supported by Jahanara Shahnawaz, and endorsed by Yusuf Khattak, the Pathan general secretary of the Pakistan Muslim League.[9] Revived in late September 1953 along with the alternative of a zonal federation for the western wing, the 'one unit' plan received its biggest push after the League's defeat in east Bengal. There was now more reason than ever to be alarmed by the implications of the

[8] Ibid., 16 November 1954.
[9] See *CAD*, V, 2 March 1949, 285.

constitutional settlement Bogra had helped negotiate. Based on the principle of parity between the two wings, one of which was divided into five units, the constitutional formula gave the Bengalis a clear preponderance in any future national parliament.

This may have been consistent with Pakistan's political arithmetic; but it was not a prospect which could appeal to a predominantly west Punjabi civil bureaucracy and army. It was comforting to learn that some Punjabi politicians, notably Daultana, were quite as worried about east Bengal making common cause with the smaller units. So the civil bureaucrats and military officials could plausibly use these politicians to promote their own institutional concerns, by now the single most important factor coming to define the imperatives of the state.

The merger of west Pakistan was simply one feature of the constitutional framework favoured by the top dogs at the centre. Its other aspects included an unicameral legislature, a presidential form of government and, of course, a strong centre. But, without the unification of west Pakistan, none of this mattered very much; the Bengali majority would still dominate the national legislature, making perfect nonsense of a strong centre, even if it remained under the control of an administrative bureaucracy and army drawn primarily from western Punjab. The one unit scheme was designed to preempt any possibility of a Bengali controlled centre; this was dangerous play for the highest stakes.[10] Before 'steamrolling' west Pakistan into one unit,[11] it seemed politic to at least appear to have the tacit consent of the provincial assemblies. But, apart from a few stray individuals who saw short-term advantages in toeing the centre's line, informed public opinion in the non-Punjabi provinces was bitterly opposed to the merger scheme. This made it even more imperative that the central government demonstrate support for its grand design. With one eye on developments in the eastern wing where the demands for a return to parliamentary

---

[10] Mirza at one of his weekly luncheon engagements with the British high commissioner elaborated on his theory of 'controlled democracy'. Power in both wings of the country would vest in the hands of a centrally appointed governor who would select a prime minister and a team of ministers, not necessarily from among the members of the assembly. Upon assuming office all members of the cabinet would resign their seats in the assembly which would have to be filled by by-elections. So the cabinet would be responsible to the governor rather than the legislature. A 'similar system would be adopted for the Centre'. Steps would also be taken to greatly 'strengthen the powers of senior civil servants'. What Mirza seemed to have in mind was a mixture of the American political system and the French administrative system of 'prefects'. (Murray to Morley[CRO], 3 December 1954, DO35/5406, PRO.)

[11] 'One Unit is a steamroller' which could not be 'stopped by small pebbles in the road', Mirza blurted out contemptuously. *Dawn*, 24 February 1955.

government were gaining ground, and the other on the Sind high court's deliberations, the central team – backed by politicians like Daultana and Yusuf Khattak – lunged forward to impress its will on the smaller provinces, initially through persuasion and failing that through outright intimidation.

In the second week of November 1954, a group of provincial politicians were summoned to Karachi and told that the centre wanted no further debate on one unit. They had either to throw in the towel or risk political oblivion. An elaborate document, purportedly written by Daultana, outlined the advantages of the scheme and promised certain safeguards to the smaller units. It would avoid fragmentation by stressing the cultural unity and economic inter-dependence of the western wing. Above all else, 'politics on a larger canvas...[would] lead to a larger [national] vision' and militate against local forms of oppression. To bring about the miracle, the Punjab would voluntarily restrict its share of representation in the west Pakistan assembly to 40 per cent (its population entitled it to 56 per cent) for ten years, and agree to Peshawar becoming the provincial capital.[12] This would require considerable horse-trading among Punjabi and non-Punjabi politicians. But, as the document correctly noted, the existing provincial services were the single biggest threat to the merger. As 'the most vocal and influential part of the population', they 'dominate[d] the intellectual atmosphere' and were 'the real focus of behind-the-scene politics'. Without a concerted attempt to buttress their interests, they could easily 'wreck the One-Unit Government' through a 'determined conspiratorial opposition'. So various nostrums were offered for a period of fifteen years: uniform pay scales, continued recruitment of the subordinate services at the local level and fixed quotas giving the smaller units more representation in the unified provincial service.[13]

For the time being, however, all this was less salient than the high-handed methods needed to bring the scheme to early fruition. Dubbed 'clearing the decks', the operation entailed isolating such trouble-makers as Abdus Sattar Pirzada, then the premier of Sind and an outspoken critic of one unit. The well-wishers of the scheme were urged to forcibly 'silence and render inoperative all opposition', taking full advantage of the fact that the 'present regime...[could] hold a pistol to achieve [a]...constitutional agreement'. It was a particularly propitious

---

[12] 'Talking Points Regarding One Unit', handed to Sardar Abdur Rashid, chief minister of the NWFP, by Chaudhri Mohammad Ali. Reproduced with certain omissions in Maniruzzaman, *The Politics of Development*, appendix V. I am grateful to Sardar Rashid for making the full text of the document available to me.

[13] Ibid.

time for such tactics. The people of Pakistan had been reduced to a 'state of hopelessness and despair' and were 'ready to accept dictation'.[14] Buoyed by these optimistic assessments the centre followed most of the recommendations to the line. On 8 November, Pirzada's ministry in Sind was dismissed and the mantle handed over to Khuhro – in league with the centre for quick personal gains and not because he believed in one unit. The chief minister of the Punjab, Firoz Khan Noon, who had become the main proponent of a zonal federation, was ordered to stop shooting from the hip. The seemingly more pliant chief minister of the NWFP, Sardar Abdur Rashid, was politely told to fall into line or face the consequences of central displeasure.

On 22 November 1954, Bogra formally announced his government's intentions to merge west Pakistan. This was promptly followed by the provincial and state assemblies rubber-stamping the one unit resolution drafted in Karachi.[15] Although the assemblies voted for the one unit resolution, central coercion not provincial consent had been the determining factor. If the political process had been allowed to take its own course, there can be little doubt that the provinces and the princely states would have resisted – perhaps broken – the centre's whip. Even in the Punjab there were pockets of resistance, contained only by the device of placing Mushtaq Gurmani in the office of governor, a vantage point from where to squash political as well as administrative opposition to one unit. Without blackmailing the Frontier into submission[16] and buying up a few Sindhi politicians, the central team for all its fiddling might well have had to bend to a political process whose dominant impulses were the very negation of what they had set themselves out to achieve.

Realising the fragility of an order based on the rejection of provincial identities, the governor-general decided to bolster the centre's hand by bringing H.S. Suhrawardy into the cabinet. The leader of the Awami League in east Bengal and a man with 'ambition and intelligence',

---

[14] Ibid.
[15] The Khairpur assembly was the first to vote for unification, followed by Bahawalpur state, the NWFP, Punjab and Sind legislatures. Identical resolutions were passed by the Quetta municipality and the shahi jirga in Baluchistan; the municipal corporation of Karachi; the rulers of the Baluchistan states union; the jirgas of the Mohmand, Waziri and Masud tribes; and the tribal *sardars* of the Khuram and Malakand agencies. Such unanimity was too good to be true.
[16] One day before going through the motions of passing the one unit resolution, the Frontier League's assembly party had voted unanimously against it. According to Sardar Rashid, who was chief minister at the time, he had been told in plain language that his failure to persuade the assembly party would simply mean the appointment of a man who could deliver the goods. (Interview with Sardar Abdur Rashid, January 1984.)

Suhrawardy was expected to use his good offices to bring round his province to the idea of one unit.[17] This would put the finishing touches on a constitution based on two provinces, parity, a measure of provincial as well as cultural autonomy and a centre restricted to four subjects (defence, foreign affairs, currency and trade). Forming party coalitions with one or both of the main parties in the United Front, Suhrawardy's Awami League and Fazlul Huq's Krishak Sramik, might enable the Muslim League to work the constitution without fundamentally altering the existing power constellation at the centre. This was entirely within the realm of possibility since the administrative centralisation of west Pakistan envisaged under the scheme would place the centre in a strong position to influence the political process in that wing. Indeed, the proposed administrative structure for the western wing was the primary motivation behind the support lent by senior civil and defence officials to the one unit system.

In mid-December, after the Sind assembly voted itself into extinction, the governor-general had established a west Pakistan administrative council under Gurmani's chairmanship.[18] Four separate subcommittees, headed by senior civil bureaucrats like Akhtar Hussain, the defence secretary, and Eric Franklin, the secretary of the establishment division, were asked to draw up proposals for the creation of a common secretariat, the organisation of its various departments, the integration of the provincial and state cadres, as well as the coordination and implementation of administrative policy. By the end of January 1955 the west Pakistan council had completed its report.[19] Based on the twin principles of greater administrative centralisation and increased concentration of power in bureaucratic hands, the proposals warmed the hearts of many senior civil servants, especially in the CSP. The most powerful individual in the new administrative structure was to be the divisional commissioner, overseeing the activities of various districts and reporting directly to provincial headquarters. The authority and responsibility vested in the post ensured that it could only be occupied

---

[17] The opinion was expressed in 'The Talking Points Regarding One Unit'. Yet Suhrawardy's relations with his fellow cabinet ministers were anything but cordial. He accused Bogra of conspiring against him and complained that he was 'surrounded in the Cabinet by a set of crooks and Fascists – he particularly mentioned Iskander Mirza'. (Murray to Morley[CRO], 27 December 1954, DO35/5406, PRO.)

[18] The council consisted of the governors and chief ministers of Punjab, Sind and the NWFP, the chief commissioner and agent to the governor-general in Baluchistan, the adviser to the ruler of Bahawalpur, the chief minister of Khairpur and the prime minister of the Baluchistan states union, (The Pakistan [establishment of council for the administration of west Pakistan] Order, 1954, *Orders of the Governor-General, 1951 – 1956*, Karachi 1957, 123 – 4.)

[19] *Imroze* (Lahore), 29 January 1955.

by someone bearing the emblem of the central superior services. So, with the merger of the existing provincial and state services, and the creation of a single secretariat, the real bearers of central authority in west Pakistan were those members of the CSP fortunate enough to be appointed divisional commissioners. In this way the centre's writ could be exercised at the lower levels of the administrative hierarchy, just where it was needed the most. This was also the best bet of wielding the big stick on provincial politicians unwilling to accept dictation by the centre.

So all in all the one unit system held out a promising future for the bureaucratic and military clique at the centre. Smelling the sweet scent of victory, the central executive confidently declared that on the eighth birthday of its independence the country, though still without a legislature, would find itself under a new constitution. The British high commissioner, who like his American counterpart kept close tabs on the 'inner ring', was of the view that while the 'responsible authorities' did not anticipate any difficulty in getting ratification of the constitution they were in 'no hurry to proceed...[with] the holding of a general election under its provisions'.[20] Both Mirza and Chaudhri Mohammad Ali were thinking of governor's rule in east Bengal, and possibly also in west Pakistan, until after the elections. This would allow the administrative services to influence the elections, if and when they were finally held.[21] But, despite these immaculate calculations, the central government was left confronting a threat which, precisely because it had been shrugged aside when it initially reared its head, was to push the country on the edge of a precipice.

On 9 February 1955, when a full bench of the Sind high court upheld Tamizuddin's appeal, no one was more dismayed than the central executive. According to the court's ruling, the governor-general had 'no power of any kind to dissolve the Constituent Assembly'.[22] Nor could he appoint a cabinet without reference to the people's representatives. By extension, the governor-general could not force a constitution by executive decree, such as the one issued to establish the west Pakistan administrative council. Nonplussed but aware that the court decision, if unchallenged, could sound the death-knell for their future plans, the central coterie pretended to make light of the matter. After consulting

[20] A.C.B. Symon [British high commissioner] to Swinton[CRO], 18 January 1955, DO35/5406, PRO.
[21] Chaudhri Mohammad Ali believed that even if parliamentary government was introduced before the elections it would be necessary to reimpose section 92a in 'both Units immediately prior and during the elections'. (Symon's note, 7 January 1955, ibid.)

with the Punjabi chief justice of Pakistan, Mohammad Munir, the governor-general heaved a sigh of relief.[23·] Justice Munir was in sympathy with the centre and ready to overrule the lower court's decision. With judicial partiality towards the chief executive as the new element in the game, the central government formally appealed to the federal court and, at the same time, instructed the official constitutional machinery to continue firing on all cylinders.

All eyes were now on the federal court. On 21 March 1955, the court ruled by four to one that the Sind high court had no jurisdiction to issue a writ in Tamizuddin's favour. The federal court did not, as the chief justice intimated, consider whether the governor-general had rightly dissolved the constituent assembly; it merely overruled the lower court's decision on the grounds that section 223a under which it had heard the appeal did not have the governor-general's assent and was, therefore, not part of the law.

It was a momentous ruling. The people of Pakistan now discovered that the constituent assembly had never been a fully sovereign body. Since it had also served as the federal legislature it was deemed to operate under the restrictions specified in section 6(3) of the independence bill of 1947. A close reading of that section, however, makes it amply clear that the provision for the governor-general's 'full power of assent' was not tantamount to a power of veto on constitutional matters. If anything it had been inserted with the deliberate aim of underscoring Pakistan's independence from the British sovereign despite its status as a dominion. Yet it had seemed reasonable to the federal judges to interpret the clause otherwise. And this in spite of the fact that, for the past seven years, the rules of procedure for the constituent assembly – formulated while Jinnah was alive – stated that the governor-general's assent was not necessary for a bill to be placed on the statute book.[24]

After the federal court's verdict, Pakistan was not only without a parliament but as many as forty-six acts had lost their legal sanction. At least three major court cases had been decided on the argument that laws passed by the constituent assembly did not require the governor-

---

[22] Cited in G.W. Choudhury, *Constitutional Development in Pakistan* (second edition), London 1969, 86.

[23] It is not clear when the governor-general made his approach. But that his meeting with the chief justice did take place is a well-known fact. In a recent article, Sultan Ahmed – a former editor of *Dawn* – has alleged that Munir had 'assured the Government in advance that he would upset...[the Sind High Court's] judgement when it went before him...'. (See *Dawn*, 9 August 1986.)

[24] See federation of Pakistan vs. Tamizuddin Khan, in the *Federal Court Reports, 1956*, Karachi 1955.

general's assent. Here was a constitutional crisis with perplexing political and legal ramifications. Far from being perturbed by the implications of the court's decision, the central government was ready to gild the lily. It seemed opportune to interpret the federal court's decision as a signal to go ahead with constitution-making according to the original plan. Yet, by camouflaging their decision in technicalities rather than legalities, the four honourable judges had subtly admitted their inability to sanction the central government's intentions to enforce a constitution by executive fiat. Judicial ambivalence, however, could be turned to political advantage. So Suhrawardy, the law minister and a consistent proponent of restoring the people's 'democratic' rights, was given the job of announcing that the centre would summon a 'constituent convention' consisting of its nominees from the provincial and state legislatures; it would approve a constitution incorporating one unit as well as all the other trappings necessary to prop up central authority.[25]

This was a bolt from the dark; but the worst had still to come. The central government was gratified to learn from its British law secretary, Eric Snelson, that the governor-general could give retrospective assent to the laws that had become void as a result of the federal court's ruling.[26] This set the stage for the final act of an uncomfortably imbalanced play on the art of state-building in which the executive repeatedly undermined the legislature while the judiciary whistled away indistinctly.

Within a week of the federal court's decision, the governor-general had issued the emergency powers ordinance IX, declared a 'state of grave emergency' throughout Pakistan, and placed a blanket prohibition on all proceedings against the central government in connection with the dismissal of the first constituent assembly.[27] The ordinance empowered him to frame a constitution, to convert west Pakistan into a single unit of administration, to validate thirty-five of the forty-six laws passed by the constituent assembly but for which his assent had not been sought, to pass the central budget and, finally, to rename the eastern wing 'east Pakistan'.[28] The assumption of sweeping powers by the centre saw its staunchest support cut to the quick. There were calls for elections and a representative constituent assembly in consonance with the governor-general's original proclamation of 24 October 1954. These

---

[25] *The Pakistan Observer* (Dacca), 22 March 1955, cited in Rahman, *Public Opinion and Political Development in Pakistan*, 162.

[26] *Dawn*, 23 March 1955, also in ibid.

[27] *Dawn*, 28 March 1955.

[28] Choudhury, *Constitutional Development in Pakistan*, 87–8.

were endorsed by an unexpected quarter – the federal court itself. The relief operation was occasioned by the court's decision on another major constitutional case – Usif Patel vs. the crown.

On 13 April 1955, a full bench of the federal court with justice Munir in the chair, declared that, while the governor-general could 'give or withhold assent' to bills passed by the constituent assembly, he could 'neither claim powers which he never possessed nor claim to succeed to the powers of that Assembly'.[29] In other words, in the absence of a constituent assembly, the governor-general could not validate laws retrospectively. So the section of the emergency ordinance giving him such powers was held to be *ultra vires*. The chief justice also maintained that the court's decision on the Tamizuddin case had been 'grievously misunderstood'. The 'first concern' of the central government should have been to 'bring into existence another representative body to exercise the powers of the constituent assembly'. But the governor-general's ordinance made 'no reference to elections'.[30] Rebuking the government for failing to create the appropriate constitutional machinery, the chief justice now confessed that he did 'not know whether the Constituent Assembly was dissolved legally or not'. During the deliberations on the Tamizuddin case, the counsel for the government had assured the court that steps would be taken to set up a constituent assembly within a matter of ten days. But, he regretted, 'this has not been done so far'. This was wholly contrary to the law and could spell 'disaster' for the country.[31].

The federal court's Solomonic ruling threw the central government into momentary disarray. Much to its consternation, the new constitution could not be promulgated by the vote of a *nominated* assembly. So willy-nilly, the governor-general announced that the 'constituent convention' would meet on 10 May. It would consist of sixty members,[32] all to be elected by the existing provincial assemblies except for seven whom he would nominate to represent Baluchistan, Karachi, the princely states and the tribal areas. The 'convention' was to be dissolved within six months, giving the members just enough time to read and register their opinions on the draft constitution which had already been prepared. At the same time, the governor-general assumed powers to validate the thirty-five laws pending advice from the federal court.

[29] See Usif Patel vs. the crown. *Federal Court Reports*, 1955, 366.
[30] Ibid., 372
[31] *Dawn.* 14 April 1955, cited in Rahman, *Public Opinion and Political Development in Pakistan*, 166 and Choudhury, *Constitutional Development in Pakistan*, 88.
[32] There were to be thirty members from east Pakistan, including seven non-Muslims; sixteen from the Punjab; four from Sind; three from the NWFP and one each from Baluchistan, the Frontier states, Khairpur, Bahawalpur and Karachi.

Without this stop-gap measure nothing could prevent a complete breakdown of the legal and administrative system. As a result of the federal court's ruling even the provincial legislatures were illegal since they too were elected under laws which had not been properly validated.[33]

The federal judges now prevailed upon the central government to formally request their opinion on the knotty issue of whether the constituent assembly had been dissolved legally or not. Until then, the judges declared, they could not establish the legality of any alternative constitution-making body. After frenzied exchanges in smoke-filled rooms, the central government relented. The meeting of the 'constituent convention' was postponed until the federal court had devised a way out of the constitutional morass.

On 10 May 1955, the federal court pulled a rabbit out of the hat. Although the independence bill had not given the governor-general any power to dissolve the constituent assembly, four of the five federal court judges upheld the legality of his action by drawing upon the British common law doctrines of *salus populi superma lex* [safety of the people is the supreme law] and *salus republicae est superma lex* [safety of the state is the supreme law].[34] The judges were also of the view that the governor-general could validate laws retrospectively until a new constitution-making body had formally met to decide on the matter. In return for these large concessions, the governor-general and his 'council of ministers' had to make a few small sacrifices, if only for the sake of judicial credibility. The 'constituent convention' had to be called the 'constituent assembly' and the governor-general was debarred from nominating any of its members. These would have to be elected by the provincial assemblies, an unnecessary irritation for the central government since it afforded politicians an opportunity to demand 'a stiff price for their co-operation'.[35]

Ostensibly, the federal court's judgement had solved the Pakistani constitutional puzzle, forestalling martial law and restoring a semblance of 'democratic' procedures or, more aptly, their nuisance value. But by pulling the constitutional crisis out of the realm of public debate the court's decision had conveniently turned it into a bedrock of the future state structure. Insofar as the constitutional crisis was a

---

[33] A measure of the confusion in the country was the attitude of the United Front leadership. Their sheer 'delight' at discovering that governor's rule in east Pakistan had no basis in law was 'tempered by the...understanding' that the provincial legislature to which they belonged had all along been illegal. (Dacca fortnightly report no.8, 20 April 1955, DO35/5299, PRO.)

[34] Special reference no. 1 of 1955, *Federal Court Reports*, 495.

[35] Symon to secretary of state [CRO], 14 July 1955, DO35/5378, PRO.

product of the tussles between the centre and the provinces, its outcome provided legal rationale to bureaucratic and military efforts to use executive authority to undermine politicians and, if possible, to do away with the political process altogether.

Railing the political system

By the early summer of 1955, the supremacy of central authority over the provincial units was no longer in doubt. But the experience of the past seven and a half years had taught the strongmen of Karachi never to underestimate the capacity of provincial politicians to bounce back into action at the centre's expense. Now that the federal court had ruled out constitution-making by executive decree, the central leadership naturally wanted a controlling hand in elections to the constituent assembly since its members – raised to eighty[36] – were not above trying to chisel the draft constitution out of recognition. Exerting pressure on the provincial legislatures was the only way of ensuring the election of the centre's henchmen to the constituent assembly. Adept at such operations, the central team was ready to exploit the factional permutations in the provinces. They stood a better chance in west Pakistan than in east Pakistan where the United Front, though racked by divisions, was likely to resist central dictates more effectively.

There was nothing new about Karachi wanting to use provincial factionalism to further its aims. But, whereas earlier it had been content simply to play one League faction against the other, the objective now was less straightforward. The display of provincial divisiveness, towards which it was only too willing to contribute, was an excellent excuse to justify placing the political process at the service of a central government drawing strength from the administrative and coercive arms of the state rather than a popularly based national party. To put it unequivocally, the architects of state-building had long concluded that 'parliamentary government' – or rather its facade – was a necessary evil, to be tolerated until such time that the political process had been discredited or,

---

[36] The membership was raised in order to pacify Fazlul Huq, the leader of the United Front, who threatened to boycott the assembly because east Pakistan had not been given a majority of the seats. With the twenty additional seats, the composition of the assembly was:

East Pakistan	40 (9 non-Muslims)	Tribal areas	3
Punjab	21 (1 non-Muslim)	Baluchistan states union	1
NWFP	4	Frontier states	1
Sind	5 (1 non-Muslim)	Khairpur state	1
Baluchistan	1	Karachi	1
Bahawalpur	2	TOTAL	80

alternatively, those in command at the centre felt able to exercise unfettered authority over Pakistan's wayward constituent units. With this inner logic guiding their every move, it was easy to confuse future designs with existing realities. Having decided to do away with provincial identities in the western wing, the central leaders pretended they no longer existed, provoking antagonisms against the state which no amount of soft pedalling could neutralise, much less dispel.

Firoz Khan Noon, the chief minister of the Punjab, was brusquely ordered to let the Pakistan League's parliamentary board select sixteen out of the twenty-one Punjabi representatives to the constituent assembly, including six central ministers.[37] Noon dithered and sulked, but refused to surrender. So he had to be dismissed although a majority in the provincial assembly and the Punjab League council silently applauded his courageous stance against the centre. Abdul Hamid Dasti who belonged to the anti-Noon group led by Daultana – once again the centre's handyman in the Punjab – was installed as chief minister.[38] Noon retaliated by forming an independent group consisting of sixty of his supporters in the assembly; the defection split the Punjab League down the middle.[39]

In Sind, it was the central government which had given Khuhro a fresh lease in provincial politics. The Sind high court tried ridding the province of Khuhro by declaring his appointment as chief minister to be illegal. But the man was unstoppable; he refused to resign and sniggered at suggestions that he was not the authentic president of the Sind League.[40] The central government, one of whose members described Khuhro as 'a good honest crook you can rely on',[41] had no reason to regret the baneful effects of 'Khuhroism'[42] on Sindhi politics. All Khuhro had to do to validate his passport from the centre was to promote one unit and assist the election of men who would obey the centre's whip in the constituent assembly.[43]

---

[37] On 22 April, the Punjab League's assembly party allowed itself to be swayed by Daultana's impassioned appeals to accept the centre's demands. But once negotiations between the central and provincial parliamentary boards failed to make headway, Noon and his supporters took matters in hand and objected to this infringement of Punjabi rights. (*Dawn*, 23 April 1955 and 1 May 1955.)

[38] *Dawn*, 22 May 1955.

[39] Noon was eventually expelled from the League; he was to play an important role in the formation of the Republican party.

[40] In 1953, Nazimuddin had declared against Khuhro's continuing in office as president of the Sind League due to his conviction under PRODA.

[41] Acting British high commissioner to the CRO, telegram no.133, 9 November 1954, DO35/5406, PRO.

[42] The term was coined by Suhrawardy.

[43] Evidence of Khuhro's attempts to buy the centre's favour was his decision to allot 150,000 acres of land to army personnel in the Makhi Dhand area. (See *Dawn*, 22 March 1955.)

The Frontier presented more awkward problems for the central government. Although Sardar Rashid had gone along with the one unit scheme in principle, he soon began falling out with the centre over the details. With the Afghans protesting against the integration of west Pakistan[44] and the danger of revived Pathan enthusiasm for 'Pakh-tunistan', the central government hesitated before dismissing Rashid's ministry. But on 18 July, after elections to the constituent assembly, Karachi ousted Rashid and brought in Sardar Bahadur Khan, Ayub's brother and a firm supporter of the merger. Public opinion, and not just that of the Pathans, was shocked by this 'tragically cruel interference by the Centre with the democratic rights of a province'.[45]

This was not an isolated incident, but the considered policy of a central government determined to complete the final leg of a tiresome journey towards one unit. For instance, to appease the Pathans, Dr Khan Sahib was designated as the first chief minister of west Pakistan. Yet typical of the twisted thinking in the control room was the central team's hopes of getting Khan Sahib elected to the solitary seat reserved for Baluchistan in the constituent assembly. Three members of the Baluchistan shahi jirga did raise their voice against the unfairness of it all; the administration was 'not only...partial, but putting pressure upon both the members of the Shahi Jirga and the [Quetta] Municipal Committee to facilitate the election of Dr Khan Sahib'.[46]

The wails of protest from Punjabis, Sindhis, Pathans and Baluchis were interpreted by the central government as evidence that victory was near at hand. And so it was in the western wing. Matters were, of course, much trickier in the eastern wing. However much it tried, the central government could not expect to control the Bengali representatives in the constituent assembly. Since this could overturn the benefits of its hard earned successes in west Pakistan, the central government con-cluded that understandings with the United Front, from which Suhrawardy's Awami League had been expelled in April 1955, were unavoidable.[47] Bogra particularly could see advantages in grasping the

---

[44] Apart from using normal diplomatic channels to register their displeasure at the integration of NWFP with the rest of west Pakistan, the Afghan government sat back while a frenzied mob attacked the Pakistani embassy in Kabul. (*Dawn*, 31 March 1955.)

[45] *Azad*, 23 July 1955, cited in *Dawn*, 25 July 1955.

[46] *Dawn*, 9 June 1955.

[47] The reasons for the Awami League's expulsion are complex; but that was true of all Bengali politics. Three of the main leaders of the provincial Awami League – Ataur Rahman, Abul Mansur Ahmad and Mujibur Rahman were accused of conspiring to oust Huq from the leadership of the United Front, 'hob-nobbing' with the centre over his head and using 'abusive' and 'unparliamentary' language against him. (Ibid., 25 April 1955, cited in Afzal, *Political Parties in Pakistan*, 173.)

Table 5.1 *Party position in west Pakistan*

Punjab		Sind		Karachi	
Muslim League	15	Muslim League	4	Muslim League	1
Noon group	3	Minority	1	*Baluchistan*	
Opposition	2	*NWFP*		Independent	1
Minority	1	Muslim League	4	(Dr Khan Sahib)	

Source: Dawn, 22 June 1955.

Party position in east Pakistan

United Front	16	United Progressive Parliamentary party	2
Awami League	12		
Pakistan Congress	4	Muslim League	1
Scheduled Caste Federation	3	Independent Muslim League	1
Communist	1		

Source: Ibid., 23 June 1955.

nettle. Suhrawardy was his main rival for the post of prime minister. Unless able to get himself elected as east Pakistan's representative in the constituent assembly, Bogra would forfeit the right to remain in office. So he found the terms of an agreement with Fazlul Huq. In exchange for Huq's assurances about the election of Bengal's representatives to the constituent assembly, including the promise of a seat, Bogra announced the lifting of section 92a – something he had resolutely opposed. Less than two weeks before the elections to the constituent assembly, Abu Hussain Sarkar – a central minister since October 1954 – was invited to form a 'United Front' or more aptly a Krishak Sramik cabinet. Bogra's deal with Huq had opened the way for a Muslim League-'United Front'[48] coalition at the centre.

Despite the flagrant abuse of central authority to prop up its chances, the League failed to secure a majority in the constituent assembly. Predictably, it did well in west Pakistan, winning fifteen seats from the Punjab; all four from the NWFP; four from Sind and one from Karachi. Bogra was the lone Leaguer elected from east Pakistan; here the United Front and the Awami League won sixteen and twelve seats respectively (see Table 5.1). Of the old members of the constituent assembly, a mere

---

[48] Without the Awami League, the coalition which had buried the League in east Bengal was hardly 'United'; what remained of it was effectively a Krishak Sramik front.

Table 5.2 *Occupational background of members of the second constituent assembly*

	West Pakistan	East Pakistan
Landlords	28	—
Lawyers	3	20
Retired officials	5	9
Industry and Commerce	4	3
Miscellaneous	—	8

Source: Mushtaq Ahmad, *Government and Politics in Pakistan* (second edition), Karachi 1963, 115.

fourteen managed to get re-elected, largely due to the disappearance of the Muslim League in east Bengal. The social backgrounds of the members, however, were almost identical to those of the first constituent assembly; landlords dominated the west Pakistan contingent; lawyers held sway over Bengal's representatives (see Table 5.2). The east-west divide, which had made it difficult for the previous assembly to find the basis for a constitutional agreement, continued to loom large on the horizon.

Much as they had always feared, the central leadership had not been able to translate their legal successes into political victories. Even the most cosmetic form of 'democracy', they learnt to their dismay, had its inconveniences. There was talk of doing away with political parties.[49] But until then a coalition with the United Front or the Awami League was the only way the Muslim League – to which bureaucrats like Mirza and Chaudhri Mohammad Ali belonged – could continue to stake a claim in the running of the government. So on 11 August 1955, after further manoeuvrings as a result of which Bogra, Suhrawardy and even Ghulam Mohammad[50] fell by the wayside, a Muslim League-United

---

[49] As early as January 1955, Dr Khan Sahib had spoken of the irrelevance of political parties under the circumstances then prevalent in the country. (*Nawa-i-Waqt*, 11 January 1955.) For an ex-Congressman who had joined the central government without deigning to join the Muslim League, this was an understandable effort at self-justification. But the thinking was shared by some people, and not least officials in the civil and military services.

[50] Bogra because he tried to block Mirza from becoming governor-general; but in view of his past services, he was allowed to fulfill his dream of returning to Washington as Pakistan's ambassador. Suhrawardy was asked to come in as the deputy prime minister but refused to accept anything less than the prime ministership. Mirza, who had been 'endeavouring to manoeuvre Chaudhri Mohammad Ali into the position', claimed he would 'resign rather than serve under Suhrawardy'. (Symon to Laithwaite, 31 July 1955, DO35/5378, PRO.) As for Ghulam Mohammad, he was by no means outmanoeuvred; age and flagging health forced him into retirement.

Front coalition assumed office under the prime ministership of a
somewhat reluctant Chaudhri Mohammad Ali. Fazlul Huq was rewarded with the job of governor of east Pakistan. The most coveted
position of all, that of interim governor-general, went to Iskander Mirza
who with the backing of Ayub – now out of the ministry but still the
'final arbiter of the destiny of Cabinets'[51] – 'at least tacitly' used the
'threat of force [to] obtain [his] own position and...to coerce...
[Chaudhri Mohammad] Ali into accepting [the] Prime Ministership'.[52] Contrary to earlier understandings between the two wings,
both the key positions had been farmed out to west Pakistanis. This was
the price the United Front had to pay in order to prevent Suhrawardy
becoming prime minister since he could be relied upon to use his office to
dethrone the Sarkar ministry in east Pakistan. Bengali divisions had
kept the Muslim League as the dominant party at the centre. Here was
an opportunity for the bureaucratic-military alliance to use the combined voting strength of the League and the United Front to give the
draft constitution a final kick through the constituent assembly.

Yet, once the members of the new assembly began debating the future
constitution, disagreements came thick and fast. There were dissidents
within the League's ranks and the United Front, a loose conglomerate of
three parties – the Krishak Sramik, the Nizam-i-Islam and the Ganatantri Dal – who were far from agreed on the vital constitutional issues.
A stalemate would give the new governor-general the pretext for
dismissing the assembly and perhaps even imposing martial law. This
was the more likely since the 'inner ring' believed that their 'effective
power ha[d] been reduced'[53] in the aftermath of elections to the
constituent assembly and were depending 'in large measure...on army
support'.[54] Suhrawardy, now effectively the leader of the opposition,
was convinced that the 'ruling clique' which, according to him,
'consist[ed] of General Iskander Mirza and Ayub' were 'hop[ing] and
expect[ing] the current attempt to introduce the constitution by
democratic means to fail – thus preparing the way for a dictatorship'.[55]
Mirza himself conceded that he was 'not really interested in the timetable of the constitution' because, to quote him, once 'we get One Unit

[51] Hildreth's despatch to the department of state, 26 August 1955, *Foreign Relations*,
    VIII, South Asia, Washington, DC 1987, 436.
[52] Arthur Z. Gardiner [counsellor, Karachi embassy] to the department of state,
    telegram, 19 September 1955, ibid., 440.
[53] Hildreth's telegram to the department of state, 26 August 1955, ibid., 436.
[54] Gardiner's telegram to the department of state, 15 September 1955, ibid., 438.
[55] First annexure to the high commissioner's despatch no.151 to the CRO, 17 August,
    1955, DO35/5406. PRO.

through we have control and our position is strengthened'.[56] So the members of the constituent assembly, more the captives of circumstance than the conscience of constituents, no longer had the option of agreeing to disagree. The first task before them was to validate the laws which had become void due to the federal court's ruling on the Usif Patel case. With that problem safely out of the way, the assembly was allowed to chew on the west Pakistan establishment bill. Some members of the opposition, notably Firoz Khan Noon and representatives of the Awami League, accused the central government of muzzling opposition to the scheme: ministries had been dismissed, members of the provincial legislatures opposed to the idea were 'interned, externed and sent to jail'. In short, the claim that one unit had the support of the people of west Pakistan was wholly 'without foundation'. A referendum alone could settle the thorny issue.[57] But it was a losing battle; referendums and elections were not on the central government's agenda. By no means enamoured by the proposed unification of west Pakistan, the United Front adopted the posture expected of a party sharing power at the centre. When the final vote was taken, a mere thirteen votes were cast against the bill – with the exception of one lonely west Pakistani voice, all the others were by Bengalis.[58] And so, on 14 October 1955, the province of west Pakistan at long last assumed a reality. A seven member cabinet headed by Khan Sahib was formed with Gurmani as the governor of the new province.[59]

With the brightest feather firmly in its cap, the central government had less reason to be nervous about some of the other contentious issues. A twelve member sub-committee with equal number of representatives from the League and the United Front was set up to thrash out the final draft of the constitutional bill. Against a background of intense political activity by the religious parties as well as the regional autonomists in east Pakistan, the sub-committee presided over by Chaudhri Mohammad Ali tried resolving the differences between the parties in the ruling coalition. That it was not a smooth sail is suggested by the prime minister's equivocal 'warning' about the grave implications for the country in the absence of a constitutional agreement.[60] The threat, along with speculations about the reimposition of section 92a in east

---

[56] Symon to Laithwaite, 21 September 1955, DO35/5378, PRO.

[57] The Awami League peppered its case by arguing that the inclusion of Karachi into west Pakistan was unwarranted since it had been developed with central funds and, therefore, east Pakistan's resources.

[58] *CAD*, 1, 17 and 30 September 1955, 875 and 1472.

[59] Only the staunchest supporters of one unit like Daultana, Khuhro and Sardar Bahadur Khan found a place in Khan Sahib's cabinet.

[60] It was issued on 17 November 1955, cited in 'Pakistan: Last Stage of Constitution-Making', *Round Table* (London), XLVII, no.182, March 1956, 178.

Pakistan, produced the desired results. After painful negotiations during December, the two parties had saved the coalition and also managed to produce a constitutional bill which, on the face of it, accepted a federal instead of a unitary form of government and a parliamentary instead of a presidential system – the bare minimum needed to mollify the Bengalis.

On 8 January 1956, the constitutional bill was placed before the constituent assembly. A preamble based on the objectives resolution of 1949 defined Pakistan as an 'Islamic republic'. Coining a new name for the state was easy; detailing its nature and workings required 234 clauses divided into thirteen sections and another six schedules. The members of the assembly were given a week to digest the document. After twelve days of general discussion, the assembly met seventeen times to consider the clauses in detail. As many as 670 amendments were proposed, mostly by the Awami League. On 29 February, the constitution was approved; but not before a walkout staged by the opposition groups at Suhrawardy's instigation.[61] On 2 March 1956, Mirza signed the constitution bill; he did so after guaranteeing his nomination, if not his election, as the provisional president. So on 23 March 1956, exactly sixteen years after the adoption of the Lahore resolution, Pakistan formally became an 'Islamic republic' with a 'federal' constitution and a 'parliamentary system' based on the British model. The constituent assembly was to serve as the interim national assembly; general elections were promised once the legislatures in east and west Pakistan had decided whether to have joint or separate electorates – an issue over which there was still no agreement in sight.

So, after nearly nine years of agonising, Pakistan had a constitution, considered and approved by an indirectly elected constituent assembly. Together with the creation on 19 October of a three man electoral commission, this was seen as a sure sign of the government's desire to hold general elections. But Karachi's apparent commitment to 'democratic' procedure disguised many awkward realities. Intimidation, outright coercion and the extension of patronage had been critical in the central leadership's success in forcing the constitutional bill through the constituent assembly. The constitution was a stop-gap, not a first step towards free and fair elections. After a seventy-minute meeting with Mirza the British high commissioner had gained the impression that the 'Governor-General w[ould] do his best to stave off elections until he is

---

[61] Apart from the Awami League, the protesting members included Mian Iftikharuddin [Azad Pakistan party], Mahmud Ali [Ganatantri Dal] as well as the representatives of the United Progressive party and the Scheduled Caste Federation. (Callard, *Pakistan: a Political Study*, 121–2.)

completely satisfied that the people will throw up the right government, e.g. people like himself and Chaudhri Mohammad Ali'.[62] Since that was unlikely in the near future, the constitution was fitted with as many contradictions as were necessary to render it unworkable, thus consolidating bureaucratic and military control over the state apparatus. The seeds of the crisis that enveloped the state during the remaining two and a half years of 'parliamentary government' were written into this constitutional artefact. A thorough scrutiny of the main constitutional provisions makes this crystal clear.

A CONSTITUTION OF MISTAKEN IDENTITY

While emulating the government of India act of 1935 and the final draft of the first constituent assembly, the 1956 constitution faithfully reflected the tensions between the political process and the centralisation of state authority in Pakistan. Far from containing the main points of conflict or detailing a system of checks and balances, the constitutional framework was a veritable time bomb with the fuse box in the custody of the president. The powers of the president far exceeded those normally bestowed upon a ceremonial head of state in a parliamentary system, and this despite the opposition's success in forcing certain curbs. Although governor-generals had been subject to recall by London upon a simple request by parliament, the president was practically irremovable. He was to be elected by the national and provincial assemblies for a period of five years, but for no more than two terms. Impeachment procedures were laid down; yet the three-fourths majority required to give it effect was prohibitive in a country where incumbents tended to treat parliament as a bargain basement for votes.

Admittedly, there was nothing unusual about investing the president with far-reaching powers. The Indian constitution of 1950 made similar allowances. But the experience of the last nine years had shown that the chronic instability of party government in Pakistan had as much to do with inveterate meddling by the head of state, largely at the behest of interest groups within as well as outside the state apparatus, as with the lack of a grassroots political organisation. Having had to forego a presidential form of government based on the American pattern, the framers of the constitution had ingeniously superimposed it on a distorted version of the British 'parliamentary system'. Unlike a candidate for the White House, the president of the 'Islamic republic' was not nominated by an organised political machinery; nor did he require a direct mandate from the people. He was also immune from

---

[62] Symon to Laithwaite, 21 September 1955, DO35/5378, PRO.

many of the established conventions that served to check the powers of the British head of state.

The presidency of the 'Islamic republic of Pakistan' was a unique position for anyone to occupy, let alone someone of Mirza's ilk. It had nothing whatsoever to do with Pakistan's ideological leanings and the tortured debate about creating an 'Islamic state'. Appropriate nods no doubt were made to the religious lobby. The repugnancy clause precluded the adoption of any legislation contrary to Islamic law. But, true to the dominant proclivities of senior officials in the two main institutions of the state, the constitutional scribes avoided declaring Islam as the state religion. The proclamation of an 'Islamic republic' was not to be taken too literally.

The constitution's flirtations with parliamentary democracy and federalism were equally light hearted. An examination of the statutory powers of the president – whether in relation to the cabinet or the national assembly – furnishes proof of the troubles the authors of the constitution took to ensure the continued infirmity of 'parliamentary government'. In consonance with the intentions of the bureaucratic-military alliance, the constitution aimed at impressing, once and for all, the imperatives of state-building on the political process while keeping attention focused on the easily demonstrable inability of party leaders to organise or govern.

Executive authority was vested in the president who appointed and dismissed the cabinet, thus undermining its collective responsibility to the national assembly. The only stipulation against the president's powers was that he use 'discretion' and appoint as prime minister a member of the national assembly most likely to command a majority in the house. The president had enormous powers of patronage; a tremendous resource when it came to vote chopping in parliament. All cabinet, state and deputy ministers were to be selected by him from among the members of the assembly. They were to 'aid and advise' him on everything to do with the federation except where the constitution specifically empowered the president to act on his personal discretion.[63] By contrast, the prime minister was bound by 'duty', if not by gratitude, to keep the president informed of all decisions taken by the cabinet on administrative and legislative matters.[64] So, while the president had authority to interfere with the workings of the cabinet, nothing in the constitution compelled him to act on its advice. In the event of serious

---

[63] *Constitution of the Islamic Republic of Pakistan*, Karachi 1956, section IV, articles three, four, five and seven.
[64] Ibid., article forty-two.

disagreement, the head of state was certain of winning hands down, not least because the prime minister remained in office at the 'pleasure of the President'. A storm of protest in the constituent assembly did force the government benches to amend the constitutional bill so that the president could not apply the Ghulam Mohammad formula to dismiss the head of government unless 'satisfied' that he did not command the support of a majority of the members in the national assembly.[65] Yet the provision was of doubtful value; the constitution did not lay down precisely the conditions and the circumstances under which the president could justifiably decide whether or not a prime minister enjoyed the confidence of the national assembly. A mere stroke of the presidential pen could suffice to make a perfect travesty of 'parliamentary government'.

The president's relationship with the national assembly followed a similar pattern. He could summon, prorogue and dismiss the national assembly which was to consist of 310 members[66] divided equally between east and west Pakistan. The annual budget was placed before the national assembly only after the president's approval and its members could not pass a taxation bill or allocate expenditure from the federal consolidated fund without first seeking his consent.[67] The president possessed a limited veto on all bills passed by the national assembly and an absolute veto on provincial laws under his jurisdiction. And of course the head of state had full authority to issue legal ordinances while the assembly was not in session. Unless endorsed by the assembly within six weeks of its next meeting, the ordinance lapsed automatically. Nothing could prevent him from reissuing the ordinance. Alternatively, he could use his emergency powers to dismiss the national assembly and rule by ordinance for an indefinite period.

The president also appointed all the key personnel in the state hierarchy. As the supreme commander of the armed forces, he was responsible for selecting the three commanders-in-chief as well as raising, maintaining and granting commissions in the services. The members of the All-Pakistan civil services, both at the centre and in the provinces, were directly answerable to the president who supervised their appointments, transfers and dismissals. The provincial governors were chosen by the president and exercised powers identical to his with respect to the provincial ministries and assemblies. It was once again the

---

[65] Ibid., article six.
[66] Including ten seats reserved for women; five each from the two wings. (Ibid., article forty-four.)
[67] The federal consolidated fund covered all revenues and loans raised by the government of Pakistan.

president who nominated the judges of the supreme and the high courts. So, even without recourse to the emergency provisions, the president could direct and control the functioning of the entire state apparatus.

The emergency provisions under section XI of the constitution were a further menace to 'parliamentary government' and the actual workings of the federal system. It is true that most federal constitutions invest the centre with such powers. The government of India act of 1935 made ample provisions to dilute the provincial autonomy it so proudly introduced; the Indian constitution is no exception. Yet the 1956 constitution improved on these examples, making the emergency provisions more stringent and, as some members of the constituent assembly complained bitterly, upsetting the delicate balance between the centre and provinces before federalism had begun operating in earnest. Six articles of the constitution delineated the powers of the president in periods of political and financial instability without defining the meaning of an 'emergency'. This was just as well. The state had been lurching from one 'emergency' to another ever since its creation; spelling out the term would have made it impossible to counter allegations that with the emergency provisions the president could at a wink sully the workings of the political process.

Under article 191, the president could proclaim a state of emergency if the 'security or economic life of Pakistan' or any of its parts was 'threatened by war... external aggression... or...internal disturbance' which was 'beyond the power of a Provincial Government to control'.[68] It was simple to understand 'war' and 'external aggression'. But in Pakistan, periods of economic instability and internal disturbances were everyday occurrences. So under this provision the president could at any time intervene in provincial affairs, disrupt the political process and take charge of the entire administration – except the high courts – either directly or through the governor. Under these conditions, the national assembly in principle was to assume all powers for provincial legislation. But the proclamation was to be placed before the federal parliament for approval 'as soon as conditions ma[de] it practicable for the President to summon that Assembly'.[69] To put it plainly, the president could suspend the political process *indefinitely* in the provinces as well as at the centre![70] Articles 193 and 194 equipped the president with extraordinary powers to deal with two other types of emergency. The first, a

---

[68] Ibid., article 191 (1).
[69] Ibid., article 191 (6).
[70] Under article fifty-one the national assembly had to meet at least twice a year, but it was not clear whether this would be binding on the president in a period of emergency.

breakdown of the constitutional machinery in a province, was identical to section 93 of the 1935 act and section 92a of the interim constitution – that bugbear of provincial autonomists. The second could be invoked if the financial stability of the state or any of its constituent units was endangered and it became necessary for the federal government to issue guidelines on 'financial propriety' to the provinces. Both articles, however, required the sanction of the national assembly within sixty days for a period extending no longer than six months. Interestingly enough, the constitution made no provision for the suspension of constitutional government at the centre. But, together with article 191 and the president's power to dismiss the prime minister and the national assembly, the omission was inconsequential.

If the president's relationship with the cabinet and the national assembly cast serious doubts about the authenticity of the Pakistani 'parliamentary system', the emergency provisions call for extreme circumspection about the federal principles of the 1956 constitution. The president's emergency powers raise a question of fundamental and perennial importance in any understanding of the Pakistani state: was the federalism of the 1956 constitution a mere smoke-screen which enabled its authors to furtively inject the spirit and the substance of an essentially unitary system of government?

Prima facie the 1956 constitution was federal in form. It had to be if provincial sentiments, especially those of the eastern wing, were to be assuaged. Above all, without concessions to the units of the federation, the central government would have had no choice except to bid farewell to democratic pretences and enforce the constitution by executive fiat, something it had been discouraged from doing not because it cared a whit about legal niceties but simply because it was still developing the necessary props for its dictatorial predilections. So the constitution-makers made concessions with one hand and cancelled them with the other. To impress the central government's *bona fides*, the constitution went further than the government of India act of 1935 in granting legislative autonomy to the provinces and, what was more, investing them with residual powers. The subjects on the provincial list were increased from fifty-five to ninety-four. This might seem to suggest a trend towards the decentralisation of authority. But the federal government continued to exercise control over the most important subjects and, together with its financial and administrative powers, could offset the effects of any devolution. Clause after clause in the constitution emphasised the priority of federal legislation over the provincial; this applied to subjects on the concurrent list and a special provision rendered a provincial law void if it contravened legislation enacted by the national parliament. A mere increase in the number of subjects on the provincial list had made no difference to the federal centre's supremacy in the legislative realm.

In any event, legislative autonomy by itself cannot be seen as indicative of how power is apportioned between the centre and the constituent units in a federal system. By far the more important determinants of the relationship are the financial and administrative arrangements. The 1956 constitution, predictably enough, stood pat on the principles of the 1935 act which had been improved upon by the interim constitution to give the federal government primacy in the allocation of financial resources and control over the administrative machinery. Revenues from customs, export and excise duties, and taxes on incomes other than agriculture, as well as the sales tax, all were channelled into the federal treasury. The provinces were entitled to half of the proceeds from the sales tax and a share of the income tax. But, with their total annual expenditure exceeding that of the federal government on items other than national defence, they were left in a sorry financial condition. Despite the Raisman award of 1953, financial bickerings between the central and provincial governments had continued unabated. The award had left the provinces more dependent on but less satisfied with their share of receipts from central taxes. In 1954–5, 37 per cent of east Bengal's revenues were derived from central taxes; the figure for Punjab was 22 per cent; 17 per cent for NWFP and 19 per cent for Sind.[71] Instead of devising a way to ease the friction, the constitution provided for the establishment, eventually, of a national finance commission which was to make recommendations on central and provincial allocations from export duties on jute and cotton, and taxes on income and sales.[72] Short of an immediate increase in their share of these principal taxes, the provinces had no way of making ends meet except through central grants-in-aid or loans. With national defence eating larger and larger slices of the central revenues, grants were difficult to come by. To raise an external or an internal loan, provinces had to enter into lengthy and often futile negotiations with officials in the central finance ministry, an experience which could convert the staunchest nationalists into the most rabid advocates of provincial autonomy. That this autonomy had to extend beyond

---

[71] See *Explanatory Memorandum on the Budget, 1957–58* and the annual budget statements of the governments of east Bengal, Punjab, the NWFP and Sind. Reproduced in Andrus and Mohammad, *The Economy of Pakistan*, chapter XIX.

[72] It was to consist of the central and provincial finance ministers and individuals appointed by the president after consultations with the governors. (*Constitution of the Islamic Republic of Pakistan*, 1956, article 118.)

legislation to include a degree of financial and administrative decentralisation is illustrated by the case of industries, one of the subjects transferred to the provincial list. Without resources and licences – both of which required circumventing reams of red tape in the federal bureaucracy – provincial legislation for the establishment of industries had no effective meaning.

And, indeed, it was in the delegation of administrative powers between the centre and the provinces that the 1956 constitution came closest to betraying the real nature of the proposed state structure. Quite apart from the president's powers to invoke an emergency, article 126 gave the central government powers to direct provincial governments on how to administer their affairs even in normal times. For instance, the federal government could issue guidelines to the provincial government for 'preventing any grave menace to the peace or tranquillity or economic life of Pakistan, or any part thereof.[73] Recognising the absurdity of trying to administer east Pakistan from Karachi, the constitution allowed the federal centre to delegate power to provincial governments. But this was by no means a concession to provincial autonomy. It was seen to be feasible only because the federal centre appointed the governors – the chief executive authority in the provinces. With the governor to execute its commands and members of the All-Pakistan civil service manning most of the key jobs in the provincial administration, the centre could devolve powers without loosening its reins on the units of the federation. Even without recourse to article 126 or the emergency provisions, the governor and CSP officers in the provinces were the best guarantee for the continued exercise of unitary control by the federal centre. Like the 1935 act the new constitution ensured that the governor could not be removed by either the provincial ministry or the legislature while article 181 precluded them from taking disciplinary action against any member of the central civil service.

Clearly then, the 1956 constitution does not recommend itself as a coherent framework for either a parliamentary or a federal system of government. And, although a big leap in the direction they had wanted it to take, the constitution was less than perfect from the point of view of the bureaucratic and military axis. The need for a semblance of a national consensus had prevented them from installing a system of 'controlled democracy'. But the 'capacity of the Centre to resist pressure from below' was deemed to be 'far less than it was', not least because the inauguration of the constitution had given a 'strong fillip' to '"democratic" sentiment', a term which in the Pakistani context did not

[73] Ibid., article 126 (c).

'mean...the participation of the masses in government but rather the control of the senior politicians by the more numerous junior ones'.[74] This was why the authors of the constitution, while appearing to concede demands for a parliamentary and federal structure, incorporated as many loopholes as were needed to ensure that the state functioned as nearly in accordance with a presidential and unitary form of government as was possible. That there was plenty of room for serious confusion of constitutional authority and responsibility, not to mention a hardening of centre-province tensions, in such a system of government hardly needs stressing. But the extent to which the ambiguities served the purposes of those who were by now effectively carrying the central mantle has to be seen in the manner in which the 1956 constitution helped fashion the dialectic between the political process and state consolidation.

Centre-province disequilibrium

Insofar as the 1956 constitution facilitated state consolidation during the two and a half years that it remained in operation, it did so by accentuating centre-province and inter-provincial tensions – administrative as well as political. Taking the implicit unitarianism of the administrative arrangements under the constitution as the cardinal principle in its relations with the units of the federation, the centre was able to keep the scales tipped in its favour. But the advantages accruing from its vast administrative powers, especially when put to use in trouncing political opposition in the provinces, were qualified by the adverse reactions which these invariably one-sided victories elicited in the constituent units. Eager to expedite the consolidation of central authority for various reasons, among which the integration of Pakistan's diverse peoples into 'one nation' was the least well considered, the state managers in Karachi had occasionally to puzzle over the rather parochial reception to some of their policies.

It was tempting to dub all criticisms of the centre's policies as treason, high and low. Allegations of a Punjabi conspiracy to do down other linguistic groups, however, posed thornier problems. Uncovenanted beneficiaries of the uneven development fostered by the colonial state for purposes of its own, Punjabis from the middle and upper economic strata had a stranglehold over the most important civil and military jobs. This was an embarrassing truth which could not be wished away by the

---

[74] Annexure to the British high commissioner's despatch no.22, 28 April 1956, DO35/5406, PRO.

device of establishing a quota system to ensure better representation for the provinces. But despite similarities in their socio-economic and educational backgrounds, there was little real love lost between state bureaucrats and the variegated landlord politicians of the Punjab. Familiarity bred contempt as often as it encouraged alliances. As for a conscious collusion against non-Punjabis, that implied a convergence of class and occupational interests – difficult to forge and quite impossible to sustain. The relationship between the Punjab administration and the provincial leadership was strewn with as many instances of conflict as of collaboration.

Yet charges of collusion are best sustained when the proof lies not in its actual existence but in the realities shaping the perceptions of those who consider themselves to be its victims. As late as 1956 there was no Bengali above the rank of joint secretary in the central secretariat. Of the 741 top jobs in the federal government, 93 per cent were held by west Pakistanis with the Punjabis and Urdu-speaking migrants claiming the plums.[75] The rapid expansion of the central government in the 1950s, however, did open up job opportunities for non-Punjabis in the lower echelons. In 1949, there were a dozen central ministries; by 1957 the number had risen to twenty with twice as many central government employees than in 1950.[76] Bengalis and Pathans did fare a little better at the junior levels of the administrative hierarchy. But Sindhis and Baluchis continued to experience the cold winds of exclusion since Punjabis and Urdu-speakers had not failed to net their share of the job harvest. So for the Bengalis, Sindhis, Pathans and Baluchis, the mutuality of interest between the Punjab and the centre seemed palpable enough. It was not uncommon for district and divisional commissioners, and in some cases even the provincial chief secretaries, to carry the Punjabi label on one brow and the centre's colours on the other. Consequently, central policies insensitive, or perhaps too sensitive, to their political, economic and cultural aspirations were seen as part of Punjabi expansionism rather than as a concomitant of state interventionism.

This is why consolidating central authority by manipulating the administrative machinery was so fraught with consequences for the stability of the state. For one thing, the internal structures of the state were not above reproducing provincial jealousies. A mere 25 per cent of the senior posts in the provincial governments were reserved for

---

[75] *CAD* no.52, 1 January 1956 1843–4.
[76] C.M. Ahmed, *The Civil Service in Pakistan* (second edition), Dacca 1969, 84.

members of the provincial civil service;[77] the rest had all to be filled by CSP officers, Punjabis or Urdu-speaking Muhajirs in the main. So, although members of the Punjab civil service harboured as many resentments against the CSP as the other provincial services, non-Punjabi officials saw it as Punjabi favouritism on the part of the central government.[78] With non-Punjabis at odds with Punjabi CSP officers, and Punjabi-Muhajir tensions within the CSP itself, inter-service rivalries – most notably between the generalist administrators of the central superior services and the specialist services – presented themselves in deeply parochial shades.

Apart from issuing periodic sermons about burying the evils of provincialism, the centre's star strategists spent few sleepless nights musing over the alarming provincial and linguistic cleavages both within and outside the state apparatus. If anything, they were now more single-minded than ever about streamlining the structures of central authority, maximising its insulation from these deplorable manifestations of parochialism and, thereby, ensuring its autonomy of action in times of political and economic crises. In short, ripples in the political system were not to be allowed to either delay the consolidation of central power or dictate the manner in which it was exercised. The confidence flowed from the knowledge that Pakistan's predominantly Punjabi army – that ultimate rod of order – so long as it remained under the command of general Ayub, could be relied upon to use the sledgehammer to swat as many flies as was necessary to hold up the centre against an imminent disintegration.

This was a dangerously negative line of reasoning since the army had by no means escaped the bane of professional jealousies and the lure of kickbacks afforded by the initiation in 1954 of the American sponsored mutual defence assistance programme. Two senior members of the army command were retired when they protested against giving Ayub a second term as commander-in-chief.[79] Opposition to Ayub was not restricted to those in the upper echelons with ambitions of replacing him. As Mirza was to acknowledge in the spring of 1956, 'General Ayub was not now quite so popular with the Army since he was showing much

---

[77] The percentage could change if CSP officers, always short in supply, were not available for service in the provinces, (See Callard, *Pakistan: a Political Study*, 293.)

[78] In June 1956 after one unit had come into operation, the Punjab provincial civil service (executive branch) association suggested that the CSP be restricted to jobs in the central agencies. (*The Pakistan Times*, 29 June 1956, cited in ibid., 296, fn.1.)

[79] They were lt. general Yousuf and major general Adnan Khan. (See telegram from American consul general [Lahore] to the department of state, 4 October 1955, *Foreign Relations*, VIII, 444.)

too much favouritism'.[80] Pakistan's politicians held no monopoly over factionalism and corruption. Rival ambitions for power and position within the army were matched by temptations of illicit wealth which on occasion proved irresistible. Upon discovering that Pakistan's military shopping lists included uniforms, the US ambassador had 'suspicions' that certain 'Pakistan military circles...[were] favour[ing] procurement of some stuff outside rather than making it here because there was more chance for a rake-off'.[81] It was for reasons such as these that its principal benefactors in the international arena were increasingly of the view that the Pakistan army 'may not be the sound element for stability our policy assumes it is'.[82] But from the domestic angle of vision reliance on the army, however fractious and unstable in reality, was consistent with the logic of expediency that was coming to be accepted unquestioningly even by politicians – whether Punjabi, Bengali, Pathan, Sindhi or Baluch – who managed temporarily to ally with the bureaucratic-military combine in the exercise of state authority. With few exceptions, these politicians had either risen to national prominence during the preindependence period or made their way up by striking deals which not infrequently involved selling out the very local and provincial interests they claimed to represent. So like the bureaucratic administrators they too had reason to discourage the growth of organised parties and the holding of elections since these might give political leaders with solid local and provincial bases of support an opportunity to strike from below. This meant that civil bureaucrats and military officials could continue to keep the institutional balance of power tilted against the political leadership; muffling the voices of those who even after learning the hard truths about central imperatives could still think in terms of redressing some of the outstanding provincial grievances.[83] As the tactics adopted to push one unit loudly hinted, the institutional imbalances within the state apparatus had practically blurred the distinction between coercion and consensus in national politics.

But even politics of coercion demand a modicum of consistency. As long as the political system continued to be based on the broad principles of 'parliamentary government', however devoid of substance, it was impossible to keep the centre wholly insulated from developments

---

[80] Symon to Garner, 28 April 1956, DO35/5406, PRO.

[81] Memorandum of conversation between Hildreth and Chaudhri Mohammad Ali, 30 March 1955, *Foreign Relations*, VIII, 426–7.

[82] Telegram from the American consul general [Lahore] to the department of state, ibid., 444.

[83] Suhrawardy is a notable example, although he too was not above compromising Bengali interests for the will-o'-the-wisp at the centre.

at the provincial and the local levels of society. So however much the lack of organised politics suited the interests of the bureaucratic-military cabal and their allies outside the state structure – the business groups especially – it did not ensure the continuity or coherence of government at the centre. Short of actually dismantling political parties and imposing a system of 'controlled politics' – so strongly advocated by the president himself – the new constitutional framework seemed certain to heighten centre-province and inter-provincial animosities. The fact that inter-provincial jealousies made a joint front against the centre extremely unlikely was cold comfort. In the absence of a nationally recruited administrative bureaucracy and army, or a political party organisation enjoying support throughout the country, the centre was bound to find itself in the anomalous situation where despite sweeping constitutional powers it could neither completely benefit from the fragmentation of politics in the federal units nor prevent them impairing the inner workings of the state structure itself. It was partly in recognition of this danger that the 1956 constitution's directive principles committed the state to the goal of achieving parity of representation between east and west Pakistan 'in all spheres of [the] Federal administration' and a policy of encouraging 'people from all parts of Pakistan to participate in the defence services of the country'.[84] But the statement of objectives alone does not assure implementation. And, in any case, the directive principles of state policy in the constitution, were not enforceable in any court of law. Understandably, but in the circumstances facing Pakistan somewhat unfortunately, the directive principles had nothing to say about the need to strengthen the role of parliament and encourage the emergence of stable national political parties. It is not too far-fetched to assert that a mention along these lines, however unusual a feature of constitution-making, would have brought the 1956 constitution closer to the nub of the problems confronting the state than the copious irrelevance of some of its other provisions.

No special genius is required to see that consolidating central authority in a multi-linguistic and unevenly developed polity without nationally based political party structures matching those of the administrative machinery can prove fatal for the internal stability of the state. In Pakistan, the need for nationwide party organisations was doubly imperative since inadequate representation in the civil and the military institutions of the state, and the exclusion from decision-making this entailed, was a major source of discontentment among non-Punjabis. Yet after the promulgation of the 1956 constitution far from

---

[84] *The Constitution of the Islamic Republic of Pakistan*, article thirty-one.

facilitating the development of such organisations, successive political groupings at the centre not only assisted the decay of the Muslim League but with help from the administrative services did their level best to forestall the emergence of any alternative party commanding support in all the provinces. Using the 1956 constitution as a cover to consolidate central authority on the one hand, and weakening the political party system on the other was a sure recipe for a crisis of the state. Those who concocted it might have foreseen some but not all of the consequences. So the task of unravelling the various threads linking state consolidation with the dominant strains in the political process has by default to be carried out by the historian of Pakistan in order to show how politicians with nondescript bases of support joined forces with the preeminent powers in the civil and defence services to drive the state to the brink of a crisis which, if it was to be defused, required central powers even greater than those invested in the president's hands by the 1956 constitution.

FEDERAL POLITICS IN FLUX

Chaudhri Mohammad Ali's brief but eventful stint as prime minister was the first round in the unedifying spectacles which led to the abrogation of the 1956 constitution and the imposition of direct military rule. A civil servant at the helm of a multi-party coalition was a departure from the established norms of 'parliamentary government';[85] but it was not to be the only one. Lacking an independent base of support the prime minister shared the president's antipathy to parties and provincial politics. But unlike the chief executive Chaudhri Mohammad Ali had abiding faith in constitutional government. So there was an 'inherent potential [for] conflict' between the president and the prime minister, a fact not lost on provincial politicians manoeuvring to occupy strategic positions prior to the holding of general elections.[86] Mindful of the dangers to their own position, the prime minister and the president despite disagreements on the finer points sought to work a parliamentary and federal system of government by undermining political parties and by trying to distance the centre from the ensuing instability in the provinces.

---

[85] The British high commissioner's view that 'it would be deplorable' if a civil servant like Chaudhri Mohammad Ali became prime minister was not shared by officials in the CRO on the grounds that Bogra's fall from grace would result in a 'slightly less warm attitude to the United States' without any major shift in Pakistan's foreign policy. (See extract from Symon's letter to Laithwaite, 21 April 1955 and Morley's minute of 15 August 1955, DO35/5406, PRO.)

[86] Gardiner's telegram to the department of state, *Foreign Relations*, VIII, 440.

This unique approach to parliamentary democracy and federalism was not quite the best one for a state racked by confusions and contradictions. The existence of a Muslim League-United Front coalition itself bore testimony to the crucial importance of political party alignments in the provinces for the stability of government at the centre. But, having chalked out the shortest route to 'controlled democracy', the president prevailed upon the prime minister to ignore the voices from the political wilderness and concentrate instead on consolidating central authority. This was soon to land the prime minister in a plethora of troubles, not least among which were embarrassing criticisms of his policies by the Muslim League, the party in whose name he had assumed office.

It is difficult to disagree with the contention that the League, which was 'not a political party' but a 'collection of gangs', had 'no soul to be damned and no body to be kicked'.[87] Yet in the absence of a viable alternative the League's name could still rally the largest number of sinners in the political arenas of west Pakistan. With the establishment of one unit and the need to elect members of the west Pakistan legislative assembly, half-hearted attempts were made to revitalise the League. In late January 1956, Sardar Abdur Rab Nishtar was elected president of the Muslim League at the behest of the prime minister who dominated the entire proceedings of the League council. Not one of the five items on its agenda dealt with the outstanding constitutional issues of the day. Instead the council focused its attention on adopting an amendment to the League constitution restricting government ministers, both at the centre and the provinces, from holding an office in the party. This was a reversion to the 1948 constitution, a portent for the relationship between parties and government envisaged by the inner circles at the centre. As Chaudhri Mohammad Ali soon learnt to his dismay, foregoing the position of party president made it impossible to prevent the League council from airing opinions contrary to government policy. After the elections to the west Pakistan assembly, the prime minister found himself seriously at odds with his own party. He had submitted to Mirza's line that elections to the new assembly should be held on a non-party basis. It was the only way of keeping Dr Khan Sahib as chief minister in the western wing, something which was desirable from the centre's point of view because he could be useful in pacifying Pathan feelings against being lumped with Punjabis and also because this old

---

[87] D.W.S. Hunt [deputy British high commissioner, Lahore] to J.M.C. James [Karachi], 16 April 1956, DO35/5411, PRO.

Congress stalwart was momentarily in Mirza's good books.[88]

By the time the central government finalised the election guidelines, candidates to the west Pakistan assembly had to disavow party affiliations and rely exclusively on manipulating factional alliances in the districts to secure a seat at the provincial level. Making districts the focal point of electioneering was consistent with the administrative centralisation which had all along been the main driving force behind the one unit scheme. It gave district commissioners a chance to vet candidates, weeding out those likely to evade central dictates. The principle of non-party elections had the additional merit of pitting rival provincial factions against each other, a development which fitted in splendidly with the overall objective of enhancing administrative autonomy and diminishing that of party politicians. Although the elections resulted in the success of factional alliances supportive of one unit, the vast majority of the new members of the west Pakistan assembly were simply old Leaguers without the label. In the Punjab, the abstention of Mamdot and Noon from the running saw Daultana and Gurmani's men returned to the assembly; in the NWFP, victory fell on Sardar Bahadur Khan and Dr Khan Sahib's factions and in Sind the battle was essentially fought out between the two rival gangs led by Khuhro and Ghulam Ali Talpur. Delighted to see so many familiar faces in the west Pakistan assembly, the Muslim League council authorised its president to instruct his party men to form a League parliamentary party. They did so willingly since Khan Sahib was not one of them and, therefore, could restrict their access to the key sources of patronage in the province.

Sensing doom, Khan Sahib on Mirza's advice began probing the possibility of setting up a one unit party in the assembly. But the League's majority was undeniable. So Chaudhri Mohammad Ali implored the leaders of the main factions, namely Daultana, Khuhro and Sardar Bahadur, who by the way had jumped at the opportunity of joining Khan Sahib's cabinet, to accept a non-party chief minister. But the League president was having none of this; members of the parliamentary party could not overrule the working committee's decision. Hoping for an even better deal, Daultana, Khuhro and Sardar Bahadur astutely changed tack, thus bringing the crisis to a head. Mirza

---

[88] Khan Sahib was Abdul Ghaffar Khan's brother, the leader of the Red Shirt movement and the most strident propagandist of 'Pakhtunistan'. Moreover, while soliciting support for one unit the job had been promised to a representative of the smaller provinces for a period of ten years. But then a promise had also been made to make Peshawar the seat of the provincial capital; the attractions of Lahore, however, proved to be irresistible.

was convinced that Daultana, whose 'real object' was to become prime minister and get Nishtar in as president, had arranged 'some sort of an alliance' between Sardar Bahadur and his brother, general Ayub, by accusing Dr Khan Sahib of 'wishing to bring about Pushtoonistan'.[89] Having only recently reassured the American ambassador of 'absolute certainty' on the commander-in-chief's loyalty to him,[90] Mirza understandably had 'no doubt' that 'Ayub could be brought to see reason'.[91] But his suspicion that Daultana and Nishtar were working a double-cross had been confirmed on 2 April when Sardar Bahadur Khan was elected leader of the League parliamentary party and, with a view to his forming a new ministry, the six existing Leaguers in Khan Sahib's ministry were told to resign. However irritating for Mirza, this crack of the party whip placed the prime minister in a real dilemma. He now had either to disown his own party's verdict or part company with Mirza and Gurmani who were conniving actively to keep Khan Sahib in office. Once he had chosen to back the powers that be, Chaudhri Mohammad Ali found himself in the uncomfortable role of a prime minister assisting in the undoing of his own party.

After scotching the Daultana-Nishtar revolt in the spring of 1956, the presidential, prime ministerial and gubernatorial triumvirate administered a series of shocks to the political process in west Pakistan. While the Muslim League was the main casualty, the broader repercussions on the state were serious enough to warrant an account of the new political standards which the central government was helping establish under the flimsy guise of furthering Pakistan's national interests.[92] As a first step, Khan Sahib secured Gurmani's blessings to reform his cabinet by launching an impressive job creation scheme aimed at delinking as many members from the League assembly party as was possible.[93] Since Daultana, Khuhro and Sardar Bahadur had tendered their resignation,

---

[89] Symon to Garner, 28 April 1956, DO35/5406, PRO.
[90] Hildreth's telegram to the department of state, 17 February 1956, *Foreign Relations*, VIII, 459.
[91] Symon to Garner, 28 April 1956, DO35/5406, PRO.
[92] A firm supporter of Mirza's tactics, the British high commissioner thought it would be 'highly dangerous' if 'unity within the Muslim League was to be purchased at the price of abandoning...the hopes of better government' under Dr Khan Sahib whose 'disappearance' would be 'a matter for serious concern in the wider interests of Pakistan'. (See annexure to British high commissioner's despatch no.22 of 28 April 1956, ibid.) But as the deputy high commissioner in Lahore had warned, 'it would be a mistake to see all virtue on one side and all vice on the other'. (Hunt to James in Karachi, 16 April 1956, DO35/5411, PRO.)
[93] Upon closer scrutiny it appeared that with the exception of Dr Khan Sahib the reformed cabinet – Gurmani's gang in the main – consisted of at least '4 crooks and 2 boneheads'. (See minute on p.1 of ibid., no date; initials not legible.)

he was able to rope eight members of the League parliamentary group into his non-party corral. On 23 April, at a meeting attended by the prime minister the Pakistan Muslim League's working committee decided to expel the Leaguers who had flouted party discipline by joining Khan Sahib's ministry. The more important resolution, however, was the demand for the immediate removal of the governor on grounds of his unconstitutional behaviour.[94] These resolutions posed a stern test for the prime minister. Unable to sustain his equivocal position, Chaudhri Mohammad Ali was forced to come out into the open. Frankly admitting his lack of commitment to the League, he argued that his primary responsibility was to the cabinet and parliament, not to 'the resolution of any political party'.[95] The contradiction was startling. Here was a prime minister claiming responsibility to the coalition government as a whole but refusing to honour the policies of one of its component units. Moreover, by backing a non-party chief minister, he was holding office in the name of a party which had now gone into opposition in not just one but both wings of the federation. The taming of the prime minister was one instance only of a more widespread rot whose stains can still be seen on the fragile edifice of Pakistan's political system.

With both Mirza and Gurmani acting as midwives, Khan Sahib announced the birth of the Republican party, a misnomer for a collection of League dissidents and others attracted by the magnetic pull of power and promises of land grants, route permits, licences and other such nostrums. That it was a product of a 'palace' intrigue was well-known; that it could break the League's record in jobbery came as a blow to those who still clung to the view that 'parliamentary government' under the 1956 constitution if given a fair chance would eventually turn out to be something better than a cruel hoax. Khan Sahib's patrons wanted to be absolutely certain of his ability to survive a League onslaught in the assembly. So Gurmani postponed the meeting of the west Pakistan assembly to give the chief minister time to buy more votes by offers of ministerial posts or official patronage. The campaign, which could not have been conducted without Mirza's sanction, threw the recently integrated provincial administration into utter confusion. Civil servants were ordered to bolster the Republican party's fortunes; those who failed or challenged the orders were promptly transferred or demoted. The police were deployed to evict tenants and intimidate MLAs who showed a reluctance to bite the Republican bait. If there had

---

[94] *The Pakistan Times*, 24 and 26 April 1956.
[95] Ibid., 15 May 1956.

been any possibility of winning popular support for one unit, these strong arm tactics to succour a party which had never done a day's work at the grassroots level destroyed it once and for ever.

All this naturally provoked a barrage of criticism in the popular press.[96] Instead of feigning contriteness about the public disclosures of their nefarious activities, the well-wishers of the Republican party entered still more dangerous terrain. Firoz Khan Noon, a recruit to the Republican party and a man on whose 'obliging shoulders, hidden hands ha[d] often fixed their own guns', called for a two month suspension of the constitution in order to resolve the political battles in west Pakistan.[97] The proposal was savaged by the media and there were calls for a national election. If not for Chaudhri Mohammad Ali's 'vacillating' – he 'could be persuaded to agree to something in the morning, but had developed a habit of getting cold feet by the evening'[98] – Mirza and Gurmani may well have ignored public opinion and taken steps along some such line. It certainly would have saved them the disappointment of discovering the shortfalls of political coercion.

On 19 May 1956, when the west Pakistan assembly finally met, it was evenly divided between Republican and League supporters. The acting chairman of the assembly cast his vote in favour of the Republican nominee, and so Khan Sahib's ministry survived. Bemoaning the state of affairs where the stability of a ministerial coterie was being bought at the expense of creating all round political anarchy, one prominent daily concluded that the constitution had been 'reduced to a farce...the people continue[d] to be betrayed...[while] the world laughs'.[99] Even inside Pakistan it was difficult to shed tears for this sham parading as democracy. The central government took the major brunt of journalistic abuse; it was accused of trying 'artificial insemination with democracy',[100] and stultifying the political process to place in office a party which had no roots among the people.[101]

By the end of June, the Republican party's tentacles had extended to the centre. Twenty-two Muslim Leaguers defected and formed a Republican core in the national assembly. This made Chaudhri Mohammad Ali's position more untenable than ever. However, he was

[96] See Rahman, *Public Opinion and Political Development in Pakistan*, 178–87.
[97] *Dawn*, 8 and 9 May 1956, cited in ibid., 185.
[98] As Mirza regretted to tell the British high commissioner. (See Symon to Laithwaite, 14 May 1956, DO35/5407, PRO.)
[99] *Dawn*, 24 May 1956, cited in Rahman, *Public Opinion and Political Development in Pakistan*, 185–6.
[100] Ibid.
[101] *The Pakistan Times*, 18 July 1956, cited in ibid., 186–7.

rewarded for past services when the deserters promised to give him their backing. So a man who had proudly proclaimed himself above selfish party politics was now the leader of a coalition government which depended on the shifting sands of League, Republican and United Front support. In private this disheartened and lonely man, who had written his political epitaph and was now digging the grave, complained bitterly about the 'poor calibre of his cabinet colleagues' and the 'interminable political manoeuvrings' which prevented him from concentrating on administrative matters.[102] No less candid in public, Chaudhri Mohammad Ali deplored the manner in which the centre was being turned into a 'sport of provincial politics'.[103] It would have been nearer the mark if he had admitted that the absence of sportsmanship in the provinces was due largely to the unexpected consequences of central policies he himself had helped formulate. But for this bureaucrat caught in the minefield of west Pakistani politics, the fatal stumble came with the fall of the United Front ministry in east Pakistan, a development which finally forced him to concede that the centre's immunity from provincial wrangles, which he had sought by disowning the League and resisting the Republican embrace, was inadmissible under the 1956 constitutional framework.

In east Pakistan, Sarkar's United Front ministry had been kept in office for the same reasons and through the same devices as Khan Sahib's Republican ministry in Lahore. But there were some important differences. Unlike its counterpart in the western wing, the Sarkar ministry was the main pillar of the coalition at the centre. So in many respects the United Front government was an even greater beneficiary of central imperatives than Khan Sahib's. Fazlul Huq – the former leader of the United Front and the governor of east Pakistan – did his unconstitutional best to ward off all threats to the Sarkar ministry. It was not too difficult to postpone meetings of the assembly indefinitely. Despite cries of foul play, the loudest of which came from Suhrawardy, the governor with the centre's approval remained unmoved. A meeting of the assembly was eventually called in the third week of May because the provincial budget had to be passed before 31 May. The assembly hall was packed to the roof, inadequately ventilated and so poor acoustically that it was impossible to follow the proceedings. Understandably frustrated, the members showed scant respect for the speaker's authority, 'shouting at the top of their voices or jostling for the use of the all-

---

[102] Minute by H.A.F. Rumbold, 27 June 1956, DO35/5407, PRO.
[103] *The Pakistan Observer*, 29 July 1956, cited in Rahman, *Public Opinion and Political Development in Pakistan*, 187.

important microphone'.[104] So no sooner had a member of the Awami League raised a point of order questioning the constitutionality of Sarkar's presentation of the budget than the United Front speaker adjourned the assembly. Later that day Mirza suspended the east Pakistan assembly, imposed president's rule and sanctioned the provincial budget for another three months.

Within a week presidential rule had been lifted and Sarkar was back in office. The Awami League protested and began exploring ways of ousting the ministry through the usual methods – popular campaigns and alliances of convenience. The food crisis and floods provided the ammunition for the first, constitutional issues the rationale for the second. All the centre could do to counter the fire and fury of the Awami League's movement was to hand over the provincial food distribution machinery to the army.[105] It was an immensely unpopular move. The army's 'operation service first' failed to bring down prices in several parts of the province while individuals were summarily arrested and sentenced by army food magistrates.[106] Under pressure the Sarkar ministry issued a revised food control ordinance replacing army food magistrates with special civil magistrates on the day the provincial assembly reconvened.[107] Sarkar and Huq might have played for a postponement if not for the fact that the provincial budget had to be passed before 31 August. Not ones to concede the game easily, on 13 August, when the assembly began its proceedings, the members were greeted with the United Front speaker reading the governor's prorogation order.

The governor and the central bosses, not without some prodding from army headquarters, had clearly overplayed their hand. Chaudhri Mohammad Ali's presence in Dacca on the eve of the session had not gone unnoticed.[108] *Dawn* summed up the situation beautifully: 'A Centre which tolerates such flagrant partisanship and abuse of power on the part of its provincial governors can be dubbed as one of two things – weaklings or secret abetters'.[109] The central government in Karachi fitted both descriptions. With the central government under fire for its pro-Western stance on the Suez crisis and himself facing a bitter personal campaign led by the Muslim League, the prime minister wobbled in characteristic style and finally told Sarkar to obtain a vote of

[104] Dacca fortnightly report no. 11 for period ending 30 May 1956, DO35/5299, PRO.
[105] *The Pakistan Times*, 1 July 1956.
[106] Dacca fortnightly report no.14 for period 28 June to 28 July 1956, DO35/5299, PRO.
[107] Dacca fortnightly report no.17 for period 9-22 August 1956, ibid.
[108] *The Pakistan Times*, 16 August 1956, cited in Rahman, *Public Opinion and Political Development in Pakistan*, 227.
[109] *Dawn*, 16 August 1956, in ibid.

confidence or resign. On 30 August 1956, Sarkar preferred to resign than be humiliated by the assembly. The formation of an Awami League ministry under Ataur Rahman Khan left Chaudhri Mohammad Ali with no safer passage than to quit. Mirza who after a recent visit to Dacca had been forced to acknowledge the Awami League's popularity also 'concluded that the time to dispense with Mr. Mohammad Ali had come'.[110] On 8 September 1956, although he still had a majority in the national assembly, Chaudhri Mohammad Ali resigned. The date is something of a watershed in the history of party politics in Pakistan since it officially registered the total elimination of the Muslim League from governments at the centre as well as in the two provinces. Four days later Suhrawardy formed an Awami League-Republican ministry at the centre. So ostensibly the centre had come to reflect the political configuration in the federal units. But the flux of federal politics under the previous ministry had set a pattern for the future which a general election alone could change.

The economy of alliance

The upper echelons of the state apparatus, both civil and military, backed by an increasingly vocal business lobby in west Pakistan had strong reservations about a general election. It might lead to a Bengali-dominated configuration wresting power in Karachi. Even if the Bengalis and their allies in the smaller units of west Pakistan could be stopped short of storming the centre, there was no guarantee that any alternative political combination would be either stable or dependable enough to hold the ring and promote state imperatives as defined and dictated by the bureaucratic-military combine. For these architects of state consolidation, a compelling argument against allowing the political process its head was the already precarious condition of the national economy. Although now more dependent on US technical, military and commodity aid than ever, there was considerable acrimony over the precise terms and uses of this aid. The donors saw the dispensing of aid as a zero-sum game; more for the military meant less for economic reconstruction. Pakistani military and bureaucratic officials contested this formulation and pressed for increased aid levels in both categories. But they soon learnt about the limited options of recipients. The Pakistan economy had to be better regulated and controlled if it was to qualify for larger inflows of foreign assistance. Without an external relief operation nothing could prevent the simmering economic discontent-

---

[110] Acting British high commissioner to CRO, 12 October 1956, DO35/5407, PRO.

ments from breaking open the fragile structures of authority which the mandarins and the praetorian guard – admittedly in consort with a few political stragglers and nascent industrialists – had so recently and so painfully cobbled together.

Yet here was the rub. Nowhere had the consequences of the disjunction between the political process and the imperatives of state consolidation been felt more acutely than in the realm of economic decision-making. The absence of stable and popularly based governments at the centre capable of keeping firm checks on the demands of military headquarters and the activities of a sprawling administrative machinery had been as great, if not a greater, obstacle to sound economic planning than the shortage of finance and trained personnel. The economic policies of successive central governments had been a mirror image of the shifting balance of power within the state apparatus. The decision to promote industry at the expense of the agrarian sector flowed directly from the need to enlarge the resource base of the state to meet the financial requirements of the military establishment. Building a state structure largely geared to sustaining a political economy of defence in a country where agriculture accounted for over 60 per cent of the gross national income was not without attendant political risks. It was to defuse these that Pakistan had joined US sponsored military alliances with alacrity. But increased inflows of foreign aid made the goals of national economic planning more illusory, setting off a chain reaction in which the search for political stability became more elusive, relations between state and society more discordant, and the likelihood of direct military intervention more imminent. A review of the attempts at planned development and the effects these had on the economy, both before and after the formalisation of Pakistan's ties with the United States, illustrate the points fairly and squarely.

Since the Colombo plan of 1950, the government of Pakistan had been trying – with varying degrees of enthusiasm and ineptitude – to get the engine of economic development rolling. In 1951, its confidence shored by the windfall from jute and cotton export earnings following the Korean war boom, the central government launched a six-year plan – later supplemented by an even more ambitious two-year priority programme – in the vain hope of paralleling the loud successes India was registering under its first five year plan. Yet, by the last quarter of 1952, a sharp drop in Pakistan's export earnings had forced the government to lower its sights and settle for downward adjustments in the economy. In 1953 the Pakistani economy was in all manner of difficulty: strict import controls; depleting inventories of essential consumer goods; an inflationary spiral; a serious food shortage; not to mention balance of payments difficulties and rapidly falling foreign exchange reserves. In the spring of that year the central government under severe popular pressure tried its hand at combating inflation. But its inability to make do without deficit financing, together with the ineffectiveness and corruption of the administrative apparatus as well as the increasing entrenchment of the 'forces of personal profit' in the Pakistani political structure,[111] ensured that the price controls came to no avail. The government's austerity programme also proved to be something of a non-starter. Unable to balance its accounts, much less regulate the distribution machinery, the central government had to assess the costs and benefits of trying to bridge the gap between supply and demand by relaxing import controls on a range of consumer items. With Pakistan's foreign reserves well below the safety level, it was difficult for the central government to meet the need for more consumer imports without slashing back on either defence or development expenditure.

It was a classic dilemma of economic decision-making. Early in 1953, the central government's specially constituted economic appraisal committee frankly conceded that Pakistan's annual expenditure on defence and civil administration was wholly out of line with its available resources. Between 1947–8 and 1952–3, defence alone accounted for 51 per cent to 71 per cent of the central government's total revenue expenditure, and 16 per cent to 48 per cent of the total capital expenditure. During the same period expenditure on civil administration rose from 16 per cent to 20 per cent of the total revenue expenditure of the central government.[112] In short, any government austerity programme failing to economise on defence and administrative expenditure would be ineffectual. As the authors of the report boldly declared, a 'correct balance' could only be achieved through a 'minimum expenditure on defence consistent with security' and 'the maximum expenditure on development consistent with resources'. After all, 'development alone c[ould] sustain the expenditure on defence'. The committee also proposed that expenditure on civil administration be brought down to 15 per cent or, better still, 12.5 per cent of the total revenues since 'no organisation...[could] afford to spend such a large proportion of its income on administration...at a time when income is declining'.[113]

---

[111] American embassy [Karachi] to the department of state, 4 January 1954, NND.842909, RG 59, Box 5568, 890D.10/1-454, NA.
[112] *Report of the Economic Appraisal Committee*, Karachi 1953, paras. 426 and 427.
[113] Ibid.

The 1953–4 budget made some cursory nods in the right direction.[114] But GHQ's sharp reaction to accepting its share of the proposed cuts, especially the prospect of forcibly retrenching some 40,000 army personnel, was the best guarantee against further decreases in the military budget. In the mid-fifties the 'major problem' with American aid was the 'division of money between economic aid...and defence support'. General Sexton, the chief of the military assistance advisory group [MAAG] in Pakistan, was 'constantly struggling' for more money for the military 'against suggestions [that] the money should be spent for additional irrigation'.[115] By 1958, as an American intelligence report astutely noted, 'the Pakistani army ha[d] developed as a pressure group' and would 'continue to have priority over economic development for appropriations', irrespective of the Indian factor.[116] Unwilling to incur the wrath of military headquarters, the central government concluded that the only alternative to continued shortages of consumer imports, and all the political risks that this entailed, was to whittle down the allocations for provincial development projects and double the incentives to private enterprise in the hope that this might at least keep the engine running.

In May 1953 the central government had been forced to scrap the six year development plan and the two-year priority programme adopted with much pomp in 1951. A planning board which now replaced the development board was asked to review the economic conditions with a view towards 'promulgating a more realistic economic development programme' for the five years commencing 1 April 1954.[117] The planning board was also to recommend how to make the administrative machinery more conducive to the implementation of the proposed plan. The shots of realism were administered by foreign economic experts, Americans in the main. During FY 1953–4 there were already over a hundred US experts and advisers working in Pakistan under the technical assistance programme. Their diagnosis of the principal cause of Pakistan's economic troubles was simple enough: the administrative machinery was 'completely uncoordinated'. Relations between the central government and the different provincial governments had not been 'clarified or made administratively effective'. Worse still, there was

---

[114] See above, p. 178.
[115] Memorandum by the American assistant secretary of defence for international security affairs, 17 February 1955, *Foreign Relations*, VIII, 418.
[116] 'Pakistan's Current Economic Situation and Prospects', report no. 7706 of office of intelligence research and analysis, department of state, 15 May 1958, NA.
[117] See American embassy [Karachi] despatch no. 1102, 24 June 1953, NND.842909, RG 59, Box 5542, 890D.00/6-2453, NA.

no clear cut delineation of responsibility between the different ministries. But there was hope yet; Pakistani officials were keen to secure American advice which was 'continuing to be rendered on a great number of activities not covered by [the] project agreements'.[118]

This suggests that, even before it had formally joined the South East Asian treaty organisation (1954) and the Baghdad pact (1955), the Americans had gained a toehold in the administrative operations of the Pakistani state. But this privileged access was not without a cost. In view of Pakistan's dire economic predicament, the United States had now to consider whether it 'should or could assume... responsibility for the successful administration, external financing and technical effectiveness of some 35–40 per cent of Pakistan's total development programme'. Fortunately in 1954–5 American dollar funds were expected to be double those in 1953–4. By using aid to 'exercise a major influence on...[Pakistan's] financial development', and, by bolstering both its public administration and defence services, the United States could help 'buttress [its] political and economic stability during the immediate period of crisis' while at the same time securing the main purpose of American interests in this strategically useful corner of the world.[119] The assumption of such wide responsibility by the United States could not be made palatable to the Congress and the American people without formally associating Pakistan in the struggle against Communism. In February 1954, the announcement of a Turkish-Pakistan agreement to cooperate on matters of mutual security interest – a precursor to the Baghdad pact of 1955 – along with Karachi's tacit assurances of joining a South East Asian defence organisation was promptly followed by Washington's formal decision to grant a limited amount of military aid to Karachi.

General Ayub, who played a pivotal role in the negotiations with Washington, was 'dejected' and 'broken hearted' by the size of the American aid package.[120] Looking for something over $300 million, he managed to extract an initial promise of no more than $25 million. The members of the US military mission, which arrived in Pakistan during the spring of 1954, had made it known that many of the defence units would have to be built up from 'scratch' and equipped with American

---

[118] American embassy [Karachi], despatch no. 20, 8 July 1953, NND.842909, RG 59, Box 5545, 890D.00.TA/7-953, NA.

[119] American embassy [Karachi] to the department of state, 12 August 1953, NND.842909, Box 5542, 890D.00/8-1253, NA.

[120] Memorandum of conversation between the deputy director of South Asian affairs office and the Pakistani ambassador, Amjad Ali, 6 August 1954, *Foreign Relations*, 1952–4, XI, II, Africa and South Asia, Washington, DC 1983, 1860.

equipment.[121] Maintaining American equipment while shifting from the British tactical doctrine of military organisation was bound to be a costly affair. In fact, the 'greater the [amount of American military] aid, [the] greater the costs to Pakistan'.[122] Under the terms of the mutual defence assistance programme, agreed upon in October 1954, the US committed itself to helping the Pakistan army enlarge and equip five and a half divisions for an estimated cost of $171 million over a period of three years. But by early 1955 the programme had run into a jumble of red tape. Each side blamed the other upon discovering that the actual cost of the programme would be well in excess of the amount allocated. Ayub and Akhtar Hussain, the defence secretary, were dismayed by the slow pace at which the military programme was developing. The Americans for their part argued that the delay stemmed from Pakistan's economic difficulties and its inability to raise the additional troops required to absorb the military equipment. Any acceleration of the programme would demand increased economic aid or the diversion of counterpart funds under the PL 480 programme for military purposes.

The limited amount of 'World War II obsolete equipment'[123] which had arrived could not but give rise to suspicions in Ayub's mind that the US was resorting to 'double talk'.[124] Indications that Washington was thinking of completing the programme in five to eight years using $171 million as the ceiling irrespective of the force levels it would maintain elicited a vehement reaction from Rawalpindi. Ayub felt 'let down'. He was 'in no position [to] answer growing feeling in Army circles that [the]...US [was] engaging in "political opportunism" with Pakistan' and now, he lamented, stood to 'lose my trousers'.[125] The American ambassador and MAAG's chief of the army section were both anxious to spare Ayub the humiliation. Hildreth warned Washington of grave political implications if the mutual defence assistance programme fell short of expectations. The men running Pakistan were 'more favourable to US and free world interest than any possible alternative in sight'. With the political opposition and the press already charging the

---

121 Extract of letter from the British embassy [Washington] to K.R. Crook [CRO], 28 July 1954, DEFE7/153, PRO. For an account of the British reaction to the American entry into Pakistan, see A. Jalal 'Towards the Baghdad Pact: South Asia and Middle East Defence in the Cold War', *International History Review*, XI, August 1989, 3.

122 Hildreth to the department of state, 9 August 1954, *Foreign Relations*, 1952–4, XI, 11, 1862.

123 As Akhtar Hussain asserted (See brigadier general Brown [MAAG's chief of the army section] to John K. Wilson Jr. [office of the secretary of defence], 18 November, 1955, Admiral Radford File (1953–7), RG 218, Box 15, 091 Pak, NA.)

124 Ibid.

125 American consul general's telegram [Lahore], 4 October 1955, *Foreign Relations*, VIII, 444.

government with selling Pakistan for a 'mess of porridge[sic]' it would be a political blunder not to strengthen the ruling group, Ayub in particular.[126] General Brown concurred. While Ayub's 'blackmail' and pressure tactics were to be regretted, Brown accused the state department of 'attempts to reach desirable political and diplomatic objectives...[without] count[ing] the cost realistically until the waiter comes up with the bill'.[127] The ceiling of $171 million was eventually raised. But not before Hildreth had rejected pleas by Ayub and Mirza that 'they did not want any support for military aid to come out of economic funds or counterpart funds because that only made the rest of Pakistan angry at the proportion of funds the military was receiving'.[128] So even the military establishment was sensitive to some of the dangers inherent in creating a political economy of defence.

Yet Pakistan was in the throes of a financial crisis; an awkward position from which to refuse anything on offer, especially if it carried the possibility of increased aid levels in the future. As Dulles had grimly noted long ago, the government of Pakistan would have to find ways of enlarging its economic base and raising domestic resources for military expenditure. It could, of course, have all the American advice it wanted to place its economy on the road to planned capitalist development.[129] The first gush of advice was already in the pipeline. As early as July 1953, the central government had sounded off the Ford foundation. Pakistan wanted an international team of experts to assist the planning board prepare the first five year plan. The request met with an enthusiastic response from Harvard's Littauer School. In December 1953, the government of Pakistan signed an agreement with the Ford foundation which, in turn, formalised its understandings with Harvard.[130]

In April 1954, the Harvard advisory group began operations in Pakistan. It is no secret that the HAG role in the preparation of the first five year plan – first made public in May 1956, revised in April 1957 and eventually finalised in May 1958 – 'far exceeded simply advising an effectively functioning Pakistani staff'. Yet it is less well known that the plan, still hailed in some quarters as a masterstroke of economic analysis, was based on the 'best guesses'; the paucity of accurate

---

[126] Hildreth's telegram to the department of state, 30 June 1955, ibid., 430–2.

[127] Brown to Wilson, 18 November, 1955, Admiral Radford File (1953–7), RG 218, Box 15, 091 Pak, NA.

[128] Hildreth's despatch no. 608 to the department of state, 31 March 1955, *Foreign Relations*, VIII, 426, fn. 2.

[129] Dulles to American embassy [Karachi], 20 August 1954, *Foreign Relations*, 1952–4, XI, II, 1865–6.

[130] For an account of the activities of the Ford foundation and HAG in Pakistan see George Rosen, *Western Economists and Eastern Societies: Agents of Change in South Asia, 1950–1970*, Oxford 1985, parts I and III.

statistical information was in inverse proportion to the 'idle speculation' and 'wishful thinking' of the proposals submitted by the warring central and provincial ministries.[131] It is important to consider the context, economic and political, in which the plan was prepared, chopped and changed. As a first step, the plan needs setting against the economic trends of the preplan period. Between 1949–50 and 1954–5, the national income rose by 15.2 per cent at constant prices, or 2.9 per cent annually. But during this period, the agricultural sector was stagnant; recording a dismal average annual growth rate of 1.3 per cent at a time when population was growing by 2.4 per cent. A decline in average per capita agricultural production, together with the fall in agricultural prices after 1952, had seen per capita income dropping appreciably in the sector where over 80 per cent of the Pakistani population was bunched. Such increase in the per capita income as seems to have occurred was due largely to the high growth rates achieved by the industrial sector which, because it had an extremely low base for a start, cannot be seen as an indicator of the salubrious condition of the Pakistani economy.

Among the many structural barriers to the growth of the national economy was the continuing low rates of national savings, matched by alarmingly high rates of private consumption expenditure. Estimated to be less than 6 per cent of the annual gross national income, the savings rate was well below the 9 per cent to 10 per cent seen to be necessary to maintain full employment at the existing rates of population growth. With defence and civil administration swallowing most of the foreign aid as well as nearly 80 per cent of its annual revenue, and increased debt servicing liabilities, the central government had to seriously consider reforming the taxation structure. Yet the dramatic fall in world prices of its two main export crops, jute and cotton, foreclosed the possibility of raising indirect taxes which already provided approximately 73 per cent of its ordinary revenues as well as those of the provincial governments. Increasingly the role of direct taxes in public finance was out of the question; it would almost certainly erode the government's support among the propertied classes. Cutting back on foreign consumer goods and promoting import-substitution industries seemed to offer a way out of the vicious rut. But import-substitution policies aimed at the production of consumer rather than capital goods far from increasing the rate of domestic saving enhanced the consumption levels of the well-to-do and the rich further still. So the only real alternative to easing financial hardship was to rely on a mixture of deficit financing and ever

---

[131] This was the revelation of David Bell, a key adviser of the HAG; cited in ibid., 154.

larger inflows of foreign aid. The high rates of inflation that followed
from this policy saw real wages plummeting.[132]

This in brief was the stark context in which the planning board, fitted
with the best minds Harvard could put on offer, had to formulate its
proposals. Consequently, it was difficult to work out a systematic course
for the attainment of the plan's five main objectives:[133] (1) to raise the
national income by 20 per cent during the plan period, (2) to improve the
balance of payments, (3) to improve employment opportunities, (4) to
expand social services, and (5) to quickly increase the rate of development in east Pakistan and other less-developed regions in the country.
The last of these objectives, and potentially the most explosive
politically, was a precondition for achieving the others, while the third
and the fourth were directly dependent on the success of the first two. If
the experience of the preplan period gave cause for scepticism about the
realism underlying the first two objectives, there were even firmer
grounds to doubt the central government's capacity or will to try and
narrow the highly differential rates of development in the two wings.
During the better part of the fifties, the average annual growth rate of
the gross domestic product in east Pakistan was a mere 0.2 per cent,
compared with 3.6 per cent in west Pakistan. And while per capita
incomes in the western wing were increasing marginally – by 0.8 per
cent – they were declining in the eastern wing at the rate of approximately 0.3 per cent per annum.[134] As the cost of living in the east was
generally higher than in the west these figures understate the full extent
of the disparity between them.

The central government's economic policies were in large part
responsible for the virtual absence of any development in east Pakistan.
Exporters of agricultural produce in the eastern wing had been the
principal victims of a policy that kept the rupee overvalued in order to
lower the import costs of military items for the defence establishment
and capital goods for prospective industrialists in west Pakistan.
According to one estimate, between 1950–1 and 1957–8, that is even
after the first five year plan was supposedly in operation, east Pakistan
was able to secure only 35 per cent of the total import licences issued by
the central government. Unable to reap the benefits of the central
government's import-substitution drive, and the recipient of a mere 25

---

[132] See N. Hamid, 'The Burden of Capitalist Growth: A Study of Real Wages and
Consumption in Pakistan', *Pakistan Economic and Social Review*, Spring 1974.
[133] *The First Five Year Plan, 1955–60* (draft), Karachi 1956.
[134] Emajuddin Ahmed, *Bureaucratic Elites in Segmented Economic Growth: Bangladesh
and Pakistan*, Dacca 1980, 118–19.

per cent of the total foreign imports,[135] east Pakistan had to meet its requirements by purchasing west Pakistani consumer manufactures. Apart from being of inferior quality, these were priced 40 per cent higher than in the world market. Figures for inter-regional trade suggest that at least 2 per cent of east Pakistan's average annual income was being syphoned off by west Pakistan.[136] With less than a quarter of the total investment in the country, east Pakistan's annual per capita development and revenue expenditure averaged Rs. 22.08 and Rs. 37.75 respectively. By contrast, the annual per capita development and revenue expenditure in west Pakistan averaged around Rs. 108.03 and Rs. 201 respectively.[137] The allocation of foreign aid and loans followed a similar pattern with east Pakistan receiving about 17 per cent of the total development aid and no more than a third of American commodity assistance.[138]

Short of a major realignment at the centre, east Pakistan's predominantly agrarian economy was unlikely to fare better under the first five year plan. It is true that the plan assigned the highest priority to the needs of the ailing agrarian sector, solemnly stressing the need to impose a ceiling of 150 acres for irrigated and 450 acres for non-irrigated land in west Pakistan and the completion of reforms in east Pakistan by 1956. Yet, even while calling for a balanced approach to development, the authors of the plan had taken care to add that this be brought about 'by stimulating agricultur[e]...rather than by curtailing industrial progress'.[139] This hints at the ideological bias underlying the 'modernisation' theories which inspired foreign wizards through their travails in economic development planning in Pakistan and elsewhere during the fifties and the sixties. It also clearly hints at the central government's likely response to the recommendations for agrarian reform. Interested merely in extracting the maximum surplus from the agricultural sector to finance the rapid industrialisation which the twin demands of the Pakistani business groups[140] and the defence establishment necessitated, it was not about to risk tampering with existing social relations in the countryside.

All this needs bearing in mind while considering the plan's growth targets, as well as its resource estimates and actual allocations to the

---

[135] Ibid., 126–7.
[136] John H. Power, 'Industrialization in Pakistan: A Case of Frustrated Take Off?', *Pakistan Development Review*, Summer 1963, III, no. 2, 205.
[137] Emajuddin Ahmed, *Bureaucratic Elites*, 122.
[138] Cited in ibid., 122–3.
[139] *The First Five Year Plan (1955–1960)*, outline of the plan (draft), Karachi, May 1956, 5.
[140] See Rashid Amjad, 'Role of Industrial Houses in Pakistan's Power Structure', *Pakistan Administrative Staff College Journal*, XII, June 1974.

different sectors of the economy. These targets were based on very rough estimates of public and private savings during 1955 and 1960. The public sector's average annual income, after allowing for the devaluation of the rupee in July 1955, was believed to be in the order of Rs. 2,308 million. Of this as much as Rs. 2,008 or 87 per cent represented non-development expenditure with defence, civil administration and debt reservicing together accounting for as much as Rs. 1,547 million or 77 per cent. This left a mere Rs. 300 million as the total annual saving of the public sector, Rs. 1,500 million over a period of five years. 'Private savings were calculated to be around Rs. 1,180 million per annum, a total of Rs. 5,900 million. Together with the Rs. 3,800 million projected as the total foreign grants and loans to the public sector, and an estimated Rs. 400 million as the net import of new foreign investments in the private sector, the total development outlay for the plan came to approximately Rs. 11,600 million.[141] So about 36 per cent of the development expenditure under Pakistan's first five year plan was to be financed by foreign capital.

In making the allocations to the different sectors and regions of the economy, the planning board had strictly followed the central government's guidelines. The public sector's share of the total development outlay was Rs. 8,000 million, or 69 per cent, with the private sector claiming the rest. Only after setting public sector expenditure targets higher than the available resources – an insurance for full use – did the plan make the following allocations between the centre and the provinces (see Table 5.3).

These figures belie claims that the first five year plan's allocation of development resources aimed at rectifying the step-motherly treatment

Table 5.3 *Budgetary allocations between the centre and the provinces*

	In millions of Rupees	%
Centre (including Karachi)	2731	30
West Pakistan	3503	38
East Pakistan	3002	32
TOTAL	9236	

Source: The First Five Year Plan (1955–60), outline of the plan (draft), Karachi, May 1956, Table 4, 13–4.

[141] *The First Five Year Plan (1955–60)*, outline of the plan (draft), 12.

meted out to the eastern wing. All the more so since, despite much ado about the agricultural sector, the Cinderella of the Pakistani economy, the industrial sector continued to have top priority in the allocation of resources. About 26 per cent of the total public and private expenditure was to be in the industrial sector which,[142] it was hoped, would grow by as much as 60 per cent during the plan period.[143] By contrast, agriculture had to settle for 11 per cent of all investments to attain the planned target of a 2.5 per cent annual growth rate.

Clearly then, the first five year plan was an attempt to confirm, correct and coordinate rather than to radically change the tenor of the central government's past economic policies. The mere fact that the final version of the plan was made public just six months before the military takeover demands a closer scrutiny of the political and structural obstacles in the way of its implementation. As the foremost proponents of a state consolidation based on minimal disruptions from the political process, the bureaucratic and military axis had found natural allies among business groups in Karachi. A new state – aspiring to become a regional military power but lacking the corresponding industrial base – was propitious soil for a magnificent dovetailing of interests between the few seeking power for its own sake and the many more anxious simply for the joys of unfettered profit-making. The swift transformation of merchant capitalists and traders into 'ruthless...industrial entrepreneurs',[144] a process which accompanied the virtual eclipse of the landlord-ridden Muslim League and the rise to dominance of the bureaucracy and the military during the early fifties in Pakistan, is one of the more striking instances of the modern state's role in class formation.

But it was not always easy for the state to meet the competing claims of the business groups in Karachi and their less affluent cousins in the Punjab without undermining its own imperatives. All the more so since nothing could prevent rival business factions from organising into pressure groups or manipulating their social connections with members of the administrative bureaucracy. By 1955 certainly, if not even earlier, the state had become an arena where contradictory interests vied to influence economic policies in general and the distribution of licences in

---

[142] Ibid., 36.

[143] *The First Five Year Plan, (1955–1960)*, Karachi 1958, 17.

[144] Gustav F. Papanek, 'The Development of Entrepreneurs', *The American Economic Review*, LII, 1962, 54. For the sociological background of the Karachi business communities see Hanna Papanek, 'Pakistan's Big Businessmen: Muslim Separatism, Entrepreneurs, and Partial Mobilization', *Economic Development and Cultural Change*, 21, October 1972.

particular with little or no heed to the broader national interests so essential for its stability. The most influential pressure group in the capital was the managing committee of the federation of chambers of commerce and industry, an organisation representing the interests of west Pakistani 'robber barons'[145] who controlled as much as 96 per cent of the Muslim owned private industries,[146] and nearly 80 per cent of the assets of the private banks and insurance companies in the country.[147] The close ties between the federation and the big industrial houses on the one hand, and between them and government agencies like the Pakistan industrial development corporation on the other, had a decisive bearing on economic decision-making. With privileged access to the administrative bureaucracy and the additional advantage of holding simultaneous positions in the directorates of a number of industrial concerns, the members of the managing committee of the chambers of commerce and industry were able – jointly and severally – to keep effective checks on the government's import and labour policies.

By the middle of the 1950s, however, falling profits and an overall slowing down in industrial growth rates had cut short the honeymoon for obvious reasons. The initial spurt in industrial profits was due to the imposition of import controls. While these pulled the government out of a difficult foreign exchange position and also protected indigenous manufactures, the policy of keeping the rupee overvalued brought down the prices of agricultural exports with depressing effects on both wages and domestic demand. In the absence of an expanding domestic market or a concerted effort at exporting surplus Pakistani manufactures, the potential for high growth rates in the industrial sector were limited. The arrival of new industrial competitors worsened the trend. There were other reasons why industrial growth rates had begun grinding to a halt. Successive crop failures and the need to import food forced the government to tighten controls on foreign exchange. Private investors faced a wall of bureaucratic restrictions; they were unable to use their rupee resources to import spare parts and raw materials for existing industries, much less obtain licences to acquire new machinery. Signs of increasing unrest among industrial workers – the result of rising prices

---

[145] This popular reference to west Pakistan's emerging industrial entrepreneurs was coined by Gustav F. Papanek in *Pakistan's Development, Social Goals and Private Incentives*, Harvard 1967.

[146] Maniruzzaman, 'Group Interests in Pakistan Politics, 1947–58', *Pacific Affairs*, 39, Spring-Summer 1966, 89.

[147] Rashid Amjad, 'Industrial Concentration and Economic Power', in Hassan Gardezi and Jamil Rashid (eds.), *Pakistan, The Roots of Dictatorship: The Political Economy of a Praetorian State*, London 1983, 247–8.

and falling wages as well as the government's failure to introduce any progressive labour legislation – lent weight to the oft-repeated argument that major changes were now required to take Pakistan into its second stage of industrialisation.

On 31 July 1955, the decision to devalue the rupee[148] gave the first inkling of the government's willingness to countenance modifications in its industrial policy. The planning board which was by now involved in the preparation of the national budget had prevailed upon the government to accept the view, held by prominent Karachi based industrialists and unequivocally endorsed by the HAG, that import-substitution had run its course and the time had come to augment foreign exchange earnings through the maximisation of exports. As the white paper on the budget of 1956–7 put it, Pakistan had not only attained the status of a 'semi-industrialized' economy but was in a position to 'encourage exports of manufactured goods on an internationally competitive basis'.[149] The government's aggressive new tune and reports of a balance of payments surplus in 1955 let loose a chorus of demands for more liberal foreign exchange allocations and larger quotas of import licences. This, the representatives of private capital argued, was not only consistent with the shift of emphasis from saving to earning foreign exchange on manufactured exports but also with the government's implicit acknowledgement that the country had moved from being a mere associate on the peripheries to full membership in the international capitalist system. Not all of the government's financial advisers were convinced.[150] Pakistan was still reeling on the peripheries and had to use every opportunity to maintain and consolidate foreign exchange reserves – its only hope of one day kicking the habit of deficit financing and an unashamed reliance on foreign aid.

Unresolved disagreements within the administration between the so-called 'expansionists' and 'consolidators' about the pace at which Pakistan could safely proceed with industrialisation and export-promotion was frustrating for Karachi's business magnates. Having made handsome profits from import-substitution, they now were ready to take advantage of the government's export-promotion drive and invest in heavy industries. So they had to persuade the relevant

---

[148] Before 31 July 1955, the Pakistani rupee was valued at $0.30225; with the devaluation it equalled $0.21.

[149] *White Paper on the Budget of Pakistan for 1956–7*, cited in Andrus and Mohammad, *The Economy of Pakistan*, 303.

[150] 'Plea for a More Liberal Spending of Foreign Exchange', by Jafar Naqvi, *The Pakistan Times*, 8 May 1956.

government departments and ministries either to cut back on import licences for prospective small- and medium-scale industries or increase the availability of foreign exchange. The first option was politically unfeasible since with Suhrawardy in the saddle the centre could not turn a deaf ear to the demands of east Pakistani business groups for parity in the allocation of foreign exchange and import licences for both small- and medium-scale industrial machinery, exactly what the Punjabi business interests had been clamouring for all along.[151] A new export promotion scheme announced in October 1956 slightly liberalised the government's policy on foreign exchange allocations for industrial raw materials and spare parts. But it fell short of the expectations of big business. Much to their dismay the chairman of the planning board, Zahid Hussain, dismissed calls for a 'spectacular heavy industries programme'; the country had to first become self-sufficient in food and solvent in foreign exchange before private capital could be allowed to reach out for this pie in the sky.[152]

So the bigwigs of Karachi business had to wait for the big time when there would be opportunities galore to multiply profits. But even now their predicament was far from hopeless; a divided and corrupt administrative bureaucracy could always be relied upon to find loopholes to slip an odd import licence for heavy industrial machinery. In any event, Ghulam Farooq, the chairman of the Pakistan industrial development corporation [PIDC] and the leader of the 'expansionists', was in favour of encouraging investments in heavy industry. Opposing him were 'consolidators' like Chaudhri Mohammad Ali and Zahid Hussain. And, while there was 'some hope' that the 'consolidators' would 'prevail', there was a very real 'danger' that even this school of thought might 'not face up to the severe pruning of the present industrial programme' necessitated by consolidation. Alternatively, under pressure from the 'expansionists' they might be eventually 'driven to make so many exceptions to a policy of consolidation as to make nonsense of it'.[153]

The extent to which these conflicting political considerations delayed the government's approval of the revised draft plan becomes clearer in the light of the structural obstacles – some inherent, others recent

---

[151] See p. 258.

[152] *The Pakistan Times*, 7 November 1956, The non-CSP chairman of the planning board Zahid Hussain had drafted the first five year plan's controversial sections on land reforms and administrative reorganisation. He was unlikely to withstand the inevitable two-pronged attack by west Pakistani landlords and the Pakistan civil service cadres long enough to frustrate the ambitions of private capital.

[153] Symon to Garner, 1 February 1955, DO35/5378, PRO.

inventions – facing the Pakistani economy. The sheer enormity of the agricultural sector and its continuing importance in determining the overall performance of the economy, good or bad, was one of the inescapable realities which the state managers could ill afford to deny. And indeed, even before they could complete the first round of self-congratulations on the positive effects of the devaluation decision – between 1954–5 and 1955–6 Pakistan's exports increased by 68.5 per cent – the tables had turned on them.[154] In 1956–7, the value of exports fell by over 10 per cent despite a 9 per cent and 18.3 per cent rise in cotton and jute prices respectively. With 56.4 per cent of the cotton crop and 15.5 per cent of the jute production being consumed by indigenous industry, it was possible to explain the respective fall of 30 per cent and 28 per cent in their exports. Yet, contrary to expectations, the loss of export earnings from raw jute and cotton had not been offset by increased foreign exchange earnings from jute manufactures or cotton twist and yarn.[155] Pakistan had a long way to go before its semi-manufactured goods could squeeze through the half-closed doors of the international market.

There were darker clouds on the domestic economic horizon. Crop failures in 1956–7 saw rice and wheat disappearing from the bazaars. This worsened the inflationary pressures that had followed in the wake of the rupee devaluation: larger incomes from cash crops had seen increased demands for foodgrains in Pakistan's overpopulated and underfed rural areas. Anxious to stem the drift towards political unrest, the government not only bought food imports at much higher rupee costs but also introduced price subsidies, thus imposing an excruciating burden on an exchequer crippled by escalated rates of defence and administrative expenditure. The creation of paper money to meet the government's current account deficit, nearly 40 per cent of which was due to food subsidies alone,[156] saw the inflationary spiral assuming monstrous proportions. The salutary effects of increased inflows of agricultural commodity assistance from the United States, the United Nations and other private agencies were cancelled by the triple curse of hoarding, black-marketeering and smuggling across the borders with India. Floods in the last quarter of 1957, destroying some 100,000 tons of wheat, brought the country to the verge of bankruptcy. The state

[154] Calculated from figures on Pakistan's balance of trade in Andrus and Mohammad, *The Economy of Pakistan*, table 29, 104.
[155] 'Pakistan's Current Economic Situation and Prospects', report no. 7706 of the office of intelligence research and analysis, department of state, 15 May 1958, NA, 4.
[156] Ibid., 5.

bank issued a warning against further increases in the money supply. To print more treasury bills the government would first have to secure legislative approval. Its deficit financing was attaining the maximum level contemplated under the five year plan. Liberal allocations of import licences and higher payments on government account had forced the foreign exchange reserves down to nothing. If Pakistan's disputed claims against the reserve bank of India for approximately Rs. 490 million are excluded, the reserve ratio stood ominously close to the 30 per cent statutory minimum in gold and foreign exchange necessary to back currency in circulation.

The government had no choice but to lower the growth targets under the first five year plan. Realising that its own, as well as the cumulative effects of past economic failures, had badly damaged the people's confidence in the viability of the state, there was little point risking cuts in either defence or administrative expenditure. And so the country had once again to sacrifice chunks of development expenditure for defence and administrative purposes. Insofar as this postponed recovery in the agricultural sector, it diluted and even reversed the much vaunted successes of the industrial sector. In May 1958, when the final version of the first five year plan was made public, the growth target for gross national income had been reduced to 15 per cent. This meant an average annual growth rate of about 2.9 per cent. But with the economy in tatters and its main component, the agricultural sector, groaning on account of neglect and exploitation, the actual achievements during the five years in which the plan was ostensibly in operation were much lower than even the revised targets. With a 1.4 per cent growth in agriculture, as opposed to the planned 2.5 per cent, the gross national product increased by only 2.4 per cent annually, well below the original target of 4 per cent provided for in the May 1956 draft.

So the reassuring presence of American economic advisers, larger doses of aid and imported models for 'progress' notwithstanding, yet another attempt at planned economic development was ending in fiasco. It was easy to lay the blame on Pakistan's chronic political instability. Yet, for all the truth in that charge, it would be a travesty of history to argue that the state's strategic self-perceptions – shaped by regional and international compulsions – and the chosen path for its economic development had not contributed to, and even expedited, the fragment-ation of politics in Pakistan. Development policies aimed at channelling the energies and productive resources of a predominantly agricultural society to create a political economy tailored to meet the demands of the defence establishment are not the sparks that kindle the imagination of a people.[157] Knowledge of Pakistan's growing ability to deter India's military might, however gratifying, was no substitute, and never was to be, for resolving the problems of bread, clothing and shelter.

If pursuing an economic development policy bereft of popular support had its inconveniences, recourse to the electoral process was politically inexpedient – for bureaucrats, military commanders, members of big business and some elements of the landed gentry in west Pakistan, quite as much as for Pakistan's sponsors in the international arena. The political crisis enveloping the country during 1956 and 1958 was not just an expression of popular discontentment with corrupt politicians and an ineffective system of government, but a severe indictment of the state's economic and foreign policies.

The state under political siege

Between September 1956 and October 1958 three prime ministers belonging to as many parties tried steadying the course of political developments. But the antinomies of the political process and state consolidation defeated them. The swings in ministerial fortunes must, therefore, be seen in the context of a growing uneasiness in the relationship between the political process and a state structure within which the non-elected institutions had already acquired clear dominance. The last two years of 'parliamentary government' wrought greater fragmentation of politics at the top which, together with the general worsening of economic conditions and the polarisation of social relations below, gave an unprecedented pitch to intra-provincial as well as centre-province tensions. The institutions of the state, both civil and military, were obvious arenas for the reproduction of these tensions. By the autumn of 1958, it was not simply the central cabinet but the state itself that was under a political siege. The origins of the state of martial rule can be traced further only by assessing the multiple challenges to the state's authority and its capacity, or lack of, to cope with them in the twenty-five months preceding the military intervention.

---

[157] As the American ambassador James M. Langley, who took over from Hildreth on 1 May 1957, acknowledged, the military establishment was such a 'drain' on the Pakistani economy that inflows of US aid at best helped 'maintain precarious living standards'. Since it was 'difficult for the man in the street to appreciate a benefit which has to be measured in almost negative terms', pro-US sentiments were confined to only that 'very small upper crust' who were doing well out of American assistance. (James M. Langley to assistant secretary of state for Near Eastern, South Asian and African affairs, 27 December 1957, *Foreign Relations*, VIII, 488.)

SUHRAWARDY'S MINISTRY (12 SEPTEMBER 1956– 11 OCTOBER 1957)

As the only Bengali of national stature who could claim a base of support in the eastern wing, Suhrawardy's prime ministership might appear to be a healthy departure from the norms of 'parliamentary government' in Pakistan. It was certainly a welcome development to have as prime minister a man who despite an 'inexhaustible appetite for the bright lights and gay life of cafe society'[158] was not only a 'politician to the finger tips'[159] but one with a penchant for stirring oratory. All in all the prospects for the political process 'look[ed] much more hopeful' under Suhrawardy even if 'it seem[ed] to be the last chance'.[160] And indeed, coinciding with mounting political and economic discontents as well as a rising crescendo against Pakistan's pro-Western foreign policy, Suhrawardy's term in office furnishes further evidence – if such evidence is still needed – of how an overweening president acting independently or at the behest of a small coterie was able at each step to subvert the political process until the need for an alternative system of government seemed unavoidable. Even before he had reconciled himself to having Suhrawardy as prime minister, Mirza was finding 'the constitutional limitations' on his emergency powers 'extremely frustrating'. If he acted under articles 191 or 193 of the constitution he was liable to be 'faced by an appeal to the Courts'. Since in his view the constitution was 'unworkable as it stood', Mirza was ready to 'impose martial law if necessary' rather than 'see Pakistan disintegrate'.[161]

So although many notches above Bogra in political stature, Suhrawardy, once at the centre, was an easy prey for Mirza – a past master at political intrigue. He qualified for office only after accepting all three of Mirza's conditions: (1) that he would not alter Pakistan's pro-Western foreign policy (2) that he would not meddle with the army,[162] and (3) that he would keep the left-wing of the Awami League led by Maulana Bhashani firmly in harness. As Mirza told his British and American friends: 'If the Prime Minister plays tricks, so can I. If he tries

---

[158] Symon to secretary of state [CRO], 14 July 1955, DO35/5378, PRO.

[159] James [acting British high commissioner] to secretary of state [CRO], 12 October 1956, DO35/5407, PRO. The American embassy in Pakistan, also recognising his political potential, had instructed its officers to 'maintain pleasant social contact with Suhrawardy'. (Hildreth's telegram to the department of state, 12 August 1955, *Foreign Relations*, VIII, 435.)

[160] This was the assessment of Roger Howroyd, a senior British civil servant who had been serving the government of Pakistan since 1947. (Howroyd to Laithwaite, 10 September 1956, DO35/5407, PRO.)

[161] James to Laithwaite, 18 August 1956, ibid.

[162] Suhrawardy had only recently asserted that his 'first step' as prime minister would be to 'dismiss Ayub'. (James to the CRO, telegram no.1342, 23 August 1956, ibid.)

to tamper with our stand...I shall show him that he will have a revolution on his hands'.[163] The president's astonishing confidence flowed from his belief that the army and the civil service were behind him and also from the very nature of Suhrawardy coalition ministry.

A man of populist pretensions, some of them genuine, Suhrawardy had slotted himself into office by forging an alliance with the oldest of the old guard.[164] As the senior partners in the coalition, the Republican landed heavyweights had no stomach for the prime minister's populism, much less for the mild palliatives he was wont to offer to keep the left-wingers in the Awami League in low swing. Suhrawardy's handling of the burning political questions of the day established him as the reluctant mouthpiece of men who, having created the Republican party on the ruins of the Muslim League in west Pakistan, needed some sort of a footing in the eastern wing to legitimise their claims to power at the centre. But, if being a Bengali was Suhrawardy's best credential, the Republican bosses and their backers within the presidency and the state bureaucracy were determined to miss no opportunity to convert the prime minister to the logic of central and, if possible, west Pakistani imperatives. Put less politely, the only acceptable Bengali in office in Karachi was a captive Bengali!

And so the one-time godfather of the Calcutta underworld began learning the captivating truths about prime ministerial office in the Pakistani state system. But for a remarkable reserve of political guile, a natural resilience, and an ambition matching that of the existing power brokers in Karachi, Suhrawardy may not have passed the initial tests of his new calling with such flying colours. However with Mirza acting mufti, there is reason to consider both the nature of the challenges and the response Suhrawardy was able to muster, especially since the prime minister's efforts to manoeuvre on purely political issues had a bearing on his ability to deal with the economy, the one issue upon whose cut and thrust all else ultimately depended.

The controversy over the appropriate electoral system for Pakistan, whether joint or separate, revived itself almost as soon as Suhrawardy completed muttering the oath of office. A long-standing proponent of

---

[163] See James to the secretary of state [CRO], 16 October 1956, ibid., and Hildreth's telegram to the department of state, 24 September 1956, *Foreign Relations*, VIII, 470–1.

[164] In September 1956, there were seventy-seven members in the national assembly; fifty-two in favour of the new coalition and twenty-five opposed. Of the government MLAs, a mere fourteen belonged to the Awami League. Even with the addition of one Ganatantri Dal member and seven Hindu MLAs from east Pakistan, the Republicans – twenty-seven of them from west Pakistan and three from east Pakistan – had a clear edge over Suhrawardy.

joint electorates, Suhrawardy became premier after the west Pakistan assembly had plumped in favour of separate electorates by a joint Republican and Muslim League vote of 122 against ten cast by G.M. Syed's Sindhi Awami Mahaz and the Hindu MLAs. In west Pakistan, opposition to joint electorates bordered on the fanatical. According to the Muslim League and religious parties like the Jamat-i-Islami, anyone espousing the cause was a traitor to Islam since the Hindu minority of east Pakistan wanted to do away with separate electorates simply in order to better exploit divisions among Muslims. The irony of a majority demanding electoral safeguards against a minority was completely lost on these champions of an Islamic Pakistan.

Attempts to link the electorate issue with Islam were embarrassing for the new prime minister. Not only his own party, but a majority opinion in east Pakistan vehemently supported joint electorates. On 1 October 1956, the east Pakistan assembly pronounced overwhelmingly in favour of joint electorates. This brought Mirza flying to Dacca where the national assembly was to meet to decide the matter. Presidential instructions were given to the Republicans; they were not to oppose the east wingers, much less question his fantastic proposal that the two parts of the country be allowed to choose different electoral systems. On 10 October, the electorate amendment act recommending separate electorates for west Pakistan and joint electorates for east Pakistan was passed in the national assembly by forty-eight to nineteen votes. The prime minister was left gasping at the president's nerve, but delighted himself in the privileged knowledge that joint electorates eventually would be enforced in both wings of the country. Saved by the presidential bell, Suhrawardy was temporarily beholden to the master. He realised that there were more advantages in keeping his fences with the president in good repair than pressing the Awami League's demands too insistently. The compromise distanced him from the party. This suited the central coterie since it left the prime minister with little choice except to harp their tunes unquestioningly. Suhrawardy's dramatic *volte-face* on foreign policy and the one unit system suggest how power at the national level can convert the most rabid provincialist into a dyed-in-the-wool centralist.

Since Nasser's nationalisation of the Suez canal in July 1956, public opinion was restive about the central government's pro-Western policies. Chaudhri Mohammad Ali's government had been rocked by a series of public demonstrations against Pakistan's failure to lend its unequivocal support to the Egyptians. In Lahore a meeting attended by 300,000 – the largest ever since partition and an indication that tempers were being fed by the unrelenting economic distress – called upon the government to not only revise its Suez policy but to also withdraw from the commonwealth, SEATO and the Baghdad pact.[165] In east Pakistan, Suhrawardy's Awami League was in the vanguard of the movement for a drastic reorientation of Pakistan's foreign policy. Ignoring the party's position, one which he himself had helped define, Suhrawardy in his first public address as premier vowed to abide by and strengthen Pakistan's military agreement with the Western powers. Coming from this crusader of non-alignment, the declaration was particularly disheartening for the Awami League. Its president, Abdul Hamid Khan Bhashani, the pro-Chinese leader of the Bengal peasantry, took the opportunity to steel up the left-wing of the party to launch an attack on the premier's blatant sell-out. Susceptible to such pressure Suhrawardy tried distancing his government from Britain's Suez policy only to be reminded by Mirza of the terms of his contract.[166] In November 1956, the Anglo-French and Israeli invasion of the Suez zone saw Bhashani leading a protest strike in Dacca; angry mobs tried burning down the British and French consulates. Passions in west Pakistan ran apace. Although he had a better grip over the west Pakistan Awami League, Suhrawardy had here to bear the brunt of public fury stirred up, paradoxically enough, by the Muslim League. Desperately trying to spring back into action, the Muslim League now took to flooding the press with texts of resolutions against Pakistan's foreign policy, arguing that compromises made by its governments owed nothing to the opinion of party workers.

By the end of 1956, foreign policy had become central to the public debate in Pakistan. While a thorn in the flesh for the central government, the thrust of the arguments against Pakistan's pro-Western foreign policy could be blunted by pointing the finger at India and all the machinations that were associated with that name in the popular imagination. On 17 November, the Kashmir constituent assembly took the big step of declaring itself as an integral part of the Indian union; the amendment to the constitution was to become effective from 26 January 1957. Rudely shocked by this unilateral declaration, even the sharpest opponents of the government's foreign policy decided to keep mum while the United Nations security council deliberated on the legitimacy

---

[165] *Dawn*, 17 August 1956.

[166] Suhrawardy had tried to delay sending Pakistan's representative to the second users' conference in London on the pretext of wanting to first consult the governments of other Muslim states. It was an admirable, if futile, attempt. Mirza 'repeated with great firmness his determination to keep Suhrawardy on the rails' through 'strong action if necessary'. Interestingly enough, Mirza 'hope[d] that if he had to take over the country people in Britain and America would not say he had done so for personal ends'. (James to the CRO, telegram, 22 September 1956, DO35/5407, PRO.)

of the move. This left the field open to those who believed that Indian perfidy was the best vindication of Pakistan's pro-Western tilt. The convenient turn of events gave Suhrawardy the opening he needed to secure the national assembly's endorsement for the centre's foreign policy. Towards the end of February 1957, he defended Pakistan's 'pactomania' with a passion worthy of a Bengali. With Kashmir on their minds and such convincing theatrics from the prime minister, the members of the national assembly could hardly avoid endorsing the government's foreign policy. Even the opposition benches thought it politic to abstain; the final vote showed forty in favour and only two against Pakistan's existing foreign policy. It was a mixed blessing for Suhrawardy. Facing Bhashani's revolt in the Awami League and a reassertion of east Pakistan's provincial autonomy demands, he had taken the precaution of securing the west Pakistan Awami League's approval for his government's, or more aptly the centre's, foreign policy. This precipitated a series of desertions from the Sind and NWFP branches of the Awami League. Suhrawardy saw no reason to lament the development; the turn-coats wanted to undo the one unit system, an issue on which he was even less able to follow a line independent of his patrons at the centre.

Opposition to one unit was older than the system itself. In August 1956, six minor parties in the west Pakistan assembly – the Sindhi Awami Mahaz, the Red Shirts, the Azad party, the Sind Hari committee, the Wrore Pakhtun and the Ustaman Gal – had formed the Pakistan National party with the explicit purpose of abolishing one unit and introducing radical agrarian reforms. It was the first ever merger of parties in Pakistan's history. More significantly for the politics of west Pakistan, the PNP with its dozen or so votes in the assembly held the balance between the Republicans and the Muslim League. This acted as a spur to the anti-one unit movement with the two main parties see-sawing inexorably between opposing and supporting the system. With one eye on the shifting positions in the west Pakistan assembly and the other on the pro-one unit lobby at the centre, Suhrawardy hesitated before supporting one unit more emphatically. The revelation weakened his hold over the rump of the Awami League in west Pakistan and foreclosed his joining the key anglers in the Muslim League and the Republican party as they trawled for support in the smaller provinces. Under the laws governing the balance of power within the Pakistani state system, hanging on to prime ministerial office seemed to be inconsistent with enjoying the support of a popularly based party organisation.

Not a man to let set-backs destroy his morale, Suhrawardy thought his political fortunes might change if he scored some successes on the economic front. Pandering to the demands of east Pakistani commercial and trading organisations, as well as alleviating the food shortage in the country could outweigh the ill-effects of his lapses on political and foreign policy issues. On 18 November, at Suhrawardy's behest, Abul Mansur Ahmad – the Awami League minister for commerce and industries – announced a series of concessions for small-and medium-scale business groups in east Pakistan. These included parity in the allocation of foreign exchange between the two wings and a review of the existing categories of importers to facilitate the entry of newcomers from east Pakistan as well as from areas in west Pakistan which had hitherto been underrepresented.[167] The move was hailed by east Pakistani commercial and trading groups. But it landed Suhrawardy in deep trouble with the industrial magnates of Karachi. Already put off by the slackening of the government's aid-to-private industry programme, they were not about to accept cuts in their import quotas. Accusing the Awami League of provincialism, the president of the federation of chambers of commerce and industry lodged a strong protest with Mirza.[168] This was one item only in the charge-sheet which the west Pakistani business groups were to place on the president's desk just prior to Suhrawardy's fall.

The prime minister's efforts to find lasting solutions for the food problem never got off the ground. But they damaged such standing as he had with the west Pakistani rural lords. Suhrawardy had given the food and agriculture portfolio to an Awami Leaguer with a view to alleviating the acute shortage of rice in east Pakistan. Since the food crisis in the country was linked with the need for major agrarian reforms, Suhrawardy encouraged his party to investigate the problem in a big way. In January 1957, an Awami League conference in Dacca called for agrarian reforms and a constitutional amendment legalising the state's confiscation of land without compensation.[169] West Pakistani landlords protested against this unIslamic attitude towards private property. The reaction, however, was rooted in developments beyond the Awami League's paper proposal. During the summer of 1956, they had been startled by the sight of nearly 2,000 tenants demonstrating in the streets of Lahore against illegal evictions. Instigated by the Awami Jamhoor party, an extension of the Azad party and the left-wing of the Awami

[167] *Dawn*, 19 November 1956.
[168] See Maniruzzaman, 'Group Interests in Pakistan Politics, 1947–58', *Pacific Affairs*, 39, Spring-Summer 1966, 90.
[169] See Gankovsky, *A History of Pakistan*, 279.

League, the march was a resounding success. Not only did it electrify populist parties and the main labour unions in the province but, and this was what worried the rural lords, the west Pakistan government actually conceded some of the demands in principle. Fearing that the Awami League's outlandish suggestions might set alight the Punjabi and Sindhi rural areas, they decided to set up the west Pakistan zarai [agricultural] federation[170] – an organisation with no concern other than to ward off all threats to the existing agrarian structure. Its appearance on the scene was greeted warmly by much of the top Republican leadership; a clear hint of its pedigree.

The prime minister had been issued a sharp warning. Certainly not much more was heard of the Awami League's agrarian proposals. Hedging his bets, Suhrawardy took the easier – but for the state more expensive – route of allocating small sums of money to the agricultural sector. Yet these fits of largesse were no substitute for the miracles Suhrawardy needed to refashion his public image. For one thing, unrest in the rural areas was comparatively more muted than the upsurge of organised labour activity in both wings of the country. Since the summer of 1956, striking workers had been demanding cost of living allowances, higher wages and better terms of employment. But, with the west Pakistani industrialists planning how best to axe him, the prime minister dared not put his name to the mildest of labour reforms. Having seen the futility of going against the grain of the dominant power bloc in west Pakistan, Suhrawardy, like so many of his predecessors, now turned to the stick instead of the carrot – the easiest recipe for clinging to political office in the Pakistani context.

Suhrawardy's capitulations and the consequent dip in his popularity meant that Mirza could be more dismissive of the prime minister. With no influence whatsoever on the Republican gaggle, Suhrawardy was reduced to rubber-stamping a series of presidential and gubernatorial confabulations which, breath-taking though they were, served to discredit and eventually dismantle the tottering edifice of provincial politics in west Pakistan. By early 1957, the movement for the dismemberment of the one unit system had come to dominate politics in west Pakistan. Even the Republicans, already divided on the question of Khan Sahib's successor, had been affected. Facing an almost certain no-confidence motion on the issue the chief minister succeeded in postponing a meeting of the provincial assembly until March when, short of presidential rule, there was no getting around legislative approval for the annual budget. But on 20 March, before the budget had been passed,

170 Ibid.

thirty members of the Republican party crossed over to the opposition benches. Having lost his majority, Khan Sahib called upon the centre to impose president's rule; Mirza obliged willingly.

Constitutional propriety demanded that the governor call upon the Muslim League leader to form a new ministry. But this would have upset the coalition at the centre as well as the one unit arrangements so vital for the continued dominance of the bureaucratic-military axis. Suhrawardy's line that president's rule was necessary to ratify the provincial budget cut no ice with the national press, at one in condemning this latest attempt to subvert the constitution. His bluff called, Mirza embarked upon a renewed attack on the British parliamentary system; it was completely unsuited to Pakistani conditions and the sooner it was replaced by a modified version of the American system the better it would be for the country.[171] Khan Sahib had even more radical ideas. What Pakistan needed, he asserted, was the suspension of all political parties and the setting up of a revolutionary council to preside over the affairs of the state for a period of at least five years.[172] The military command must have made a mental note of this interesting suggestion.

In the meantime, Mirza – once again exceeding his presidential brief – began exploring the possibilities of bringing the Republicans back to power. Realising that a Muslim League ministry in west Pakistan would mark the end of his term in office, Suhrawardy declared that a Republican ministry could be restored only if the president's 'party' was able to prove the support of at least 160 MLAs. Deeply worried about the fading magic of his tactical manoeuvres, Mirza ordered the Republicans to show their strength. They did so by means more foul than fair. In the first week of July 1957, a 'party' which was incapable of winning power through the ballot box had conjured up support to form a ministry. Sardar Abdur Rashid was inducted to replace Khan Sahib as party leader and on 15 July, against a background of protest, a Republican ministry was returned to office.

On the face of it, Mirza's high handedness had saved the Republican-Awami League coalition at the centre. But, in point of fact, the president had only secured the Republican position; Suhrawardy by now was redundant. Developments in east Pakistan underlined his irrelevance. In early April, the east Pakistan assembly had passed a resolution calling for full autonomy, especially in matters to do with finance. This had been followed in quick succession by the left-wing of the Awami League

[171] See *Dawn*, 25 March 1957.
[172] *The Pakistan Times*, 9 August 1957.

demanding autonomy in all spheres except foreign affairs, defence and currency. More disturbingly, some members of the Awami League ministry in east Pakistan were thought to be assisting their Hindu supporters in smuggling currency and gold, as well as rice and other consumer goods worth fifty to seventy crores of rupees each year across the 2,000 mile long border with India.[173] In May 1957, the army had to be called in once again to clamp down on the operations and, more specifically, to bring a halt to the inordinate rise in the price of rice.[174] The formation of the National Awami party in July 1957 underlined Suhrawardy's dispensability to the custodians of national imperatives. Consisting of Awami League dissidents led by Bhashani, the Ganatantri Dal and the anti-one unit PNP, the NAP's populist rhetoric and anti-American propaganda was a menace to the bureaucratic and military axis at the centre. NAP was equally dangerous for the Republicans. On 14 September, the west Pakistan assembly was scheduled to meet to give a vote of confidence to the Republican ministry. Sensing defeat, the Republican stalwarts decided to negotiate an agreement with NAP. According to the terms, the Republicans would support the move to substitute one unit with a zonal federation of linguistically and culturally autonomous units; in return NAP would give its vote of confidence to the ministry. It was a typically Pakistani political accommodation, one devoid of any principles.

On 17 September 1957, the west Pakistan assembly voted by 170 against four to abolish one unit. A transparent ploy to keep the Republicans in office, the vote could not have been taken without a wink from Mirza. And indeed no sooner had the assembly recorded its decision than Mirza and Suhrawardy, supposedly at Ayub's insistence, publicly denounced the anti-one unit resolution.[175] This took away some of the bite from jubilant statements by NAP leaders and claims by some Awami Leaguers that the dismantling of one unit would be accompanied by east Pakistan demanding representation in the national assembly and in the services according to its population, as well as a larger share in the allocation of finances.[176] Suhrawardy was now the running dog of military headquarters and the central bureaucracy in the fight to save one unit. Seizing the moment, the Republicans informed Mirza of their decision to withdraw support for the coalition at the centre. With big business groups in Karachi lobbying against

[173] *Dawn*, 24 April 1957.
[174] Ibid., 17 May 1957.
[175] Colonel Mohammad Ahmad, *My Chief*, Lahore 1960, 96.
[176] *Dawn*, 9 October 1957.

Suhrawardy's decision to distribute the better part of $10 million of ICA[177] aid to east Pakistani and new industrialists, and to establish a national shipping corporation despite fierce opposition from the shipowners' association and the federation of chambers and commerce and industry,[178] Mirza had absolutely no qualms demanding the prime minister's resignation. On 10 October, his request to seek a vote of confidence in the national assembly turned down and under threat of dismissal, Suhrawardy resigned.

I.I. Chundrigar's ministry reserves a special place in Pakistani history. Ousted before many had registered its existence, the ministry's brief stay in office was simply another episode in the unsightly muddles parading under the appellation of national politics. The leader of the Muslim League party in the national assembly, Chundrigar had served the state in various capacities. A close friend of Mirza with known sympathies for west Pakistani big business, Chundrigar qualified easily for the job of prime minister. So, once Mirza invited him to form the government, the Republicans wisely dropped their claim to be the largest single party in the national assembly and formed a coalition with the Muslim League. While refusing to accept Chundrigar's humiliating suggestion that they merge with the League, the Republican bosses agreed to support his party's line on one unit and separate electorates. With Chaudhri Mohammad Ali's Nizam-i-Islam and one faction of the Krishak Sramik pitching in, Chundrigar had no problems making his way into office.

Staying there was another matter. Seeing that his days might be numbered, Chundrigar lost no time reversing Suhrawardy's decision on the allocation of the $10 million of ICA aid; the creation of a national shipping corporation was also put into cold storage. The west Pakistani industrial magnates were understandably relieved. East Pakistani business circles for their part reacted by giving unqualified support to the demands for provincial autonomy. The rift between the two wings of the country was now complete.

Under the circumstances, it was pure folly to revive the electorate controversy. But, with his party fighting street battles against the proponents of joint electorates, Chundrigar had to try and modify the electoral amendment act. Declaring that his government would not be

---

[177] The International Cooperation Administration agency set up to manage American foreign aid.
[178] Maniruzzaman, 'Group Interests in Pakistan Politics', *Pacific Affairs*, 39, Spring-Summer 1966, 90–1.

'cowed down by threats of bloodshed in the event of a change in the Electoral Law' was tantamount to equating the issue with a vote of confidence for the coalition ministry.[179] Called upon to ratify their understanding with the Muslim League, the Republicans dithered but finally refused to reopen the electorate issue. So Chundrigar had to resign. He did so one day after approving the prevention of smuggling (special powers) ordinance no. xviii (1957) which gave the army absolute powers to conduct the anti-smuggling drive – popularly known as 'operation closed door' – in east Pakistan.[180] Whether in recognition of this or his previous record of service to the establishment, Mirza gave Chundrigar another chance to form a government. He failed because no major grouping in the national assembly was prepared to form a coalition on the issue of separate electorates alone.[181]

NOON'S MINISTRY (16 DECEMBER 1957 – 7 OCTOBER 1958)

Firoz Khan Noon was the last in the line of prime ministers called upon to stay the course of Pakistani politics. The leader of the twenty-one member Republican grouping in the national assembly, Noon proved his majority by forging alliances of convenience with as many as five different political groupings – the Awami League, the National Awami party, the Krishak Sramik party, the National Congress and the Scheduled Caste Federation.[182] A coalition dependent upon the support of a motley half a dozen parliamentary blocs was not likely to throw up a stable government. The Awami League and the National Awami party, in any case, showed their contempt for the Republican-led coalition by refusing to join the cabinet. It was a superb tactical move by Suhrawardy and the NAP leadership. Until more Bengalis were brought in, the central government could not be considered representative – the best insurance that Noon would remain vulnerable to pressure from parties with bases of support in the eastern wing. By holding out a

---

[179] *Dawn*, 18 November 1957.
[180] Ibid., 11 December 1957.
[181] Ibid., 14 December 1957.
[182] In December 1957 the party position in the national assembly for the time being was as follows:

Republicans	21	Muslim League	15
Awami League	13	Nizam-i-Islam	3
National Awami party	4	People's Progressive party	1
Krishak Sramik	6		
Pakistan National Congress	4	Independents	8
Scheduled Caste Federation	2	TOTAL	77*

*There were three vacant seats.

constant threat to withdraw support for the ruling coalition, Suhrawardy was able to reassert himself as a national leader as well as
prolong the tenure of the Awami League ministry in Dacca. The NAP
did quite as well; with twenty-nine votes in the 310 member east Pakistan
assembly it kept both the Republicans and the Awami League on its
tenterhooks.

Times were changing. The centre's earlier success in manipulating
provincial factions was losing its cutting edge. Not because provincial
politicians had found a way to parry central dictates. Far from it. One
large result of the economic crises of the late fifties and the consequent
polarisation of social relations was that the splintered provincial
groupings were most reluctant to toe the centre's line without first
extracting concessions to improve their chances in the forthcoming
general elections. These political manoeuvres and the consequent
impression of political instability had been inherent in the very interim
nature of the period between the passage of the constitution and the
holding of national elections.[183] Although as hopelessly divided as ever,
provincial politicians were now simply bidding for higher stakes, stirring
just enough trouble to keep the centre perpetually off balance.

Incessant bargaining between the centre and the provinces had dire
implications for the administrative machinery. The imposition of one
unit instead of easing administrative operations in west Pakistan had
accentuated tensions between Punjabi and non-Punjabi civil servants.
The policy of posting members of the old provincial cadres to different
parts of the unified province was immensely unpopular, especially
among Pathan and Sindhi civil servants who unlike their Punjabi fellows
preferred to work in familiar surroundings. In east Pakistan, animosities
between members of the provincial service and their mainly Punjabi
superiors remained unmitigated. Riddled with regional and professional
jealousies, the administrative structure was neither efficient nor reliable.
The frequent use of the police to quash political opponents and the ever
increasing concentration of power in bureaucratic hands – whether to
issue licences, sanction government contracts, funnel chunks of foreign
aid or to supervise various development projects – had exposed the
entire administration to malpractices once considered the exclusive
preserve of the politicians. Since the astronomical rise in the cost of
living had hit the salaried groups, anyone not making extra rupees under

---

[183] As the British high commissioner, by now a seasoned observer of Pakistan, noted: the
'impression of undue political instability...[was] not a fair reflection of the situation'.
He agreed with Suhrawardy that a 'basically stable political situation' could emerge
only after the elections. (Symon to secretary of state [CRO], 3 May 1957, DO35/5408,
PRO.)

the table found few sympathisers. With corruption rampant in the higher, middle and lower echelons of the administrative machinery, the state's ability to counter the multiple challenges to its authority was calling for a chain of command quite different from the one in existence. The army's 'operation closed door' in east Pakistan, so aptly named, was ominously hinting at the shape of things to come.

Realising that the odds were against him, Noon began by putting his weight behind the army's anti-smuggling operations in east Pakistan. But combined pressures from the Awami League, NAP and the Hindu members of the national assembly forced the government benches to accept a much watered down version of the anti-smuggling ordinance issued in December 1957.[184] Checkmated by his east Pakistani friends, Noon thought he might at least try keeping a semblance of control over his equally obstreperous supporters in west Pakistan. Heightened activity by the newly formed All-Pakistan peasant association, with Bhashani at the helm, had seen Lahore being flooded by evicted tenants and thousands of landless agricultural labourers demanding immediate government action.[185] The prime minister's reassuring statement that his government would not tolerate any radical agrarian reform did nothing to assuage the landlords. Instead of burying their differences and rallying under the Republican umbrella, many landlords had begun gravitating towards the more extreme religious and communal groupings. Even if incapable of acquiring mass electoral support, these parties could at least be relied upon to support the status quo unlike the Republicans for whom power justified the most inglorious of compromises.

With support for the Republicans diminishing rapidly and no sign of a consolidated landlord bloc emerging to fight the general elections, Mirza took matters in hand. As he told the British prime minister, Harold Macmillan, if left-wing forces won the elections he had 'no intention' of allowing them to 'form a government' and 'would take drastic steps...to prevent this'.[186] Having repeatedly failed in his efforts to create a 'national government',[187] Mirza after December 1957 began trying to bring the Muslim League and the Republicans into an electoral coalition.[188] Among the terms laid down by him was an undertaking by

---

[184] *Dawn*, 5 January 1958, cited in Afzal, *Political Parties in Pakistan*, 226.

[185] *The Pakistan Times*, 10 and 11 March 1958, cited in Gankovsky, *A History of Pakistan*, 298.

[186] Record of conversation between the British prime minister and Iskander Mirza, 30 October 1957, DO35/6520, PRO.

[187] See Symon to Garner, 28 April 1956, DO35/5406, PRO.

[188] Note by Mirza on the terms of an electoral agreement between the Muslim League and the Republicans, December 1957 [in the author's possession].

the Muslim League to support the Republican ministry in west Pakistan through the budget session in March 1958. In addition, the two parties were to agree to hold joint meetings during the election campaign and, most problematic of all, draw up a combined list of candidates.[189] Towards the end of February 1958, Daultana formally responded to the president's suggestion. The Muslim League was ready to form a coalition with the Republicans at the centre as well as in the west Pakistan assembly. But Daultana, who once reportedly declared that 'intrigue is in my blood',[190] carefully avoided committing himself to the point which, all said and done, was the nub of Mirza's proposal – namely that both parties agree on a common list of candidates. Daultana simply left it to a special committee to take all the final decisions.[191] By March the two parties had failed to find common ground. So the Muslim League under the fiery leadership of Khan Abdul Qayum Khan signed a vague sixteen-point socio-economic programme with the National Awami party in the hope of toppling the Republican ministry.[192] Just what Mirza dreaded the most.

Although the Muslim League-NAP agreement went the way of all such understandings between political parties in Pakistan, the overall situation in west Pakistan held out few hopes for a Republican victory at the polls. Even to make a respectable showing, the Republicans needed a chief minister with sufficient cunning to manipulate the administrative arrangements under one unit during the elections. Sardar Abdur Rashid was deemed to be too weak-kneed. So Mirza helped engineer his downfall, bringing in Muzaffar Ali Qizilbash, a Punjabi and a Shia like the president, as chief minister. Once again denied the comforts of high office, the Muslim League launched a blistering campaign against Mirza; Qayum Khan led the circus, enthralling his audience by hitting home some plain truths – for instance dubbing the central coalition as 'an employment exchange for unemployed politicians'.[193] The election campaign was now well and truly on its way.

If developments in west Pakistan gave Mirza good reason to want to banish the spectre of elections, thus the frequent postponement of the schedule, the downfall of four ministries in east Pakistan within six months came as a welcome bonus. In March 1958, a reconciliation between the two factions of the Krishak Sramik party under Sarkar's

[189] Ibid.
[190] B.J. Greenhill [Karachi] to Morley [CRO], 8 December 1953, DO35/5326, PRO.
[191] Daultana to Mirza, 20 February 1958, cited in 'Iskander Mirza Speaks: An Autobiography', *Meyaar* (Lahore), 29 May–5 June 1976, 18–9.
[192] *Dawn*, 19 March 1958.
[193] *Morning News* (Karachi), 9 April 1958.

leadership spelt doom for Ataur Rahman's Awami League ministry. Ataur Rahman's request that the assembly be prorogued was used as a pretext by the governor, Fazlul Huq, to send the ministry packing. Huq, the founding father of the Krishak Sramik party, contravened central advice and swore Sarkar in as the new chief minister. Suhrawardy responded by threatening to withdraw support from the coalition at the centre. So, within twelve hours of the news of the ministerial change reaching Karachi, Huq had been replaced with a new governor who, predictably enough, dismissed Sarkar and brought back Ataur Rahman.

Encouraged by the events, a parliamentary board headed by Bhashani drew up a five point programme which was to serve as the basis for NAP's future understandings with other parties. It included the demolition of one unit; an independent foreign policy; early elections on the basis of joint electorates; complete autonomy for all the provinces and the implementation of all the unfulfilled items of the United Front's original twenty-one point programme.[194] Suhrawardy's intervention prevented the provincial Awami League from accepting the NAP's stance on one unit and foreign policy. On 18 June, Ataur Rahman's ministry was defeated because NAP members, who held the balance in the assembly, opted to stay neutral. Two days later Sarkar was back in office for seventy-two long hours. The provincial Awami League leadership now decided to ignore Suhrawardy's directives and came to terms with NAP. Together they defeated Sarkar's ministry. This time the centre reacted by slapping section 193 on the province. It was not until 25 August that Ataur Rahman, not without help from Suhrawardy at the centre, managed to form a new ministry. The Awami League again tried curtailing the speaker's powers. On 20 September, in an atmosphere that might have intimidated the goondas of Dacca, Shahid Ali – the deputy speaker – made the fatal mistake of announcing that an Awami League motion declaring the speaker to be of 'unsound mind' had carried. Twenty-four hours after the event, the east Pakistan assembly had been turned into a battlefield. The respectable members of the legislature gave vent to their frustrations by hurling each other across the floor; the deputy speaker was a favourite catch. And while many were wounded, Shahid Ali never recovered. His death a few days later marked the beginning of the end for the parliamentary system, such as it existed, in Pakistan.

If it had been an isolated incident, the central government might have weathered the storm by simply extending the army's brief in the

[194] *Dawn*, 4 June 1958.

province. But the astonishing happenings in the Bengal assembly were symtomatic of wider trends in Pakistani politics which, and this needs special emphasising, reflected a crisis rooted in the very nature of the state structure. As long as that structure was in the process of formation, appeals to the centres of the international system had allowed the ruling clique to partly neutralise Pakistan's political and economic crises. Now contradictions within the structure of the state itself were constraining their room for manoeuvre. Impending elections had made the alleviation of centre-province tensions particularly urgent. Yet this was quite inconsistent with the imperatives of sustaining a political economy of defence. To complicate matters, the international system was no longer seen by their patrons to be threatened by a communist hurricane. So the interplay of international and domestic compulsions was pointing to quite a different set of tactics and strategies to perpetuate the status quo than those which not so long ago had been deployed to give the non-elected institutions a dominant role in the state structure.

Amazed by the 'increasingly byzantine and sterile characteristics of political activities', Washington's recently appointed ambassador James M. Langley quickly concluded that the time had come to 'rethink...[the US] approach to the Pakistan problem' because 'military strength, without a sound economic and political base, does not constitute real strength in South Asia or elsewhere'.[195] He was echoing the changing foreign policy perceptions of key figures in the American establishment. By early 1957 president Eisenhower was telling his national security council that 'in some instances the neutrality of a foreign nation was to the direct advantage of the United States'. The US had made a 'terrible error' keeping Pakistan as a military ally while 'doing practically nothing' for its people.[196] But having bet on the military and the bureaucracy in Pakistan it was now impossible to avoid facing up to the consequences. Suggestions by some American diplomats in Pakistan that Washington try and steer Mirza away from his authoritarian tendencies were countered by the argument that this would defeat US purposes by reviving the old slogan: the 'real Prime Minister [of Pakistan] is named Hildreth'.[197] In any event, the state department and the joint chiefs of staff had not been seeing eye to eye on who was their 'best man' – Mirza or Ayub. The state department thought Mirza was

---

[195] Langley's telegram to the department of state, 1 November 1957, *Foreign Relations*, VIII, 486.
[196] Memorandum of discussion at 308th meeting of the national security council, 3 January 1957, ibid., 25–6.
[197] Carvel Painter [American consul, Lahore] to the department of state, 24 May 1957, ibid., 480, fn. 4.

'more competent' than Ayub, a view generally shared by the British,[198] while the joint chiefs of staff thought Mirza was 'no match for Ayub' so far as 'honesty and directness' were concerned.[199] The American foreign and defence establishments, however, were agreed on one thing. They would back the military and bureaucratic combination most capable of restoring a semblance of stability in a country in which they had invested so much for so little.

So while 'seeking to extricate' the US from 'the present worrisome situation' there could be no question of turning back on 'those elements which, for whatever motive, and however imperfect' were America's 'closest friends and supporters'. Consequently, any attempt at balancing Pakistan's military and economic requirements had to 'be conducted *by and with* Mirza and General Ayub and at all costs *not against them*'. Past American investments in the Pakistan military were in 'danger of being wiped out if something...[was] not done to arrest the current deterioration in many aspects of Pakistani life'. In the American ambassador's colourful metaphor: '...in Pakistan we have an unruly horse by the tail and are confronted with the dilemma of trying to tame it before we can let go safely....I have the uneasy feeling that far from being tamed this horse we assumed to be so friendly has actually grown wilder of late'.[200]

It is true that on the eve of a long awaited general election the political scene in the country had become a trifle more chaotic. Given the deterioration of economic conditions in the country, it would have been remarkable indeed if the various political groupings – whether in or out of office – had not tried to show a greater responsiveness to the disaffections of their prospective constituents by intensifying pressures on the centre for more financial support to the provinces. Yet the centre which for so long had dodged the issue of elections was now to face them when its revenues were falling and defence and civil administration expenditures were rising. Barely able to remain solvent, the centre could meet the provinces half way only by slashing the budgets of the two institutions which were the best hope the state had for surviving assaults from below. This double paradox – the need to dole out funds to allay some of the provincial grievances just prior to the elections and the impossibility of finding the finances without cutting back on defence and

---

[198] Mirza was 'the one Pakistani in whom we can have real confidence', Symon told the British prime minister. (Symon to Macmillan, 19 September 1957, DO35/6520, PRO.)

[199] Memorandum on discussions between the department of state and joint chiefs of staff, 14 January 1955, *Foreign Relations*, VIII, 412.

[200] Langley to assistant secretary of state for Near Eastern, South Asian and African affairs, 27 December 1957, ibid., 487

civil administration – was the crisis of the state which the October 1958 military intervention aimed at dispelling if not altogether resolving.

Historians of Pakistan have so far shied away from analysing the first military takeover as a response to a crisis stemming in large part from the nature of the state structure itself. Focusing on the unseemly doings of politicians may be less controversial, even entertaining, but hopelessly inadequate if taken as the sole basis for an analysis of what actually prompted the October 1958 coup. Without a clear reading of the evolving dialectic between state authority and the political process in the final months before the military action, it is impossible to understand the failure of Pakistan's experiment with 'parliamentary democracy', much less give it a decent burial.

March 1958 was not just the month which saw police cordons protecting the provincial assembly chambers in both wings of the country. It was the month when the central and the provincial budgets were debated in all three houses. Amjad Ali, the finance minister, had been lumbered with the task of announcing the national budget for FY 1958–9. In an unusual move during an election year, the finance minister proposed a whole series of taxes and, most shockingly, suggested reducing incentives to business. The taxes were not expected to raise more than Rs. 4.5 million in central revenues. But they were greeted by an almost universal outcry. The critics were at a loss for adjectives to describe the budget. It was 'gloomy, desperate and unwise',[201] the 'most anti-people budget ever presented in the history of Pakistan'.[202] Business interests for their part saw it as a wanton attempt to strangulate industry.[203] A number of trade associations observed token strikes. The unkindest cut for the government was the decision by the board of directors of the Karachi stock exchange to close down business for three days.[204] Interestingly enough, increased allocations for both defence and civil administration – and the main reason for the centre's taxation proposals – were only mildly criticised; an indication of the extent to which the so-called representatives of the people had resigned them-

---

[201] This was the view of Tamizuddin Khan, the president of the east Pakistan Muslim League. (*Morning News*, 1 March 1958.)

[202] Ibid., 13 March 1958.

[203] Under the new taxation structure, public limited companies would have to pay 66.66 per cent of their income in taxes as opposed to 50 per cent in the previous year; private limited companies were faced with the dismal prospect of the state taking away 73 per cent instead of 60 per cent of their income. Moreover, the business profits tax was no longer deductible from the total income; this would increase the incidence of taxation for public companies by 16 per cent and for private companies by 20 per cent (Ibid.)

[204] Ibid.

selves to letting these two main institutions of the state get the better part of the national revenue.

The central government's bombshell was followed by the two provincial governments declaring deficit budgets for FY 1958–9. The east Pakistani deficit of Rs. 4 crore was to be financed by the provincial government raising Rs. 2 crores from fresh levies on fourteen items; the central government was expected to finance the deficit on capital account.[205] The opposition's demand that the Awami League ministry circulate the finance bill to elicit public opinion lit the fuse for the explosions that occurred in the assembly towards the end of September 1958. The west Pakistani deficit was smaller than that of the eastern wing, but larger than the combined deficits of all the provinces prior to one unit. Though the provincial government proposed to finance part of the deficit through new taxes on eight items,[206] the centre had unavoidably to lend a helping hand.

Declaring budgetary deficits was a well-established method by which provincial governments could try and twist the centre's arm for bigger financial packages. A sensible device, considering that the provinces had to surrender all the main taxes to the centre. But in a context where the centre's finances were perilously low, provincial deficits could not but be seen as vengeful or, at the very best, irresponsible. Even if the monetary shortfalls accurately represented the problems confronting the provincial governments – a fact not necessarily proven by the imposition of new taxes alone – the ensuing pressures on the centre plunged the state into a crisis; financial in nature; political in manifestation.

By the summer of 1958, the central government was in dire straits. Drastic economy measures had led to cut-backs in industrial imports with the result that factories in the Karachi area were operating at a mere 35 per cent of their existing capacity.[207] Despite the availability of thousands of acres of land in Punjab and Sind for cultivation, the government had been unable to finalise the allotments due to conflicting claims by refugee associations, local landlords and the spokesmen of the indigenous peasantry on the one hand, and of army personnel and members of the civil bureaucracy on the other. Since it had also not been able to weed out the inveterate hoarders and the wily smugglers in the country, the food shortages had to be met by continuing to import heavily on government account. Towards the end of June, with the economy in shambles, the finance minister resorted to special pleading. Attributing the country's precarious foreign exchange position to

[205] Ibid., 15 March 1958.
[206] Ibid., 22 March 1958.
[207] Cited in Gankovsky, *A History of Pakistan*, 294.

recessionary trends in international markets, Amjad Ali called for 'a united effort at all levels – public, business and official'.[208] But with the cost of living index soaring to new heights – partly a result of the government's decision to abolish price controls – no one was moved by the finance minister's performance, least of all in east Pakistan where rice was selling at unaffordable prices.

As if to remind the central government that confessions about the state's economic dilemmas did not mean immunity from public accountability, labour unions in both the private and the public sector had taken to orchestrating their demands more militantly. During May and June 1958, despite the state's draconian labour laws, workers at a foreign oil concern in west Pakistan organised one of the most effective strikes in the country's history.[209] It was followed by school teachers, the telegraph workers union and other government employees going on strike to demand better wages. Encouraged by the waves of unrest, student unions across the country sprang into action. Even the urban intelligentsia – accustomed to keeping their noses buried in the sand – were ready to take to the streets. The people were in revolt: demanding early elections, a life worth living and a foreign policy meriting their respect.

Leading in eloquence, if not necessarily in mass support, was Qayum Khan, the president of the Muslim League. Demanding early elections and an independent foreign policy, Qayum taxed Mirza's nerves to breaking point. In Mirza's very own words: 'We had reached a point where public meetings were being held outside the President's House...politicians shouted abuses and threats at me personally, while the loudspeakers directed the speech straight at my house.'[210] If Mirza was under siege planning his next moves from above, Qayum was hard at work below. He had kept the Muslim League out of the all-parties conference which agreed to postpone elections from November 1958 to February 1959. When the leaders of the Kashmir liberation movement were arrested for planning to send armed volunteers into Indian Kashmir, Qayum seized the opportunity to lash out at Pakistan's allies. But when in the early summer of 1958 'a group of junior Army officers warned him' that 'the Army's senior officers would not allow the scheduled elections to take place' and 'declared themselves ready to strike first with Muslim League backing, he discouraged them'.[211]

[208] *Morning News*, 26 June 1958.
[209] See Gankovsky, *A History of Pakistan*, 296–7.
[210] 'Iskander Mirza Speaks: An Autobiography', in *Meyaar*, 5–12 June 1976, 48.
[211] American consulate [Peshawar] to the department of state, despatch no. 11, 29 October 1958, NND.867414, RG 59, Box 3865, NA. For further corroboration of Qayum's disclosure, see American embassy [Karachi] to the department of state, despatch no. 446, 14 November 1958, ibid.

While cautiously declining help from pro-Muslim League army officers, Qayum demanded a review of Pakistan's foreign policy in the national assembly and threatened to launch 'direct action' if the government refused to announce a firm date for elections. Short of elections, Qayum announced publicly, nothing could save Pakistan from a military takeover similar to the July 1958 coup by Iraqi junior officers.[212]

Frequent references to the anti-Western Iraqi coup, the revival of public debate on Kashmir and bitter attacks on foreign policy by all the opposition parties, not to mention the strong-arm tactics of the Muslim League's national guards, inflamed an already deeply embittered military high command. Ever since the Noon ministry had succumbed to political pressures and weakened the army's control over the anti-smuggling operations in east Pakistan, the military command was on red alert. While it had succeeded in getting an increase in the military budget for 1958–59, the strident demands for provincial autonomy in east Pakistan was cause enough to view the prospect of a general election with apprehension. On 20 September, the central government's ban on all para-military organisations led to clashes between Muslim League workers and the police in Karachi. Three days later the facade of parliamentary democracy in east Pakistan came crashing down. Mindful of the effects of these events on army discipline – intelligence reports indicated that a group of younger officers was planning to stage a coup – the military high command was ready to take decisive measures.

The military high command's growing resolve to takeover the state apparatus was communicated to Washington between mid-May and mid-September 1958. Despite the close links Washington had nurtured with the top brass of the Pakistani military, a military coup was initially not the US ambassador's preferred strategy. The 'best hope of keeping [Pakistan's] foreign policy oriented to the West', Langley had believed, was to 'have Mirza in office, as well as Suhrawardy'. Washington had to 'decide' whether the 'United States should discreetly attempt to affect the course of the elections'; he hoped the state department would have 'the principal say...even if the decision were to be such that *another agency* were charged with this precarious assignment'.[213] But already by 19 May 1958, Ayub and Mirza in separate conversations with the US ambassador had conveyed their opinion that 'only a dictatorship would work in Pakistan'. While the two had their own reasons for promoting such a line, there was evidence of institutional 'pressure within the Army to seize power....from officers just below Ayub, both Generals and

[212] *The Pakistan Times*, 1 September 1958.
[213] Langley to Frederic P. Bartlett [SOA], 28 April 1958, NND.867414, RG 59, Box 3873, NA [emphasis added].

Brigadiers'.[214] The final decision for a direct military intervention was taken by Ayub and Mirza with the support of other top ranking military officers on or about 15 September 1958.

On 24 September 1958, Mirza for 'the third time in one week ...criticized...the workings of democracy in Pakistan'.[215] Three days later he expressed deep concern about the attitude of 'officers in lower echelons' of the army.[216] It was on 4 October 1958 that Mirza 'confirmed' to Langley that 'he would take over the Government of Pakistan probably within a week and simultaneously proclaim martial law'. Interestingly, he claimed that the takeover was designed 'to prevent an army seizure of power in Pakistan'.[217] US officials noted that Mirza had taken them 'into his confidence almost as soon as his plan of action was formulated and agreed to by the key military leaders involved'.[218]

Quite unaware of the intrigues in military and diplomatic circles during late September 1958, the prime minister Firoz Khan Noon in a last ditch attempt to save his government went in for a massive expansion of the central cabinet, increasing the number of ministers from fourteen to twenty-six in order to satisfy Suhrawardy's Awami League. Within days, unhappy with their portfolios, the Awami League ministers resigned. And so the final act of Pakistan's tragic experiment with 'parliamentary government' ended as an unrelieved farce. But not before the appearance of the army as the only reliable guarantor of the state's integrity. On 6 October, the Khan of Kalat reacted to the building of military bases in Baluchistan by seceding from Pakistan. The revolt was scotched; the army had made its point loudly and clearly.

By the early morning hours of 8 October 1958, Ayub with Mirza's connivance had staged a successful coup. Before the people could hear of the news, the makers of the coup thought it politic to secure the

---

[214] American embassy [Karachi] to the department of state, despatch no. 394, 28 October 1958, NND.867414, RG 59, Box 3865, NA. On the personal side of things, Mirza had sensed his waning control over the Republican flock and his inability to influence the electoral process. Ayub, apparently, had become 'a convert to dictatorship' during the summer of 1958 when the Muslim League leader, Ghazanfar Ali Khan, began inciting army officers in the Lahore area against him. But Ayub was not alone. The decision for a military takeover was supported among others by lt. general Musa [army chief of staff], major general Yahya [chief of the general staff, GHQ], lt. general Sheikh [commanding eighth division, Quetta], major general Jilani [commanding army staff college, Quetta] and major general Umrao [commanding general east Pakistan]. (See Langley to the secretary of state, telegram no. 791, 6 October 1958 and telegram no. 1155, 8 November 1958, ibid.)

[215] American embassy [Karachi] to the secretary of state, telegram no. 682, 24 September 1958, ibid.

[216] Langley to the secretary of state, telegram no. 721, 27 September 1958, ibid.

[217] Langley to the secretary of state, telegram no. 775, 4 October 1958, ibid.

[218] Bartlett [SOA] to William M. Rountree [NEA], 7 October 1958, ibid.

blessings of Pakistan's foreign allies. Mirza summoned the American ambassador and the British high commissioner along with a handful of other foreign dignitaries. Pakistan, he asserted in Ayub's presence, had been placed under martial law. But irrespective of changes at the domestic level, the new government 'would be even more pro-west than before'.[219] In short, the gap between popular opinion and state policy, which had so worried its allies of late, would not be allowed to detract from Pakistan's stance in the international arena. Armed with the legitimacy they deemed to be important, Mirza at Ayub's behest, issued a proclamation suspending the constitution, dismissing the central and provincial governments, dissolving the three assemblies, banning all political parties, postponing elections indefinitely and placing Noon as well as other members of the central cabinet under house arrest. Not a shot was fired in protest against the imposition of martial law.

The only hitch, as everyone realised, was that the 'duumvirate' of Ayub and Mirza could not last long. Neither had a solid constituency of support, but Ayub 'with his direct control over the army' had a clear edge over Mirza.[220] The US ambassador nevertheless thought 'it desirable' that Mirza, a civilian, 'emerge as top man'.[221] Yet Washington thought the 'wisest course' would be to 'take a rather neutral position between the two potential contenders for power, while being friendly and equally frank with both of them.'[222] Nervous about his own future, the irrepressible Mirza tried enlisting the support of the air force and Ayub's rivals within the army. He allegedly made an unsuccessful attempt to order air commodore Rabb, the chief of staff of the Pakistan air force, to arrest four generals close to Ayub, including major general Yahya Khan.[223]

Ayub, by this time, had the 'army behind him in two ways': it 'support[ed] him fully on the one hand, but on the other it also tend[ed]

[219] Langley to the secretary of state, telegram no. 816, 8 October 1958, ibid. Significantly, while the Americans 'knew of the impending coup' the British high commissioner was not informed 'until after it happened'. However, the high commissioner had tipped off his government on 2 August 1958 that 'a coup was in the offing'. (American consulate [Dacca] to the department of state, despatch no. 221, 24 November 1958, NND.867414, RG 59, Box 3866, NA.)

[220] Langley to the secretary of state, telegram no. 827, 8 October 1958, NND.867414, RG 59, Box 3865, NA.

[221] Langley to the secretary of state, telegram no. 942, 17 October 1958, ibid.

[222] Bartlett [SOA] to Rountree [NEA], 24 October 1958, ibid.

[223] American consulate [Peshawar] to the department of state, despatch no. 32, 1 April 1959, NND.867414, RG 59, Box 3866, NA. For further confirmation cf. Mohammad Asghar Khan, *Generals in Politics: Pakistan 1958–1982*, New Delhi 1983, 8–9. The newly appointed commerce minister, Zulfiqar Ali Bhutto, thought that the 'greatest credence should be given to the report that the immediate cause of Mirza's downfall was his...attempt to work out some type of alliance with General Musa'. (American embassy [Karachi] to the department of state, despatch no. 445, 14 November 1958, NND.867414, RG 59, Box 3865, NA.)

to push him forward'.[224] On 27 October 1958, Ayub at a meeting with generals Azam Khan, Burki and Sheikh, all members of the central cabinet, decided to rid himself of Mirza and assume complete control over the affairs of the state. Mirza was sent into exile – 'banished without warning' – as he was to ruefully reminisce many years later.[225] Ayub in the saddle quickly set about proving to sceptics that he was not merely the army's 'front man' but 'absolute master' in Pakistan.[226]

[224] American embassy [Karachi] to the secretary of state, telegram no. 1085, 31 October 1958, ibid.
[225] 'Iskander Mirza Speaks: An Autobiography', *Meyaar*, 12–19 June 1976.
[226] Langley to the secretary of state, telegram no. 1155, 8 November 1958, NND.867414, RG 59, Box 3865, NA.

6

State and society in the balance: Islam as ideology and culture

This study has so far focused on the dialectic of state-building and political processes in Pakistan. Political processes are an important, perhaps the most important, gauge in assessing interactions between state and society. But in the absence either of organised parties or other forms of institutionalised structures involving increasingly larger sections of society in the formulation of state policies, they alone cannot offer the insights needed to unravel the complexities of the relationship. So, without losing sight of politics and economics, the analysis has now to turn to considering the relationship between state and society in Pakistan at the level of ideology and culture.

That relationship, it must be reiterated, was grounded in a historical context where the state did not organically emerge from socio-economic structures existing below but began at the top by constructing a wholly new central government which could then impose authority on areas hitherto ruled from New Delhi. The very fact that the British transferred power in India to two centralised high commands instead of the provincial and the local bosses whose support they had so long solicited and used to strengthen their raj meant that the institutionalisation and consolidation of a new political centre over the Muslim-majority areas was implicitly a question of society accommodating itself to a state whose structures of authority were as uncertain as its claims to legitimacy were vague and ambiguous.

This is where Islam proved to have its uses. Its babel of tongues notwithstanding, Pakistan was predominantly Muslim; more to the point, the better remembered slogans of the movement that had brought about its creation were shrouded in religious terms. But, contrary to established wisdoms about Pakistan, the role of Islam in the processes leading up to the partition of India was to amplify and dignify what remained from first to last a political struggle launched by the Muslim League under the secular leadership of Mohammad Ali Jinnah. This is not to deny the uses made by Jinnah and the League of religion or even to suggest that the catchall – 'Pakistan' – did not come to be associated with Islam in the popular imagination.[1] Yet the 'two nation' theory

---

[1] See chapter 1 below and A. Jalal, *The Sole Spokesman*.

which provided the basis for Jinnah and the League's case was essentially a strategy aimed at deriving maximum mileage out of Muslims being a separate political category, albeit one which repudiated the minority status it had served to institutionalise. An array of religious groups, the Jamat-i-Islami, the Ahrars and the Khaksars for instance, opposed the demand for Pakistan on account of its being insufficiently imbued with the tenets of religion. After partition, these same groups became the loudest proponents of an 'Islamic state'.

Proclaiming Islam, however defined, as the ideology of the state proved to be an irresistible expedient for the temporal authorities quite as much as for the religious, although for very different reasons. It emphasised Pakistan's distinctiveness in relation to India; gave the appearance – if not the reality – of unity to an otherwise disparate people and allowed the state more room in which to manoeuvre its way towards establishing dominance over a society with highly localised and fragmented structures of authority. With the collapse of the Muslim League, such as it had existed, the ambiguities of Islam seemed to offer the best hope of lending legitimacy to a state which, because it had only the most tenuous roots in society, was coming to base its authority on an administrative rather than a political centralisation. The success or failure of the Islamic recipe in legitimising the state as well as facilitating its accommodation by society has to be assessed at two levels – Islam as an all pervasive ideology and as the leitmotif of an otherwise variegated culture.

Accommodating the state in Pakistani society: the uses of Islam as ideology

Even before the civil bureaucracy and the military establishment had triumphed over party politicians at the centre, the absence of a nationally based political party had begun posing awkward dilemmas for the legitimacy of the new state. Linguistically diverse, culturally diffuse, and riddled with economic disparities of an extreme sort, the Pakistani social milieu was susceptible to just the kind of particularisms which have militated against centripetal trends in many parts of the developing world. Here, as elsewhere, the principal loyalties were to the family and *biraderi* groups or the elaborate patron-client networks operating at the local or provincial levels, not to the authority of a far away central government. Without a concerted drive to educate and mobilise the people – not a priority of the Pakistani state, and never to become one – identification and incorporation with distant structures of authority demanded official patronage which, unfortunately, was available only in very limited amounts to a desperately poor central government. The Islamic pretensions of the Muslim League's leadership, even if unable to make a direct contribution to the consolidation of the state, could be put to use in disguising those largely material exigencies that underpin structures of power and authority.

Within the very first year of independence it had become apparent that the fit between state and society would be none too easy. Those responsible for constructing the new central government were at odds with the provincial bosses on such vital issues as the allocation of power and resources. Tensions between the centre and the provinces, disputes with India, to say nothing of the anxieties about the protection of life and property following the disturbances and massive dislocations of partition, were all ingredients for an acute insecurity complex – one that reflected itself in the policies of the state quite as much as in the attitudes of the upper strata in society.

Religiosity, simply professed or actually practised, is a perfect anaesthetic for those seized by insecurities. In Pakistan, the coupling of religion and insecurities found expression in statements by the most unlikely of all people – Mohammad Ali Jinnah himself. Using the occasion of the Prophet's birthday to address the Sind bar association, Jinnah exhorted his audience to eschew narrow-minded provincialism and prepare themselves to 'sacrifice and die in order to make Pakistan [a] truly great Islamic State' – a radical departure from his famous speech six months earlier at the first meeting of the Pakistan constituent assembly.[2] Speaking extemporaneously, Jinnah had tried laying down the broad ground rules for the relationship between state and society in Pakistan:

You are free to go to your temples, you are free to go to your mosques or to any other place of worship in this State of Pakistan....You may belong to any religion or caste or creed – that has nothing to do with the business of the State.... We are starting with this fundamental principle that we are all citizens and equal citizens of one State.[3]

One can either conclude that the definition of an 'Islamic State' in the Quaid-i-Azam's personal lexicon was wholly unique or that the travails of office as Pakistan's first governor-general had weakened his resolve never to take the path of least resistance on matters to do with religion. If the truth lies somewhere in between, the conclusion must still be that

[2] Cited in the British high commissioner's report to the CRO for the period 22 to 28 January 1948, L/WS/1/1599, IOL.

[3] Jinnah's speech to the Pakistan constituent assembly, 11 August 1947, in *Speeches of Quaid-i-Azam Mohammad Ali Jinnah as Governor-General of Pakistan*, Karachi 1948, 10.

Jinnah – the secularist – was above all else a hardened politician, ready to take refuge in Islam to survive the cross-fire of provincialism and religious extremism.

Jinnah and his lieutenants had some narrow escapes while attempting to stamp out the fires of provincialism with solemn messages of religious unity without sparking off an Islamic conflagration. The earliest instance of this was the reaction to statements by central leaders, including Jinnah and Liaquat, that Urdu would be the official language of the state. For the Bengali majority this was not merely an insult to their language and culture, but an outright denial of their status as equal citizens of Pakistan. This was a poor omen for the integration of Pakistan's far flung and linguistically distinct provinces, especially since the influx of millions of refugees, many of whom were Urdu-speakers, had accentuated the sense of provincial exclusivity and attachment to regional languages in the western wing as well.

Instead of retracting from their position on the language issue, the central leaders, taking their cues from Jinnah's motto of 'UNITY, FAITH and DISCIPLINE', hit out against forces of provincialism. These they argued were seeking to disrupt Pakistan in collusion with India. Liaquat Ali Khan spent one whole day in the sizzling heat of June holding up the banner of Islamic unity, sacrifice, discipline and loyalty to the Pakistan government while lambasting an enervated Sindhi audience for wanting to prevent Karachi becoming a federal territory. However much it smacked of an incipient authoritarianism, the principal loyalties of the people had to be to the centre and its policies, good or bad. Labelling most criticisms of the centre's policies as Indian inspired and refusing to tolerate even the mildest expression of provincial loyalties reflected the insecurities of the state managers. As one dismayed commentator noted, from Jinnah downwards the Muslim League's leadership showed a 'petulant resentment of all criticism'; their 'persecution complex' and 'evidence of some basic disequilibrium' had found a favourite outlet in the theme of Pakistan being 'beset by enemies on every side and menaced by saboteurs within'.[4]

Illusions nurture still more fantastic illusions. The equation of Islam and the central government encouraged arguments, some more pious than others, about Islam's potential leavening effects on all forms of social divisiveness. Its categorical pronouncements on the right to own private property, matched by a very broadly defined concept of social justice, could preempt moves by ungodly communist ideologues to promote class conflict. For the landlords of west Pakistan, anxious to

---

[4] British high commissioner's monthly appreciation for May 1948, L/WS/1/1599, IOL.

cut short all moves towards agrarian reforms, for the trading and commercial groups, determined to make a killing without let or hindrance, for the urban propertied classes, looking to secure and augment their wealth, and for a state needing to consolidate and expedite the processes of capital accumulation, Islam offered a moral escape from one too many awkward realities. As Liaquat Ali Khan pontificated, the people of Pakistan should 'follow the teachings of the [P]rophet and not those of Marx, Stalin or Churchill[sic]'.[5]

Of course nothing in the game of power politics is without its costs. Adopted as a ploy to defuse potentially explosive socio-economic issues, Islam soon became the main point of contention between a handful of individuals who, their ideological differences notwithstanding, were drawn mainly from the educated strata in urban society. In a predominantly illiterate and rural setting, this qualified as the 'public debate'. So while the overwhelming majority of Pakistani society carried on with life as they had always done – avoiding, accepting and rarely, if ever, activity accommodating the state – a dazzling array of religious ideologues took the opportunity to make a concerted bid for power against a ruling clique whose inherent secularism even if moderated by its conservatism never seemed to quite add up to the orthodox Islamic world view.

The Shariat or the 'mullah' lobby within the Muslim League and the Jamiat-ul-Ulema-i-Islam – formed by the ulema of Deoband who had supported the demand for Pakistan – were among the first to call for an Islamic constitution. Under the system of government proposed by these orthodox proponents of an 'Islamic state', sovereignty would belong to Allah, not the people. In other words, there was no place for a sovereign legislature in Pakistan. Some of the more practical, and the 'fundamentalists' in particular, were ready to concede law-making powers to the representatives of the people in matters not covered by either the Quran or the Sharia. But there was still no avoiding the fact of a theocracy since the ulema and the mullahs – Allah's viceregents amidst a sea of lesser mortals – would be the ultimate judges of whether the laws of the state were in accordance with the teachings and the spirit of Islam.

This line was echoed by an array of religious groups: by the Jamiat-ul-Ulema-i-Pakistan, which in contrast to the strictly orthodox line of the JUI, presented Islam in the populist traditions of the Barelvi ulema; by Maulana Maududi's Islamic fundamentalist party, the Jamat-i-Islami;

---

[5] Cited in British high commissioner's report to the CRO for the period 22–8 January 1948, ibid.

and also by the Majlis-i-Ahrar and the Khaksars. Having by and large opposed the League's demand for Pakistan, these religious groupings needed to reestablish their credentials as loyal citizens of the state, not to mention build political bases of support among the more religious segments of the urban lower middle-classes – the commercial and trading groups in particular. While by no means unanimous in their definitions of what constituted an 'Islamic State', they were at one in condemning the unIslamic life styles of Pakistan's most influential managers – the politicians quite as much as the civil and military officials. A common allegation, partly justified, was that, so long as Pakistan remained the preserve of men who flouted the teachings of the Holy Quran and the Sunnah, the Islamic rhetoric in state policies would never quite materialise.

Apart from being embarrassing, these charges undermined the policy of claiming legitimacy for state authority on the basis of Islam. One way to blunt the edge of the attack was to accuse the religious groups of obscurantism and proffer a more 'progressive' face of Islam. Khaliquzzaman, then the president of the Muslim League and an aspiring pan-Islamicist, dubbed the advocates of 'Shariat government' 'hypocrites' who had no purpose other than to exploit the catch-phrase for personal ends. True Islamic democracy, according to him, could only be established by the constituent assembly and the Muslim League when the people had been properly educated.

To demonstrate the government's good intentions, these statements were followed up by studiously ambiguous discussions on the future of the educational system – an early and unrelieved victim of the debate about Islam and the state of Pakistan. Fazlur Rahman, the education minister in Pakistan's first cabinet, declared that educational methods in the future would be permeated by an 'Islamic ideology'. Not only that, the state would harness the film and broadcasting media to transform the outlook of the people, the young and the old, as it continued to thunder ahead to bring about ideological uniformity. Eminent scholars were to be recruited to rewrite history and other textbooks from an Islamic point of view. The real howler was a proposal to base the educational system as well as the affairs of the state on Arabic instead of Urdu. Fazlur Rahman – a Bengali, and understandably worried about the effects of the language controversy on his own political standing – was among the most enthusiastic proponents of the idea. It is not just the benefit of hindsight that make these abortive proposals appear so tragically comical. The more perceptive could see that these confusions parading as ideology were 'designed chiefly as a sop to the Maulvis' and, with the notable exception of reinventing history, 'would not be translated into practice'.[6] By the end of 1949, even Fazlur Rahman was bemoaning the negligible progress made in Islamising the educational system. Although he had given up some of his old ideas about Arabic, he was now all in favour of using mosques as centres of education and making the appointment of *imams* a direct responsibility of the state. If the proposal had been adopted in earnest, which it was not except piecemeal by the government of the NWFP, the state may well have succeeded in establishing real control over some of the more influential maulvis at the local as well as the provincial levels. So Rahman's ingenuity notwithstanding, the educational system – twisted this way or that – was not likely to prepare the ground for an 'Islamic democracy'.

If anything, the state's palpably crude attempts at Islamic social engineering gave religious bigotry its head as never before. In a step that baffled the more discerning citizens of the state, Liaquat Ali Khan issued an official injunction urging Muslims to observe the ramazan fasts in letter and in spirit. Someone thought it would be a good thing if this was followed up with a law forcing hotels and restaurants to go out of business during the hours of the fast. And, while this was quietly swept under the carpet, the suggestion together with the prime minister's public utterances about appropriate Islamic behaviour in the holy month of ramazan unwittingly set the pattern for an open display of religious intolerance. In later years, the month of ramazan frequently saw angry mobs attacking restaurants serving meals at mid-day with the police conveniently making an after the event appearance. In the NWFP where religion often became a pretext for some typically Pathan entertainments, fastbreakers had often to suffer the indignity of having their faces blackened before being paraded in the bazaars with the tacit support of the local police. Encouraged by these activities, a magistrate in the Haripur district of the province sentenced three persons to one year rigorous imprisonment for a breach of the peace; they had been caught eating in public. This display of Islamic fervour by state officials who privately and, in some cases, publicly ignored most of the Quranic injunctions was quietly deprecated by the educated few. Belonging to the upper rungs of the social hierarchy where the enthusiasm for ramazan was visibly muted, these were the 'liberal' citizens of Pakistan who, for reasons of their own, wanted to see the state resisting the path of religious extremism without overstepping the parameters of conservatism. But on the issue of ramazan, neither they nor the better known

---

[6] British high commissioner's opdom no. 46, 3–9 June 1948, L/WS/1/1599, IOL.

public personalities had the courage of their convictions to condemn the state's pandering to religious extremism.

A trifle hypocritical no doubt, it was consistent with the terms of the accommodation worked out between the state and the dominant classes within the initial years of independence. According to the terms, the state's social pronouncements would always be in the Islamic idiom. But it would not neglect to protect the rights of its liberal citizens to deviate from the literal interpretations of the Islamic world view. In other words, the state would tolerate Muslims from all walks of life so long as its own Islamic credentials were not called into question.

The state's response to the demand for a total prohibition on the consumption of alcohol illustrates the point. By the spring of 1949, all the provincial governments had passed tentative laws against the sale of alcoholic beverages in public places.[7] Karachi, significantly enough, was spared the inconvenience. But even the provincial police services, perpetually on the look out for ways to make extra rupees, could see that the prohibition law was more in the form of a social gimmick to placate the zealots. Consequently, the main effect of Pakistan's first experiment with prohibition was the appearance of stills in strategic places and, naturally, plenty of opportunities for illicit money-making.

These examples are all based on the initial few years of independence, since this was the period when Pakistan's leaders were most concerned about establishing the state's claims as the ultimate guarantor of an Islamic social order. Unable to present a coherent world view that could inspire or weld together a people who were showing growing signs of disunity and disarray they readily adopted the concept of an 'Islamic state'. But they had no intention whatsoever of facilitating a form of government in which they were destined to become supplicants to the religious guardians. So the clouds of Islamic fervour, far from filling in the vacuum of a social consensus, merely obfuscated the fact that the construction of the state was proceeding in a veritable ideological wilderness.

This is borne out by the various attempts to find common ground between the orthodox, fundamentalist and modernist views on the role of Islam in the political and social structures of the state during the nine long years of constitution-making in Pakistan. In March 1949 the objectives resolution, which served as the preamble for the constitution eventually adopted in 1956, took the momentous step of conceding Allah's sovereignty over the entire universe. But when it came to Pakistan, the authors betrayed their leanings by inserting that Allah in

---

[7] *Nawa-i-Waqt*, 1 April 1949.

His infinite wisdom had taken care to delegate authority to the people on condition that it be exercised 'within the limit prescribed by Him as sacred trust'. After these measured nods, the rest of the resolution proceeded to reject the notion of an 'Islamic state' as a religious theocracy. Pakistan was to be a 'sovereign, independent state'; power would be wielded by the chosen representatives of the people, not by the religious leaders. The state would be based on Islamic principles of democracy; there would be freedom, equality, tolerance and social justice for all, including the minorities.[8] Yet at the same time it would be the duty of the state to ensure that Muslims at various levels of society lived in accordance with the teachings of Islam, individually as well as collectively.[9] This loosely worded provision was to become the source of much confusion about the relationship between state and society in Pakistan. The mover of the resolution – the prime minister himself – seemed to be in two minds about what it was intended to imply. To begin with, Liaquat interpreted it as meaning that the state could not rest at being a 'neutral observer' and would actively work towards creating a 'new social order' so that Pakistan could become the perfect 'laboratory' of Islam. But he ended by declaring that the goal before Pakistan was 'to build up a truly liberal Government where the greatest amount of freedom...[would] be given to all its members'.[10]

Liaquat then slipped up further while holding out an olive branch to the Hindu members of the assembly. He urged them not to pay any heed to the 'mischievous propaganda' of the 'maniacs', 'these so-called Ulemas' who not only wanted to deny non-Muslims the right to equal citizenship but were all 'out to disrupt Pakistan' by 'misrepresent[ing] the whole ideology of Islam' and creating doubts about the 'bona fides of the Mussalman...'.[11] One of his lieutenants tried to clear the air by suggesting that the resolution was simply aiming for the 'establishment of a moral state' whose sovereignty would be circumscribed by the Islamic rectitude of the people.[12]

The resolution nonetheless was open to varied interpretations. While marking a victory for the modernists it had given the orthodox and the fundamentalists the opening they needed to continue lashing out against anything and everything that attested to the state's failure to remodel Pakistani society along Islamic lines. Their snipings kept up the pressure on the government. Even inside the constituent assembly, members were

---

[8] *CAD*, V, 1949, 1–2.
[9] Ibid.
[10] Ibid., 12 March 1949.
[11] Ibid.
[12] Ibid.

heard accusing the government of duplicity; its surplus budgets were 'deficit spiritually' since no allocations had been made towards establishing 'religious ideals' in Pakistani society. While government condemned all forms of unIslamic behaviour, 'many high officials and well-placed non-officials ha[d]...not been able to give up the habit of drinking and dancing'. This was 'adversely affecting the morale of the people', already shocked by the availability of obscene literature at book-stalls and street-corners in all major cities in the country. It was surely 'a contradiction in terms to talk of an Islamic state and do the reverse in matters of dress, food and drink, etc.'. As 'architects of an Islamic state', the members of the constituent assembly had to 'cast...[their] head[s] down in shame'.[13]

These were uncomfortable moments for Pakistan's early managers. By declaring a national consensus on the need to base Pakistani society on the Quran and the Sunnah, something which cut against the grain of their own proclivities, they had wantonly inspired a bitter and irresolvable debate on what constituted an 'Islamic state'. It was actually more a dialogue of the deaf than a debate; no one was minded to hear the opposite point of view except under duress.

This made it easier for the religious groups to exploit the political and ideological divisions to claim a larger stake in the structuring of power and authority at each step in the constitution-making. But, except for a brief period when Nazimuddin was in office, they were thwarted in their efforts by a civil bureaucracy and military studded at the top with men of essentially secular leanings, and also by politicians who had found a temporary haven in the highest offices of the state. The very guarded lip service paid to Islam in the 1956 constitution bears testimony to the fact. So despite a proven ability to rouse religious passions among the poor and the lowly – during the anti-Ahmediya riots in 1953 for instance – the ulemas, the maulanas and the religious laymen of Pakistan had to bide time before the bureaucratic-military state that was in the making had reason to throw its resources behind the cause so dear to their hearts.

Until then the role of Islam in the state was open to conjecture. So the people of Pakistan, or rather those patient enough to follow an 'ideological debate' which, with the passage of time seemed less and less relevant to their socio-economic needs, resigned themselves to the discomforting knowledge that terms like Islam and Muslim were neither straightforward nor uncontroversial. Under the circumstances, it was difficult to fashion any concept of a Pakistani national identity, whether

[13] Ibid., I, 4, 19 March 1952.

Islamic or Muslim; it almost certainly would be torn to shreds by some shade of orthodox, fundamentalist, modernist or secular opinion. Basing Pakistan's identity on a territorial nationalism may well have been a sensible proposition if not for the state's insecurities and the implacable faith of its architects in the advantages to be gained from claiming authority over a single and ideologically unified nation. But, since the attempt to legitimise that authority by recourse to an all-pervasive, if undefinable, religious ideology had not quite worked out as intended, it remains to be seen whether the equation of the state and Islam could perhaps at the level of culture lend some unity of purpose to Pakistani society.

An uncertain resource: Islam as culture in Pakistani society

It is one thing to admit Islam's undeniable hold on the psyches of the Pakistani people. Quite another to argue that its impact is everywhere uniform and unaffected by gradations in socio-economic structures both within and between the different regions of Pakistan. There nevertheless have been few comprehensive studies on Islam as practised by Pakistanis belonging to the various classes and regions, in rural and urban areas alike. The lacuna follows from the emphasis on Islam as a total way of life. Intended to blur the distinction between religion and culture, the assertion is not without its stumbling-blocks. Inter and intra-regional diversities in Pakistan seem to imply that Islam either falls short of providing a complete world view for the mass of the people or, equally palpable, that its fusion with local cultures is so complete as to confound the task of bringing about a national integration on the basis of religion alone.

Though overwhelmingly Muslim, the underpinnings of Pakistani society have been defined by regional cultures, some more well-developed than others. While all absorbed Islam, none was wholly absorbed by it. Despite Islam's egalitarian creed, Muslims remain divided by class, caste, tribal and clan affiliations, to say nothing of the inherited differences of rank and privilege. In varying measure, the vast majority of Pakistani Muslims retain an unconscious attachment to local traditions and symbols, not uncommonly of Hindu origin. The syncretic weave is most visible in the Punjab, Sind and Bengal, where for centuries before partition Muslims and Hindus had lived cheek by jowl – resisting as well as adopting one another's social mores. In the NWFP and Baluchistan, where Hindus were wholly outnumbered by Muslims, Islam had to accommodate the customs of a largely tribal and pastoral people.

During the nineteenth and early twentieth centuries, orthodox and fundamentalist movements, which often had tacit or active support from the urban intelligentsia, sought to weed out unIslamic and superstitious practices in popular religion. But, in the fifties, there is no evidence to suggest that 'high Islam' was displacing little rural traditions, certainly in the Punjab and Sind where landlords frequently combine the functions of local religious leaders – the *pirs* and the *sajjada nashins*. By acting as intermediaries between God and the people, the *pirs* and *sajjada nashins* of Punjab and Sind undermine a major precept of orthodox and fundamentalist belief. Their success in withstanding repeated assaults from the largely urban based crusaders of 'pure Islam' has as much to do with the trappings of socio-economic power in the countryside as with the susceptibility of the illiterate peasantry to a spirituality which is immediately accessible, not straight-jacketed by religious scriptures.

In east Bengal, more than elsewhere in Pakistan, the religion of the peasantry is a hybrid; the rituals of religion are unqualifiedly Islamic while the superstitions are shot through with symbols and practices borrowed from Hinduism. The marriage of religion and tribal forms of social organisation in the NWFP may have produced the most 'orthodox' variant of Islam in Pakistan, but one coloured by the teachings of local mullahs with a none too remarkable reputation for serious Islamic learning. In Baluchistan, the temporal authority of the tribal leadership undercuts the role of the mullahs, making for a rather more casual attitude towards Islam among a largely nomadic people.

So local differences notwithstanding, the intermeshing of religious rituals with popular culture has meant that for Pakistan's predominantly rural population Islam assumes spiritual rather than doctrinal connotations. Even in those parts of the country where mullahs and mosques rather than *pirs* and shrines are the main points of religious reference, observance of the five pillars of Islam – the oath, praying five times a day, fasting during ramazan, alms-giving and the pilgrimage to Mecca – has more to do with personal belief, considerations of social stature and material capacity than with a sense of belonging and responsibility to the local or the wider community of Allah. Forging a feeling of national solidarity out of such an atomistic group of religious devotees, already set apart by economic, linguistic and cultural differences, is a proposition difficult to sustain much less substantiate.

If the role of Islam in the multifarious popular cultures of Pakistan's rural landscape was a barrier to the purposes of national integration, there remained the possibility of the more orthodox and fundamentalist versions practised in the urban areas providing the foundations for at least a partial bridging of the gap. With more and more of the rural unemployed joining the ranks of the urban working class, a process well in evidence by the fifties, the superimposition of doctrinal Islam on popular culture might conceivably have been carried out under the auspices of the state. But, insofar as 'urbanisation' could act as a catalyst in merging together popular and doctrinal Islam within regions or provinces, there was still the problem of extending that union to the national level.

Attempts towards that end were no doubt made by the champions of an Islamic ideology, both within and outside the state apparatus. But the uses which the state could make of the available ideological instruments – the broadcasting media, the educational system and the sprawling network of mosques – could have proved effective only in a context where there was a measure of agreement about the form of Islam to be introduced in Pakistan. In the absence of any consensus on that score, the initiative belonged to the religious groups, each professing its own interpretations of Islam and exploiting doctrinal, sectarian as well as linguistic differences in the working and lower middle-class quarters of the urban areas. The anti-Ahmediya riots of 1953 are a stern reminder of the devastating effects of doctrinal differences on urban society. Instead of becoming the melting pot for popular and doctrinal Islam, Pakistan's urban centres were being turned by orthodox and fundamentalist groups into powder kegs of religious extremism. Islam far from acting as a cement for national integration was assisting cultural fragmentation.

And, while paradoxes are not unusual for Pakistan, the role played by the religious groups in that process was facilitated by the very symbols which the state in consort with the dominant classes had deployed to emphasise the Islamic cultural unity of its people. Urdu and the aristocratic culture of Mughal India were presented as the indubitable link between the people of Pakistan and their Islamic heritage. The implicit denial of the Islamic elements in regional languages and cultures provoked the sharpest reaction in east Bengal. But the effects on urban culture were more directly felt in the western wing, in Sind especially where most of the Urdu-speaking Muhajir population was bunched. Prior to partition, Urdu speakers constituted less than 1 per cent of the total population of Sind; by the time of the 1951 census the figure had shot up to 12 per cent.[14] During the late fifties over half of the inhabitants of Karachi claimed Urdu as their mother-tongue.[15] It is no

---

[14] *Census of Pakistan*, V, 108.
[15] Ibid.

small coincidence that religious groups like the Jamiat-ul-Ulema-i-Pakistan and the Jamat-i-Islami made their earliest headway among the Muhajir population of Karachi. Believing their sacrifices for Pakistan to be greater than those of the indigenous inhabitants and bitter about the lives they had been forced to leave behind in India, the Muhajirs were perfect grist for the religious opposition's mill. This alliance of many conveniences, dignified by Islam and claims of linguistic and cultural superiority, evoked resentments from Sindhis quite as much as from Punjabis, Pathans, Gujaratis and Baluchis settled in Karachi. If competing with the generally better qualified Muhajirs for jobs, housing and official patronage lay at the root of the resentments, the state's sponsorship of Urdu and the culture associated with it was an obvious target.

It is true that anti-Muhajir feelings were strongest in Karachi and Sind. Yet it would be a mistake to underestimate the tensions between native speakers of Urdu and other linguistic groups in west Pakistan. Despite their knowledge of Urdu educated Punjabis have often felt out of their depths in the company of Muhajirs using the mother-tongue with the deliberate intent of stressing a superiority in cultural upbringing. So, although in the initial flush of patriotism many urban educated Punjabi families embraced Urdu, they carefully avoided the linguistic nuances and cultural affectations of the more high brow among the Muhajirs. Urdu is less commonly used by urban educated Pathans who pride themselves in the knowledge that Pushto is the oldest regional language in west Pakistan. In Baluchistan, Urdu is seen by many to be an alien implant; a language often understood but rarely used by the upper crust of provincial society, whether Baluchi, Brahui or Pathan.

So efforts by the religious zealots to make political capital out of Urdu in order to strengthen support for an Islamic state among the Muhajirs only served to alienate other linguistic groups. Except in the Punjab where the age-old connection between the educated strata and Aligarh allowed for the spread of a parochial variant of Urdu in the urban areas, movements to promote regional languages gained momentum in Sind, the NWFP and Baluchistan. Neither religious dogma, nor the adopted language and cultural pretensions of the ruling alliance were sufficient to paper over the permutations of Islamic beliefs and linguistic affinities in Pakistan. Having carelessly chosen a set of national symbols which denigrated the religious and cultural sentiments of a vast majority of the population, the architects of state consolidation had now to try and stem the tide of social fragmentation with still more desperate methods.

It was in the eastern wing where the equation between Pakistan, Islam, Urdu and the cultural traditions of Mughal India had the most devastating impact on national unity. Not insignificantly, this was also the one province where state officials openly sought assistance from religious parties while seeking to foster a sense of Pakistani national unity. But past experience had shown that commitment to causes alone was no assurance for success. What was really needed were considerable inflows of money. Since the central government was unable to offer anything more than token support, it seemed natural enough to try and promote the cause of Islam and national unity by knocking on the doors of Pakistan's friends in the international arena. Towards the end of November 1950, American officials in Dacca were surprised by the unannounced arrival of two members of the Jamiat-ul-Ulema-i-Islam with a letter of introduction from the governor, Firoz Khan Noon. Deeply perturbed by signs of an emergent Bengali nationalism, the JUI wanted the Americans to produce a sum of Rs. 10,000 'to help meet their costs in promulgating the anti-Communist line' as well as Urdu pamphlets on the 'treatment of Muslims in Russia' to demonstrate 'how Islam...[was being] crushed under the Communist system'. The Americans asked for time to consult and consider before putting the JUI on the US payroll, but took the opportunity to hand out propaganda literature in Urdu for circulation among Bengali-speakers. When the American consul general approached the governor, Noon showed his sense of propriety by declaring that the funds should be provided directly 'by the local Government and not by the United States'.[16]

Religious parties in opposition in west Pakistan were less fortunate than the east Bengal wing of the JUI. But they made up for it by being resourceful. Before long some of them had begun sounding out the Americans for financial and other forms of morale boosting assistance. The Jamat-i-Islami was 'anxious to get information on...[its] organization in the hands of the American Embassy', maintaining it was the victim of 'false propaganda...[by] the Muslim League'. As early as November 1951, Jamat officials were extending warm invitations to American diplomats to attend their annual session.[17]

These overtures led some Americans to do a bit of cautious thinking about using Islam to promote their national interests. There were 'great possibilities in encouraging adherents [of] Islam...in spiritual...assertion against communist nihilism'. While there was 'no objection' to combining religion and politics 'where practicable and desirable', it was 'preferable [to] keep politics and religion on separate

[16] Withers to Warren, 28 November 1950, NND.842430, RG 84, Box 7, File 350–Pak. Pol. 1950, NA.
[17] Report on the Jamat-i-Islami, NND.842430, RG 84, Box 12, File 320–Pak. Pol.1951, NA.

but parallel tracks leading to the same destination'.[18] But, since the Americans were convinced that Islamic parties like the Jamat-i-Islami were 'not a powerful force in Pakistan politics...',[19] there was no immediate danger of Washington deploying Islam as a convenient prop for its own purposes.

For the managers of the Pakistani state, however, there was no real alternative except to continue making increasingly more cynical uses of Islam. This entailed issuing seasonal statements urging the people to order their lives according to the high ideals of Islam, condemning the spread of corruption with catchy quotes from the Quran and making a big play for religious piety during ramazan. The rhetoric was couched in an idiom designed to reinforce Islamic sentiments, but one which was sufficiently ambiguous as to allow the 'liberal' citizens to get on with their lives unaffected by the counter-propaganda of the religious parties. It was a typically Pakistani posture – morally upright in appearance, but in reality tolerating, nurturing, even admiring of those discreet enough to get away with living blissfully in sin. As a member of Pakistan's first constituent assembly put it aptly: 'we are very emphatic about accepting everything Islamic and rejecting and detesting anything un-Islamic but in our practical life, we...do...the reverse'.[20]

And indeed, while over 80 per cent of the population in the rural areas remained oblivious and, at best, indifferent to the state's religious posturing, those in the urban centres interpreted it variously. This helped ensure that, as in the rural hinterlands, the practice of Islam in the urban areas would be eclectic with, of course, suitable smatterings of religious rituals just to keep up appearances. It was right and proper for even the most liberal urban families to employ a maulvi for their children's religious education which involved a compulsory reading of the Quran from beginning to end in Arabic, usually without a translation. Exposed to Arabic while speaking a regional language or dialect at home and learning English and Urdu in schools, and in Baluchistan also Persian, most of the first generation of upper-and middle-class Pakistanis grew up being literate not in one language but practically illiterate in at least four. But then they could hardly have escaped bearing the brunt of the confused experiments of their parents' generation to find an acceptable conjunction between Islam, nationalism and 'modernity'.

Karachi's educated upper- and middle-classes took the lead in finding more and more improbable syntheses between Islam and cosmopolitan

[18] R.A. Hare to the secretary of state, 14 April 1952, ibid., File 320–Pak. Pol.1952.
[19] Report on the Jamat-i-Islami, ibid., File 320-Pak. Pol.1951.
[20] *CAD*, I, 4, 19 March 1952, 251.

social concepts. An enterprising attempt was a banquet hosted by the Indonesian ambassador which began with recitations from the Holy Quran and ended with a strip-tease act – 'an unintended irruption from the Hotel Cabaret'.[21] Even in the more conservative setting of Lahore, fewer and fewer upper- and middle- class women were observing *purdah*. And this at a time when Abdur Rab Nishtar, known for his religious orthodoxy, was governor of the Punjab. According to one rough estimate, 60 per cent of the central government servants above the rank of deputy secretary liked bringing their wives to mixed gatherings.[22] But, insofar as the position of Pakistani women can serve as a yard-stick,[23] these signs of 'liberalism' creeping into the upper- and middle-class strata of urban society have to be taken with a modicum of scepticism. With a handful of notable exceptions, attending social functions with their husbands was an occasion to parade the newest additions to the wardrobe – a *shalwar-kameez* modelled on the latest fashions in Paris, New York, Rome, London and New Delhi – not an opportunity to broaden mental horizons. That would have been contrary to the rampant anti-intellectualism of the upper layers of educated Pakistani society. To her credit, Rana Liaquat Ali Khan did try to stir educated women to participate in patriotic causes. Her efforts included organising a Pakistan women's national guard. She met with 'half-hearted support from the official and middle classes', was totally ignored by the *burqa* clad lower middle-class women, while 'a body of opinion' wanted to be altogether 'rid of the Begum and of her new-fangled experiments'. For Rana Liaquat Ali Khan, it was worse than that. The mullahs of Karachi never failed to make 'pejorative references to her in their sermons'.[24]

The clash between 'mullahism', a derogatory term for the forces of religious conservatism, and the so-called 'Westernised' strata, who according to the fundamentalist ideologue Maududi were the long-sufferers of a most lethal form of 'white jaundice',[25] was to become more

---

[21] 'Mullahs and their influence in Pakistan', prepared by J. McCormick [British high commission, Karachi]; enclosure to Grafftey-Smith's letter to Attlee, 14 February 1951, DO35/3185, PRO.

[22] Ibid.

[23] The relationship between women and the state in Pakistan has been an especially intriguing one. The state's stance on women's place in society has often been a measure of its religious rectitude. Women's attitudes have been marked by both subservience and resistance to society and state. For a more detailed study of the triumvirate of Islam, women and the state in Pakistan see A. Jalal, 'The Convenience of Subservience: Women and the State of Pakistan' in Deniz Kandiyoti (ed.), *Islam, Women and the State* (forthcoming).

[24] 'Mullahs and their influence in Pakistan', by McCormick, DO35/3185, PRO.

[25] S.A.A. Maududi, *Purdah and the Status of Women in Islam* (eighth edition), Al-Ashari (trans.), Lahore 1986, 211.

ferocious. Conducted both within and outside the state apparatus, it has militated against Islam giving a sense of cohesion to urban, much less rural, society in Pakistan. This is to be expected. While the religious conservatives label efforts to accommodate the Islamic way of life with ideas borrowed from the West as blasphemous, the 'Westernised' elements remain firmly of the view that a synthesis is not only desirable but an imperative of the twentieth century which neither the Pakistani state nor society can afford to ignore. The debate continues to rage on, both at the level of ideology and everyday culture. For the swelling ranks of confirmed pessimists in Pakistan, the prospect of its outliving the existing state structure seems perfectly plausible.

7

The state of martial rule, 1958 to the present: towards a conceptual framework

Since 1958 recurring cycles of military intervention, consolidation and collapse have dominated Pakistani history, fashioning as well as refashioning relations between state and society with telling effect. The frequency of military rule in Pakistan is commonly attributed to weaknesses in its political party system and to difficulties inherent in welding together a linguistically and culturally heterogeneous society. But such explanations have done more to obfuscate than to lay bare the complex dynamics which have served to make military rule the norm rather than the exception in Pakistan. Insofar as exceptions prove the rule, these dynamics when traced to the period before the first military intervention point to an altogether different explanation of an outcome which has compelled quite as much as it has eluded analyses of Pakistan.

It was during the first decade of independence that an interplay of domestic, regional and international factors saw the civil bureaucracy and the army gradually registering their dominance over parties and politicians within the evolving structure of the state. While allowing the state a relative autonomy of action in directing the course of political and economic developments, the shifts in the institutional balance of power by their very nature militated against forging organic links with society. With decision-making firmly in the hands of a ruling alliance drawn mainly from the top echelons of the bureaucracy and the army, although loosely tied to dominant classes and interest groups, there was no obvious equation between the actual wielding of state authority and the structures of economic power and social control. Consequently, the relative autonomy of the Pakistani state from the internal class structure came to rest in large part on the closely nurtured connections of its senior state officials – civil and military – with the centres of the international capitalist system.

Yet in the absence of organised channels for the articulation of socio-political and economic interests, except through a highly centralised administrative apparatus, the legitimacy and effectiveness of state authority in a complex and stratified society like Pakistan was perpetually at risk. By choosing to manipulate their international connections to mould the administrative machinery and pursue specific strategies for development, the bureaucratic-military axis grossly underestimated the need for popular bases of support. The very fact of a military takeover in October 1958 suggests that, in spite of the dominance of the bureaucracy and the army, the internal structures of the state were still fluid enough to be threatened by political forces. Regionalised and fragmented though these were, they could challenge the state's claims to legitimacy and exploit latent tensions both within and between the central and the provincial arms of the civil service.

So it is better to avoid the oft-repeated assertion that the collapse of the 'parliamentary system' in Pakistan flowed from the 'power vacuum' created by a faction-ridden and corrupt leadership at the helm of political parties with no real bases of popular support. A more convincing explanation for the military takeover of October 1958 might lie in the equally plausible, if paradoxical, situation where the consolidation of authority under bureaucratic and army auspices ended up undermining the relative autonomy of the state in Pakistani society. This raises three overlapping questions: (1) what were the domestic, regional and international compulsions under which an already dominant military establishment had to assume control of the state apparatus, (2) to what extent did this alter or confirm developments underway since the initial years of independence, and (3) what have been the implications of the first military takeover for the state and its relations with society during the subsequent three decades of Pakistani history?

One can begin to address such large questions only after sketching the broad contours of a conceptual framework in which to place the relationship between state and society in post-colonial Pakistan. This chapter does so by boldly projecting up to the present the five interrelated themes which informed the analysis of the years preceding the military intervention of 1958 – namely, tensions between the centre and the provinces, the absence of a well-organised national political party, the role of the civil bureaucracy and the army in bolstering central authority, the extent to which the international connections of senior civil and army officers influenced internal developments and the uses made of Islam to give legitimacy to the state, not to mention lend a semblance of cohesion to a linguistically and culturally disparate people.

There has always been an interesting correlation between the emphasis given to the unifying principles of Islam and anxieties about the legitimacy of the Pakistani state. But, despite references to an 'Islamic ideology' which they never cared to define, the state managers could not expect to legitimise authority without at least appearing to serve the interests of society as a whole. This confronted them with contradictions inherent in the role of any state: the need to safeguard diverse socio-economic interests while at the same time furthering its own institutional concerns and those of the dominant classes. It is a formidable problem even for states with well-established organisational structures and relatively low levels of social stratification. In Pakistan, not only was the society highly stratified, but the state had to establish its structures of authority and legitimacy both at the same time. Minor revamping of the two main institutions of the colonial state – the civil bureaucracy and the army – could provide the basis for the exercise of state authority. Confirming its legitimacy in a society riddled with economic disparities, as well as a multiplicity of religious and ideological beliefs, was rather more problematic. However much they tried, the issue of state legitimacy could not be resolved by deference to the Islamic galleries alone. It was bound to crop up at each twist to the political saga and at each turn of the economic key. All the more so because 'legitimacy' far from being an abstract concept is a loose label for those complex webs of realities which order and define relations between state and society everywhere in the world. Coming to grips with some of these realities might explain why the legitimacy of the Pakistani state has been so open to question and why the responses to periodic threats from below have tended to be based on outright repression, softened only by the infusion of Islamic rhetoric.

Very soon after independence those who set about creating a new central government apparatus found themselves on the horns of a grave dilemma: the domestic political imperatives of the state were at variance with the strategic and economic consequences of the partition of India. The Muslim League – the only potential political vehicle linking the central leadership and the provincial, district and local levels of society – was the least well-organised in the areas which became part of Pakistan. It was difficult to transform the Muslim League into a popularly organised party without diverting financial resources into the provinces, the principal arenas of political activity and also the most badly affected by the massive dislocations accompanying partition. Military hostilities with India gave the centre a powerful pretext to extract resources from the provinces to finance the defence and administrative needs of the state. Discord between the centre and the provinces, especially east Bengal, followed naturally with serious implications for the political stability of the state. It was against a background of unmitigated strains in relations with India, chronic fiscal problems, heightening grievances in the constituent units, tensions between the central and the provincial governments, the decay of the Muslim League such as it existed and, not least, the shift in the institutional balance of power in favour of the civil bureaucracy and the army that Pakistan joined the international system firmly on the side of the Western allies.

After 1954 the state's growing involvement in American inspired international security arrangements closely matched its efforts to make deeper forays into the domestic economy and society. Far from easing the central government's financial worries inflows of American military aid increased the maintenance costs of the defence establishment. Administrative overheads also showed a steady upward climb and this despite the lack of any coordination between the central and the provincial governments. To confound the problem, the political and economic crises of the mid-fifties made it unfeasible to cut back on the already modest allocations for provincial development. The defence establishment for its part was wont to jerk up its annual budgetary requirements upon learning about an advance in weapons technology. So there was no real option except to enlarge the economic base to raise domestic revenues. Assured of American advice and a moderate flow of financial assistance each year, and encouraged by signs of willingness among business groups at long last to take investment risks, the state managers were ready to begin streamlining the administrative machinery with a view to better regulating and controlling the domestic economy, as well as coordinating the activities of the central and the provincial governments. But in setting their sights on building a state structure geared to sustaining a political economy of defence they neglected to take account of the complex social dynamics underlying the political process.

An important gauge of society's responses to the cut and thrust of state policies, the political process had been curbed but not crushed. Detailed analysis of the fifties has shown how Pakistan's predominantly Punjabi civil bureaucracy and army manipulated their international connections and the opportunities afforded by endemic provincial factionalism to consolidate state authority at the expense of the political process. There is no denying their success in thwarting the growth of organised parties with bases of support in all the provinces of Pakistan. But, so long as the facade of 'parliamentary government' was kept alive, there was nothing to stop the mushrooming of small- and medium-size oppositional groupings. More to the point, these could after a national election conceivably coalesce together to endanger, if not altogether undo, a state structure which was being designed to give primacy to the institutional interests of the bureaucratic-military axis and its allies – in particular among Karachi based industrialists and some prominent Punjabi landed and business families.

The chaos and fragmentation of Pakistani politics, therefore, cannot be blamed on the well-advertised lack of principled leadership and disciplined parties alone. A more convincing explanation would have to consider whether the underpinnings of power at the local, district and provincial levels of Pakistani society were at all conducive to basing state authority and an externally stimulated economic development strategy on an administrative as opposed to a political centralisation. The fierce opposition of the non-Punjabi provinces to the imposition of the one unit system in west Pakistan was a warning against basing state authority on an administrative centralisation while the political system was purportedly federal in structure. Yet it was the absence of any effective system of local self-government in the territories constituting Pakistan,[1] in the west more so than in the east, which offers the more striking comment on the bankruptcy of the methods adopted by the state to extend its sway over both economy and society. Without some institutional mechanisms like elected union and district boards and municipal and town committees to associate rural and urban society with the operations of the local bureaucracy, administrative centralisation was more likely to hamper than facilitate the implementation of development programmes.

Between 1947 and 1955, while planned development was still on the drawing-boards, an inordinate increase in the responsibilities of district officers saw local administration deteriorating rapidly. Unless relieved of some of their judicial and revenue functions it was difficult for district officers to supervise the grandiose development programmes that were in the offing. With the coming of one unit in 1955 district administration took a turn for the worse. While district officers were placed under the direct control of divisional commissioners, no steps were taken to delegate responsibility to officials lower down the administrative hierarchy. Not surprisingly, by the end of the fifties administration in most districts had 'reached a state of chaos and confusion'.[2] And, if this

---

[1] At the time of partition, there were forty-seven municipalities, fifteen district boards and 3,600 union boards in the eastern wing to provide civic amenities for a population of over fifty million people. The situation in west Pakistan was much worse. In Sind, the NWFP and Baluchistan, local self-government was virtually non-existent. West Punjab had some sixty-three municipal committees, fifteen district boards, forty-two town committees, 3,544 village panchayats and twenty-two notified area committees. But most of these existed on paper. Insofar as the district boards in west Punjab can be seen as indicative of the general trend, the majority of the members were elected while the chairmanship remained the exclusive preserve of a nominated civil official, usually the all-powerful and badly over-worked district officer. (Shahid A. Rizvi, 'Development of Local Government in Indo-Pakistan from 1688 to 1958', *Journal of the Pakistan Historical Society*, XXI, II, April 1973, 140.)

[2] Najmul Abedin, *Local Administration and Politics in Modernising Societies: Bangladesh and Pakistan*, Dacca 1973, 148.

was a poor omen for the implementation of the central government's development programme outlined in the first five year plan, the condition of the local self-government bodies seemed an even better guarantee for disaster – in the western wing certainly. By 1957-8, twenty out of thirty-four district boards and 58 per cent of the municipal councils in west Pakistan had been suspended and placed under the direct control of civil administrators appointed by the provincial and the central governments.[3] There were various reasons for scrapping the local self-government bodies, not least among which were frequent power struggles between government officials and the local landlords who, despite inveterate factionalism, were at one against the state encroaching on their personal domains. Keeping rural boards moribund and, thus, safely out of the reach of the local notables may have been consistent with the drive for an administrative centralisation. But it also encouraged the rural lords to look more favourably upon political parties as a way of circumventing the local administration and advancing their interests at the provincial and the central levels. The prospect of a national election gave further impetus to the trend. Indeed, one of the reasons why elections to local bodies were so rare was that these gave political parties an opening through which to try and make a dent in the rural areas. The urban municipalities were already 'buzz[ing] with the factional squabbles of the upper classes',[4] often with the backing of rival political parties. For the bureaucratic-military axis to have allowed political parties to mobilise the rural areas prior to the consolidation of the administrative machinery was tantamount to losing the old world with no absolute certainty of holding on to the new.

By 1957-8, a deepening fiscal crisis, together with the lack of an effective infrastructure to implement economic development policies, and mounting social and political grievances had underlined the constraints on the relative autonomy of the state. Under the circumstances, the bureaucratic-military axis and their allies outside the state apparatus were understandably apprehensive about the upsurge in political activity on the eve of promised national elections. There was the danger of the non-Punjabi electorate in west Pakistan voting for parties committed to dismantling the one unit system. In east Pakistan, parties calling for greater provincial autonomy were likely to romp home with handsome margins. To add to the difficulties, even parties which could be expected to support the status quo were not above exploiting popular sentiments by demanding a non-aligned foreign

---

[3] Shahid A. Rizvi, 'Development of Local Government in Indo-Pakistan from 1688 to 1958', *Journal of the Pakistan Historical Society*, XXI, 11, April 1973, 142–3.
[4] Ibid.

policy and an immediate settlement of the Kashmir dispute. These trends, unless checked, were bound to recoil on Pakistan's relations with the United States and possibly lead to a suspension of military and economic aid.

There were strong domestic, regional and international compulsions for the bureaucratic-military axis to want to depoliticise Pakistani society before it slipped into the era of mass mobilisation. And, while it was the political and economic crises of 1958 which brought matters to a head, thinking along these lines was in evidence long before the actual military intervention. As early as 1954, general Ayub Khan had put his name to a memorandum outlining a constitutional framework based on the nebulous concept of 'controlled democracy'. The commander-in-chief was then defence minister in Bogra's cabinet. It would not be too far-fetched to suggest that the proposal if not actually prepared by them had the backing of senior civil bureaucrats in Karachi. Clearly then, by intervening in October 1958, the military high command was not simply coming to 'the aid of civil society' or attempting to fill the 'power vacuum' created by the political leadership. With the dominance of the army and the civil bureaucracy already well established in the state apparatus, the notion of a 'power vacuum' is an unsustainable one. The constraints on the state's autonomy of action – whether on account of domestic, regional or international factors – all point to the inescapable conclusion that the Pakistan army entered the political arena with the explicit intention of countering threats to its alliance with the civil bureaucracy and certain dominant social and economic classes. That in doing so it was merely trying to confirm developments, the rough basis for which had been laid as early as 1951, can be seen in the military regime's efforts to take the sting out of the political process by a selective mobilisation under the supervision of the administrative bureaucracy.

Between 1958 and 1971 two different military rulers tried consolidating state authority and implementing externally stimulated development strategies without being inconvenienced by unstable ministerial coalitions which had so characterised Pakistan's first decade after independence. Both relied on the support of a predominantly Punjabi army and civil bureaucracy and, through the extension of differential patronage, on social and economic groups with political bases that were neither very extensive nor wholly independent as to pose a serious threat to the stability of the regimes. But, while the first military regime under general Ayub was unceremoniously swept out of office by a mass urban uprising, that of general Yahya Khan ended ignominiously with the disintegration of the country. The collapse of the two regimes is a resounding comment on the limitations of state consolidation under military and bureaucratic auspices as well as the resilience of political opposition, whether organised or semi-organised, in societies subjected to systematic depoliticisation.

The paradox is all the greater because, when general Ayub began building his new order, the civil bureaucracy and the army seemed to be the regime's best bet for survival. Anxious to put the country back on the rails, Ayub vowed to root out the ills besetting Pakistani society with a flourish of regulations. None was drastic enough to qualify being revolutionary. Indeed the one with the most far reaching effects – the basic democracies order of 1959 – displayed shades of nineteenth-century Riponian thinking! Fittingly announced on the first anniversary of the military takeover, it was intended to expedite rural development, improve social welfare facilities, and create a new politically conscious class of leaders with administrative skills and the wherewithal to mobilise the rural population. Stripped of these noble intentions, the basic democracies order was nothing less than an undisguised attempt to institutionalise bureaucratic control over the political process.

Some 80,000 basic democrats – 40,000 each from the two wings of the country – were to be elected on the basis of direct adult franchise to union councils and union committees in the rural and urban areas respectively. These would then indirectly elect members to the higher level local bodies – the tehsil/thana councils in the rural areas and municipal committees and cantonment boards in the urban areas, as well as the district and the divisional councils. Left at that, the proposal might have been hailed as an innovative measure to build bridges with rural society. But the basic democrats were also to serve as the electoral college for the election of the president and the provincial assemblies.[5] All the four tiers were to be controlled by the bureaucracy which was to nominate as many as half of the members to the district and the divisional councils. By tipping the balance in favour of rural politicians vetted and nurtured by the civil bureaucracy, the CSP in particular, the basic democracies system virtually disenfranchised the more volatile sections of urban society – industrial labour and the intelligentsia especially. Despite urban opposition to the proposed political system,[6] the basic democracies order was incorporated into the 1962 consti-

---

[5] On 17 February 1960, after a record vote of 95.6 per cent by the newly elected basic democrats in his favour, Ayub officially took the oath of office as president. (Lawrence Ziring, *The Ayub Era: Politics in Pakistan, 1958–69*, Syracuse 1971, 18.)

[6] Most effectively voiced in the reports of the constitution commission of 1962 and the franchise commission of 1963.

tution. Announced on 8 June 1962, at the time of the lifting of martial law, the constitution provided for a federal system of government and an all-powerful president to be elected by the basic democrats who were not about to commit hara-kiri by casting their ballots against the man to whom they owed their new privileges.

In choosing to consolidate the state's hold over society by extending the scope of bureaucratic patronage – both political and economic – to the rural localities, Ayub hoped to bolster central authority without being constrained by parties and politicians with provincial bases of support. This was part of a grand strategy to industrialise and militarise Pakistan in the quickest possible time; the general had lost no time negotiating a multi-million dollar agreement with the United States to help finance the rural development programme and give a fillip to his basic democracies system. But the strategy cut against the grain of provincial demands for greater autonomy. And, while it was intended to do just that, in a country where provincial sentiments were the highest common denominator of social dissidence and, by virtue of the composition of the civil service, a constant source of friction within the administrative machinery, placing the political process under bureaucratic control amounted to sowing the seeds of the state's possible, if not necessarily inevitable, fragmentation. The takeover of the state apparatus by the military may have put the political parties out of the running. Yet the intervention had not resolved the inherent contradictions of pursuing an externally stimulated development strategy through an administrative centralisation that ignored the federal configuration which Pakistan's social diversities necessitated.

So, if the military high command and its allies in the bureaucracy had now rid themselves of the biggest obstacle in the way of their plans to consolidate the state, they had done so only by increasing the attendant risks. By neutralising the tensions within the institutional framework of the state, by reconfirming old alliances with the dominant classes as well as creating new ones, by disqualifying old politicians and keeping a firm leash on the new recruits, the Ayub regime could certainly try and confirm the existing structures of authority. The power of the state lay in its ability to be selective in the granting of political privilege to sections of dominant socio-economic groups. The state's magnet-like quality in defining the field of political privilege made it difficult for socio-economic dominance to be sustained while resisting being drawn into its sphere of patronage.[7] State authority consolidated in this way was at best a

[7] See A. Jalal 'State Magnetism and the Field of Political Privilege in Pakistan', Myron Weiner and Ali Banuazizi (eds.), *Political Elites and the Restructuring of the Political Order in Afghanistan, Iran and Pakistan* (forthcoming).

precarious achievement. The state's role in selectively safeguarding some old privileges and intervening to create new sets of 'elites' was designed to build a limited social base of support in its search for legitimacy. But the state's accommodation with certain forms of privilege also served to exacerbate underlying social tensions. The state was liable, sooner or later, to reproduce some of these tensions within its own internal structures. This in turn could seriously undermine its ability to act coherently, perhaps force it to rely more and more on the available instruments of coercion – the police and in the last resort, the army – and so raise awkward questions about the legitimacy of state authority.

The basic democracies system aimed at a partial mobilisation of the rural areas and encouraged the localisation of political activity. With their social bases restricted to the localities and districts, and no real incentive to forge horizontal links, the BDs could not muster up the sort of mass support the regime needed to justify keeping a lid on urban opposition. By providing the rationale for the exclusion of the more recalcitrant sections of urban society from the electoral process and for the extension of patronage to those deemed to be less threatening politically, the basic democracies system was more likely to polarise than help integrate Pakistani society. As the bedrock of the strategy of depoliticisation, the basic democracies system confronted the regime with dilemmas of a fundamental nature. To effectively preempt a challenge from the politically excluded strata of society it had to register successes on the economic front. Yet providing differential economic patronage to a narrowly defined political constituency – essential for the success of the BD system – while at the same time hoping for the benefits of rapid economic growth to trickle down to the rest of society were not easily reconcilable objectives. The regime, understandably enough, went about the former with enthusiasm. But it was not long before it had to grapple with the unintended consequences of a policy of depoliticisation which had to be sustained by economic strategies emphasising growth rather than redistribution.

Preoccupations with the growth-redistribution debate has tended to blur analyses of the state's critical role in the creation of socio-economic privilege. The overwhelming trend has been to focus on the location of dominant socio-economic groups in relation to the state structure. But the dissonance between the military and the bureaucracy's institutional interests and those of socio-economic groups makes it equally, if not more important, to investigate how positions within the state apparatus facilitate the relocation of functionaries of government at various levels in key socio-economic sectors. This sort of penetration of strategic social spheres was intended to buttress support for a bureaucratic-military state and to enable it to control the nature and direction of socio-economic change. But it also contributed to the generation of new tensions and conflicts. Evidence for this can be found in the effects of Ayub's social engineering in rural and urban areas alike.

The land reforms of 1959 were, on the face of it, intended to break the hold of the landed gentry in west Pakistan. But in actual fact they were aimed at ingratiating the regime with middle-sized landlords, many of whom were ex-military and civil officials. A large part of the resumed land was handed over to military and civil officials at throwaway prices. Hundreds of thousands of acres of newly irrigated land in Sind and sizeable plots of land in the urban areas were parcelled out to both military and civil officials – Punjabis in the main. Since there was nothing to prevent them reselling the land at fantastic prices in the open market, senior government employees found themselves climbing the economic ladder with startling ease. Retired military officials were assured of plum jobs in both the public and the private sector while others were absorbed into the central and provincial services – a first step to their eventual positioning in the upper layers of the main sectors of the economy. These were well and truly the halcyon days for officials of the bureaucratic-military state. Those with a penchant for wheeling and dealing could even expect to find a place alongside the regime's other most favoured groups – the business and industrial entrepreneurs.

There were certainly plenty of incentives for wanting to join the growing ranks of Pakistani entrepreneurs. Special policy measures like the bonus voucher scheme allowed businessmen to multiply their profits overnight. These could then be funnelled into large-, medium- or small-scale industrial enterprises. The second five year plan (1960–5) – the blueprint of the Ayub regime's new economic order – called for a 60 per cent growth in large-scale industry and a 25 per cent increase in small-scale industry. This was to be brought about by a two-fold increase in investment, with foreign loans and grants providing for 42 per cent of the total amount.[8] The share of industry in the gross domestic product rose from 9.2 per cent in 1959–60 to 11.4 per cent in 1964–5.[9] But a better measure of the regime's success in taking Pakistan down the road of capitalist development can be seen in the astonishing concentration of wealth. According to one rough calculation, about 66 per cent of the industrial assets and 87 per cent of the banking and insurance assets were in the hands of some two dozen families.[10] These industrial

[8] *The Second Five Year Plan (1960–65)*, Karachi 1960, 4–5.
[9] Sergei Kamanev, *The Economic Growth of Pakistan*, Lahore 1985, 30.
[10] *Dawn*, 25 April 1968.

families, together with an estimated 15,000 senior civil servants belonging to approximately 10,000 families, and about 500 generals and senior military officials,[11] formed the core of the regime's bases of support in the urban areas. But with a rise in the proportion of urban population from 17 per cent in 1951 to 22.5 per cent in 1961 – there was a three-fold increase in the numbers of industrial workers in the 1960s alone – not to mention the growing armies of the educated unemployed, the cities of Pakistan were potential tinder boxes liable to blow any regime out of existence, certainly one frankly committed to functional inequality as the guiding principle of its economic policies.

Yet, as the January 1965 presidential elections showed, there was no possibility of a concerted challenge against Ayub from within the officially recognised boundaries of the political process. And this despite attempts by a coalition of opposition parties [12] to make a dent on the BD system by selecting Fatima Jinnah, the sister of the Quaid-i-Azam, as their presidential candidate. Secure within the confines of a political system controlled by the administrative bureaucracy, Ayub failed to anticipate the rising crescendo of opposition to his rule from social groups which rapid industrial growth and 'capitalist' oriented strategies in the agrarian sector had helped create as well as marginalise. In September 1965 an inconclusive war with India exacerbated the trend. During 1965–6, expenditure on the military was increased by 17 per cent, imposing a crippling burden on an already sagging economy. The second half of the sixties saw industrial production declining, a food shortage forcing the government to import, foreign aid decreasing by 25 per cent and,[13] worst of all, rampant inflation. Deteriorating economic conditions, a cooling of relations with the United States and a seething bitterness about the post-war Tashkent accord with India exposed the regime to an ever widening spectrum of political opposition. The barrage of attacks hit the regime in just those places where it was most vulnerable. The politics of exclusion and the economics of regional and class disparity had turned the logic of functional inequality on its head.

Against a background of labour militancy and student radicalism, provincial politicians led by Sheikh Mujibur Rahman – the leader of the east Pakistani based Awami League – called for an immediate devolution of power to the constituent units. His six-point programme for provincial autonomy, justified on the grounds of growing economic disparities between the two wings and inadequate representation of the

---

[11] Angus Maddison, *Class Structure and Economic Growth: India and Pakistan Since the Moghuls*, London 1971, 143.

[12] The political parties act of 1962 had legalised the setting up of political parties.

[13] Cited in Kamanev, *The Economic Growth of Pakistan*, 31.

Bengali majority in the civil bureaucracy and the army, was seized upon by non-Punjabi politicians to demand the end of one unit. By 1967 parties belonging to the left and the right in both wings of the country were calling for universal adult franchise and the reintroduction of parliamentary government. The foundations of the regime were visibly crumbling. It was too late to rectify all the wrongs. So the regime, never very adept at the art of dangling carrots except within the limited sphere carved in consort with the CSP, had now to turn to the more heavy-handed methods of the stick. Beginning with east Pakistani demands for provincial autonomy – short-sightedly dubbed secessionist – the Ayub regime tried to quell political opposition. Mujib and thirty-four of his associates were accused of conspiring with India and, more incredulously with the United States, to bring about the secession of east Pakistan. Known as the Agartala conspiracy case, Mujib's trial inflamed Bengali opinion. By the time the regime saw wisdom in withdrawing the case, the damage had been done.

Neutralising east Pakistani demands for provincial autonomy just when economic and political disaffections in west Pakistan – in particular among industrial labour, students and urban professionals within as well as outside the state apparatus – were reaching unprecedented heights was a severe challenge for a tottering military regime. Shunned by his principal ally in the international arena, and unable to deny the sentiments of middle and junior ranking army officers against the Indo-Pakistan agreement at Tashkent, Ayub lacked the means with which to avert the crisis. His break with Zulfiqar Ali Bhutto, the foreign minister and the most outspoken critic of the Tashkent declaration, was the last straw. Mujib and Bhutto may not have had organised political machineries to counter the machinations of administrative bureaucrats loyal to Ayub, but they certainly had the stature and the guile to become the focal points of the opposition which was gathering momentum in both wings of the country.

By making more and more cynical uses of the ideological and coercive arms of the state, Ayub's government merely assisted in its own undoing.[14] The spectacle of a military regime crashing down in the very congested city streets that the strategy of depoliticisation was supposed to have washed clean lends extra irony to Ayub's final months in office. Between November 1968 and March 1969, a remarkable number of

---

[14] In October 1968 for four long weeks the regime managed to outrage the politically conscious sections of the educated urban middle-class by using the national media to celebrate its achievements during the 'decade of development'. A resounding failure in public relations, the operation left the country poorer by $30 million. (Ziring, *The Ayub Era*, 89.)

voluntary associations, many of them completely unknown, paraded their demands in the main urban centres. Students, lawyers, engineers, doctors, teachers, industrial labour, low-ranking government employees and the ulema, all joined the fray.[15] Pitched battles with police and army contingents left an estimated 250 dead in both east and west Pakistan. Significantly enough, the administrative bureaucracy – the CSP in particular – rather than Ayub was the primary target of attack. Calling for drastic administrative reforms, the elimination of the basic democracies system and the economics of functional inequality, the urban protesters served notice on Ayub and his bureaucratic associates that determining the rules of inclusion and exclusion in the electoral process are not the sum total of politics. On 25 March 1969, seeing his political epitaph if not its logic, Ayub quietly handed over power to general Yahya Khan, the commander-in-chief of the Pakistan army.

Unexpectedly lumped with the task of healing the rifts in a deeply polarised country, general Yahya Khan was in no hurry to relinquish command. But if he was to escape the fate of his predecessor Yahya had to find a way of accommodating the new social forces let loose by the bureaucratic-military state's strategies of political denial and differential economic patronage. And, since Yahya was dependent on the support of the same military and bureaucratic ruling groups as Ayub, he had to do so without disturbing the cluster of power that had for so long dominated the state apparatus. Preventing a change in the nature of the state while successfully conciliating, if not necessarily incorporating, the array of political forces ready to storm its gates was not an easily reconcilable contradiction.

Yahya started off making the right noises. His regime was to be a transitional one, committed to policies of conciliation rather than confrontation. Anxious to play the role of honest broker, Yahya carefully avoided denouncing the politicians and promised free and fair national elections followed by a transfer of power to the representatives of the people. He sanctioned some administrative reforms as well as new educational and wage policies to counter student radicalism and labour militancy. Granted under duress, these concessions were not without strings. An immediate cessation of street demonstrations and student and labour violence had to be the precondition for the announcement of an election schedule. The appeal was heeded. But the reigning calm was dangerously artificial. The ideological polarisation of Pakistani society

---

[15] For a detailed analysis of the composition of the urban mass movement see Munir Ahmed, 'The November Mass Movement in Pakistan', in *Political Sociology: Perspectives on Pakistan*, Lahore 1978, 1–56.

which the recent mass protests had brought to the surface reflected itself in the composition of the regime. While some in the council of ministers and the upper echelons of the bureaucratic-military axis wanted to neutralise left-wing groups by bringing a genuine redress of social and economic grievances, those linked with right-wing groups like the Jamat-i-Islami and big business surreptitiously worked to sabotage the reforms. Never united to begin with, the ruling alliance under pressure was acting less and less coherently. In an atmosphere of uncertainty and distrust, no level of Pakistani society remained unaffected by the massive realignment of political and economic forces that was underway.

In November 1969, Yahya unfurled his plans for a transfer of power. Polls were scheduled for the fall of 1970; political parties could kick off their election campaigns by January of that year. To allay the regionalists, the president declared the end of one unit; Bengalis were to be represented in the national assembly on the basis of population rather than parity. But his conspicuous failure to make any mention of Bengali demands for provincial autonomy betrays the military high command's aversion to the Awami League's six points, especially the explicit denial of the centre's right to raise taxes in the federating units. In March 1970, the regime showed more of its hand by proclaiming the legal framework order (LFO). A less than subtle ploy to prejudge the future shape of the constitution, it gave Yahya the veto on any document produced by the elected national assembly.[16] Together with the regime's attempts to merge the three factions of the Muslim League and come to a pre-electoral understanding with the religious parties, the LFO was part of a well-planned strategy to preempt a constitutional framework unacceptable to the military establishment and its bureaucratic allies. So, even if the regime's assumption that the elections would not throw up a clear majority for any party proved to be mistaken, the LFO was an insurance against shifts in the balance of power within the existing state structure. To put it bluntly, the Yahya regime had no intention of transferring power to any political configuration – whether from the eastern or the western half of the country – which aimed at circumscribing the interests or reducing the dominance of the two main institutions of the Pakistani state.

After the elections the strategy undoubtedly came to assume an anti-Bengali bias. But this had more to do with the composition of the senior

---

[16] The legal framework order did not as such specify the details of the future constitution. But the intentions were clear enough. The federating units could have all the autonomy they wanted so long as this did not undermine the federal government's powers to discharge its legislative, administrative and financial responsibilities and preserve the independence and integrity of Pakistan.

echelons of the military and the bureaucracy than with the supposedly irreconcilable differences between the east and west Pakistani electorates. It is true that the Yahya regime's plans to thwart east Pakistani demands for provincial autonomy had the tacit support of a number of west Pakistani parties, including Zulfiqar Ali Bhutto's Pakistan People's party. Yet this again was a direct spillover from the two decades during which the bureaucratic-military axis tried consolidating state authority by a systematic stifling of political parties which, given half a chance, might conceivably have attempted to cultivate bases of support in both wings of the country. Insofar as the social and regional bases of support of the Awami League and the PPP and the results of the elections are indicative of the extent of political polarisation between the eastern and the western halves of Pakistan, they are an unequivocal comment on the methods adopted to build the state structure in the fifties and the sixties.

Of the political parties that contested the elections,[17] the Awami League emerged as the dominant power bloc in the national assembly, securing as many as 160 out of 162 seats from east Pakistan. The PPP with its bases of support confined to the Punjab and Sind bagged eighty-one of the 138 west Pakistani seats in the national assembly. The success of two parties with regional as opposed to national bases of support might at first sight appear to have simply highlighted the age-old dilemma of power sharing between the Bengali majority and a west Pakistani dominated ruling alliance. But there was an important new twist. In the late forties and early fifties when the state was still in the process of consolidating its authority, the sharing of power between the two wings may have been a matter for the main political party or parties to settle. By 1970, this was no longer the case. The institutional stakes of the military and the bureaucracy within the existing state structure were much greater than those of the social groups represented by the Awami League and the PPP. Even if they wanted to, Mujib and Bhutto could not palpably arrive at any formula to share power without the implicit approval of the praetorian guard and the mandarins. And, while Mujib had no reason to want to square the interests of a predominantly Punjabi military and bureaucracy, the PPP's limited and fragile bases of support foreclosed the possibility of Bhutto making concessions on behalf of the west Pakistani ruling coterie.

---

[17] Among the religious parties were the Jamat-i-Islami, the Jamiat-ul-Ulema-i-Islam and the Markazi Jamiat-ul-Ulema-i-Pakistan. Parties with democratic, social-democratic and leftish pretensions included the Pakistan Democratic party, the three factions of the Muslim League – Council, Qayum and Pakistan – the Awami League, the National Awami party and the Pakistan People's party.

With the institutional balance of power in the Pakistani state as the main point of reference, an understanding of the factors that enabled the Awami League to sweep the polls in east Pakistan and a closer look at the PPP's social bases of support, it is possible to reach plausible conclusions about the reasons for the failure of the post-electoral negotiations and the tragic events which accompanied the dismemberment of the country.[18]

Undeniably, the Awami League's six-point programme for maximum provincial autonomy held out many attractions for Bengali middle-class professionals, students, small-and medium-scale businessmen, and industrial labour. But, without the support of the rural areas, these urban groups alone could not have brought about a landslide victory for the Awami League. Here the Awami League's extremely effective psychological propaganda against the centre's delayed response to the human suffering caused by the cyclone in the fall of 1970 proved to be decisive. At the helm of a movement rather than a properly organised political party, Mujib's ability to manoeuvre after the elections was strictly limited by the expectations aroused by the Awami League's programme for provincial autonomy. Whatever Mujib's own predilections for a solution within a united Pakistan, the mere hint of compromise would have lost him the adulation of the Bengali people – his best resource against an intractable west Pakistani ruling alliance.

As for the PPP, it reflected more than represented the interests of that alliance. The secret of Bhutto's success in the elections lay in piecing together a loose coalition of divergent social and economic interests. This included emergent middle-sized Punjabi farmers, landed notables from Sind and the Multan district of the Punjab, Punjabi urban middle-class professionals, the newly organised industrial workers in Karachi and the Punjab, new rural-urban migrants, and the Punjabi rural underprivileged – small landholder-cum-tenant farmers, landless field labourers and menials – whom the much vaunted 'green revolution' in the late sixties had helped politicise. Contending with such a varied constituency was difficult to say the least. The PPP's electoral victory in any case was restricted to the relatively prosperous, more urbanised and semi-industrialised parts of the Punjab.[19] So, although it had been able to

---

[18] The definitive history of this period will have to await the opening of the relevant documents in Pakistan, Bangladesh and India.

[19] See Craig Baxter and Shahid Javed Burki, 'Socio-Economic Indicators of the People's Party vote in the Punjab', *Journal of Asian Studies*, August 1975 and Philip Edward Jones, 'The Pakistan People's Party: Social Group Response and Party Development in an Era of Mass Participation', (unpublished doctoral dissertation, Fletcher School of Law and Diplomacy, April 1979, parts II and III).

make a dent on the old structures of agrarian Punjab, the hold of the rural gentry was by no means broken. Soon after the elections, the rural lords – alarmed by the PPP's promise to give land to the tillers – coalesced with the local bureaucracy and the police to carry out a spate of tenant ejections. Attacks on its rural bases of support, matched by a price spiral and a wave of worker retrenchments in large- and medium-scale industries in the urban areas, aggravated the ideological differences which had been apparent within the PPP ever since the beginning of the election campaign.[20] Bhutto had to perform a delicate balancing act in order to hold on to both the left and the right wings of his party. These considerations coloured his stance on national issues, forcing him to put out feelers to the military regime before the social tensions of the post-election period in west Pakistan combined with the Awami League's demands to destroy the PPP and, by extension, his own claims to state power.

With their domestic accounts just barely in the black, neither Mujib nor Bhutto were well-placed to make the kind of generous concessions that were needed to circumvent the calculations of the military regime. Taking advantage of the constraints the unstable nature of their constituencies imposed upon the Awami League and the PPP leadership, Yahya stalled for time. The longer the post-electoral political stalemate the better his regime's chances of overturning an electoral verdict which, if allowed to translate itself into control over the state apparatus, was bound to diminish the position of the bureaucratic-military axis and its allies among certain west Pakistani landed and business families.

If Mujib was a difficult customer, Bhutto's weaknesses were there to be exploited. Appearing to go along with Bhutto's demand that the six-point programme be debated prior to convening the national assembly, Yahya just about succeeded in shifting responsibility for the delay in the transfer of power on the PPP's shoulders. But on 25 March 1971, by ordering the army on to scotch the east Pakistani reaction to an indefinite postponement in the meeting of the national assembly, general Yahya Khan revealed the inner thinking of the bureaucratic-military axis. Unbowed by the loss of legitimacy, first registered during the 1968–9 urban uprisings and confirmed by the 1970 election results, it was making a last ditch attempt to perpetuate its authority on the noble pretext of saving the integrity of the state. The army's campaign against Bengali resistance – a tragic mixture of human folly and capacity for

[20] Jones, 'The Pakistan People's Party: Social Group Response and Party Development in an Era of Mass Participation', 627.

brutality – was abruptly cut short by Indian military intervention and the disintegration of Pakistan.

The breakaway of east Pakistan following the army's humiliating defeat at the hands of its Indian counterpart lent urgency to old uncertainties about the state's capacity to survive. Yet the context had been altered dramatically by the socio-economic transformations during Ayub's decade of 'development' and consolidation. The state had no longer simply to search for ways to bolster its existing structures of authority. The problem now was how to make them more receptive and resilient to the demands and challenges of a society that had begun inching its way from old to newer, and comparatively less stable, forms of organisation. It was a classical dilemma for a state officiating over a society in flux, if not in actual transition. For the Pakistani state, the difficulties were compounded by the chilling knowledge that the nub of the tensions in its remaining territories bore a striking resemblance to those which had just resulted in a bloody civil war and the secession of its eastern wing.

Whoever was daring enough to pick up the gauntlet thrown by a disgraced military regime had to shoulder an awesome set of responsibilities. Rebuilding a state apparatus is quite as difficult as creating one anew, not least because of tenacious resistance from the institutional king-makers of yesteryears. Equally formidable was the need to restore the morale of a people shocked at being defeated by an enemy whom they had always regarded as the biggest threat to their security. Fortunately, skilful manipulation of symbols necessary for a psychic uplift came naturally to Bhutto, a political jackal whose party had the lion's share in the Punjab and Sind assemblies but no real influence in either NWFP or Baluchistan. The PPP's self-avowed 'populism' – whether the tingling proclamation, 'Islam is our faith, democracy is our polity, socialism is our economy, All power to the people', or the catchall 'roti, kapra aur makan' (food, clothing and housing) for all and sundry – seemed designed to allay the social discontents so menacing for the stability of the state. As the civilian leader with the largest following, Bhutto was an obvious choice for a military high command which, once saner counsels prevailed, accepted that vacating the political arena willingly would leave the door open until the time was ripe to capture it again.

In power, Bhutto began perfecting the art of political jugglery; a favourite game for a politician to whom the safest investments smelt uncannily enough like wasting assets. This may have been a dangerous way of perceiving a world he was out to reform. But for a man who

claimed to have been swept into power by a popular wave, not by a
temporary loss of military nerve, it was understandable. Amazingly
successful in bringing a variety of disaffected interest groups under the
PPP's wing – thus the aptness of the label 'populism' for his style of
politics – Bhutto had now to find a way of keeping the conflicting
ideological strands they represented from clashing in louder discord.
And he had to do so without weakening his own position *vis-à-vis* the
civil bureaucracy and the army – the bent but unbroken crutches for the
effective exercise of state power, especially at the centre where most of it
was concentrated.

So, even if it can be argued that he was holding the centre stage on
account of the PPP, Bhutto's survival there depended on the deals he
could strike with the civil bureaucracy and the army. The cooperation of
one was a precondition for the implementation of his ambitious reform
programmes, while the tacit support of the other was vital for the very
survival of his regime. Pakistan might have entered the era of mass
participation or 'populism', whatever the preferred term, but the
structure of the state, though it reflected the tensions generated by the
changes, had not as yet been brought into conformity with an emergent
social reality. Extending his control over the mandarins and the
praetorian guard, jealously watching his seemingly impregnable hold
over the underprivileged social groups, and also placating the dominant
interest groups – petrified by his populist rhetoric – without toning
down his party's promises required more cunning and tact than is
possible in a single life-time.

A gifted, pragmatic and shrewd politician, Bhutto certainly tried his
hand at reforming state institutions – the civil bureaucracy, the police
and the military. But he mistook reforms allowing him to deploy the
magnetic power of the state to broaden his constituency with reforms
aimed at altering existing institutional imbalances. So, while taking a
variety of steps to neutralize the military's threat to his regime,[21] Bhutto
failed to slash the defence budget and instead sanctioned increases in the
cost of maintaining the coercive arms of the state. In 1973 he abolished
the CSP, merged it into a linear all-Pakistan unified grade structure and
introduced lateral entry, ostensibly to attract talent into the administrative services but actually as a means of distributing political patronage.
The rapid expansion of the public sector following Bhutto's populist
measures – whether land reforms, new legislation safeguarding the
interests of labour, the nationalisation of heavy and capital intensive

---

[21] See Hasan Askari Rizvi, *The Military and Politics in Pakistan: 1947–86*, Lahore 1986,
chapter 10.

industrial units, banks and selected educational institutions – saw the regime more dependent than ever on the administrative bureaucracy. Bhutto sought to keep the upper hand by allowing the new recruits as well as professional civil servants to exploit the new job opportunities to gain entry into the higher ranks of the economic strata.

Bhutto was seeking to build a core group of supporters who could counter his opponents within the military and the bureaucracy. In a similar vein he used reforms as a means of punishing opponents and rewarding supporters while at the same time widening his own popular base of support.[22] It was not long before socio-economic groups most threatened by the PPP's reforms were joining the party. The magnetic attraction of state patronage, as Bhutto had learnt from his years as minister in Ayub's cabinet, was the best means of controlling those most likely to sabotage his party's populist policies. But Bhutto overplayed his hand. By weeding out the radicals and bringing in members of the landed gentry into the PPP he alienated loyal party workers anxious to capitalize on the support generated by the regime's land and labour reforms among the rural and urban underprivileged. Bhutto's intolerance of criticism from party loyalists, just in case this gave them a chance to carve out independent bases of support, is a poignant comment on his almost paranoid distrust of the veteran power brokers at the centre and their allies among the dominant socio-economic strata. In denying PPP workers the latitude they needed to convert the party's support into a truly well-organised political machinery, Bhutto missed a unique opportunity to create the popularly based institutional counterweight he so clearly needed to check the civil bureaucracy and army's dominance of the state apparatus.

This negated the potential effects of some of his more successful foreign policy measures on the state's internal power configuration. In June 1972, his agreement with Indira Gandhi at Simla placed Indo-Pakistan relations on a more congenial footing; a conceivable prelude to recasting the state's regional defence imperatives and restricting the influence of army headquarters on domestic politics. An old champion of non-alignment, Bhutto took concerted steps to reduce Pakistan's dependence on the Western allies, the United States in particular. His decision to take Pakistan out of the British commonwealth and SEATO, his overtures to the Islamic and Eastern bloc countries as well as his pro-China policy, might have antagonised London and Washington – the main centres of patronage for the Pakistani civil and defence establish-

[22] See Omar Noman, *The Political Economy of Pakistan, 1947–85*, London 1988, part II, chapter 2.

ments. But they improved his standing with a people who even in the aftermath of military defeat remained wedded to the idea of a non-aligned foreign policy. Sadly for Bhutto, support for his bold new directions in the regional and the international arenas could not wholly offset the disappointments with the PPP's policies on the domestic front.

Existing analyses of the Bhutto period are at one in concluding that his regime's flirtations with 'populism' were haphazard in the extreme and, ultimately, proved counter-productive in a society where the emergence of new interest groups did not entail the displacement of those that were already well-entrenched.[23] Yet in doing so they have placed rather more emphasis on Bhutto and his seemingly voracious appetite for power than on the contradictory constraints which the context imposed upon him. There is no disputing the fact that, while heightening mass awareness of the leavening effects their political leverage could have on existing socio-economic disparities, Bhutto failed to deliver the matching goods. He failed not merely on account of a spurious commitment to reforms, as some of his more relentless critics never tire pointing out, but due to the structural limitations of the state and the disparate nature of the PPP's constituency – a product of Ayub's politics of exclusion and the peculiar blend of 'populism' Bhutto had to bandy about in order to take advantage of mass discontents in the late sixties and early seventies. Whatever the pitfalls of the PPP's 'populism' in bringing about real social change it unleashed storms of expectations and counter-expectations. As even his critics concede, despite the nominal impact of many of the PPP's reforms, Bhutto was immensely popular among the rural and urban under-privileged. But growing criticisms from an urban intelligentsia who had spotted the blot in his democratic facade, to say nothing of those conniving to oust him from office, saw Bhutto relying increasingly on the coercive instruments of the state – especially the federal security force (FSF) which he had set up in May 1973 with the explicit intention of limiting his reliance on the army. For someone who liked to boast a knowledge of history, Bhutto made the all too familiar error of seeing coercion as the best means to acquiring greater autonomy of action.

In February 1973, he summarily dismissed the National Awami party and Jamiat-ul-Ulema-i-Islam government in Baluchistan. The NAP-

---

[23] See Jones, 'The Pakistan People's Party: Social Group Response and Party Development in an Era of Mass Participation', especially the epilogue. For a more detailed analysis of the PPP's years in office, see Maliha Lodhi, 'Politics in Pakistan During the Bhutto Era' (unpublished manuscript, no date]. Among the published works are Shahid Javed Burki, *State and Society in Pakistan, 1971–77*, London 1980; and Khalid B. Sayeed, *Politics in Pakistan: the Nature and Direction of Change*, New York 1980.

JUI government in the NWFP resigned in protest. This made nonsense of the PPP's claim that the 1973 constitution unlike those of 1956 and 1962 had the consent of all the main opposition parties and granted more autonomy to the provinces than ever before. After ridding himself of the non-PPP governments in Baluchistan and the NWFP, Bhutto began honouring the 1973 constitution more in the breach than in the observance. So, although Bhutto took special care to incorporate a provision making future military interventions unconstitutional, he had no qualms letting the army out of the barracks to put down Baluchi tribesmen in armed revolt against the federal government. By December 1973, the Pakistan army was once again in the political picture fighting a full-scale civil war to protect the integrity of the state. But there were two important differences. Instead of chasing Bengali guerrillas in the swamps of the Sundarbans it had to contend with the no less determined Marri, Mengal and Bizenjo tribesmen in the mountainous terrain of Baluchistan. And, most important of all, instead of acting on behalf of a military regime it had to take orders from a civilian government whose leaders ought to have known that the martial spirit once given its head stops at nothing short of total solutions, negative or positive.

During the remaining three and half years of his regime, Bhutto was to overrule most, if not all, the premises on which he had started building a new popular order in Pakistan. Proud of portraying himself in the secularist traditions of the Quaid-i-Azam, Bhutto – the Quaid-i-Awam (the leader of the people) – might have shrugged off charges by religious parties that his rule was 'unIslamic'. But the oil boom in 1973 saw an externally financed religious opposition growing both in confidence and strength. Bitter about the adverse effects of Bhutto's policies on their own socio-economic interests as well as those of the constituencies they represented,[24] the Islamic parties – most notably the fundamentalist Jamat-i-Islami – had been fanning the religious sensibilities of a people dispirited by military defeat. The claim that it was not the ineffectiveness of religion to weld together Pakistan's diverse constituent units but the state's lack of Islamic morality which had led to the disintegration of the country touched sympathetic chords across broad sections of society. It provided consolation for the more religious lower middle-classes – the small shopkeepers and petty merchants, teachers, the semi-professional and educated unemployed.[25] As the 1972 language riots between Urdu

[24] See Maliha Lodhi, 'Politics in Pakistan During the Bhutto Period', 150—1.
[25] Mumtaz Ahmad, 'Ideology, Power, and Protest: Toward Explaining Islamic Revivalism in Pakistan', unpublished paper prepared for a workshop on Islamic revivalism at the Centre for Strategic and International Studies, Georgetown University, 4 January 1986, 18–9.

and Sindhi speakers in Karachi had shown, such a line could spark off violent anti-government demonstrations.

The calls for an 'Islamic revival' held out temptations for a wide spectrum of social groups. Industrialists and big business affected by nationalisation and the PPP's labour reforms began contributing generously to the opposition's coffers. Bhutto's promise of a new spate of agrarian reforms sent panic waves among the landed gentry. In the summer of 1976, the nationalisation of agro-processing industrial units completely alienated the middlemen who provided the main bases of support for the religious parties. Sections of the urban middle-classes infuriated by runaway inflation and the scant respect shown by the regime for civil liberties also began looking for alternatives to the PPP. Instead of addressing the causes of the opposition, Bhutto tried establishing his regime's Islamic credentials by cynically making concessions to the religious parties. By giving more substance to the Islamic umbrella than the divergent and materially based interests accommodated under it warranted, Bhutto further antagonised the left. Yet he had wisely kept his lines open to the rural and urban under-privileged. The PPP's reforms may have been inadequate, but they were sufficiently popular to offset the negative perceptions of Bhutto's political accommodations with segments of the dominant socio-economic groups – big landlords in particular.

In 1977, Bhutto decided to renew his mandate in the obvious hope of improving the PPP's position in parliament and the provincial as-semblies. Despite his attempts to distance himself from the politics of the radical left – more PPP tickets were handed out to members of the rural gentry than in 1970 – none of his many opponents was ready to see this as a sign of his having turned over a new leaf. Bhutto found himself facing a nine party opposition coalition[26] which had nothing in common except the objective of dismantling his regime. Bhutto won the elections. Charging his regime with extensive rigging and calling for a *Nizam-i-Mustafa* (the system of the Prophet Mohammad), the opposition Pakistan National Alliance launched a meticulously planned and well-financed post-electoral campaign. Political commentators pointed the finger at Washington. The Pakistani rupee was strangely enough rising against the dollar during the election campaign and the Carter administration was publicly opposing Bhutto's intentions to proceed

---

[26] Representing a broad political spectrum from the extreme right to the left – it included the Jamat-i-Islami, the Jamiat-ul-Ulema-i-Pakistan, the Jamiat-ul-Ulema-i-Islam, the Muslim League, the Tehriq-i-Istiqlal, the Pakistan Democratic party, the National Democratic party, the Khaksar Tehriq and the Muslim Conference.

with the nuclear programme.[27] Bhutto himself accused the United States of encouraging his opponents to overthrow his regime.[28] The international factor was as ever seen to be looming large on the domestic political horizon.

Between March and July 1977, Pakistani cities and market towns were rocked by violent demonstrations. A broad cross-section of Pakistani society was represented. Industrial labour was conspicuous by its absence but its place had been more than adequately filled by commercial and trading groups, the main constituents of the religious parties. Unable to meet the PNA's demands that he step down and less able still to control the passions in the streets, bazaars and mohallas of Pakistan, Bhutto the great political conjurer was falling prey to a 'populism' he had done so much to promote. On 5 July 1977, the Pakistan army was back in the political arena for the third time – a lucky number for a general in league with Allah! If not for the enduring institutional imbalances within the Pakistani state structure, street power alone could not have paved the way for a military intervention. In choosing to deploy the state's magnetic power to cajole and coerce the privileged to concede reforms for the underprivileged, Bhutto had gravely erred in failing to build the independent political institutional counterweight he needed to thwart the bureaucratic-military, industrial and commercial onslaught against his populist regime.

General Zia-ul-Huq soon dispelled the view that his was just another military takeover of the state apparatus. A devout Muslim, Zia wanted to return a 'degenerate [Pakistani] society' to the pristine purity of Islam.[29] He justified his mission by arguing that Pakistan and Islam were two sides of the same coin, and the protection and integrity of both was a task the military establishment alone was capable of performing. In case the simple, if loaded, equation between Pakistan, Islam and the military failed to convince the cussedly cynical, Zia had no difficulty turning the calls for a *Nizam-i-Mustafa* – that umbrella term used to lend unity to an opposition divided along ideological as well as economic lines for the sole purpose of overthrowing Bhutto – into a personal mandate from the people.

It was easier to assert and proclaim than to maintain and establish the legitimacy of his regime. Here the device of keeping the country under martial law until December 1985, long after the political ferment against electoral and other malpractices of the PPP regime had petered out,

---

[27] *Viewpoint* (Lahore), 27 May 1977, 5.
[28] Ibid., 13 May 1977, 23.
[29] Cited in Sayeed, *Politics in Pakistan*, 183.

proved invaluable. It gave the Zia regime the means with which to break the back of the PPP by incarcerating or sending into exile some of the more irrepressible of its leaders and supporters, and the time that was needed to convict and hang Bhutto after charging him with the murder of a political opponent's father.

After a carefully executed preemptive strike at the main source of opposition to his rule, Zia concentrated attention on neutralising potential trouble-makers as well as building a solid constituency for his military regime. Upon assuming office, he decried the 'tremendous polarisation...between the right and the left, the poor and the rich, among the students and labour, and between the haves and the have nots'.[30] With the zeal of a religious crusader, Zia declared that his regime would turf out 'anti-social' elements propagating seditious notions about class inequalities. Stern warnings to industrial labour, a blanket prohibition on strikes, police swoops on left-wing militants, loud thwacks of the stick for the rural dispossessed still harking back to the days when all power was supposed to have been vested in their hands, were all designed to win around the propertied classes. It had the further merit of keeping the state's coercive arms well-versed in the art of vigilance. Yet state repression, even when laced with his chosen interpretations of Islam, was not the only face Zia wanted to project. His was to be a severe but fair government. The rules of the game demanded that he tend to the interests of all those willing to extend their support and use them as building-blocks for the constituency he needed.

With the military in his pocket and the civil bureaucracy well within reach, Zia concentrated upon winning over the social groups who had formed the backbone of the PNA's movement against Bhutto. It was convenient that the use of Islamic symbolism by the three religious constellations in the nine-party alliance – the Jamat-i-Islami, the Jamiat-ul-Ulema-i-Pakistan and the Jamiat-ul-Ulema-i-Islam – had become the best remembered expression of the movement. So it was only natural for the general to woo their main constituencies and in this way strengthen his own case for the 'Islamisation' of the Pakistani state, economy and society.

In the Punjab, support for the religious parties came primarily from urban middle- and lower middle-class groups engaged in trade and commerce – traders, merchants, small shopkeepers as well as middlemen. Migrants from east Punjab in the main, they replaced west Punjabi

---

[30] *The Pakistan Times*, 10 April 1978, cited in ibid., 178.

Hindu and Sikh traders and moneylenders after partition.[31] In 1976, when Bhutto nationalised agro-industries, it was the middlemen supporters of the religious parties that suffered. In Sind, the Jamiat-ul-Ulema-i-Pakistan and the Jamat-i-Islami drew electoral support from the Urdu-speakers, by and large migrants from the United Provinces of India, who constituted nearly 45 per cent of the population in the province and were concentrated in the urban centres of Karachi and Hyderabad.[32] Himself a migrant from east Punjab, and so a beneficiary of the close *biraderi* ties which are a distinguishing feature of these trading and commercial groups, Zia could hardly resist the temptation of laying claims to this ready-made constituency. It was after all their money and muscle that had given the PNA's movement its momentum; they were also among the most conservative strata in the country – a perfect fit for the general's grand design to 'Islamise' Pakistani society. Yet catering to their interests by hob-nobbing with the religious parties, the Jamat-i-Islami in particular, was not without a price. While capable of bringing down governments, these were not the groups who could turn the tables of Pakistan's political arithmetic in the general's favour. Although it was the best organised party in Pakistan, the Jamat's strength lay in the ideological commitment of a small membership, not in its ability to sway large rural vote banks.

Too open an association with electorally weak parties like the Jamat could stymy his regime's claims to legitimacy. Moreover, it might put off those in the upper echelons of the military establishment who did not share Zia's enthusiasm about casting Pakistani society into an 'Islamic' mould. But here the Jamat's long-standing policy of encouraging its supporters to join the armed forces could be turned to good advantage. Since the 1965 war with India many new recruits to the officer corps have come from pro-Jamat lower middle-class families. So Zia could and did retire and isolate officers opposed to his 'Islamisation' campaign. Yet it would be a mistake to underestimate the ideological differences within the armed forces or to assume that Zia's efforts to establish a religious ethos in Pakistan's military establishment has entirely displaced the secular orientation inherited by the three services from the colonial period. Mindful of potential opposition from within his main constituency Zia had to periodically temper his 'Islamisation' policies.

Treading on fragile ground Zia began by confirming his support among middling commercial and trading groups, and at the same time

[31] See Jones, 'The Pakistan People's Party: Social Group Response and Party Development in an Era of Mass Participation', chapter XI, and Lodhi, 'Politics in Pakistan During the Bhutto Era', 151.

[32] Lodhi, 'Politics in Pakistan During the Bhutto Era', 151–2.

considered how best to throw out a line to the bigger fish. Loudly asserting that he would protect life and property with all the force at his disposal, Zia embarked on the slippery road to consolidation. He denationalised some industries and blocked the new spate of land reforms that were in the pipeline. This won him the backing of some but not all the dominant interest groups; polarisation had by now enveloped the upper and the middle quite as much as the lower layers of Pakistani society. Military rule was no doubt welcomed by the business groups, anxious to make their killings without let or hindrance from party bosses. But, in an agricultural economy where it was rural lords who mattered, martial law was a potentially constraining influence on local privileges and could mean a possibly prolonged exclusion from the direct exercise of political power at the provincial as well as the national levels. In 1979 Zia tried co-opting the landed groups by resorting to the Ayubian device of holding non-party elections to the local councils. He was taken aback by the results. Most of the winning candidates were affiliated with the PPP. Zia reacted by imposing a ban on parties and politics and postponing national elections indefinitely. In December of that year the Soviet invasion of Afghanistan gave the regime a new lease. With American military and economic aid and the spectre of an external threat to Pakistan's security providing the cover, Zia was able to use the lure of state patronage to win the backing of certain influential elements in the agricultural, industrial and trading sectors of the economy. By 1981 the general was in a position to establish a selected as opposed to an elected federal advisory council – the Majlis-i-Shoora. A symbol of 'Islamic democracy', the Shoora had no effective powers over the executive. Its main purpose was to give the regime a semblance of legitimacy by inducting members of the dominant socio-economic strata into the ambit of state patronage so as to enable Zia to safely call for elections to the national and provincial assemblies.

But not many were enamoured by the general's ideas of representative government. The urban intelligentsia and the professional groups, rather those among them who still believed in democratic freedoms or had a special antipathy to being ruled by the military, found Zia's Islamic pretensions and his political system retrogressive and hypocritical. These however were the alienated strata of a polity where the mechanics of exercising political choice had been declared 'defunct'. And so they could be ignored. The marginalised groups, in the rural as well as the urban areas, posed rather more difficult problems. The general's Islamic prescriptions to cobble together a society free of class tensions seemed irrelevant to what they needed and, in any event, were too old and effete to take a hold of their hearts and minds.

Clearly then, so long as it remained in the hands of a military ruler with limited popular support, the Pakistani state could not pretend to be acting in the general interest of society, least of all in the economic realm. Divisions among, and the conflicting demands of, the dominant interest groups was a double-edged sword. While appearing to give the state a relatively larger measure of autonomy, the fragmentation in the upper echelons of Pakistani society made its claims to legitimacy more shaky than ever. The difficulties were compounded by the fact that the state's internal structures were not only affected by the broader social tensions which Zia wanted to altogether deny but by deepening rivalries between its two main institutions – the civil bureaucracy and the army. Martial law had been accompanied by grafting military officers in key positions within the civilian administration, as well as in semi-government and autonomous organisations. The militarisation of the state apparatus made it easier for the military high command to keep watch and ward on the affairs of government. But the mere presence of civil bureaucrats livid at being superceded by military men was not a good portent for coherent state action. The more so since placing military men in key positions within the state apparatus was a first step to their location in key sectors of the economy. During the Zia era a number of enterprising army officers were able to exploit access to state authority to gain entry into the wealthy circles of society.

Blunting criticisms against the military's silent colonisation of the administration and, by virtue of legal and extra-legal economic privileges, also of society while at the same time affirming the regime's legitimacy required a powerful but innocuous remedy. Making women the focal point of the campaign for an Islamic moral order provided Zia with an ingenious recipe with which to establish the legitimacy of his regime without unduly taxing the sensibilities of Pakistan's male-dominated society. Promising to restore the sanctity of the *chador* (or the veil) and the *chardivari* (or the home) – those well-known symbols of female honour and the security of the Muslim family – the general promulgated a series of 'Islamic' laws wildly discriminatory towards women.[33] But in 1980 when Zia tried extending his social engineering to

---

[33] The Hudood ordinance of 1979 blurred the distinction between adultery and rape. It was followed by the qisas [retaliation] and diyat[blood-money] ordinance in 1980 which provided that the compensation for a woman, who had been beaten or murdered, would be only half that of a man. But the real howler was the law of evidence; it reduced the weight of a woman witness's evidence to half that of a man. For a fuller discussion of the Zia regime's policies towards women, see A. Jalal 'The Convenience of Subservience: Women and the State of Pakistan' in Kandiyoti (ed.), *Islam, Women and the State* (forthcoming).

the economic realm by introducing two Islamic taxes – *Zakat* (an alms tax) and *Ushr* (an agricultural levy) – there was a volley of criticism. His attempts to introduce 'interest free banking' were equally unpopular. Realising that 'Islamising' the economy without upsetting the established structures of power and authority was well-nigh impossible, Zia wisely opted to go into neutral gear on the economic front. So, in spite of much hue and cry over the setting up of Shariat courts in 1980, the general made sure to exclude all matters relating to the economy from their purview.[34] The brunt of Zia's Islamisation', therefore, was borne by women and religious minorities in the main.

Quite clearly, Zia's state sponsored 'Islamisation' programme cannot be seen as anything more than a token effort, and a highly spurious one at that, to establish his own legitimacy without having to court mass popular support. There was certainly no sign of a groundswell of feeling for the general's policies outside a very narrowly based political constituency and certain sections of the military and the civil bureaucracy. In December 1984, the general held a referendum to get a mandate for another five years by equating himself with Islam; the turnout was embarrassingly low. This was one of the main reasons for Zia's stubborn resistance to the demands of the opposition's Movement for the Restoration of Democracy – a conglomerate of parties as disparate as the PNA but lacking its financial clout – that he hold free elections on a party basis.

In 1985, when Zia finally decided to hold national and provincial assembly elections on a non-party basis, he was confronted with an opposition boycott led by the PPP. But by then there were enough members of the Shoora as well as the local councils eager to retain their privileged access to state authority and others for whom languishing on the margins of a system based on differential patronage was becoming increasingly untenable. The list of candidates and winners furnishes firm evidence of the Pakistani state's magnet-like qualities in determining both the shape and the scope of the political field. Although *biraderi* ties dominated the voting patterns in a number of constituencies, the electorate selectively cast negative votes against the regime's most rabid supporters. But in the absence of organised party machineries the growing maturity of the electorate was dissipated by the rules of a system designed by the bureaucratic-military axis to encourage the localisation and fragmentation of politics. Parliament was dominated by landed interests, with business groups in second place. State

---

[34] See Hamza Alavi 'Pakistan and Islam: Ethnicity and Ideology', paper presented at the South Asian Institute, University of Heidelberg, 9–12 July 1986, 30.

patronage and protection – by now a highly refined art – had ensured the emergence of a new string of politicians, albeit drawn from the same socio-economic groups that had always dominated the political arenas of west Pakistan. Elated by this endorsement of his political system Zia appointed a Sindhi landlord, Mohammad Khan Junejo, as prime minister and, in December 1985, finally lifted martial law.

Sustaining a political system dependent on state patronage and subservient to the non-elected institutions was a costly exercise. To consolidate its successful manipulation of the political process the regime resorted to the extraordinary device of handing out large sums of money to members of the national assembly ready to promote its interests. The burgeoning of a 'grants economy' had dire implications for the fiscal health of the state. Deficit financing reached unprecedented levels. Having borrowed to the hilt in international money markets the government took to selling off its savings schemes and drawing money from the banking sector in order to pour funds down the channels of state patronage. In 1977, when Zia seized power, the government's debt-reservicing charges had been roughly equal to its revenue receipts; eight years later interest payments were outstripping receipts, a gap that widened at an alarming rate once military rule donned a civilian mask. The regime's fiscal woes left it with no alternative except to mortgage the state to a small affluent crust of Pakistani society. Here was the price future generations would have to pay for the illusion of stability in the Zia era. For now the long-standing disjunction between those exercising economic clout and the actual wielders of state authority enabled the dominant military and bureaucratic institutions to keep the balance firmly tilted against its political clients. Junejo could only be as powerful as Zia wanted him to be. The instant the prime minister began flexing his political muscle he was sent packing.

Islamic posturing and expensive social engineering did not gain Zia the legitimacy and the bases of support he needed. What then were the factors that made his regime one of the longest surviving in Pakistan's history? A political opposition, albeit a gagged, divided and disorganised one, certainly existed. There were signs of tensions within the central and provincial arms of the state, a wave of popular discontent in rural Sind, a discomforting silence over the battered terrain of post-civil war Baluchistan, plenty of Punjabis disenchanted with military rule and, last but not least, the city of Karachi whose sprawling shanty towns came to be ruled by coalitions of gun runners, narcotics dealers and the local police. Undoubtedly, Zia's capacity for survival had much to do with state coercion, actual and potential; claims about the health of the economy, apparent and real; the unflagging support of a military establishment, prospering and proliferating; and the co-option of the landed and business classes in the new political arrangements designed to give the regime a civilian face. Yet all said and done, Zia's ability to perpetuate his rule had much to do with the shifts in the regional balance of power – triggered by the Iranian revolution and followed soon after by the Soviet invasion of Afghanistan. After December 1979 the military not only ruled the roost in Pakistani society but acted as the defenders of a state deemed by the United States and the Western allies to be on the 'front line' between Soviet Russia and the 'free world'. Unstinting support by the Zia regime for the Pakistani-based Afghan resistance movement entitled it to American military and economic aid worth billions of dollars. The presence of nearly three million Afghan refugees on its soil helped to fuel social conflicts and created a parallel arms and drugs economy, patronised and protected by the military's very own inter-services intelligence. The kickbacks for military and civilian defence contractors and the narcotics kings won the regime ardent supporters it could hardly afford to deny. If the fifties saw senior civil servants and army officials adopting a blueprint for a state structure geared to supporting a political economy of defence, the interplay of domestic, regional and international factors in the eighties enabled the Zia regime to bring the scheme to virtual fruition.

On 17 August 1988 Zia's death along with key senior military officers in an aircrash removed a major obstacle to the holding of free and fair elections on a party basis. But the general's eleven years in office left a daunting set of legacies, not least of which was the unquestioned supremacy of the state apparatus over the political process. The systematic assault on party based politics had seen Pakistan lapsing into the politics of local patronage in which infusions of largely illicit funds on an unprecedented scale attempted to sway voter choices. The fiscal crisis of the state and the growth of new pockets of private affluence accentuated grievances of entire provinces – especially Sind and various linguistic groups within them, most dramatically manifested by the Muhajir Qaumi Mahaz (MQM) in Karachi and Hyderabad. Restor-ation of the political process and the easing of centre-province tensions were the twin challenges confronting the political opposition to Zia's regime. The Pakistan People's party led by Benazir Bhutto sought to achieve these aims in the elections of 16 November 1988 through a partial evocation of her father's populism tempered by a pragmatic realisation of the dominance of the non-elected institutions of the state. The Islamic Democratic Alliance – a rag-tag conglomeration of nine pro-Zia political groups, including the Muslim League and the Jamat-i-Islami – tried utilising their control of the institutionalised channels of patronage to remain in power and provide a civilian face to the bureaucratic-military state. But a combination of populism and accommodations of expediency reached with sections of the landed oligarchy enabled the PPP to emerge as the largest single party in the national assembly, well ahead of the IDA (see Table 7.1). On 2 December 1988, after an agonising delay of two weeks, Benazir Bhutto was sworn in as prime minister.

Since the Zia regime had not only denied the people their fundamental right of political choice but had launched a concerted attack on the right of women to be equal citizens, there was poetic justice in the spectacle of a woman leading the country to party based parliamentary democracy. The PPP's electoral sweep in Sind and good showing in the Punjab in the national elections augured well for the alleviation of tensions in the federal equation. But its inability to do as well in the provincial elections, especially in the Punjab, opened the disconcerting prospect of the federal government facing strong opposition by the IDA in the majority province. The precarious condition of state finances and an uncertain regional environment coupled with international pressure limited the possibility of any significant departures in economic and foreign

Table 7.1 *1988 national assembly election results*

Party	Punjab	Sind	NWFP	Baluchistan	Islamabad	FATA[a]	TOTAL
PPP	52	31	8	1	1	—	93
IDA	44	—	8	2	—	—	54
JUI[b]	—	—	3	4	—	—	7
ANP[c]	—	—	2	—	—	—	2
PAI[d]	3	—	—	—	—	—	3
BNA[e]	—	—	—	2	—	—	2
JUI[f]	—	—	1	—	—	—	1
PDP[g]	1	—	—	—	—	—	1
NPP[h]	2	—	—	—	—	—	2
Independents	12	15[i]	3	2	—	8	40

Elections were held for 205 out of the 207 Muslim seats. There are in addition ten seats for minorities and twenty nominated seats for women in a house of 237.

[a] Federally Administered Tribal Areas
[b] Jamiat-ul-Ulema-i-Islam (Fazlur Rahman group)
[c] Awami National Party
[d] Pakistan Awami Ittehad
[e] Baluchistan National Alliance
[f] Jamiat-ul-Ulema-i-Islam (Darkhasti group)
[g] Pakistan Democratic party
[h] National People's Party's (Khar group)
[i] Thirteen of the seats were won by members of the Muhajir Qaumi Mahaz.

policies. The greatest challenge to the largest political party, however, stemmed from the lingering imbalance between elected and non-elected institutions in Pakistan's history. Both the military and the bureaucracy had somehow to be squared. That challenge could only be met by striking just the right balance between bold initiatives and tactful diplomacy so as to strengthen the elected institutions, specifically parliament, without provoking the military backed by its international patrons to intervene directly in the political arena. To survive and succeed an elected prime minister in the Pakistani context has almost to play the role of the leader of the opposition upholding the cause of the political process against the preexisting state structure. The extent to which the prime minister and her party successfully perform that role will in large part determine whether in 1988 a momentous return has been made to truly representative government or whether it is simply that the state of martial rule has decided temporarily not to parade in its true colours.

GLOSSARY

awab	illegal exactions
begar	unpaid services rendered by tenants and labourers to the landlords
biraderi	literally 'brotherhood', patrilineal kinship group
burqa	tent like garment worn by women, covering them from the head down to the ankles
chador	a sheet of cloth worn by women to cover the head and the body but not the face
chardivari	literally the four walls of the home
crore	one hundred lakhs or ten million
goonda	hooligan
hari	sharecropper with no occupancy rights or landless labourer in Sind
Hudood	literally the limits; used in Islamic law to establish the maximum punishment for a crime
imam	title used for Muslim religious leader
jagir	land grant
jagirdar	big landlord
khatib	preacher
khud khast	self-cultivated land
kisan	peasant; cultivator
lakh	one hundred thousand
Majlis-i-Shoora	advisory council
mandi	market
marwari	Hindu trading and moneylending group
maulvi	title used for Muslim religious leader
maund	unit of weight; approximately eighty pounds
mazdoor	labourer
mohallah	a ward or a quarter
Muhajir	literally refugee
mullah	title used for Muslim religious leader
nizam	ruler
Nizam-i-Mustafa	system of the Prophet Mohammad
panchayat	council of elders
pir	term used for spiritual guide
purdah	veil
rabi	the spring harvest

raj	kingdom, rule or sovereignty
ramazan	the Muslim month of fasting
rupee	Pakistani currency
sajjada nashin	literally one who sits on the prayer rug; custodian of a sufi shrine
sardar	chief of tribe
shahi jirga	grand meeting of all tribal sardars
shalwar-kameez	a long shirt worn over baggy trousers – the national dress of Pakistan
Shariat	Islamic law
Sunnah	teachings of the Prophet Mohammad
tehsil	sub-district
thana	police station
ulema	person versed in Islamic religious sciences
ushr	agricultural levy
wadera	term used for big landlords in Sind
waqf	Muslim religious trust
zamindar	term is used loosely for any landholder, large or small
zakat	alms tax

SELECT BIBLIOGRAPHY

Manuscript sources

India Office Library, London

Treasury Papers: L/F/.
War Office Papers: L/WS/1/.
Eric Franklin's manuscript, MSS.EUR.C.364.

Public Records Office, London

Dominion Office Papers: DO35 and DO134 series.
Foreign Office Papers: FO371 series.
Treasury Papers: T229/ and T236.
Ministry of Defence Papers: DEFE7 series.

National Archives of the USA, Washington, DC

Papers of the various departments of the US government, including the department of state, are categorised in the National Archives according to region and countries. The following declassified record groups and boxes contain important papers on Pakistan and occasionally also on other countries of South and West Asia:

NND.42424, RG 84: Box 1
NND.842423, RG 84: Box 1
NND.842424, RG 84: Boxes 1, 5 and 6
NND.842430, RG 84: Boxes 1, 4, 7, 8, 12, 36, 40, 41, 42
  RG.59: Box 424
NND.842905, RG 59: Boxes 4145 and 4147
NND.842909, RG 59: Boxes 5542, 5545, 5547, 5548, 5549, 5555, 5558, 5559, 5568, 5955, 5956, 5959 and 5970
NND.867414, RG 59: Boxes 3865, 3866 and 3873.
NND.760050, RG 59: Boxes 6016, 6018, 6019
  RG 218: Box 15.

'Pakistan's Current Economic Situation and Prospects', report no.7706 of the office of intelligence research and analysis, department of state, 15 May 1958.

Washington National Record Center, Washington, DC

US military papers are located in this separate repository. The following declassified record groups contain relevant papers on Pakistan:

Declassified 785011, RG 319, Entry 57: Box 409
Declassified 785012, RG 319, Entry 57: Box 443
Declassified 785013, RG 319: Box 447

Published sources

Speeches of Quaid-i-Azam Mohammad Ali Jinnah as Governor-General of Pakistan, Karachi 1948.
Report of the Agrarian Committee appointed by the Working Committee of the Pakistan Muslim League, published by S. Shamsul Hasan, assistant secretary of the Pakistan Muslim League, 1949.
Pirzada, Syed Sharifuddin (ed.), *Foundations of Pakistan: the All-India Muslim League Documents: 1906–1947*, II, Karachi 1970.
Foreign Relations of the United States of America, 1951, VI, II, Asia and the Pacific, Washington, DC 1977.
Foreign Relations of the United States of America, 1952–4, XI, II, Africa and South Asia, Washington, DC 1983.
Foreign Relations of the United States of America, 1955–57, VIII, South Asia, Washington, DC 1987.
Constitutional Relations Between Britain and India: The Transfer of Power 1942–7, Nicholas Mansergh and Penderel Moon (eds.), vols, X, XI, and XII, London 1981–3.

Official publications

All publications of the government of Pakistan are printed in Karachi unless otherwise stated.

Partition Proceedings, I–V.
Budget of the Central Government of Pakistan, 1947–48 (15th August to 31 March and 1948–49).
Budget of the Central Government of Pakistan, 1949–50.
Budget of the Central Government of Pakistan, 1950–51.
Budget of the Central Government of Pakistan, 1953–54.
Constituent Assembly Debates, 1947–1958, 1948–59.
Census of Pakistan, 1951, V.
Report of the Committee on Constitutional and Administrative Reforms in Baluchistan, in *CAD*, I, 1951.
Orders of the Governor-General, 1947–1950, 1951.
The Assassination of Liaquat Ali Khan: Report of the Commission of Enquiry (second edition), 1952.
The Punjab: A Review of the First Five Years (August 1947 to August 1952), Lahore 1952.

Financial Enquiry Regarding Allocation of Revenues Between the Central and Provincial Governments, report by Jeremy Raisman, 1952.

Report of the Economic Appraisal Committee, 1953.

Report of the Court of Inquiry constituted under Punjab Act II of 1954 to Enquire into the Punjab Disturbances of 1953, Lahore 1954.

Federal Court Reports, 1955, 1955.

Constitution of the Islamic Republic of Pakistan, 1956.

The First Five Year Plan (1955–1960), outline of the plan (draft), May 1956.

Explanatory Memorandum on the Budget, 1957–58.

Orders of the Governor-General, 1951–1956, 1957.

The First Five Year Plan, (1955-1960), 1958.

Report of the Land Reforms Commission for West Pakistan, Lahore 1959.

The Second Five Year Plan (1960–65), 1960.

Economy of Pakistan: 1948–68, Islamabad 1968.

Newspapers and Periodicals

Civil and Military Gazette, Lahore.
Dawn, Karachi.
Imroze, Lahore.
Khyber Mail, Peshawar.
Meyaar, Lahore.
Morning News, Karachi.
Nawa-i-Waqt, Lahore.
The New York Times, New York.
The Observer, London.
The Pakistan Observer, Dacca.
The Pakistan Times, Lahore.
Round Table, London.
Viewpoint, Lahore.

Secondary works cited

Abedin, Najmul, *Local Administration and Politics in Modernising Societies: Bangladesh and Pakistan*, Dacca 1973.

Afzal, M. Rafique, *Political Parties in Pakistan: 1947–1958*, Islamabad 1976.

Ahmad, Colonel Mohammad, *My Chief*, Lahore 1960.

Ahmad, Mumtaz, 'Ideology, Power, and Protest: Toward Explaining Islamic Revivalism in Pakistan', unpublished paper prepared for a workshop on Islamic revivalism at the Center for Strategic and International Studies, Georgetown University, 4 January 1986.

Ahmad, Mushtaq, *Government and Politics in Pakistan* (second edition), Karachi 1963.

Ahmad, Syed Nur, *From Martial Law to Martial Law, Politics in the Punjab 1919–1958*, Mahmud Ali (trans.); Craig Baxter (ed.), Colorado 1985.

Ahmed, C.M., *The Civil Service in Pakistan* (second edition), Dacca 1969.
Ahmed, Emajuddin, *Bureaucratic Elites in Segmented Economic Growth: Bangladesh and Pakistan*, Dacca 1980.
Ahmed, Munir, *The Civil Servant in Pakistan*, Oxford 1963.
  'The November Mass Movement in Pakistan' in *Political Sociology: Perspectives on Pakistan*, Lahore 1978.
Alavi, Hamza, 'The State in Postcolonial Societies: Pakistan and Bangladesh', in K. Gough and H.P. Sharma (eds.), *Imperialism and Revolution in South Asia*, New York 1973.
  'Pakistan and Islam: Ethnicity and Ideology', paper presented at the South Asian Institute, University of Heidelberg, 9–12 July 1986.
Ali, Chaudhri Mohammad, *The Emergence of Pakistan*, Lahore 1973.
Altaf, Zafar, *Pakistani Entrepreneurs: their Development, Characteristics, and Attitudes*, London 1983.
Amjad, Rashid, 'Industrial Concentration and Economic Power', in Hassan Gardezi and Jamil Rashid (eds.), *Pakistan, The Roots of Dictatorship: The Political Economy of a Praetorian State*, London 1983.
  'Role of Industrial Houses in Pakistan's Power Structure', *Pakistan Administrative Staff College Journal*, XII, June 1974.
Andrus, J. Russell and Azizali F. Mohammad, *The Economy of Pakistan*, Oxford 1958.
Aziz, K.K., *Party Politics in Pakistan: 1947–1958*, Islamabad 1976.
Baxter, Craig and Shahid Javed Burki, 'Socio-Economic Indicators of the People's Party's vote in the Punjab', *Journal of Asian Studies*, August 1975.
Binder, Leonard, *Religion and Politics in Pakistan*, Berkeley 1971.
Braibanti, Ralph, *Research on the Bureaucracy of Pakistan*, Durham 1969.
Burki, Shahid Javed, *State and Society in Pakistan, 1971–77*, London 1980.
Callard, Keith B., *Pakistan: a Political Study*, London 1957.
Choudhury, G.W., *Constitutional Development in Pakistan* (second edition), London 1969.
Gankovsky, Yu V. and L.R. Gordon-Polonskaya, *A History of Pakistan 1947–1958)*, Lahore [no date].
Hamid, N., 'The Burden of Capitalist Growth: A Study of Real Wages and Consumption in Pakistan', *Pakistan Economic and Social Review*, Spring 1974.
Jalal, A., *The Sole Spokesman: Jinnah, the Muslim League and the Demand for Pakistan*, Cambridge 1985.
  'Inheriting the Raj: Jinnah and the Governer-Generalship Issue', in *Modern Asian Studies*, 19, I, February 1985, 29–53.
  'India's Partition and the Defence of Pakistan: an Historical Perspective', *The Journal of Imperial and Commonwealth History*, XV, May 1987, 3, 289–310.
  'Towards the Baghdad Pact: South Asia and Middle East Defence in the Cold War', *International History Review*, 1, August 1989, 3.
  'The Convenience of Subservience: Women and the State of Pakistan' in

Deniz Kandiyoti (ed.), *Islam, Women and the State* (forthcoming).
'State Magnetism and the Field of Political Privilege in Pakistan', Myron
  Weiner and Ali Banuazizi (eds.), *Political and the Restructuring of
  the Political Order in Afghanistan, Iran and Pakistan* (forthcoming).
Jansson, Erland, *India, Pakistan or Pakhtunistan: The Nationalist
  Movements in the North West Frontier Province, 1937–47*, Uppsala
  1981.
Jones, Philip Edward, 'The Pakistan People's Party: Social Group Response
  and Party Development in an Era of Mass Participation', unpublished
  doctoral dissertation, Fletcher School of Law and Diplomacy, April
  1979.
Kamanev, Sergei, *The Economic Growth of Pakistan*, Lahore 1985.
Khan, Mohammad Asghar, *Generals in Politics: Pakistan 1958–1982*,
  New Delhi 1983.
Khan, Mohammad Ayub, *Friends Not Masters: A Political Autobiography*,
  Karachi 1967.
Lodhi, Maliha, 'Politics in Pakistan During the Bhutto Era', unpublished
  manuscript [no date].
Maddison, Angus, *Class Structure and Economic Growth: India and Pakistan
  Since the Moghuls*, London 1971.
Mahmood, Safdar, *Pakistan: Muslim League Ka Dar-e-Hakumat, 1947–1954*
  [Urdu], Lahore 1982.
Maniruzzaman, Talukder, *The Politics of Development: The Case of
  Pakistan, 1947–1958*, Dacca 1971.
  'Group Interests in Pakistan Politics, 1947–58', *Pacific Affairs*, 39, Spring-
  Summer 1966.
Maron, Stanley (ed.), *A survey of Pakistan society*, Berkeley 1956.
Maududi, S.A.A., *Purdah and the Status of Women in Islam* (eighth edition),
  Al-Ashari (trans.), Lahore 1986.
Mirza, Iskander, 'Iskander Mirza Speaks: An Autobiography', *Meyaar*
  (Lahore), 29 May-19 June 1976.
Noman, Omar, *The Political Economy of Pakistan, 1947–85*, London 1988.
Papanek, Gustav F., *Pakistan's Development, Social Goals and Private
  Incentives*, Harvard 1967.
  'The Development of Entrepreneurs', *The American Economic Review*,
  LII, 1962.
Papanek, Hanna, 'Pakistan's Big Businessmen: Muslim Separatism,
  Entrepreneurs, and Partial Mobilization', *Economic Development and
  Cultural Change*, 21, October 1972.
Power, John H., 'Industrialization in Pakistan: A Case of Frustrated
  Take Off?', *Pakistan Development Review*, Summer 1963, III, 2.
Rahman, Inamur, *Public Opinion and Political Development in Pakistan*,
  Karachi 1982.
Rizvi, Hasan Askari, *The Military and Politics in Pakistan: 1947–86*, Lahore
  1986.
Rizvi, Shahid A., ' Development of Local Government in Indo-Pakistan

from 1688 to 1958', *Journal of the Pakistan Historical Society*, XXI, II, April 1973.

Rosen, George, *Western Economists and Eastern Societies: Agents of Change in South Asia, 1950–1970*, Oxford 1985.

Sayeed, Khalid B., *Pakistan, the Formative Phase* (second edition), Karachi 1968.

   Politics in Pakistan: the Nature and Direction of Change, New York 1980.

Tayyib, A., *Pakistan: A Political Geography*, Oxford 1966.

Venkataramani, M.S., *The American Role in Pakistan, 1947–1958*, New Delhi 1982.

Ziring, Lawrence. *The Ayub Era: Politics in Pakistan, 1958–69*, Syracruse 1971.

INDEX

civil bureaucracy (*cont.*)
 and one unit, 191, 198–202, 229, 264
 and parties, 5, 60, 63, 74–5, 101, 114,
  123, 143, 211, 225–7, 231, 246, 296,
  298, 300, 319
 and partition process, 30–2
 patronage, 108–9, 264, 303
 and political leadership, 2, 64, 67, 74–
  5, 108–10, 113–15, 123–4, 128–9,
  131, 133, 136–40, 146, 155, 167–9,
  171–3, 175–80, 182–3, 186–7, 189,
  191–8, 202, 207, 211, 216, 223, 225,
  227, 229, 231, 233, 236, 254, 261,
  278, 295, 300–1, 307, 314–16, 319,
  325
 and political process, 1–6, 124, 136,
  175, 178–80, 192–8, 201, 207, 215–
  16, 221, 226–7, 235, 246, 275, 296,
  298, 301–3, 319, 324–5, 328
 provincial civil services, 32, 58, 75, 79–
  80, 83–4, 87–9, 90–3, 110, 115, 149,
  157, 161–2, 163fn, 165, 199–202, 209,
  223–4, 231, 264, 305, 312
 and Punjab, 1, 82, 110, 136–7, 146,
  149, 151, 154, 175, 191–2, 198, 222–
  4, 264, 298, 301, 310
 and religious leaders, 173, 216, 282,
  286, 291
 representation in central services, 1, 3,
  82, 109–10, 144, 199, 222–3, 226,
  261, 303, 306–7
 rivalries, 224, 149, 264
 secularism of, 173, 216, 283, 286, 293
 senior officials, 4, 32, 54, 63–4, 109,
  113, 115, 131, 137, 139, 172–82,
  198fn, 201–2, 223, 264, 306
 shortage of skilled personnel, 31, 109,
  236
 UP recruits, 82, 110, 223–4
'cold war', 112–13, 115–16, 121–2, 125
Communism, 73, 75, 112, 127
 and, army, 113, 115–16, 120–1
 in east Bengal, 85, 87fn, 115, 157, 159,
  188fn, 189–90, 291
 propaganda against, 115–16, 123, 239,
  280–1, 291
 in Punjab, 105, 148fn, 116–17, 119–20
constitution-making, 1, 6
 and Baluchistan, 175, 184, 209
 basic principles committee reports,
  114, 156, 173–5, 183–4
 and Bogra's formula, 184–5, 191, 197–
  8
 and bureaucratic-military axis, 173,
  175, 183–5, 191–2, 194, 196, 198,

202–5, 212, 215, 221–2, 309
 constitution (1956), 214–22, 226, 231–
  3, 253, 258, 260, 264, 275, 284, 317
 constitution (1962), 302–3, 317
 constitution (1973), 317
 'constitution convention', 204–6
 and east Bengal, 114, 156, 174, 183–5,
  190–2, 197–8, 213, 219
 first constituent assembly, 25–8, 62,
  63fn, 153, 184–6, 189, 191–2, 194,
  196–7, 279, 285–6, 292
 form of government, 1, 114, 173–4,
  183, 196, 214–15, 219, 260, 284–5,
  303
 and Islam, 114, 173–4, 184–6, 213–16,
  281, 284–6
 and national language, 114, 191
 and NWFP, 174–5
 objectives resolution (1949), 214, 284
 and one unit, 191, 195–99, 208–9, 213
 and political process, 6, 136, 140, 192,
  194–5, 197, 212, 264
 president's powers, 184–5, 197, 215–22,
  227, 253, 303
 and provincial autonomy, 114, 156,
  201, 317
 and Punjab, 153, 174–5, 183–4, 190–2
 representation in national assembly,
  114, 174, 184, 198, 201
 second constituent assembly, 196, 207–
  18
 and Sind, 175–83
 and supreme court, 203–7
 zonal federation scheme, 191, 200, 261
Cripps, Stafford, 18–19, 46
Cunningham, George, 90–1

Dasti, Abdul Hamid, 208
Daultana, Mian Mumtaz, 80–2
 and central government, 145, 153, 192
 and constitution-making, 175, 192
 and one unit, 198–9
 as Punjab chief minister, 149–54, 173,
  177
 and west Pakistan assembly, 229, 266
Dawn, 201fn, 234
defence, (see also army and military)
 and Britain, 45–6, 50–4, 76–8, 95, 111,
  117, 125–6, 129–30, 137, 171–2, 188
 common arrangements with India, 38–
  42, 50–3
 demands on central exchequer, 3, 40,
  44–5, 48–52, 54–6, 59–60, 70, 93–5,
  99–100, 178, 181, 188, 235–8, 240–1,

CAMBRIDGE SOUTH ASIAN STUDIES

These monographs are published by the Syndics of Cambridge University Press in association with the Cambridge University Centre for South Asian Studies The following books have been published in this series:

361

12931270R00223

Printed in Great Britain
by Amazon.co.uk, Ltd.,
Marston Gate.